DAILY LIFE ON

THE NINETEENTH CENTURY AMERICAN FRONTIER

Recent Titles in
The Greenwood Press "Daily Life Through History" Series

Daily Life in Elizabethan England
Jeffrey L. Singman

Daily Life in Chaucer's England
Jeffrey L. Singman and Will McLean

Daily Life in the Inca Empire
Michael A. Malpass

Daily Life in Maya Civilization
Robert J. Sharer

Daily Life in Victorian England
Sally Mitchell

Daily Life in the United States, 1960–1990: Decades of Discord
Myron A. Marty

Daily Life of the Aztecs: People of the Sun and Earth
David Carrasco with Scott Sessions

Daily Life in Ancient Mesopotamia
Karen Rhea Nemet-Nejat

Daily Life of the Ancient Greeks
Robert Garland

Daily Life During the Holocaust
Eve Nussbaum Soumerai and Carol D. Schulz

Daily Life in Civil War America
Dorothy Denneen Volo and James M. Volo

DAILY LIFE ON

THE NINETEENTH CENTURY AMERICAN FRONTIER

MARY ELLEN JONES

The Greenwood Press "Daily Life Through History" Series

GREENWOOD PRESS
Westport, Connecticut • London

Library of Congress Cataloging-in-Publication Data

Jones, Mary Ellen, 1937–
  Daily life on the nineteenth century American frontier / Mary
Ellen Jones.
    p. cm.—(The Greenwood Press "Daily life through history"
series, ISSN 1080–4749)
  Includes bibliographical references and index.
  ISBN 0–313–29634–0 (alk. paper)
  1. Frontier and pioneer life—West (U.S.) 2. West (U.S.)—Social
life and customs. I. Title. II. Series.
  F596.J585 1998
  978'.02—dc21   98–12149

British Library Cataloguing in Publication Data is available.

Library of Congress Catalog Card Number: 98–12149
ISBN: 0–313–29634–0
ISSN: 1080–4749

First published in 1998

Greenwood Press, 88 Post Road West, Westport, CT 06881
An imprint of Greenwood Publishing Group, Inc.

Printed in the United States of America

The paper used in this book complies with the
Permanent Paper Standard issued by the National
Information Standards Organization (Z39.48–1984).

10 9 8 7 6 5

Copyright Acknowledgment

The author and publisher gratefully acknowledge permission for the use of the following
material:

From Charles Preuss, *Exploring with Frémont: The Private Diaries of Charles Preuss, Cartog-
rapher for John C. Frémont on His First, Second, and Fourth Expeditions to the Far West*, trans.
and ed. by Erwin G. Gudde and Elisabeth K. Gudde (Norman: University of Oklahoma
Press, 1958). Copyright 1958 by University of Oklahoma Press, Publishing Division of the
University. Composed and printed at Norman, Oklahoma, U.S.A., by the University of
Oklahoma Press. First edition. Reprinted with permission from the University of Oklahoma
Press.

Every reasonable effort has been made to trace the owners of copyright materials in this
book, but in some instances this has proven impossible. The author and publisher will be
glad to receive information leading to more complete acknowledgments in subsequent
printings of the book and in the meantime extend their apologies for any omissions.

Among the traditional Algonquian-speaking peoples
the Olammapise
is
Principal Story-teller,
Truth Teller,
guardian and conveyer of the Nation's values,
heritage, and culture.

This book is dedicated to three olammapise:
John Jakes, in literature;
Donald R. Perkins, in public relations;
and Herman J. Viola, in history—
truth tellers all.

Contents

Acknowledgments   ix

Introduction   xi

Chronology   xiii

1. The American Frontier: Simple Stereotype, Complex Reality   1

2. Life on the Fur Frontier   11

3. Life on the Explorers' Frontier   55

4. Life on the Miners' Frontier: The New Eldorado   93

5. Life on the Land: Alien Exotics—Cowboys and Settlers   157

6. The Indian Frontier and the Frontier Regulars: The Army and the Indians on the Great Plains   211

Bibliography   253

Index   261

Acknowledgments

Writing is, ultimately, an individual wrestling with the word. Though the process is often solitary, it is never lonely, for it depends on human connections. To everyone who thus shared in the writing of this book, I am deeply grateful.

To those—in libraries and archives and museums—who interrupted already harried schedules to respond to my questions, thanks.

To those at Greenwood Press who have contributed skills and competence and encouragement, thanks.

To students in my frontier literature classes over the years who have shared and stimulated my enthusiasm for these stories, thanks.

To friends and colleagues who have offered love, excitement, laughter, and understanding, thanks.

To the olammapise who continue to inspire by example, thanks.

And, most of all, to those who lived the frontier experience, thanks.

John Gast, *American Progress*, 1872. Reproduced from the collections of the Library of Congress. The land, the bison, and the Indians eventually yielded to the spirit of Manifest Destiny, here portrayed stringing telegraph wires across the Plains and leading a parade of progress.

Introduction

The land was ours before we were the land's.

Robert Frost read this line from "The Gift Outright" at the inauguration of John Fitzgerald Kennedy, progenitor of the congerie of ideas that would be known as the New Frontier. In this poem Frost captures the complex reciprocal relationship between people and their land: they planted new crops in newly cut clearings; diverted rivers and built roads; hunted deer and buffalo and trapped beaver; mined gold and silver and other, less precious minerals; established trading posts and forts and towns. And, in the process, they changed. To survive on the land, to change the land, they had to adapt to the land. And so, gradually, they became Americans, having given themselves "outright to the land vaguely realizing westward."

Though the process continued for almost 400 years from Columbus's arrival until the 1890 declaration by the Bureau of the Census that the frontier was no more, this book concentrates on the nineteenth century, a period during which the process gained almost frightening momentum as people flooded into the trans-Appalachian and, especially, trans-Mississippi West in search of land, fortune, a new start, freedom—themselves. The focus of this book is on the fur frontier, the explorers' frontier, the gold frontier, the frontiers of the cowboy and homesteader and soldier—and of the Native Americans with whom they traded and loved and fought. Of necessity, much has been left out—the Mormon handcart brigades, the Donner Party, the migration to Oregon, western desperadoes and their sheriff nemeses. The focus, too, is on social rather than military or political history. The intent is to give a sense of the extraordinary ordinariness of surviving, prospering, failing, and dying in a new land; to explore how westering Americans "gave [themselves] outright ... to the land" and became her people while, inevitably, disowning those already bound to that same land by tradition, culture, and religion.

Chronology

1763	Proclamation of 1763. King George declares all land west of the Appalachians off limits to colonial settlers, an exercise in futility since the lure of the West is far stronger than an unenforceable proclamation.
1803	Thomas Jefferson purchases the Louisiana Territory from France.
1804–6	Lewis and Clark conduct their expedition to the Pacific and back.
1822	Rocky Mountain Fur Company is established by William Ashley; instead of establishing permanent forts, he inaugurates the annual rendezvous where trappers and Indians meet traders to barter furs for whiskey, ammunition, and supplies.
1840	The last fur trading rendezvous takes place; trade shifts from beaver to buffalo and from rendezvous to forts.
1841	Immigration to Oregon begins with a small party moving through the South Pass.
1846–48	War with Mexico.
1848	January 24. James Marshall discovers gold at Coloma, California.
1850	California statehood.
1854	Kansas-Nebraska Act; the United States acquires Indian Territory.
1860–61	The Pony Express runs between St. Joseph, Missouri, and Sacramento, California.
1861–65	The Civil War.

1861	Telegraph connection between east and west coasts makes the Pony Express obsolete.
	Theodore Judah surveys the route through the Sierra Nevada for a transcontinental railroad.
1862	Homestead Act and Transcontinental Railroad Acts are passed by Congress.
1864	Sand Creek Massacre.
1866	Long cattle drives begin; the first trail herds arrive at Abilene, Kansas, in 1867.
1868	Battle of Washita; Seventh Cavalry defeats the Cheyenne in Oklahoma.
	U.S. treaty with the Nez Percé is the last of three hundred treaties with Indians in one hundred years.
1869	May 10. The Golden Spike joins the Union Pacific and Central Pacific Railroads at Promontory Point, Utah.
1873	Barbed wire is invented.
1876	Battle of the Little Bighorn; the Seventh Cavalry, under Gen. George Armstrong Custer, is soundly defeated.
1882	Buffalo Bill Cody presents his first Wild West Show.
1889	April 22. Oklahoma land rush begins.
1890	Debacle at Wounded Knee, the last major confrontation between U.S. troops and Indians.
	The Bureau of the Census declares there is no longer any "free land"; the frontier is thus closed.
1893	Frederick Jackson Turner presents "The Significance of the Frontier in American History" at the American Historical Association meeting during the Chicago World's Fair.

1

The American Frontier: Simple Stereotype, Complex Reality

Sarah Atherton nursed her youngest, Jamie, as she stared out to the west. They'd been on the trail now for almost seven weeks and life had settled into a daily rhythm, different from home but comfortable nonetheless. Billy and Caroline had already come in from gathering buffalo chips for this evening's cook fire. Supper would be simple again—bacon and corn bread from provisions they'd bought at St. Joseph. It was late already. Even though they'd been held up this morning after an axle broke on their neighbor's wagon, they'd pressed on to find a stream for the oxen. Day by day, water was getting harder to find.

Sarah stared off to the west, her eyes burning. The dust was everywhere, and since early afternoon she'd been staring into the sun; her sunbonnet offered little protection. Her husband, Jed, had just dragged in, empty-handed, as tired as the hound dog at his heels. He'd had no luck hunting—again. Too many wagons had passed this way before them.

Jed and some of the other men trudged toward the creek. Tonight, instead of hobbling the animals and letting them find whatever blades of grass they could, they planned to pen them inside the circle of wagons. There'd been rumors. The Indians were no longer satisfied with "begging"; angered at the hordes of whites passing through their land, killing or frightening off the game, they'd begun to resort to violence. Sarah watched, lulled by Jamie's sucking.

Suddenly on the western horizon black dots appeared against the red sky. How far away Sarah couldn't tell—perspective was difficult on these treeless plains—but they grew rapidly larger. Horsemen. Indians. Riding fast.

Jed and the other men had gotten nearly all the oxen into the makeshift corral of wagons when the usually placid animals stampeded, spooked by the high-pitched yipping of the half-naked savages. Pawnees? Sioux? She couldn't tell. It didn't matter. The men dragged the final, ninth wagon into place. Too late for the live-stock, but maybe in time for the families.

Sarah passed the baby to Caroline and jumped down beside Jed behind the inside front wagon wheel. She peered between the spokes. With blood-curdling howls the Indians rode, circling on their fleet spotted ponies, so different from the draft horses she'd known back in Ohio. Faces painted, half black, half blue, doubly sinister, the Indians rode, feather headdresses streaming behind. Masters of their mounts, they rode with their knees, reaching into their quivers, notching arrows into their bow-strings, letting fly. Jed, his brother Jason, and the rest of the men returned fire . . .

Night fell. The longest of her life. Sarah wondered whether it would be her last . . .

Fire arrows had burned the canvas of six wagons. The others were ablaze, no water to put them out. Beating at the flames with a blanket, Sarah saw her house-hold goods—the children's clothing, the cherry bedstead crafted by her Pa, her few precious books—catch fire. The air reeked of scorched cornmeal, Jed's aromatic tobacco, Caroline's corncob doll. Jed lay wounded, an arrow protruding from his groin, his pants soaked in blood. A neighbor woman shrieked, her shoulder shat-tered by a gunshot. Sarah had heard the Indians could get weapons at the trading posts, and she feared the "thunk" of bullets into the wooden sides of the wagons as much as she did the mysterious noises—animals or Indians or her imagina-tion?—in the sudden silence that had fallen just beyond the circle of charred wagons.

The night seemed endless. Daybreak would bring hope, she felt. At least she could see the dangers they faced. But just before dawn the circling, shrieking savages started up again. Could this little band hold out against so many Indians? For how long? They'd drunk most of the water that the children had fetched yesterday from the creek. Some of the rest she'd used to clean wounds.

The baby whimpered. The wounded moaned. Billy and Caroline were too scared to cry. Jed lay grimly silent, counting his remaining bullets. And then, as the sun began to rise, the Indians grew uneasy, then wary. From over the slight rise to the east came new sounds—the thunder of galloping horses shod in iron, the jingle of bits and harness and the bright clarion call of an army bugle. Over the rise rode the Cavalry, blue clad, gold neckerchiefs knotted, gold and red guidon flags— and the streaming red, white, and blue. Rapid fire, pop-pop-pop. Screaming ponies felled by bullets pinned their riders. The firefight was brief. Within minutes those Indians who could galloped away.

Sarah dared breathe again—and hope. Though they'd lost a lot, they were still alive. The men would ride out with the soldiers to round up animals that had stampeded last evening. They'd get medical attention and replace supplies at the fort. And then they'd ride on—toward the West.

This image of the frontier has been bred into generations of Americans by our popular culture—from Buffalo Bill Cody's Wild West Show and Beadle's Dime Novels to John Wayne's cinema epics. Although it sug-gests *some* of the truths of America's westering process, it does not hint at the whole story. The problem is not simply its romanticizing the past. Far more significant is its fundamental imprecision and oversimplification. For this mythic American frontier is fixed in place and time: the Great Plains from roughly 1840 to 1870. In reality, it took almost 300 years for the frontier to move across a 3,000-mile-wide continent.

To focus only on the Great Plains is to ignore the continent's magnitude and the consequent diversity of relationships between man and the land. Today's fifty states incorporate an area of 3,618,770 square miles: 3,539,289 square miles of land, 79,481 square miles of water (*U.S. Atlas for the Macintosh*). In comparison, England has an area of 50,874 square miles; Great Britain, 89,041 (*Webster's New World Dictionary of the American Language*). The highest elevation in the United States is Alaska's Mt. McKinley at 20,320 feet; the lowest, Death Valley at 282 feet below sea level. Temperatures range from 134° to −86° Fahrenheit (*U.S. Atlas for the Macintosh*).

The midsection of the United States is watered by the Mississippi River, flowing 2,330 miles from northern Minnesota to the Gulf of Mexico, and its two major tributaries—the Missouri, flowing southeast from Montana for 2,465 miles, and the Ohio, flowing southwest from Pittsburgh for 981 miles. This midsection is bracketed by the Appalachian Mountains (a 1,500-mile chain, extending from southern Quebec to northern Alabama; its highest peak is Mt. Mitchell, North Carolina, at 6,711 feet) and the Rocky Mountains (extending from New Mexico to Alaska, its highest point in "the lower forty-eight" is Mt. Elbert, Colorado, at 14,431 feet) (*Webster's New World Dictionary of the American Language*). A cursory glance at a contemporary Burpee seed catalogue reveals eleven U.S. Department of Agriculture hardiness zones for plants based on average annual temperatures, though the editors warn gardeners that "even on a small property . . . many factors such as sun, wind, rainfall, snow cover, and slope (north or south facing) create changes in microclimate" (*Burpee Gardens 1996: 120th Anniversary Edition*). USA Today for June 25, 1996, notes temperature ranges from 103°/72° Fahrenheit (Tucson, Arizona) to 67°/50° Fahrenheit (Marquette, Michigan); on that day it snowed near Lake Tahoe, California.

For all the pioneers heading west, such variety in terrain and climate posed a myriad of questions. Where was a good pass through the mountains? How wide were the deserts? How early did grass flourish along a proposed route? Where were salt deposits? When was the last—and the first—major snowfall? How wide were rivers—and were there any fords making them passable? More so than for many nations, America's history has been affected by physical reality. Henry Nash Smith made this point quite succinctly: "The character of the American empire was defined not by streams of influence out of the past, not by a cultural tradition, nor by its place in a world community, but by a relation between man and nature" (*Virgin Land* 187).

It is crucial when examining the American frontier to specify what year, what decade, even what century is under consideration. Fixing the mythic American frontier experience in the thirty-year period spanning the Civil War also creates misperceptions and inaccuracies. *How* did one go west? Daniel Boone's trek into Kentucky in the early 1770s was by foot and pack horse; those taking the Oregon/California Trail between 1840 and 1860 mostly used ox-drawn wagons, though some simply walked and others transported their property in wheelbarrows or hand-carts; European immigrants to the northern Plains in the 1870s and 1880s arrived by train. With the advance of time came advances in technology, which, in turn, speeded the pace of westering. On the Missouri River, for example, during the relatively brief life span of the fur frontier, trans-portation developed from the bull boat (made of buffalo hides) to the keelboat and then the steamboat. Moreover, as time passed, travelers knew more about their routes and their destinations.

In 1492 Christopher Columbus had known where he was going but had no idea where he had arrived; when James Fenimore Cooper's father bought 40,000 acres in western New York in 1786, he had only vague knowledge beforehand as to the exact location of features such as lakes and rivers; but through the 1840s and 1850s the Corps of Topographical Engineers accomplished significant advancements in exploration, survey, and road-building efforts in the trans-Mississippi West.

Official policy toward the West also varied tremendously. The Proc-lamation of 1763 forbade settlement beyond the sources of the rivers flowing into the Atlantic, and even so exuberant an expansionist as Tho-mas Hart Benton could argue in 1825 that the Rocky Mountains were a convenient natural western boundary for the United States, a location where "the statue of the fabled god, Terminus, should be raised . . . , never to be thrown down" (qtd. in Smith, *Virgin Land* 26). Yet in 1804 Thomas Jefferson had sent Meriwether Lewis and William Clark on their expedition of exploration, following quickly on the dubiously constitu-tional 1803 Louisiana Purchase. *When* one captures a still frame of the constantly moving frontier results in vastly different pictures.

Other variables complicate the picture further. For example, was west-ering a gradual advance into contiguous territory (as occurred mainly east of the Mississippi), or did migration leap over half a continent, with most of the intervening land to be occupied later (as on the Oregon and California Trails—exacerbated by the discovery of gold)? What was the relation to the native inhabitants of the land? Although initial contact was usually benign, even friendly, relationships worsened over time— for a variety of reasons. Even during the same period, major differences occurred. During colonial times most eastern Indians preferred the French to the English because of their land policy. When whites were captured, most longed for repatriation; but others were happily assimi-lated into their new culture. And responses to atrocities such as the Sand

Creek Massacre ranged from celebrations by the citizens of Denver to condemnation by U.S. Army regulars. What means were there in the frontier West of enforcing law and order? Even though the myth portrays the Cavalry riding to the rescue, forts were often widely spaced and undermanned; many laws were blithely ignored; and new law was often made up as the situation warranted.

One of the first historians to consider such complexities, especially that of man's relation to the land, was Frederick Jackson Turner who presented his landmark essay, "The Significance of the Frontier in American History," to the American Historical Association meeting in 1893 at the Chicago World's Fair. Countering then-dominant schools of American historians, those interpreting U.S. history in light of the slavery controversy and those explaining U.S. institutions as products of English or Teutonic "germs" planted in the New World, Turner advanced a deceptively simple thesis: "The existence of an area of free land, its continuous recession, the advance of American settlement westward, explain American development." Further, he emphasized the cyclical, organic process as Americans repeatedly adapted to a new environment. "The peculiarity of American institutions is the fact that they have been compelled to adapt themselves to the changes of an expanding people—to the changes involved in crossing a continent, in winning a wilderness, and in developing at each area of this progress out of the primitive economic and political conditions of the frontier into the complexity of city life" (Turner, 3). The essay sparked discussion and debate that have continued to this day.

The catalyst stimulating Turner's thought was the statement made in an 1890 bulletin of the Superintendent of the Census: "Up to and including 1880 the country had a frontier of settlement, but at present the unsettled area has been so broken into by isolated bodies of settlement that there can hardly be said to be a frontier line. In the discussion of its extent, its westward movement, etc., it can not, therefore, any longer have a place in the census reports" (Turner, 3). Believing that until the 1890s the history of America had primarily been one of the "colonization of the Great West," Turner recognized the end of an era and the need to assess this historical Terminus.

Turner first established a clear definition of the American frontier. It is sharply different from a frontier in Europe, which was "a fortified boundary line running through dense populations." Rather, it is the "further edge of free land," defined by the Bureau of the Census as "that margin of settlement which has a density of two or more to the square mile." (For comparison, the 1990 population density of the United States was 70.33 persons per square mile.) Turner amplified: "the frontier is the outer edge of the wave—the meeting point between savagery and civilization" (4).

While Turner advanced a startling new interpretation of American history, he also reflected his time, which was more agrarian, nationalistic, and ethnocentric than the present. For instance, the two people per square mile of which the Census Bureau wrote did not include Native Americans. Implicit in differentiating between the American frontier and the European one, there is a denial of autonomy granted to sovereign states. Indians, uncounted in the census, were expected to respond to an "invasion" of their territory with greater equanimity than would, say, France invaded by Germany. Moreover, the "border between savagery and civilization" discounted Native American culture. If, indeed, one recognizes that the prevalent nineteenth century American belief was that civilization depends on agriculture (Smith, *Virgin Land* 176), government policy toward Native Americans becomes more understandable. A corollary was the tendency of many, in the East, to view as little more than barbarians those whites who chose life on the frontier.

Numerous theoretical discussions of the concept of civilization were published in Europe and America during the eighteenth century. Most argued that "all human societies pass through the same series of social stages in the course of their evolution upward from barbarism toward the goal of universal enlightenment." Some suggested that civilization begins only when a society adopts an agricultural way of life (Smith, *Virgin Land* 218; see also Beard and Beard, *Rise of American Civilization*). Thomas Jefferson described sequential stages of civilization in a passage that anticipates some of Turner's imagery:

> Let a philosophic observer commence a journey from the savages of the Rocky Mountains, eastwardly towards our sea-coast. [At that time there was only one seacoast.] These he would observe in the earliest stage of association living under no law but that of nature, [eating] and covering themselves with the flesh and skins of wild beasts. He would next find those on our frontiers in the pastoral state, raising domestic animals, to supply the defects of hunting. Then succeed our own semi-barbarous citizens, the pioneers of the advance of civilization, and so in his progress he would meet the gradual shades of improving man until he would reach his, as yet, most improved state in our seaport towns. This, in fact, is equivalent to a survey, in time, of the progress of man from the infancy of creation to the present day. (qtd. in Smith, 219)

One difference between Turner and many of the previous theorists is that rather than adopting a judgmental, moralistic, and hierarchical view of the representative stages of frontier settlement, his style is descriptive and his tone pragmatic as he examined the impact of man's interaction with the land.

Another major point in Turner's thesis is that "the frontier is the line of most rapid and effective Americanization. The wilderness masters the colonist" (5). He described how the European must adapt to his environment in virtually every aspect of culture: dress, food, tools, modes of travel, ways of thought. He must learn from the Indians how to survive, and though he may eventually master the wilderness, his experiences make him a new person, no longer European. As this process is repeated generation after generation, year after year, mile after mile, Turner argues, "the advance of the frontier has meant a steady movement away from the influence of Europe" (5).

This recurrent westering over time moved past a series of natural boundaries: the "fall line," the Alleghenies, the Mississippi and Missouri rivers, the Rocky Mountains, the deserts. If, instead of freeze-framing the procession west temporally, to a specific date, one were to assume a single physical point of view over many years, one could see a colorful procession. Turner wrote:

> Stand at Cumberland Gap and watch the procession of civilization, marching single file—the buffalo following the salt springs, the Indian, the fur-trader and hunter, the cattle-raiser, the pioneer farmer—and the frontier has passed by. Stand at South Pass in the Rockies a century later and see the same procession with wider intervals between. The unequal rate of advance compels us to distinguish the frontier into the trader's frontier, the rancher's frontier or the miner's frontier, and the farmer's frontier. When the mines and cowpens were still near the fall line, the traders' pack trains were tinkling across the Alleghenies, and the French on the Great Lakes were fortifying their posts, alarmed by the British trader's birch canoe. When the trappers scaled the Rockies, the farmer was still near the mouth of the Missouri. (10)

His observation has had profound impact on the organization of this book.

Ultimately, Turner argued, this process resulted in common traits that define the American character:

> To the frontier the American intellect owes its striking characteristics. That coarseness and strength combined with acuteness and inquisitiveness; that practical, inventive turn of mind, quick to find expedients; that masterful grasp of material things, lacking in the artistic but powerful to effect great ends; that restless, nervous energy; that dominant individualism, working for good and for evil, and withal that buoyancy and exuberance which comes with free-

dom—these are traits of the frontier, or traits called out elsewhere because of the existence of the frontier. (27)

Such observations intensify one's awareness of the diversity, complexity, and contradictions in any assessment of the American frontier experience. This variety is especially clear when one considers the reasons Americans went west. Some reasons reflect national policy (Manifest Destiny, the Lewis and Clark expedition, the 1846 war with Mexico); more reflect individual goals. Some verge on mysticism, as in Walt Whitman's poems "Pioneers, O Pioneers" and "Passage to India"; they have curiously contradictory themes of the oneness of all mankind, the wonders of technology, and a oneness with nature. (The California gold frontier suggests these themes may well be, in reality, mutually exclusive.) Other explanations reflect attempts to solve social inequities, as in the belief that the Homestead Act would attract laborers from the East, lessening the possibility of class conflict caused by workers being at the mercy of factory owners. Some raise issues of international politics: the overland emigrants of the 1840s wondered whether, once they reached California and Oregon, they would still be Americans—or Mexicans or Englishmen.

There were those who went west for religious motives: Mormons heading west to practice their religion safe from persecution, and missionaries wanting to convert and "civilize" Native Americans. Whereas many headed west to establish a permanent new life there, others, like most Forty-Niners, intended a brief, exploitative sojourn followed by a return to their homes in the East. There were fortune hunters in search of gold or land or railroad subsidies. There were tourists like Prince Maximilian von Wied, who came to hunt game and exotic experiences; and there were immigrants from Europe in search of the American dream.

Some brought civilization west. Others, like Simon Kenton, who mistakenly believed the law was after him and fled west to the wilds of Ohio, saw the West as an escape from civilization; they were, literally, outlaws. Washington Irving described them in *Astoria*: "new and mongrel races . . . the amalgamation of the 'debris' . . . of former races, civilized and savage; . . . adventurers and desperadoes of every class and country . . . ejected from the bosom of society into the wilderness" (qtd. in Smith, 177). Some Easterners viewed "all emigrants as actually or potentially criminal because of their flight from an orderly municipal life into frontier areas that were remote from centers of control" (Smith, 216). The Reverend Timothy Dwight, president of Yale, characterized the eighteenth century West as a vast septic system drawing off the depraved effluvia of New England (Smith, 216–17).

More sympathetically, Edmund Burke warned the House of Commons in 1775 about the consequences of passing unenforceable laws attempting to prevent settlement across the Alleghenies:

> If you stopped your [land] grants, what would be the consequence? The people would occupy without grants. They have already so occupied in many places. You can not station garrisons in every part of these deserts. . . . Already [settlers] have topped the Appalachian Mountains. From thence, they behold before them an immense plain, one vast, rich level meadow: a square of five hundred miles. Over this they would wander without a possibility of restraint; they would change their manners with their habits of life; would soon forget a government by which they were disowned; would become hordes of English Tartars; and, pouring down upon your unfortified frontiers a fierce and irresistible cavalry, become masters of your governors and your counselors, your collectors and comptrollers. . . . Such would, and in no long time must, be the effect of attempting to forbid as a crime and to suppress as an evil the command and blessing of Providence, 'Increase and multiply.' Such would be the . . . result of an endeavor to keep as a lair of wild beasts that earth which God, by an express charter, has given to the children of men. (Turner, 24–25)

In effect, government policy could *create* a lawless class.

Most, though, simply viewed the West as offering hope for a fresh start, for perennial rebirth, an opportunity to recover manhood, health, even virtue. In this light Timothy Flint, writing in 1827, described an agricultural utopia in the West in sharp contrast to the repressive conditions of industrial New England:

> Thousands of independent and happy yeomen, . . . who have emigrated from New England to Ohio and Indiana—with their numerous healthy and happy families about them, with the ample abundance which fills their granaries, with their young orchards, whose branches must be propped to sustain the weight of their fruit, . . . would hardly be willing to exchange their fee simple empires, their droves of cattle, horses, and domestic animals, and the ability to employ the leisure of half their time as they choose, for the interior of square stone or brick walls, to breathe floccules of cotton, and to contemplate the whirl of innumerable wheels for fourteen hours of six days of every week in the year [in the textile mills]. . . . Farmers and their children are strong, and innocent and moral almost of necessity. (qtd. in Smith, 139–40)

One can conclude, therefore, that neither while the frontier was still in existence (until 1890) nor since has there been a consensus describing or interpreting its meaning or significance. Like a kaleidoscope, the images are constantly reassembling into new patterns. The individual pieces, sometimes colorful, sometimes dull, are suspended in the fluid medium of the larger American culture. The image can, for an infinitesimal instant, be caught in time and space, but external forces—political, social, or economic—can, like the twist of a wrist, create new patterns. Thus, the daily life on the American frontier that follows is a diverse, often contradictory, always changing composite of the lives of individual Americans who, for whatever reason, sought out an ever-moving, ever-changing American frontier.

"Sarah Atherton" and her family are part of our frontier heritage—but only one part. In addition to the overlanders, mostly farmers, there were trappers and traders; explorers; miners and cowboys and soldiers; railroad construction workers and land speculators and boarding house operators; gamblers and dancers, doctors and missionaries. And there were the Indians, into whose land all the rest moved.

2

Life on the Fur Frontier

Christopher Columbus set out in 1492 to find a route to India and its riches. Although the search for a Northwest Passage persisted for another 300 years or so before it was as successful as the terrain allowed, America itself was full of natural riches that could be exploited. The first of these was fur and pelts.

Indeed, long before Spain or France or England sent explorers up tidal rivers of the eastern seacoast, overseas fishermen had established a fur trade with the Native Americans. Cartier's voyages of 1534 and 1535 found fishermen in the Gulf of St. Lawrence and on up the St. Lawrence River; having originally landed to dry their fish, they added to their ships' cargo furs procured from the Indians. Thus, the well-developed trade among Native American tribes became an embryonic international trade for furs (DeVoto, *Course of Empire* 90).

In 1764 Sir William Johnson, head of the northern section of the British Department of Indian Affairs, estimated that 10,000 Indians hunted in the watersheds of the upper Mississippi and the Great Lakes to exchange skins for British manufactured goods. In that same year Johnson estimated that traders annually bartered goods worth £100,000 for furs. A trader who was shrewd could make a 100 percent profit (Purvis, 78). When England ousted France from east of the Mississippi at the conclusion of the French and Indian War, the centers of the fur trade moved west to forts such as Detroit and Michilimackinac.

ECONOMICS

Prior to the American Revolution the North American fur trade was profitable, though the war and its antecedent disruptions caused some decline in exports. Beaver was the glamour fur, the dominant fur in the trade, but in addition the bear, fox, marten, mink, muskrat, otter, raccoon, wildcat, and wolf were trapped for their fur. In 1770, for example, 136,392 beaver worth £23,895 were exported from North America. In that same year ships carried the furs of 15,136 bears, 20,840 minks, 69,986 raccoons, and 6,581 wolves (Purvis, 79). In light of the Indian trade, it may be worth noting that in 1770 domestic rum production was 4,807,000 gallons, 30,000 of which went directly into the fur trade to supply the Indians' demand for "British milk" (Purvis, 81).

The deerskin trade was also important. In the 1580s Thomas Harriot's list of "Merchantable commodities" from the Roanoke colony included "Furres . . . great store of otters . . . [and] Deer skinnes dressed" (Furnas, 25). Growing steadily through the eighteenth century, the deerskin trade peaked in the decades before the Revolution. From 1768 to 1772, Great Britain imported an annual average of 721,558 pounds (in weight) of deerskins from its colonies south of Canada. These deerskins accounted for £69,443, or 25 percent of the exports of all thirteen colonies—more than the overseas sales of iron, naval stores, and whale oil (Purvis, 79). Already the peltry trade was part of a broad international trade; from 1790 to 1792 the destinations of American deerskins included England, Scotland, Ireland, France, Spain, Holland, Germany, and Denmark (Purvis, 80).

Beaver skins and buckskins became units of exchange in backcountry areas of the colonies, influencing not only the economy but also the language. In 1735 a trader complained about a clerk who had that day "sold only eight bucks of goods." And in 1748 the Indian agent Conrad Weiser told Ohio Indians, "Every cask of whiskey shall be sold to you for five bucks in your own town" (Furnas, 37).

Trade—in Weiser's case, deerskins for whiskey—demonstrates an important aspect of initial crosscultural contact: Europeans and Native Americans did not have the same interpretation of the value of material goods. This basis for misinterpretation dates back to 1492. Columbus's log for October 12 reads, "I want the natives to develop a friendly attitude towards us. . . . I therefore gave red caps to some and glass beads to others. They hung the beads around their necks. . . . And they took great pleasure in this and became so friendly that it was a marvel. They traded and gave everything they had with good will, but it seems they have very little and are poor in everything" (Fuson, 76). Not only does the passage suggest a political motive for trade (to "develop a friendly attitude"), which became important later as France, England, Spain, and the United States competed for the Indians' allegiance, but it suggests a sharp dichotomy between two societies' definition of wealth. To Columbus, the natives were "poor in everything"; the Arawaks, however, didn't know they were poor. Indeed, they greeted the strangers with hospitality evidenced by gift-giving: parrots, balls of cotton thread, and "a kind of dry leaf." The representatives of one society were acting out of political or economic motives; the others, out of social motives. A mercantile society was meeting one that was not.

Wilcomb Washburn suggests that the Indians had

> no particular economic need for the products first offered by the Europeans . . . but received them gratefully for their decorative, aesthetic, magical, curiosity, or amusement "value." When [they] learned what pleased the European[s], the Indian[s] generously offered [their] "products"—such as gold ornaments—in measure that astounded the European[s] who thought in economic terms. This process continued, in some degree, until the Indian[s] adopted white economic values and placed on what [they] "gave" a price appropriate to the system of [their] European trading associate[s]. (Washburn, "Symbol, Utility and Aesthetics" 50)

There's a double failure of communication at first contact, no matter where on the continent it occurs, Washburn argues. Europeans fail to comprehend the importance of gift-giving in Indian culture—to establish rank or prestige, to mark important occasions in an individual's life, or to symbolize specific messages in intertribal diplomacy. Robert Rogers as governor at Michilimackinac argued strongly with his superiors that gifts should be given. However, they opposed giving "something for nothing," unable to understand the Indians' psychological and social values. As a corollary, many Indians, who had lived in harmony and balance with nature, could not understand whites' voracious demand for beaver. In 1804 a Mandan observed to Charles Mackenzie of the North West Company, "White people do not know how to live. [To seek beaver] they leave their houses in small parties, they risk their lives on the great waters, among strange nations [tribes], who will take them for enemies. What is the use of beaver? Do they make gun-powder for them? Do they preserve them from sickness? Do they serve them beyond the grave?" (Lavender, *Fist* 36).

Moreover, the European trade goods initially seemed to have little utilitarian value to the Indian. Washburn cites Thomas McCleish, the chief of the Hudson's Bay Company Fort York. He wrote in 1728 that the Indians turned practical, utilitarian objects into decorative ones:

"They always convert [kettles] in making fine [decorative] handcuffs and pouches which is of greater value with them than twice the price of the kettle" (Washburn, "Symbol, Utility and Aesthetics" 52).

The Europeans needed to create a demand in order to get their potential customers hooked. Once a dependency on European goods was established, the fur trade would be more profitable. Once the Indians learned that trade goods could make life easier, those goods would gain value. After all, making a canoe by cutting a tree with a sharpened stone and hollowing out the log with fire was simplified with a metal ax. Sewing was easier with a metal needle and silk or linen thread than with a bone awl and thread made of split animal sinew. An iron or copper kettle made cooking easier. Unlike an earthenware pot, it didn't break; it held water better than the most water-tight woven basket; it could be placed directly over the fire. Leather clothing, as David Thompson, mapmaker for the North West Company, noted, "when wet sticks to the skin and is very uncomfortable, requires time to dry, with caution to keep its shape. . . . Every [Indian] is glad . . . to change his leather dress, for one of woolen manufacture of England" (qtd. in Lavender, *Fist* 24).

Liquor could also make life easier—or seem to—and, despite protests of wise native leaders, missionaries, and governments, it soon became a staple in the fur trade.

Across the entire continent of North America, the fur trade was the "cutting edge of the frontier process." It had high potential for profit. Because furs were "low bulk and high demand," transportation costs over great distances could be offset. Moreover, when the Indian remained the primary "producer of the product" (i.e., did the trapping), there need not be a line item for salaries, as was required in the system inaugurated by William Ashley and followed by his successors (Wishart, 18).

The fur trader in America was, thus, a revolutionary force, creating ever-changing patterns of stability and instability among three major elements: the land itself, the Native Americans, and the Europeans or Euro-Americans. As we shall see, the land itself (geography, topography, plants, animals, and climate) was at first daunting to the newcomers. At every step the Euro-Americans had to learn how to survive in this land before they could prosper. And although the skills and knowledge learned at Michilimackinac, for example, could be adapted farther west, the diaries, logs, and journals of trappers and traders make constant reference to bitter cold, starvation when meat animals disappeared from a locale, and dangers of frostbite and snowblindness.

The Native American populations—with much broader experience— were well adapted to nature. Not only did they live in harmony with it, but it was intertwined with their religious beliefs and practices. Unlike Europeans, the Native Americans had no concept of land as private property, though individual tribes did have recognized hunting grounds. To them, although nature provided food, clothing, and shelter, it was not to be despoiled. Thus, in colonial times the eastern Indians in general preferred the French to the English because of policies of land use. Whereas the English cleared the land of trees for farms and settlements, the French tended to leave the forest intact. But corruption also came with trade. In 1804 a Mandan observed to a trader, "In my young days there were no white men, and we knew no wants. . . . The white people came, they brought with them some good, but they brought the small pox, and they brought evil liquors; then Indians since diminish and they are no longer happy" (Lavender, *Fist* 431, n.2).

Despite their superior technology, the Euro-Americans were, at every stage of the advancing frontier, inept, naive greenhorns who had to learn how to survive in the wilderness and among its peoples. The transformation into one who knew enough to survive was often punctuated by formal, though rowdy, initiation ceremonies. A new trapper, for example, was dunked in the Missouri when his keelboat reached the mouth of the Platte. For the trade out of Michilimackinac, the initiation was at Grand Portage, where those who were to winter in the wilderness, the *hivernants*, were recognized as an elite distinct from those who would turn back to the fort. John Macdonnel, a trader, describes his initiation. After water was sprinkled in his face from a "small cedar Bow," he vowed, among other things, "never to kiss a *voyageur*'s wife against her own free will." The ceremony was accompanied by gunshots "fired one after another in an Indian manner" and by sharing a "two gallon keg" (DeVoto, *Course of Empire* 241).

The land was changing the man. And already a reciprocal change had occurred. The Indians were now armed with guns—though they shot them "in an Indian manner." Euro-Americans and Native Americans were heading west together to trap—for business, not merely for subsistence—an activity that would in turn change the land. Not one of the three elements—the land, the Native American, or the Euro-American— would ever be the same again.

As revolutionary as the fur trade was in ecological or cultural terms, it was also inextricably bound up in international politics.

France was the pioneer nation in building the American fur trade. As the historian Hiram Chittenden notes, early exploration was linked to trade: Joliet, who with Marquette discovered the upper Mississippi, was a trader, and LaSalle, while exploring new territory, sent back furs (Chittenden, 85). When the English successfully challenged the French for control of the continent during the French and Indian War (1754–1760), the border forts were turned over to the English. But treaties alone did not bring peace, and Indians of the border territory remained suspicious of English land-grabbing tendencies. In 1763, Indians of Pontiac's confederacy attacked western forts from Pittsburgh to Michilimackinac. The fall of the latter fort bears recounting. The Indians lured the British commander and many of his troops outside to watch a game of *bagataway*, called *le jeu de la cross* by Canadian *voyageurs*. As the game continued, squaws entered the fort with guns and tomahawks under their blankets. Seemingly accidentally, the ball sailed into the fort. Players followed it, seizing their weapons—and the fort. None of the fort's French-Canadian traders were harmed, but almost every Englishman died. One of the few survivors, Alexander Henry, described what he saw from his hiding place: "The dead were scalped and mangled; the dying were writhing and shrieking under the unsatiated knife and tomahawk; and from the bodies of some, ripped open, their butchers were drinking the blood, scooped up in the hollow of joined hands and quaffed amid shouts of rage and victory" (Lavender, *Fist* 9).

Although a similarly detailed examination of other instances of the sweep of frontier history is impossible here, several observations can be made. Although by the Treaty of Paris following the Revolutionary War, English forts south of the border with Canada became American, all geographic boundaries hadn't been determined. (In the Great Lakes area the canoe trade route became the international boundary, but western borders were disputed.) Thus, economic control—through trade—was imperative. The Louisiana Purchase increased exponentially the area in which exploration, trade, and diplomacy were linked. Though Astoria, John Jacob Astor's post on the Columbia River, failed as a step in his developing monopoly of the fur trade, it gave the United States another basis for claiming Oregon (DeVoto, *Course of Empire* 539). From the Atlantic to the Pacific, the fur trade was at one time or another a factor in international affairs.

Ultimately, however, the fur trade was big business. Unlike others who ventured into unsettled territories—missionaries or military officers, for example—the goal of those directing the fur trade was acquisition of money. In contrast to those in more settled regions who trapped for pin-money—farmers or storekeepers, for example—the goal was big money, vast profits, a monopoly if possible. The fact that the fur trade was a complex organization as hierarchical as modern corporations, enmeshed in a pattern of international trade spanning the globe, will become evident in the following discussion. It is also clear that whereas the goal of those directing the companies was profit, the daily lives of those in the field were often challenging, uncomfortable, and dangerous.

THE MONTREAL-MICHILIMACKINAC FUR TRADING SYSTEM

The historian Bernard DeVoto describes the annual fur fair at Montreal, New France:

> Savage and Christian pageantry, high mass and dancers in worship
> of the bears, Jesuit sermons and Indian oratory, breechclouts and
> velvet breeches, nuns, war chiefs, woods-runners, ceremonious
> banquets, tribal debauches, the nights crimson with fire, musical
> with river songs, hideous with the chanting and the yelping of the
> braves. (*Course of Empire* 97)

Colorful enough, this meeting of continental and world markets. Further
inland on the St. Lawrence River–Great Lakes water system, at the point
where Lakes Huron and Michigan cut Michigan into parts, lies Fort
Michimilackinac (or Mackinac) on the island of the same name. Life there
was generally boring and brutal, as Robert Rogers's wife Elizabeth discovered when she arrived expecting the glamorous life of a colonial governor's wife. (Kenneth Roberts's novel *Northwest Passage* describes life
there well.) The boredom, however, was frequently broken by events in
the annual trade cycle, the result of a rationally organized, adequately
capitalized, complex business adapting to conditions of extreme weather
and diverse cultural expectations. The fort was also a living illustration
of a hard-won policy: to set up trading posts near the Indians to provide
them necessities so they could spend most of their time trapping rather
than traveling, to increase their desire for European goods, and to prevent them from being seduced by rival traders coming up the Mississippi.

By 1800 housing was mixed on the island: a few rich individuals had
erected white clapboard houses, but most dwellings were less attractive—constructed of logs set upright in the ground, plastered over, and
roofed in cedar. At either end of the village were Indian camps, "of
round-topped huts, the intervening spaces littered with beached canoes,
cooking tripods, sleds, fur-drying racks" and dogs everywhere (Lavender, *Fist* 21).

Throughout most of the year the food was boring, consisting of fish
from the lakes, game traded from the Indians, lyed corn bought from
Indians of the Michigan peninsula, and maple sugar that was made in
spring by the residents. After Fort Michilimackinac had been transferred
to the Americans, foodstuffs were easier to come by. Buffalo, Erie, and
Cleveland became supply ports for schooners loaded with flour, Monon-
gahela whiskey, tobacco, kegged butter, lyed corn, and pickled meat
(Lavender, *Fist* 57–58).

With the arrival of spring, the ice melted from the lakes
and the first merchandise canoes arrived from Montreal, *Voyageurs,*
bringing heavy Mackinac blankets made in England, *Hivernants,*
their sizes designated by "points," or black lines woven *and the*
into the edges. (A three-point blanket measured 6'6" by *Hierarchy of*
5'6"; as the number of points decreased, so did the size *the Fur Trade*
of the blanket.) Also among the trade goods were axes and needles and

looking glasses; traps and bullet molds, skinning knives and flints, powder and lead; vermilion and black silk handkerchiefs, bright ribbons, and silver trinkets—items to satisfy vanity as well as utility. Goods came also for the *voyageurs*: "red caps, striped shirts, warm capotes, playing cards ... short-stemmed pipes" and tobacco twisted into one- or two-pound "carrots" (Lavender, *Fist* 25). Always there were eight-gallon kegs of West Indies rum or Pennsylvania whiskey or a very concentrated wine that could be diluted 1:3 with water before drinking. The arrival of the *voyageurs* with these goods was intentionally dramatic. Before they came into view they beached their canoes, shaved, and changed into pink and white shirts, bright sashes, and beaded pouches.

From the west came the canoes of the *hivernants*, bringing in the winter's catch of pelts. Faces ravaged by frostbite, stinking from the pelts and infrequent baths, wearing feathers in their caps to announce their combative prowess, they surged ashore. They prayed at the parish church and beat each other bloody in fistfights (the champion of one group taking on the champion of another) for yet another feather; they sang and laughed and drank and visited the Indian squaws. In short, they made up for the winter's denials and hardships by making the most of the brief time between the sale of their furs and their setting out again. In the brief interval, many also lost much of their money and contracted venereal disease. It was all a grand release from winter's deprivations.

There was a clear hierarchy in the fur trade. At the top were the merchants, the policy makers, the decision makers—in Montreal, mainly. Not hands-on men, they received and processed information. From the west by summer expresses came estimates of the year's take in beaver, muskrats, otter; from London and Leipzig came information about demand, based on fashion trends or economic conditions or dislocations in shipping caused by war or politics. On the basis of such information the merchants adjusted exchange rates (how many tin kettles should one of the traders in the field pay for a pack of beaver skins?), ordered trade goods from around the world (blue beads from Venice, woolen goods from England, vermilion from Canton), and entertained representatives from European fur houses (as well as John Jacob Astor from New York) who were placing orders to fulfill their requirements.

Clerks were indispensable, whether in Montreal or Michilimackinac. They supervised the opening of bales of fur, counted the pelts, had them beaten free of moths and dust, graded them according to quality, and sorted them into lots of equal quality to be packed into bundles that were branded with each merchant's own mark. They prepared shipping invoices and rounded up *voyageurs* to load the bundles aboard craft for shipment east. They copied their employers' business correspondence and trade inventory, and they prepared lists for European suppliers. They negotiated with local craftspeople—tailors and seamstresses, blacksmiths and boat builders—for locally produced products: axes and traps from bar iron, wool capotes (hooded cloaks or coats) and trousers, oil-cloth for covering the goods, new boats and canoes.

After the fall of New France, the merchants and clerks were primarily Scots and Englishmen who scorned the *voyageurs*, whom they found to be "dirty, profane, excitable, noisy, forever talking, forever singing, of volatile anger and quick delight, comradely with Indians who were even grimier than they" (DeVoto, *Course of Empire* 241). The *voyageurs* were French Canadians who were used to poverty and hard work. Roman Catholic, they were blessed by the local priest as they started west— though it was said that their swearing shocked the Indians (DeVoto, *Course of Empire* 241). Providing the muscle to move the furs and trade goods, they were divided into two distinct classes. The *hivernants*, con-sidered the elite, signed on for three- to five-year stints in the interior. The others were pejoratively called *mangeurs de lard*, or pork eaters, who powered the canoes to Michilimackinac and back to Montreal.

Voyageurs of both categories signed an indenture that bound them to their employer. (Many were illiterate, merely making their mark or an X.) A pork eater might be paid as little as $64–$80 for a season's work. In addition, he received equipment—blanket, shirt, pants, handkerchiefs, and tobacco—according to his bargaining ability. Unlike his post finery, his working clothing included an ordinary "red wool cap, long shirt, Indian breechclout, trousers, or perhaps deerskin leggings" (Lavender, *Fist* 55).

At the bottom of the hierarchy was the Indian who did the actual trapping and on whom all the rest depended.

Dependable, swift transportation was essential to this trade system, whose annual cycle was significantly **Transportation** shortened by ice on northern lakes and rivers. Though some winter transportation was accomplished by dogsled, the bulk of the freight—both furs and trade goods—was transported by water.

Manufactured goods came to Montreal by ship, but the trip to the interior was mostly by canoe. These were not ten- or twelve-foot personal canoes; they were much larger, modeled on the war canoes of the Far Nations. As far as the Grand Portage out of Lake Superior, traders used the *canots du maître*—up to six feet wide and thirty-five to forty feet long, capable of carrying four tons of goods and a crew of fourteen. Beyond the Grand Portage the *canot du nord* was used—smaller (twenty-five feet long with a crew of up to ten) and more manageable. Both canoes were made of local materials. The frame was made of slats of red cedar; strips of birch bark ¼" thick were laced to it with *watape*, a thread made from spruce roots. When finished, the canoe was waterproofed with melted pine resin. *Voyageurs* took a supply of this resin on the trip, for seams had to be treated daily. The *voyageurs* painted the paddles in bright reds and greens and white, and they often added bright geometric designs or a painting of an Indian profile to the bow faces.

The strength and skill of the *voyageurs* were fundamental to a successful trading venture. Along the way the canoes often had to be taken through dangerous "white water," extremely hazardous since the birch bark—which could be punctured by a misplaced moccasined foot—was vulnerable to the slightest contact with a snag or a rock. If the canoe should turn over in churning rapids, it meant not only loss of goods but often loss of life. Rarely was it possible to swim to shore; indeed, small wooden crosses on the shore spoke silent requiems. The *voyageurs* wore amulets and chanted incantations, appeasing both Christian and Indian deities for protection (DeVoto, *Course of Empire* 238–40; Lavender, *Fist* 27–28, 55–57, 374).

The positions of bowman and steersman required the greatest skill and responsibility; they consequently got higher pay than the "middleman." On the lakes in still water, the former could paddle canoes at six miles per hour; every sixteen-hour day they thrust their paddles into the lake 56,700 times. If there was a following wind, they would rig an oilcloth sail and make nine miles per hour. The 900-mile trip required three weeks to a month, though the light express canoes used for carrying urgent messages could make it in half that time.

The *voyageurs* needed not only skill and endurance but also strength because of portages, places where the canoes had to be taken out of the water and carried over land to more navigable water. Grand Portage, between Lake Superior and Rainy Lake, was nine miles long—a ten-day carry. (The *canot du maître* itself weighed about 500 pounds, not to mention its maximum four tons of lading.) On portages *voyageurs* changed from moccasins, which could not stand up to rocky conditions, to shoes made of ox-hide. They carried the cargo on their backs, wearing leather tumplines around their foreheads to balance the pack in place.

The goods, thus, had to be packed so that a man could carry them. The standard bale, whether of goods or fur, weighed ninety pounds. Alcohol, which arrived in Montreal in barrels, was transferred to eight-gallon kegs. The normal load was two bales stacked one atop the other, though folk legend has it that some heroic types managed to carry as many as five or six. (Incidentally, the job of the clerks who packed the bales was fairly complex, for beyond the relatively simple job of making them the right weight, they had to include a variety of goods in each pack to facilitate the job of the trader. Thus, rather than packing one bale full of blankets and another full of knives, trinkets, and gunpowder, both of which would have to be opened by the trader, subjecting him to casual theft by light-fingered customers, the clerk packed into each bale a whole range of goods.)

In addition to portaging, each night's camp required a good deal of work from the *voyageurs*. The birch bark would not withstand the canoe's being run ashore; moreover, seams had to be recaulked each night. Thus, *voyageurs* would bring the canoe near shore, leap out into the cold water to stop its progress, carry the bourgeois (or merchant-trader) and his translator ashore (hierarchy was rigid; these men did not engage in manual labor), unload the canoe, and then carry it ashore. In the morning the process was reversed.

Such extraordinary physical activity consumed an enormous number of calories. Twice each day the *voyageurs* ate a quart of lyed corn, flavored with bear oil or buffalo fat and boiled into a thick soup. For those on their first trip out of Montreal who couldn't quite stomach this meal, there were dried peas boiled with fat pork into which ship's biscuit was crumbled (Lavender, *Fist* 28). There was rum at night and, for the trader and clerk, tea and wine.

Such a life may sound bone-grindingly weary. But there were respites that actually contributed to a greater efficiency. Depending on distance or time or difficulty of the water, there were occasional rest stops called "pipes." And there were songs (sometimes sung in unison, sometimes in dialogue with the steersman) to keep the paddles moving in rhythm; they were, however, also recreational, their lyrics ranging from the naive to the obscene.

Without the *voyageur*, the Montreal-Michilimackinac trading system would not have worked. One trader, John Johnston, described the labor of a portage in which everyone was plagued by mosquitoes. In addition to demonstrating the hierarchy (he watches as they work), the passage attests to the machismo and esprit de corps of the *voyageurs*:

> I who had nothing else to do but defend myself . . . was left a perfect spectacle of deformity, my eyes closed up, and my mouth distorted in a most frightful manner; judge then the condition of the poor men, engaged in carrying baggage . . . with their faces, necks and breasts exposed, and the blood and sweat in commingled streams running from them. But they seemed to mind it very little, making game of some young men whose first trip it was, whom they . . . treated with great contempt if they expressed pain or fatigue. (Lavender, *Fist* 57)

Of this system in the last decades of the eighteenth century, Bernard DeVoto wrote:

> This was the first North American business that required large scale organization. In the course of the next two decades problems of control, supply, finance, routing, and traffic control produced a system remarkably like that of any big corporation today. It was an

elaborate and exquisitely interdependent system, so delicately adjusted that only experts could keep any part of it going and so
expensive in the overhead that combinations were inevitable.
(*Course of Empire* 238)

THE ROCKY MOUNTAIN FUR TRADING SYSTEM

Two comparably complex systems with similar mercantile goals but
different organization, shaped by the ecosystems they exploited, had
their heyday from 1806 to 1840 in the Rocky Mountains and on the upper
Missouri River. Once again, the trading system and the daily life of those
within it were powerfully influenced by geography, typography,
weather, flora and fauna, and the indigenous Native American population. Though there are obvious points of connection and overlap between
the two, the Rocky Mountain system illustrates life in the field and the
Upper Missouri system illustrates life in the fort.

Central to the Rocky Mountain trading system was the rendezvous,
an annual meeting of traders and trappers at a prearranged place and
time (usually in July) in the mountains. The exchange of goods and furs
was thus in sharp contrast to that of either the Michilimackinac or the
Upper Missouri systems, where such exchange was done mostly in forts.
The Rocky Mountain system was predicated on the willingness of white
trappers to stay in the mountains for extended times. (When Jim Bridger
finally returned to St. Louis, he had been in the mountains for seventeen
years.) The Rocky Mountain system was also in sharp contrast to the
system of the English Hudson's Bay Company, which also trapped far
into the transmontane region of the Snake River. However, the Hudson's
Bay Company sent brigades from the Columbia to the interior on an
annual or biennial basis. A good deal of their effort and time was thus
expended in traveling to and from the best trapping streams. The Rocky
Mountain system was, in contrast, more efficient because of the special-
ization of roles. Those who trapped, trapped; others delivered the goods
to rendezvous and returned to St. Louis with the fur. It was William
Ashley who created the rendezvous system, supplying men in the field
with pack trains brought to predetermined spots.

River Transport— William Ashley's initial experience in the western
William Ashley's fur trade was on the Missouri River. He received his
Experiences first trading license on April 11, 1822; it was renewed
in 1823 when William Clark, superintendent of In-
dian Affairs at St. Louis, granted Ashley and his partner, Andrew Henry, a license good for five years to trade with the
Arikaras, Mandans, Blackfeet, and Crow "within and west of the Rocky
Mountains." Records indicate that they posted a bond of $5,000 guar-
anteeing their adherence to U.S. law and indicating a capital of $40,000.

Preparatory to their first ascent of the Missouri, the partners advertised in the *Missouri Gazette & Public Advertiser* for one hundred "enterprising young men" to ascend the Missouri River and be employed for "one, two, or three" years in the fur trade.

The trip upstream was arduous, and not all the "enterprising young men" were happy to have answered the ad. One of them, Daniel L. Potts, wrote to a friend back in Pennsylvania:

> I embarked for the Rocky Mountains . . . for the purpose of hunting and traping [*sic*] and trading with the Indians in the company of about one hundred men. We hoisted our sails on the third of April 1822 at Saint Lewis and arived at Cedar fort about the middle of July when we were reduced to the sad necessity of eating any thing we could catch as our provision where exhausted and no game to be had, being advanced five hundred miles above the fronteers, we were glad to get a Dog to eat and I have seen some geather the skins of Dogs up through the Camp sing[e] and roast them and eat hearty this so discouraged me that I was determined to turn tail up stream and bear my cours down in company with eight others and by the way lost from the others without gun amunition provition or even cloths to my back on account being four hundred miles from aney white people or even knowing where to find Indians. . . . young Birds, frogs, and Snakes where exceptable food with me and not means of fire I in the course of a few days fortunately fell in with a party of Indians who treated me with great humanity and tarried with them four days and then fell in with a trader who conducted me within 350 miles of the fronteers he being able to give me but little aid I tarried but three days when I started with provition consisting of only ¾ of a pound of Buffaloe suet and arived at the fronteers in six days [w]here by eating too much and starvation I was taken with a severe spell of sickness which all but took my life. (Morgan, *West* 7–8)

Ashley's experiences weren't much more pleasant. His first boat, on which Potts traveled, sank after hitting a snag or tree submerged in the river; he lost $10,000 in provisions, ammunition, guns, and traps. A second boat started out in May under Jedediah Smith. His journal notes that while "turning a point full of sawyers, the boat by an unexpected turn brought the top of her mast against a tree that hung over the water and wheeling with the side to a powerful current was swept under in a moment" (Morgan, *West* 12). Despite the bravery of "two active men" who jumped into the current and rescued a few goods, including several hand mirrors, Ashley suffered another $10,000 loss. The final straw occurred on June 2, 1823, when Ashley, aboard the keelboat *Rocky Moun-*

tain, was attacked by the Arikaras. The incident involved a good deal of duplicity, for the "Ricaree" principal chief, The Bear, invited Ashley to dinner after an apparently successful bartering for horses. Ashley later wrote:

> I hesitated for a moment, but at length concluded to accept it, as I did not wish them to know that I apprehended the least danger from them. I took with me my interpreter and went to the lodge of the chief, where I was treated with every appearance of friendship by him. . . . The next morning just before day light, I was informed that the Indians had killed one of my men . . . and in all probability would attack the boats in a few minutes. (Morgan, *West* 26)

They did, and in the fighting that ensued Ashley lost twelve men killed and eleven wounded. That the attack was instigated by British traders (competition between countries and companies was fierce) was strongly supported by the fact that there were 600 warriors; "about three fourths of them are armed with London Fusils that carry a ball of great accuracy" (Morgan, *West* 27). Two days later Ashley wrote to Major Benjamin O'Fallon at Fort Atkinson requesting a military presence on the upper Missouri.

The Overland Route— Charles Larpenteur's Account
Though Ashley and his successors—Jedediah Smith, William Sublette and Robert Campbell, of the Rocky Mountain Company—made some use of river transport, most travel was overland following the Missouri north to Ft. Atkinson, then turning west along the North Platte and across South Pass. It was an arduous trip for man and beast. Charles Larpenteur, a French immigrant who at age 21 decided to try his luck in the "Far West" near St. Louis and who subsequently spent forty years in the fur trade, describes his first sight of

> all that beaver—all those mountain men unloading their mules, in their strange mountain costume—most of their garments of buck-skin and buffalo hide, but all so well greased and worn that it took close examination to tell what they were made of. To see the mules rolling and dusting is interesting and shocking at the same time; most of them, having carried their burdens of 200 pounds' weight for about 2,000 miles, return with scarcely any skin on their backs; they are peeled from withers to tail, raw underneath from use of the surcingle, and many are also lame. (Larpenteur, 7)

Soon thereafter Larpenteur signed a contract with Sublette and Campbell. At St. Charles he was assigned to a "mess" of nine first-rate old *voyageurs*—French boys from Cahokia, the French trade establishment across the river from St. Louis. Each man was given three mules, one to ride and two as pack animals. (In other outfits the riding animal was a horse.) Larpenteur's mule, named Simon, was better than most in that he only occasionally bucked Larpenteur off. The pack mules were loaded with "liquor Guns Powder led Blanket Pantaloons Shirts capos [capotes, or cape-like outer garments] Beaver Traps . . . raisins [and] chocolatte" (Larpenteur, 134). The men's personal possessions were spartan, to save space for trade goods. They were not allowed to "carry more than one pair of three pound [three point Mackinac] blankets for bedding." (Other records indicate that each man was issued for his animals two halters, at least one sixteen-foot rein, one saddle, one saddle blanket, one bear-skin cover, one bridle, and a two-foot wooden stake with a pointed iron socket at one end and an iron band at the other—to be used in picketing the animals. All such items of equipment were entered in account books against the individual's name. Sunder, 62–63)

For the first three or four days the mules kicked off the packs and ran away, producing a good deal of laughter at the expense of those who had to catch their animals and replace the packs; even after the mules had, in general, accepted the daily routine, there was a runaway nearly every day. Food for members of the supply train consisted of bacon and hard-tack—no sugar or coffee—for three or four days, after which each man received a "small piece of sheep meat." (This supply train was accompanied by a drove of sheep on foot.) This was to be their daily fare until they reached buffalo country.

After the supply train had been en route for about a week, the group of forty men was divided into guard details, each on duty every third day. After the animals had been picketed inside the camp circle, the guards were posted on the perimeter. Because Indians were known to creep up to camps and shoot men wandering into the plain, guards were required to stay at their posts. After a full day on the trail it was difficult to stay awake for the two and a half hour shift of guard duty, so every twenty minutes the guards were required to call out "All's well" to prove they were awake. If the captain of the guard found a man asleep, he immediately took his gun away. In the morning the miscreant was fined $5 and "three walks"—required to go on foot for three days (Larpenteur, 14–17).

Trail discipline also required that men work reasonably well together. Etienne Provost disciplined feisty new recruits full of macho bluster and quarrelsomeness. He'd form them all into a crude circle and require the braggarts to fight. Each victor was challenged until only one man—who had knocked all the others into submission—was left. Provost awarded him a red belt in token of his "championship," and the problem of fist-fights was settled (Hafen, vol. 6, 384–85).

The men's dietary tedium was broken three days after they reached the Platte, when hunters came in with much-anticipated buffalo meat. It was cut up and set to boil in kettles. The only fuel available was "the stalks of some large dried weeds, the wild sunflower" (Larpenteur, 19). When the meat was finally deemed cooked, "preparations were made to dish it out; but, as we had no pans, a clean place was looked for on the grass, and the contents of the kettle were poured out. All hands seated around the pile hauled out their butcher knives, opened their little sacks of salt, and then began operations" (Larpenteur, 20). This first buffalo, however, was so tough it was literally unchewable. Later, when they had killed fat cows, the veterans warned the greenhorns that "we should now get a sickness called . . . *le mal de vache*; it is caused by eating too much fat meat alone, and some are known to have died of it" (Larpenteur, 21).

The Bourgeois in St. Louis   And so it went, on to the mountain rendezvous. It is no wonder that many of the bourgeois, the entrepreneurs, eventually preferred living in comparative comfort in St. Louis. The city was the major collecting and dispensing depot for the fur trade. It is estimated that annually from 1807 to 1840 an average of $200,000–$300,000 in furs was channeled to the East Coast and Europe from this city (Wishart, 207). DeVoto calls St. Louis "the mistress of the western waters," a town "more cosmopolitan than any other place in America" in 1833. Indians and trappers and *voyageurs* wandered its cobblestone streets, but there was also an aristocracy whose roots preceded the Louisiana Purchase—the Chouteaus, Bertholds, Prattes, Cérrés and Cabannés. Along the river the wharves of the new steamboats extended out into the Mississippi. Above a flat that was often flooded in springtime, warehouses had been built; nearby were the "large structures of gray and yellow stone which always smelled to heaven"—the warehouses where the pelts were stored prior to shipment to New York, London, Athens, Constantinople, St. Petersburg, and Canton (DeVoto, *Across the Wide Missouri* 16). Few businesses in St. Louis were separate from the fur trade. To some travelers in 1834, St. Louis with its "well-kept gardens and well-dressed better citizens" was little different from any eastern city. But other travelers noticed the unpaved roads, sometimes with carcasses of dead animals in the gutters. The houses of poorer residents were surrounded by pools of muddy water in which children floated toy boats (Sunder, 138).

In the spring of 1832, Washington Irving spent a night at the St. Louis home of Auguste Pierre Chouteau. His journal records his impressions, fragmentary and impressionistic:

Come in sight of Col's house—white log house with Piazza, surrounded by trees. Come to beautiful, clear river, group of Indian nymphs half naked on banks—with horses near—arrival at house—

old negro runs to open gate—mouth from ear to ear—group of Indians round tree in court yard—roasting venison—horses tethered near—negroes run to shake hand and take horses—some have handkerchief across head—half breeds—squaws—negro girls running and giggling—dogs of all kinds—hens flying and cackling—wild turkeys, tamed geese—Piazza with buffalo skin thrown over railing—room with guns—rifles.

Supper, venison stakes, roast beef, bread, cakes, coffee—waited on by half breed—sister of Mr. Chouteau's concubine—adjourn to another room—pass thro open hall in which Indians are seated on floor. They come into the room—two bring chairs—the other seats himself on the floor with his knees to his chin—another Indian glares in at the window. House formed of logs—a room at each end—an open hall with staircase in the centre—other rooms above—in the two rooms on the ground floor two beds in each room with curtains—white washed log walls—tables of various kinds—Indian ornaments &c.

Half breeds loitering about the house—dogs and cats of all kinds strolling about the hall or sleeping among harness at one end of the piazza.... A quarter mile from the Col's house is his race course on a beautiful little level Prarie. He has a great number of horses which the blacks drive by the house in a drove. (qtd. in Hafen, vol. 9, 82)

Clearly the lifestyle of one of St. Louis's leading citizens was vastly different from that of the mountain men upon whom his wealth depended.

There were three main categories of trappers in the Rocky Mountain system: the *engagés*, supplied and salaried by the companies whose furs were the property of the company; the skin trappers, outfitted by the company on credit, who paid off their debt at the end of the season and kept whatever balance there was for themselves; and the free trappers, who worked alone or in small groups, owed no allegiance to any particular company, and sold their furs to the highest bidder (Wishart, 125). Collectively they constitute the mountain man, a unique American type epitomized for many by Kit Carson, Tom Fitzpatrick, and Jim Bridger. The mountain man was "the proudest of all the titles worn by the Americans who lived their lives out beyond the settlements" (DeVoto, *Year* 58).

The Mountain Man

Not everyone so thoroughly admired the mountain man. David J. Wishart, an economic historian writing on the fur trade, identifies three stereotypes of the mountain man that, like all stereotypes, have some basis in truth. The trapper is portrayed by some as an "epic hero who confronted and partially tamed the wilderness" (Wishart, 206). This is the type DeVoto calls the Long Hunter, "the man who knew the wilderness

An old-time mountain man with his ponies. Courtesy of the Denver Public Library, Western History Collection.

and ... held the admiration of the settlements," the man skilled in "woodcraft, forest craft, and river craft," the man "in flight from the sound of an axe ... [living] under a doom which he himself created, but westward he went free" (*Year* 59). This is the man captured by James Fenimore Cooper as Natty Bumppo.

The trapper has also been seen as an outsider, a renegade, a "daring but degraded character who was escaping the strictures of a civilized society" (Wishart, 206). James Clyman describes searching for *engagés* in "grog shops and other sinks of degredation" (Morgan, *West* 23). The fact that some *engagés* were thieves is revealed in a story he tells. One day when their keelboat was drawn up near a settlement, the men went out hunting and came back with "plenty of game Eggs Fowls Turkeys and what not." They built a fire ashore, dressed, cooked and ate their dinner, and then burned the leftovers. The next morning settlers arrived at the keelboat, looking for their poultry. Clyman gave them permission to search the boat, but nothing was found. Later in the day when the wind rose enough to be useful in propelling the boat, the sails were ordered unfurled and "out dropped pigs and poultry in abundance. A man was ordered to Jump in the Skiff and pick up the pigs and poultry" (Morgan, *West* 23).

There is further evidence of the mountain man as socially dysfunctional. One of the later, less well known mountain men was described as "nutty as a pet coon; [he] ate dirt and it killed him" (Hafen, vol. 5, 322). One trader, Edwin Denig, saw the trappers as a " 'desperate set of men more outlandish and more brutal than the traders and more than half-Indian in appearance and habits" (Wishart, 206).

Peter Skene Ogden, a trader for the Hudson's Bay Company, had a low opinion of Americans in the field; his superior, George Simpson, wrote that they are

> generally speaking people of the worst character, run-aways from Jails, and outcasts from Society, who take all their bad qualities along with them: this "motley crew" acknowledge no master, will conform to no rules or regulations, and are never on their guard so that they are frequently cut off and their camps plundered. When they fall in with friendly Indians, their conduct is so indiscreet that they scarcely ever fail to make enemies of them, and it is a well known fact, that War parties frequently pass our Camps without offering the least annoyance; yet will haunt and watch an American camp, for Days and Weeks, until a favorable opportunity occurs to make an attack. (Ogden, 18 n.4)

Even Francis Parkman, who came to consider Henry Chatillon not only the mountain man par excellence but also a friend, called the profession in general "the half savage men who spend their lives in trapping among the Rocky Mountains" (DeVoto, *Year* 65).

The historian William H. Goetzmann has offered another category for the mountain man: a "Jacksonian man," an "expectant capitalist" like most other Americans of that time. He argues that the primary motive for participating in the fur trade was to accumulate capital rapidly; such capital could then be invested in other ventures. Ashley, Sublette, and Campbell are illustrative of such entrepreneurial behavior, with subsequent ventures into banking, politics, coal mining, and stock breeding.

Finally, Bernard DeVoto could see the mountain man as simultaneous victim and victimizer. He argues:

> They were agents of as ruthless a commerce as any in human history; they were its exploited agents. The companies hired them— or traded with the highest order of them, the free trappers . . . — on terms of the companies' making, paid them off in the companies' goods, valued at the companies' prices deep in the mountains. They worked in a peonage like the greasers they despised, the freed Negroes of the South, or the sharecroppers of our day. The companies outfitted them and sent them out to lose their traps, their horses, and frequently their scalps—to come back broke and go deeper into debt for next year's outfit. Their trade capitalized starvation, was known to practice land piracy, and at need incited Indians against competitors. It made war on Indians who traded with competitors and debauched the rest with the raw alcohol that was called whiskey in the mountains. . . . The Indians went down before tin tubs curved to fit a packsaddle and filled with alcohol at fifty cents a gallon. . . . And, as they went down, took with them through the hole in the earth the scalps of mountain men. (*Year of Decision* 64)

There is no single description that fits all mountain men. They were of many nations. Aside from Americans (mostly from the Midwest and the upper South), Osborne Russell met Irish, French, Portuguese, and Canadian trappers. Some, like Jim Bridger, were illiterate, though that did not mean barbaric. During the winter of 1863–64 at Fort Laramie, Bridger asked an officer what was the "best book" ever written. Learning it was Shakespeare, Bridger went to the main emigrant road, stopped a wagon train, and paid for a volume of Shakespeare with a yoke of oxen. He then hired a German boy at $40 per month to read to him (Hafen, vol. 6, 99). Others, like Charles Larpenteur and Osborne Russell, were literate, leaving their journals as vivid firsthand accounts of the life of the mountain men.

Most Rocky Mountain trapping parties were small, ranging from six to eight men. By experience they had learned that a party large enough to defend itself against hostile Indians was too large to trap beaver successfully. Thus, each individual had to learn a wide variety of skills if he was to survive. DeVoto argues that the mountain man's combination of knowledge and skill honed through experience was the "most complex of the wilderness crafts practiced on this continent" (*Across the Wide Missouri* 159). What sorts of things need he be able to notice, evaluate, and act on if he were to be successful?

> Why do you follow the ridges into or out of unfamiliar country? What do you do for a companion who has collapsed from want of water while crossing a desert? How do you get meat when you find yourself without gunpowder in a country barren of game? What tribe of Indians made this trail, how many were in the band, what errand were they on, were they going to it or coming back from it, how far from home were they, were their horses laden, how many horses did they have and why, how many squaws accompanied them, and what mood were they in? . . . A branch floats down a stream—is this natural, or the work of animals, or of Indians or trappers? Another branch or a bush or even a pebble is out of place—why? . . . Buffalo are moving downwind, an elk is in an unlikely place or posture, too many magpies are hollering, a wolf's howl is off key—what does it mean?
>
> All this (with much more) is a continuous reference and checking along the margin or in the background of the trapper's consciousness while he practices his crafts as hunter, wrangler, furrier, freighter, tanner, cordwainer, smith, gunmaker, dowser, merchant. The result is a high-level integration of faculties. The mountain man had mastered his conditions—how well is apparent as soon as soldiers, goldseekers, or emigrants come into his country and suffer where he has lived comfortably and die where he has been in no danger. (DeVoto, *Across the Wide Missouri* 159–60)

Knowledge of the Beaver—A Mountain Man's Requisite Skill. More specifically, the mountain man had to know the beaver. The beaver is a strict monogamist, the family unit being a colony consisting of a male and a female and their young. Rocky Mountain beaver mate in February and have two to four cubs in late May or early June. The beaver reaches physical maturity—a weight of thirty to sixty pounds—at about two and a half years of age. When the cubs are fully grown they are driven from their parents' lodge to establish their own colony. Beaver prefer sluggish streams and small lakes but avoid areas that are likely to flood as well as rapid streams that might wash out their homes. Aspen, the preferred food of the beaver, rarely grows more than 100 feet from water; thus, the beaver need not wander far from its home pond. In summer the beaver also eats sedge, cattail roots, and water lilies. Where such conditions prevail, the beaver constructs either a lodge of branches plastered with mud or a den hollowed out of the riverbank. One of the best trapping grounds was in Blackfoot country at the three forks of the Missouri. Absaroka, the land of the Crows in the valleys of the Bighorn, Rosebud, Powder, and Tongue rivers, was also prime trapping country.

The very traits of the beaver led to its depletion. Because the pelt demanded by European markets was not the dark brown outer fur but rather the barbed, fibrous underhair, the prime trapping season was spring, although fall was also busy. However, during the summer the beaver pelt was too thin. Thus, some of the heaviest trapping was done during mating and whelping season. Moreover, the sedentary nature of the beaver made them relatively easy to catch; they were so plentiful in Absaroka that Indians reportedly could kill them with clubs. To this scene the trapper brought the improved technology of the steel trap (Wishart, 27–33).

Because of the beaver's nocturnal habits, traps were usually placed at sunset. Joe Meek describes the process:

> [The trapper] has an ordinary trap weighing five pounds, attached to a chain five feet long, with a swivel and ring at the end, which plays round what is called the float, a dry stick of wood, about six feet long. The trapper wades out into the stream, which is shallow, and cuts with his knife a bed for the trap, five or six inches under water. He then takes the float out the whole length of the chain in the direction of the centre of the stream, and drives it into the mud, so fast that the beaver cannot draw it out; at the same time tying the other end by a thong to the bank. A small stick or twig, dipped in musk or castor, serves as bait, and is placed so as to hang directly above the trap, which is now set. The trapper then throws water plentifully over the adjacent bank to conceal any footprints or scent by which the beaver would be alarmed, and going to some distance wades out of the stream. (Wishart, 180)

The beaver would be attracted to the castoreum, and the trap would snap shut on its foot. Unless it chewed off its foot it would drown, weighted down by the trap. Peter Skene Ogden noted in his journal for June 4, 1829, "Our traps have given us but five beaver, and four of this number were with only three feet each, having been already taken in the traps and made their escape" (Ogden, 157).

The mountain man then collected the traps at dawn.

The beaver was skinned immediately and along with the perineal glands, which yield the castoreum, and the tail, which was considered a delicacy, the pelt was carried back to the main camp. There the camp-keepers performed the relatively simple task of processing the pelt. First the flesh side of the skin was scraped clean. Then the skin was stretched on willow hoops and dried in the sun for a day. Finally the pelts were folded, fur inward, marked with the company's insignia, and compacted into bundles of 60 to 80 skins in preparation for transportation. (Wishart, 181)

All this the rookie had to learn before he earned the name of mountain man.

Other Skills of the Mountain Man. The learning wasn't always easy. Osborne Russell describes his failed first attempt to hunt a buffalo for meat. Despite his "elegant" rifle he could only wound the buffalo, reloading and shooting as fast as he could "until I had driven 25 bullets at, in, and about him." The animal still would not drop, and Russell was "obliged to give it up as a bad job and retreat to our encampment without meat" (Russell, 5–6). Later he mastered survival skills. He could keep himself warm by scraping away knee-deep snow, making a bed with cedar boughs, and rolling up with a companion in the one blanket they had to share (73). He could serve as mentor for a young companion wounded slightly by an arrow who whined in inexperience: "Oh dear we shall die here, we shall never get out of these mountains." Russell replied: "If you [persist] in thinking so you will die but I can crawl from this place upon my hands and one knee and kill 2 or 3 Elk and make a shelter of the skins dry the meat until we get able to travel." Russell's analysis of his companion is a tribute to his own skills as a mountain man. "He was not so much to blame [for his defeatism] as he was a young man who had been brot up in Missouri the pet of the family and had never done or learned much of anything but horseracing and gambling" (Russell, 103–4).

Additionally, the mountain man needed to know how to find and gather salt, repair guns, construct a bullboat, disguise and camouflage a cache where he stored goods and furs, treat wounds, and cure minor illnesses. It was also a plus to know how to swim; surprisingly, not all mountain men could. Moreover, communication was essential to trade and safety, and many mountain men were adept in one or more Indian languages. (While William Ashley was in the mountains during the summer of 1825 he compiled a list of "Names of Animals & Etc. in the Ute Language," the earliest effort at a Ute vocabulary. This compilation was of great interest to ethnologists [Morgan, *West* 115, 281].)

The mountain man also had to adapt to new equipment and unfamiliar living conditions. Osborne Russell describes the basic equipment of the trapper:

> A trapper's equipment is generally . . . one Animal upon which is placed one or two Epishemores a riding Saddle and bridle a sack containing six Beaver traps a blanket with an extra pair of Mocasins his powder horn and bullet pouch with a belt to which is attached a Tobacco sack with a pipe and implements for making fire with sometimes a hatchet fastened to the Pommel of his saddle his personal dress is a flannel or cotton shirt (if he is fortunate enough to obtain one, if not Antelope skin answers the purpose of over and under shirt) a pair of leather breeches with Blanket or smoked Buffaloe skin, leggings, a coat made of Blanket or Buffaloe robe a hat or Cap of wool, Buffaloe or otter skin his hose are pieces of Blanket lapped round his feet which are covered with a pair of Maccassins made of Dressed Deer Elk or Buffaloe skins with his long hair falling loosely over his shoulders complets his uniform. He then mounts and places his rifle before him on his Saddle. (Russell, 82)

Transportation in the Mountains In the mountains, transportation was usually by horse and mule. Thus, the mountain man had to care for his animals as well as himself. Especially during winter, with deep snows and sub-zero temperatures, the job wasn't easy—nor was survival easy for the animal. Ogden describes horses pawing through the snow to reach the grass beneath; on the coldest nights, the snow was so encrusted that the horses could not break through it, and morning found them still starving.

Often, when buffalo had consumed all available grass, trappers fed their animals the bark from sweet cottonwood trees. They seemed to thrive on it. William Ashley considered cottonwood bark "quite as nutritious as Timothy hay," and Joe Meek commented that "the animals fatten upon it quite as well as upon oats" (Wishart, 188). However, the bark did not keep them in the best condition, as Jed Smith notes in an October 1822 journal entry: "Forced to eat this bark from necessity . . . horses soon become verry fond of it and require little other assistance than the felling of the trees and strange as it may appear to those unacquainted with such things they become fat and will keep so during the winter if not used. But the fat acquired by this food is not permanent and is worn off by a few days of hard riding" (Morgan, *West* 39). Sometimes not even the bark was available. Ashley notes in his journal that once for a period of nine days his horses went without cottonwood.

Moreover, trappers had to worry about their horses being stolen. In much of the Rocky Mountain/northern Plains area, the Indians were extraordinarily adept horse thieves. Thus, it was common practice to let the horses graze for a while after camp was made, but generally they were tethered, or picketed—and sometimes hobbled—for the night. Russell tells us that "there is a proverb among mountaineers 'It is better to count ribs than tracks' "; that is, "it is better to fasten a horse at night untill you can count his ribs with poverty than turn him loose to fatten and count his tracks after an Indian has stolen him" (Russell, 56). However, because the horses and mules had acute senses of smell, they sometimes functioned as sentinels. Their snorting and whinnying when spooked by approaching Indians served to alert the camp.

Although riding and pack animals were brought from the jumping off points, their theft, exhaustion, or death often required replacements. Occasionally exhausted horses fell into ice-choked streams and drowned. Trading with the Indians, especially the Nez Percé, helped replenish the number, though sometimes the new animals were less than perfectly broken. The rate of exchange in the Snake River country averaged fifteen "made" beaver skins for one two-year-old horse (Ogden, 6).

For the men, too, the search for food was crucial to survival. Although Ashley's account books with trappers indicate that he **Food** brought to rendezvous some products for the trappers' personal use, one could not survive from July to July on them. In his records of an early rendezvous there are repeated references to coffee, sugar, and tobacco; two for pepper; one for flour, and one for soap; such items are clearly in the category of luxuries (Morgan, *West* 118–29).

Whereas saltpork, bacon, lyed corn, and seabiscuits were available to men on the keelboats, men in the mountains hunted most of their own food: black bear, deer, elk, mountain sheep, raccoons, wild turkeys, and, as bees were plentiful in some locales, honey. Once Ashley notes a "good supper" of a boiled wild goose. Often there were great herds of buffalo, too, which could be shot almost at will. Occasionally this butcher shop on the hoof provided an element of danger, even in camp; General Henry Atkinson described in his journal entry for September 14, 1825, how a buffalo bull ran through camp, almost knocking down the tent of Major Stephen Watts Kearney (Morgan, *West* 133–34).

Bread and vegetables were out of the question in the mountains, except for a kind of turnip root; thus, even "poor bull meat" was consumed. Osborne Russell describes a campsite during the winter of 1835–36. At any time of day one could find a fire going atop a bed of coals and ashes, a camp keeper periodically poking the ashes and rolling out "a ponderous mass of Buff beef," which, when hit with a club, "bounds 5 or 6 feet from the ground like a huge ball of gum elastic." This beating knocks off the ashes, preparatory to hacking the meat into huge slices that the trappers would chew while sitting around the fire, looking forward to the fat cows of summer's good grass (Russell, 239–40). At a more felicitous camp he describes "a large fire . . . encircled with Elk's ribs and meat cut in slices supported by sticks down which the grease ran in torrents" (Russell, 45). Other menus included a stew of bear meat and mutton seasoned with pepper and salt, roasted buffalo tongue, and Indian pemmican (dried meat and "fruit pounded together," mixed with buffalo marrow).

Often, for purposes of trade or diplomacy, trappers were invited to Indian lodges. Russell describes such entertainment at Christmas dinner 1838:

> [My host] was a French man with a flat head wife and one child. [Others at the festivities included a half-breed Iowa and his Nez Percé wife, a half-breed Cree, his Nez Percé wife and two children, and fifteen lodges of Snake Indians.] Three of the party spoke English but very broken therefore that language was made but little use of as I was familiar with the Canadian French and Indian tongue. About 1 oclk we sat down to dinner in the lodge where I staid which was the most spacious being about 36 ft., in circumference at the base with a fire built in the center around this sat on clean Epishemores all who claimed kin to the white man (or to use their own expression all that were gens d'esprit) with their legs crossed in true Turkish style—and now for the dinner. The first dish that came on was a large tin pan 18 inches in diameter rounding full of stewed Elk meat. The next dish was similar to the first heaped up with boiled Deer meat (or as the whites would call it Venison a term not used in the Mountains) The 3rd and 4th dishes were equal in size to the first containing a boiled flour pudding prepared with dried fruit accompanied by 4 quarts of sauce made of the juice of some sour berries and sugar Then came the cakes followed by about six gallons of strong Coffee already sweetened with tin cups and pans to drink out of large chips or pieces of Bark Supplying the places of plates. On being ready the butcher knives were drawn and the eating commenced at the word given by the landlady as all dinners are accompanied with conversation this was not deficient in this respect. The principal topics which was discussed was the political affairs of the Rocky Mountains The state of governments among the different tribes, the personal characters of the most distinguished warriors Chiefs etc. (Russell, 114–15).

Such celebrations were rare. During inclement weather or when too many hunters had scared away game, mountain men would literally be starving. That—and the sheer number of calories expended in ordinary physical activity—meant well-developed appetites. When a buffalo was shot the tongue was taken first, then the "boss," a small hump on the back of the neck, the hump ribs, then the flesh between the spine and the ribs, and the "lower belly fat"—considered one of the greatest delicacies. The mountain man would probably take the liver too and such portions of the intestines as his tastes suggested. Then he would "butcher out the thigh bone and use it to crack such other bones as might provide the best marrow." Francis Chardon especially enjoyed "nuts"—the original Rocky Mountain oysters. Many whites would eat the liver raw as soon as it was butchered out, seasoning it with the gall or sometimes with gunpowder. The trapper ate whatever meat was available, from his "own moccasins, parfleche, and lariats, in 'starvin' times,' on through the wide variety of mountain game . . . [including some special tidbits:] boiled beaver tail, 'panther,' and as an acquired taste young Oglala puppy." DeVoto notes that the mountain man boiled some cuts and seared or sautéed others; but most buffalo was slowly roasted, each man to his own fire, unless the trappers were divided into messes with their own cooks. The meat was skewered on a ramrod or a stick.

No man with more tableware than his belt-knife—gravy, juices, and blood running down his face, forearms, and shirt. He wolfed the meat and never reached repletion. Eight pounds a day was standard ration for the Hudson's Bay Company employees, but when meat was plentiful, a man might eat eight pounds for dinner, then wake a few hours later, build up the fire, and eat as much more. . . . Moreover, to the grease that stained the mountaineer's garments were added the marrow scooped from bones and the melted fat that was gulped by the pint. Kidney fat could be drunk without limit; one was more moderate with the tastier but oily belly fat, which might be automatically regurgitated if taken in quantity, although such a rejection interrupted no one's gourmandizing very long. (*Across the Wide Missouri* 41–42)

Nor were table manners carefully observed in the mountains. Frederick Ruxton described one extraordinary feeding. Two mountain men, seated opposite each other on epishemores, or saddle blankets, were enjoying one of the treats, *boudin* (guts) lightly seared above the fire. Squeezing the contents just ahead of their teeth, they began at opposite ends of the intestines, the pile of coiled guts between them. As the pile decreased in size, it became a kind of game between the two to make sure the other didn't get more than his fair share. Ruxton continues:

Every now and then, overcome by the unblushing attempts of his partner to bolt a vigorous mouthful [the mountain man] would suddenly jerk back his head, drawing out at the same moment, by the retreating motion, several yards of *boudin* from his neighbor's stomach (for the greasy viand required no mastication and was bolted whole) and, snapping up the ravished portions, greedily swallowed them. (qtd. in DeVoto, *Across the Wide Missouri* 41)

	Constant danger and discomfort marked life in the field.

Danger and Disease

Constant danger and discomfort marked life in the field. There are frequent references to frostbite, frozen feet, and snowblindness, voracious mosquitoes and horseflies, and intermittent fever, probably malaria. Grizzly bears were a major threat; Jedediah Smith had one ear torn almost completely off. Charles Larpenteur recalls an incident when a rabid wolf invaded a camp; there are frequent references in the literature to people being bitten by such wolves. If one didn't drown in the rivers, he could become seriously indisposed with dysentery from drinking their waters impregnated with alkali and Glauber's salts. Trying to escape from a wounded buffalo, William Ashley fell off a cliff on April 25, 1825. The following day he wrote, "I never suffered from bodily pain as much as the last night"; he and his men didn't get under way that day until almost noon, and references to his pain appear in his journal until April 30 (Morgan, *West* 107). Osborne Russell describes the danger of eating beaver soon after they have consumed "poisonous roots": one becomes sick at the stomach, his whole system filled with cramps and pains—though he knows of no one who has thus died (Russell, 124). Rheumatism was almost a given from wading in icy streams.

Moreover, there was often danger from the Indians. Many historians believe that the extreme antipathy of the Blackfeet can be traced to the fact that the only Indian killed during Lewis and Clark's expedition belonged to that tribe. The competition among fur companies and countries may also have contributed to this danger; the American Fur Company is suspected of instigating attacks on rival companies to drive them from the field. The Indians' motives, however, were of little interest once an attack was under way. John Colter, for example, was chased naked through Yellowstone by Indians.

Obviously, the mountain man was on his own to cure illness or heal wounds. No doctors were available. Ogden described bleeding a sick man. Russell treated an arrow wound sustained in a battle with Blackfeet by bathing in salt water and applying a salve of beaver's oil and castoreum. When, on the overland trip back from Astoria, Ramsay Crooks was so sick he couldn't travel, Robert Stuart purged him with castor oil and built him a sweat lodge. Perhaps most graphic is James Clyman's account of the surgery on Jim Bridger following his encounter with a grizzly. The bear had taken almost his entire head in his mouth—from the left eye to the right ear, which was nearly torn from his head. After stitching up a scalp wound, Clyman did rudimentary plastic surgery: "I put in my needle stiching it through and through and over and over laying the lacerated parts togather as nice as I could with my hands"—all without benefit of anesthesia. "[T]his gave us a lisson on the charcter of the grissle Baare which we did not forget" (Morgan, *West* 78).

For all this work and suffering, the individual trappers' pay may seem small in comparison to the figures cited by the traders **Wages** for the value of furs arriving in St. Louis. Nathaniel Wyeth wrote that "a good hunter can take an average of 120 skins in a year . . . worth in Boston about $1000." Yet such hunters could be hired for about "$400 payable in goods at an average 600 per ct. profit" (Wishart, 197–98). Although Jim Bridger was paid $3,317.13 by Pratte, Chouteau, and Company for two years' service, this was very unusual. Independent trappers spent a huge proportion of their earnings on provisions. At the 1836 rendezvous Russell paid $2 a pint for sugar and coffee, $2 a pound for tobacco, $4 for a pint of alcohol, $5 for a cotton shirt, and $20 for a blanket. In the mountains, horses cost as much as $500 each. In return, trappers were paid $4 or $5 a pound for beaver (Russell, *Journal* 60).

Relations with Indians were also an important part of the mountain man's life. Perhaps most important, **Relations with** they provided the role model for survival in the **American Indians** mountains. The Easterner, the European, the Midwesterner who hoped to thrive in the fur trade had to master the skills the Indians had perfected long ago. In many ways the mountain man had to become an Indian. As Jim Beckwourth, a mulatto trapper who became a lesser chief among the Crows, said, "though the Indian could never become a white man, the white man lapsed easily into an Indian."

> He dressed like an Indian, in blankets, robes, buckskins, and moccasins, and it was sometimes his humor to grease his hair and stripe his face with vermilion. He lived like an Indian in bark huts or skin lodges, and married a succession of squaws. He thought like an Indian, propitiating the demons of the wild, making medicine, and consulting the omens. He had on call a brutality as instant as the Indian's and rather more relentless. The Indians who had proved themselves his friends were his friends just so long as they seemed to be; all others were to be shot and scalped on sight. It was the Indian law, no violence to be left unavenged. (DeVoto, *Year of Decision* 65)

Despite the violence or possibility of violence, there was much intermarriage—or at least sexual relations—between the races owing to the absence of white women. Russell's Christmas dinner was in the lodge of a French man with a Flathead wife and mixed-breed child. Recreational sex, during winter camp and especially at rendezvous, carried the risk of venereal disease. The general lustiness of the whites caused one of the chiefs to ask Henry Brackenridge, "Did white people have no women of their own?" (Lavender, *Fist* 158). A. B. Guthrie Jr. presents a "cure" for venereal disease in the novel *The Big Sky*: the protagonist, Boone Caudill, applies beaver fur to his genitals as a kind of poultice for the infection he picked up in St. Louis.

The Rendezvous The high point of the year for mountain men was the annual rendezvous. Held in July at a site determined the previous year, it was part bacchanalian festival, part business convention. For men who had spent most of the previous year alone or with a party of six to eight trappers, this was a time of socializing, prodigious eating and drinking, meeting friends not seen for a year, and uproarious laughter at tall tales spun from their year's narrow escapes. It was a time, too, of brawling and fighting, of quick coupling with Indian women, of emotional release for both white and Indian. Washburn suggests the rendezvous was also the epitome of a successful fusion of Euro-American and Native American trade rituals ("Symbol" 50–54).

The painter Alfred Jacob Miller, one of the best chroniclers of the fur trade, captured the essence of the 1837 Green River rendezvous in his notebook:

> The first day is devoted to "High Jinks," a species of Saturnalia, in which feasting, drinking, and gambling form prominent parts. . . . The following days exhibit the strongest contrast to this. The Fur Company's great tent is raised;—the Indians erect their picturesque white lodges;—the accumulated furs of the hunting season are brought forth and the Company's tent is a besieged and busy place. (Wishart, 197)

Not all visitors were so enthralled by the rendezvous, however. A missionary wife, Mrs. Myra Eells, traveling west to Oregon with one of the wagon trains, describes the Independence Day celebration at the 1838 Snake River rendezvous:

> Captain Bridger's Company comes in about ten o'clock with drums and firing—an apology for a scalp dance. After they had given Captain Drip's Company a shout, fifteen or twenty Mountain men and Indians came to our tent, with drumming, firing, and dancing. If I might make a comparison, I should say they looked like the emissaries of the devil, worshipping their own master. They had the scalp of a Blackfoot Indian, which they carried for a color, all rejoicing in the fate of the Blackfeet, in consequence of the small pox. (Hafen, vol. 6, 94)

The primary purpose of the rendezvous was to exchange a year's worth of goods and furs without the expense of maintaining a trading post or fort. Until 1840 the rendezvous remained "the hub and distinguishing feature of the Rocky Mountain Trapping System" (Wishart, 191).

The supply trains left Lexington or Independence, Missouri, in April or May, avoiding the bitter cold and snow of winter and capitalizing on the spring grass—which would later be parched by the summer heat—as forage for the pack animals. The supply column usually consisted of fifty to seventy men and over one hundred pack animals. After 1832 some wagons and two-wheeled carts were also used, drawn by oxen, horses, and mules (Wishart, 194). Nathaniel Wyeth estimated the cost of mounting such an expedition in 1832 at $11,382 (Wishart, 195).

When the supply caravan arrived at the rendezvous site, trading began. William Ashley kept scrupulously careful accounts for each trapper with whom he did business. From them we can learn, for instance, that a Mr. Godan arrived at rendezvous owing Ashley $86.50. He brought in forty-six beaver worth $3 each for $138. He purchased $7.75 worth of sugar and coffee, two knives for $3, two packets of beads for $10, a dozen rings for $2, a half-dozen awls for $1, a yard of cloth for $6, a dozen flints for $1, tobacco worth $7.75, a fire steel for $1, and powder and lead for $12.50, leaving him a profit for his year of $51.50 (Morgan, *West* 123). When one examines the articles of agreement between Ashley and the firm of Smith, Jackson, and Sublette, which bought his trapping interests, we get a clear indication of the inventory and costs of items brought to the 1826 rendezvous:

Gunpowder of the first and second quality at one dollar fifty per pound

Lead one dollar per pound

Shot at one dollar twenty five cents per pound

Three point blankets at nine dollars each

Green ditto at Eleven dollars each

Scarlet cloth at six dollars per yard

Blue ditto common quality from four to five dollars per yard

Butcher Knives at seventy five cents each

two and a half point Blankets at Seven dollars each

North West Fusils at twenty four dollars each

tin Kettles different sizes at two dollars per pound

Sheet Iron Kettles at two dollars twenty five cents per pound

Squaw axes at two dollars fifty cents each

Beaver traps at nine dollars each

Sugar at one dollar per pound

Coffee at one dollar twenty five cents per pound

flour at one dollar per pound

Alspice at one dollar fifty cents per pound

Raisins at one dollar fifty cents per pound

Grey cloth at common quality at five dollars per yard

flannels common quality at one dollar fifty cents per yard

calicoes assorted at one dollar per yard

domestic cotton at one dollar twenty five cents per yard

Thread assorted at three dollars per pound

finger rings at five dollars per Gross

Beads assorted at two dollars fifty cents per pound

Vermillion at three dollars per pound

files assorted at two dollars fifty cents per pound

fourth proof rum reduced at thirteen dollars fifteen cents per Gallon

Bridles assorted seven dollars each

spurs at two dollars per pair

Horse shoes and nails at two dollars per pound

tin pans assorted at two dollars per pound

hand kerchiefs assorted at one dollar fifty cents each

ribbons assorted at three dollars per bolt

Buttons at five dollars per Gross

Looking glasses at fifty cents each

flints at fifty cents per dozen

mockacine alls [awls] at twenty five cents per dozen

Tabacco at one dollar twenty five cents per pound

Copper Kettles at three dollars per pound

Iron Buckles at three dollars per pound

fire steels at two dollars per pound

Dried fruit at one dollar and fifty cents per pound

Washing soap at one dollar twenty five cents per pound

Shaving soap at two dollars per pound

first quality James River Tobacco at one dollar seventy five cents
per pound

Steel Bracelets at one dollar fifty cents per pair

Long Brass wire at two dollars per pound (Morgan, *West* 151–52)

This detailed listing of Ashley's going-out-of business sale provides insights into mark-ups when compared to the prices trappers paid; moreover, it indicates quite clearly how demands for Euro-American goods had been created among western Indians.

The rendezvous system, developed by trial and error during 1823–24, had been formalized into an effective pattern by 1825 and flourished for about a decade until its decline was caused by a multitude of factors: severe economic conditions in the East, depletion of the beaver population, increasing dominance of the American Fur Company with its Upper Missouri forts, and changing fashion trends. The last Green River rendezvous was held in 1840.

THE UPPER MISSOURI TRADING SYSTEM

If the rendezvous was the distinguishing feature of the Rocky Mountain Trading System, the string of forts and their riverine access were chief characteristics of the Upper Missouri Trading System. As trade moved further and further into the interior, the forts were built farther and farther up the Missouri: Ft. Osage (1808), Ft. Leavenworth (1827), Ft. Atkinson (1819–20), Ft. Tecumseh (1822 or 1823), Ft. Pierre (1832), Ft. Clark (1831), Ft. Union (1829), Ft. William (1833), Ft. Piegan (1831–32), and Ft. MacKenzie (1832). In contrast, only Ft. Laramie on the North Platte served the Rocky Mountain system.

Transportation to and from these forts was almost exclusively by water. The Missouri River was extremely **Transportation** hard to navigate safely. Its channel runs through a hard **to and from** flood plain, so its course changes frequently and rapidly. **the Forts** In dry seasons—much of the year—the river is shallow; moreover, trees washed into the river create dangerous snags capable of impaling boats; where there were bends in the river (at frequently changing locations due to eroding banks), the water formed sand and gravel bars on which boats could run aground. The continuous navigation season was from mid-March to late June—the period after river ice had melted and while the river volume was augmented by late spring snowmelt in the Rockies and by early summer rain. Navigation was closed starting in late June when the water level dropped; fall brought ice to the river again (Wishart, 83).

The keelboat dominated river transportation for the first three decades of the nineteenth century. The boats were expensive; built in Pittsburgh or Louisville shipyards, they cost $2,000–$3,000 each. They averaged 60–80 feet in length and 16–18 feet in width. They had full decks, careful framing, and, for stability, a heavy keel from bow to stern. Because the Missouri was often low, they were built with shallow draft. Consequently their holds were only three to four feet deep; their storage space

River scene showing flatboat and two keelboats. From the Collection of The Public Library of Cincinnati and Hamilton County.

was increased by adding a four-to five-foot cargo box that occupied most of the front and rear decks. Amidships was a mast from which a square sail could be raised on the rare occasions when there was a useful tail-wind. More usually the keelboat was propelled by muscle—sometimes by oars but more frequently by poling or cordelling. When poling, each man plunged his pole into the river bottom and then walked the length of the boat. When cordelling, the crew waded ashore and then, with the rope attached to the mast, literally dragged the keelboat upstream. This was brute labor, the equivalent of the work of mules on the Erie Canal. Moreover it was dangerous, for here, unlike on the canal, there was no smooth towpath. Men clambered over fallen trees, slipped in the mud, fell into the river along collapsing banks; they were also vulnerable to Indian attack and to mosquitoes and rattlesnakes. At the end of the day those who were unused to such work "trembled all over, and returned to the vessel" (Maximilian, vol. 23, 30).

In addition, cordelling was expensive for it required at least twenty men per boat and thus a fairly heavy outlay for wages and food. Dinner was served early (4:00 P.M.) and consisted of salt pork, pemmican, hard ship's biscuit, and coffee (Maximilian, vol. 23, 27) supplemented by game shot by the ship's hunters. Occasionally there were real treats; Maximilian describes a porcupine caught alive and killed aboard ship: "Our engagés [declared] that it was a great delicacy" (Maximilian, vol. 23, 49). Both food and wages involved a cash outlay for the boat's owners, for the crew, hired in St. Louis each spring, demanded cash advances against their salaries and refused payment in marked-up goods the company used in its Indian country trade. Expense also resulted from a relatively small load—only twenty to thirty tons of cargo—and the fact that a trip upstream to the mouth of the Yellowstone required an entire season. The return trip was less arduous, taking advantage of the force of the current, but still somewhat dangerous as keelboats could capsize; great skill was needed in steering (Lavender, *Fist* 89, 391; Wishart, 83–84).

Another kind of boat on the Missouri was the Mackinaw, a large flat-bottomed type of boat built at boatyards upstream near Forts Pierre, Clark, and Union. These boats made only the downstream trip, being broken up and sold for firewood (at $4 or $5 each) in St. Louis. John Jacob Astor describes four Mackinaw boats sent downstream from Ft. Pierre in 1843 carrying 10,000 bison robes: "These boats are strong and broad, the tops, or roofs are covered with the bent branches of trees, and these are covered by water-proof Buffalo hides, each has four oarsmen and a steerman, who manages the boat standing on a broad board, the helm is about ten feet long and the rudder itself five or six feet long" (Wishart, 85).

There were, in addition, a number of other craft at work on the Missouri and its tributaries. The bull boat, constructed by sewing buffalo robes together over a round frame of willow poles and then waterproofing it with a mixture of tallow and ashes had a very shallow draft of only a few inches and carried 5,000–6,000 pounds of furs. Dugouts hollowed out of cottonwood trunks were used for short hauls between trading posts and for conveying low-volume, high-value products such as honey and bear oil. Pirogues—two canoes fastened together and decked over with planks—were propelled much like keelboats (Wishart, 85–86).

The advent of the steamboat to the Missouri reduced the time and minimized the effort of the trip, though it was still vulnerable to river conditions such as snags, sandbars, and changing channels. The first steamboat was the *Yellowstone*, built in Louisville for the American Fur Company in 1831. Its second journey in 1832 convinced even conservative skeptics that it was a viable means of transport; it left St. Louis on March 26 and arrived at Ft. Union on June 17. Later steamboats reduced that time. The steamboats were able to make the round trip (bringing in supplies and taking out furs) in one season. Moreover, they carried a far greater volume, usually an advantage. But when the *Assiniboine* caught fire in 1835 and a cargo of furs worth between $60,000 and $80,000 was lost, owners realized the disadvantage of putting all their furs into one boat.

Such difficulties were far from rare. Maximilian describes an incident aboard the *Yellowstone* on its third annual voyage upstream:

> About ten o'clock we had an alarm of fire on board: the upper deck had been set on fire by the iron pipe of the chimney of the great cabin. We immediately lay to, and, by breaking up the deck, the danger was soon over, which, however, was not inconsiderable, as we had many barrels of powder on board. We had scarcely got over this trouble when another arose; the current of the swollen river was so strong, that we long contended against it to no purpose, in order to turn a certain point of land while, at the same time, the high west wind was against us, and both together threw the vessel back three times on the south coast. The first shock was so violent, that the lower deck gallery was broken to pieces. Our second attempt succeeded no better; part of the paddle-box was broken, and carried away by the current. We were now obliged to land forty men to tow the vessel. (Maximilian, vol. 22, 368)

Above Ft. Union goods were transferred to keelboats, for waters there weren't navigable by steamboats until after 1840. Despite their advantages of speed and volume, the steamboats wreaked ecological havoc on the riparine woodlands. A steamboat consumed 25–30 cords of wood a day. Woodcutters supplying the boats had denuded the river of cedar and cottonwood trees, the best fuels, so that by 1840 steamboats relied increasingly on driftwood and decaying logs from old trading posts (Wishart, 85–87).

What was life like in the string of forts connected by this river transportation system? It was, on the one hand, rela- **Life in** tively more comfortable than life in the field, although Max- **the Forts** imilian describes cold so extreme indoors at Ft. Clark that despite panes of glass in the windows of his room—distinct evidence of advancing civilization—Karl Bodmer's paints froze. Moreover, while standing in front of the fireplace the men were roasted on one side and frozen on the other. In addition, life could be lonely at the forts, especially during winter, but when the Missouri opened in spring and when the Indians arrived bringing bison hides to trade, life soon became hectic. Following a long season of tedium, the arrival of the boats was a cause for great celebration. Life at the forts could be dangerous, too: fires occasionally threatened to explode stores of gunpowder, and simmering antagonisms between rival Indian tribes sometimes threatened to boil over when both arrived at the fort at the same time.

Always there was work to be done, regardless of the season. Wishart divides the labor into three categories: production and trading, subsistence, and post maintenance and local industry. Francis Chardon's *Journal at Fort Clark, 1834–1839*, records the endless chores at the fort: making hay, cleaning out the icehouse, gathering wood, hunting meat, protecting the horses from theft, daubing houses (whitewashing them with white clay), making charcoal, blacksmithing, making dog travois, cutting ice, shoeing horses, cutting the flatboat out of the frozen river, covering the warehouse and store with dirt for insulation, taking inventory, making butter, castrating the bull calf, repairing carts, writing letters, repairing the warehouse roof, drying hay after a rain, reconciling the ledger and the inventory, cutting axle trees for carts, caulking boats, making canoes, sawing logs into planks, and cleaning the fort. Of course, Chardon did not do all this himself, but he was responsible for organizing others—his clerks as well as *engagés* and Indians and half-breeds who worked around the fort. It is significant that most of these activities were only peripherally concerned with acquiring and preparing pelts—in the case of the Upper Missouri trade, primarily bison robes. In this trade system the acquisition and preparation of the fur was done almost exclusively by the Indians.

In late summer (August and September) Chardon, like other traders on the Upper Missouri, distributed hunting and trap- **Hunting** ping equipment and trade goods—on credit—to the Indians. The debt was to be repaid at the end of the season in furs. Whereas the beaver pelt was the standard unit of exchange in the Rockies, on the Upper Missouri it was the buffalo "robe" (a well-fleeced, wooly skin).

As in the Rockies, the annual hunting cycle was closely linked to nature. Fur traders were interested in the robes of cows and young bulls taken during the winter from November to February when the fur was thick. It is estimated that only one-quarter of the winter kill went into the fur trade; the remainder was used to supply the Indians' needs for meat, clothing, housing, sewing materials, utensils, glue, and so forth (Wishart, 26). Moreover, the hunt adhered to Indian law. Osborne Russell noted that, among the Crows, "laws for killing Buffalo are most rigidly enforced. No person is allowed to hunt Buffalo in the vicinity of where the village is stationed without first obtaining leave of the council" (Russell, 147). Anyone—white or Indian—violating this rule was punished by the tribal policemen. This was yet another reason why the buffalo hunt was done almost exclusively by the Indians.

Processing the kill was done by Indian women. The hide was tanned on one side only until it was pliable; the plush fur was left on the other. Wishart describes the process: "Each step was dictated by custom and ritual. The hide was halved, scraped clean with the shinbone of an elk, dried in the sun in the summer or over a small fire in the winter, and rubbed with a mixture of liver and brains until it was soft and pliable and ready to trade" (Wishart, 97). The quantity of robes available for trade thus depended not on how many buffalo the men could shoot but on how many hides the women could prepare. Tanning a bison hide was more labor intensive than curing a beaver pelt; thus, the demand for labor was greater in the Missouri River trade system than in the Rocky Mountain system. The increased demand for women's labor resulted in significant changes in Indian society: the time spent by women in traditional work such as farming decreased; the practice of polygamy increased, for several wives were needed to keep up with a man's hunting; and a greater division of socioeconomic classes occurred, for only wealthier Indians could afford more than one wife.

After the hides were prepared they were packed into bundles that were carried by dog or horse travois (two poles joined by a sling for carrying the burden, fastened by leather cords to the animal's harness and dragged behind the animal).

Trading in the Forts   The arrival of a trading party at a fort involved much ceremony. The trader raised the American flag and fired the cannon to properly recognize and honor the chief. Chardon describes the arrival of the Rees: "Received them with the Honors of War, fired 10 Salutes from my four pounder, and hoisted the Flag" and then "set the men to Cooking a feast of 10 Kittles [kettles] for the Rees." The honor was reciprocated, as the Rees invited him to a feast. "Six dogs lost their lives for the feast." Next Chardon gave them a feast of corn accompanied by "a great deal of good talk, great Promises Made on both sides" (Chardon, 109).

This, however, did not mean that he *liked* the Rees, for his entry for the following day reads, "Commenced trading with the Horrid tribe" (110). That evening "the Ree ladies gave us a splendid dance." Chardon could not concentrate only on the Rees, however; within the same week he recorded the arrival of a messenger from the Crow camp, four Gros Ventres "arrived from War" with the news that a large band of Sioux were only two to three days' travel away, and the Mandans returned to their village just outside the fort with plenty of meat. Not only does this suggest the need for some fluency in a number of Indian languages and customs—or the presence of interpreters—but it also implies the very real possibility of danger to traders when representatives of rival, even warring, tribes appeared at a fort simultaneously.

In many forts, trading was done in the corridor formed between the inner and outer gates. In such forts Indians were rarely, if ever, allowed into the inner square, primarily for fear of theft rather than of gratuitous violence.

Daily life could be hard at a trade fort. Chardon mentions, for example, getting down to his last flour months **Hardships** before resupply was possible; the weather was so harsh that **in the Forts** his black mule froze and the traders were literally imprisoned in the fort. The year 1836 brought starving times for men and horses. Chardon was involved in a perpetual battle with rats; each month in his journal he records how many he killed that month as well as the grand total. His last "rat inventory" in April 1839 states: "Killed 90 rats this month—total 3,729." Maximilian succinctly explains Chardon's fixation with rats—and one of the less healthy effects of international trade:

> There were a few tame cats in the fort, but not sufficient to reduce the great number of rats. These animals (the Norway rats) were so numerous and troublesome that no kind of provision was safe from their voracity; their favorite food was maize, among which they committed sad havoc; and it was calculated that they daily devoured five bushels or 250 pounds. There were often from 500 to 800 bushels of corn in the loft at a time. The rats were brought hither by the American ships. (Maximilian, vol. 23, 235)

Despite the hardship, life at the forts was more comfortable than in the field. Food was more varied; many forts had their **Food in** own vegetable gardens and all traded with the Indians for **the Forts** corn. Chardon mentions a variety of foods available at Fort Clark: bread, milk (an extraordinary treat for visiting trappers), cherries brought in by Indian women, sweet corn, peas, potatoes, squash and beans from the vegetable garden, eggs, and sturgeon and catfish from the river. All these were in addition to the meat—buffalo, elk, bear, goose, and deer—procured by hunting. Chardon kept a cow and chickens for milk and eggs.

Leisure Time in the Forts At the forts there was far more entertainment than in the field. During winter camp in the Rockies some of the men played cards and gambled and read, and dreamed of rendezvous. At the forts there was occasionally time for a leisurely walk or horseback ride. Some played chess, bet on horse races, or wrote their own lyrics to songs popular back in the States, such as the Jim Crow song. There were festive dinners for guests such as Maximilian or other traders passing through, or to celebrate Charboneau's wedding. Holidays were celebrated—the Fourth of July, All Saints Day, Andrew Jackson's birthday, the Feast of the Epiphany, Christmas, and New Years. The fact that such festivities were a desperate effort to break the monotony is evident in Chardon's entry for December 25, 1834:

Christmas comes but once a year, and when it comes it brings good cheer. But not here! As every thing seems the same. No New faces. No News, and worst of all No Cattle [buffalo] Last Night [at] ½ past 10 O'Clock we partook of a fine supper Prepared by Old Charboneau, consisting of Meat pies, bread, fricassied pheasants Boiled tongues, roast beef—and coffee—the brilliant assembly consisted of Indns Half Breeds, Canadians, Squaws, and children, to have taken a Birds eye view, of the whole group, seated at the festive board, would of astonished any, but those who are accustomed to such sights, to of seen in what little time, the Contents of the table was dispatched, some as much as seven to nine cups of coffee, and the rest of it in like proportion, good luck for the Cooks that they were of the Number seated at the table, or their share would of been scant—as every one had done Honour to his plate. (Chardon, 18)

As always, part of the trade with the Indians involved dances—the bull dance, the bear dance—in return for which entertainment the trader was expected to give some presents—a few knives or some tobacco. Chardon drew the line, however, and refused to allow the scalp dance to be performed at the fort; he was trying to curtail, discourage, or at least not encourage the killings. But the monotony of the dancing, day after day, caused him to write, finally, "I wish to God dancing is over" (49).

Medicine in the Forts As in the field, there were medical problems at the forts. Men got into fistfights. Chardon almost broke his leg falling off his horse. Chardon's wife (he had four, sequentially) and the blacksmith came down with severe diarrhea, which he treated with "a few drops of lodanum & camphor—25 drops of the former and 15 of the latter" (45). Some of his hunters, including Charboneau, came down with "something like the Cholic" (50). There are references in his journal to venereal disease: "Jos. Desnogé arrived from beaver hunting, not being able to continue, having caught the Venerial" (106), and indicating his recognition of the efficacy of Indian medicine, "Sent Hunot down to toe Ree camp, to be cured of the Venereal" (149). "An Old Woman of the [Mandan] village tired of this World hung herself last night" (106). There were other deaths close to Chardon: that of his wife Tchon-su-mons-ka ("the Sand Bar"), a Teton Sioux, and their son, Andrew Jackson Chardon—of smallpox.

Life at the forts demonstrated the interdependence of the traders and the Indians. Both cultures were changed; most severely and permanently was the Indians'.

Cultural Impacts on the American Indians

The first major cultural dislocation was caused by alcohol, a staple in the fur trade from colonial times onward. In the West almost a decade before the first rendezvous, Major Thomas Biddle warned of the corrupting influences of the fur trade and advocated strict government control to prevent them. Though the U.S. government abandoned Biddle's idea for government factories or posts, laws were passed forbidding the importation of alcohol into Indian territory for the purpose of trade. There were, however, creative circumventions of the law. When in 1831 William Sublette got a two-year trading license from William Clark, he also received a "passport" to carry up to 450 gallons of whiskey "for the special use of his boatmen" (Sunder, 102). However, he was going *overland* to the Rockies. Despite the fact that the Blackfeet preferred West Indies rum, James Kipp at Ft. Piegan concocted "Blackfoot rum" by adding water, ginger, red pepper, and molasses to a barrel of "high wine" (thirty-two or thirty-three gallons of almost pure alcohol) (Lavender, *Fist* 395). Along with the dry goods in the hold of the *Yellowstone* when she left St. Louis in 1832 were "1500 gallons of alcohol duly authorized by William Clark as intended for the company employees" (Lavender, *Fist* 406). And when the prohibition against carrying alcohol into the Upper Missouri became enforced more rigorously, Kenneth MacKenzie set up his own still at Ft. Union to make what he needed from Indian corn (Lavender, *Fist* 415).

A second major cultural impact is seen in the third volume of Maximilian's journal. His ethnographic studies during his 1832–34 stay included a compilation of vocabularies—some brief, some extensive—of at least fifteen different Indian languages. Most words are basic: parts of the body, names of animals, counting words. But it is of interest that in almost every language there were, by 1834, words for *gunpowder*; *spirits* (alcohol, not divine beings), which in Assiniboine translated "fire-water";

gun or *rifle*; and *American*, which in Blackfoot, Omaha, Dakota, and Mandan was, literally, "long-knife." To the two indigenous words in Mandan
for *ball* (the object and the game women played with it) was added the
meaning "bullet," which is the same word as is used for *lead*. Most tribes
apparently did not have a word for *money*. In Oto, however, it is translated as "white metal" and in Mandan as "that-which-the-white-men-
love-very-much" (Maximilian, vol. 24, 210–312). Clearly the fur trade had
had a strong influence on Native American language, a central element
of culture.

Disease, specifically smallpox, had the most disastrous impact. The
most catastrophic epidemic swept like wildfire through the Mandan in
1837. The steamboat *St. Peter's* arrived at Ft. Clark late on Sunday, June
18, unloaded merchandise on June 19, and left early on June 20 for Ft.
Union. Life went on normally—celebration of the Fourth of July, Indian
trade, rainfall, dances, Indians drying meat—until, on July 14, there is
an ominous entry in Chardon's journal: "a young Mandan died to day
of the Small Pox—several others has caught it" (121). By July 25 smallpox
had broken out in the Mandan camp. On the next day Chardon reports
that "the 4 Bears (Mandan) has caught the small pox, and got crazy and
disappeared from camp" (123). Each day the death count among the
Mandan rose, and the disease began to spread to other tribes. As the
disease ravaged them, they began to blame Chardon in particular and
whites in general. "They threaten Death and Destruction to us all at this
place, saying that I was the cause of the small pox Makeing its appearance in this country—One of our best friends in the Village (The Four
Bears) died to day, regretted by all who knew him"—this was Chardon's
entry for Sunday, July 30.

Despite his occasional ambivalence toward the Indians, Chardon recorded Four Bears' final speech. With the virtual extinction of the Mandans, the speech marks the end of a comparatively idyllic relationship
between the races.

**Speech of the 4 Bears a Mandan Warrior to the Arricarees and Mandans,
30th July 1837**

My Friends, one and all, Listen to what I have to say—Ever since
I can remember, I have loved the Whites. I have lived With them
ever since I was a Boy, and to the best of my Knowledge, I have
never Wronged a White Man, on the contrary, I have always Protected them from the insults of Others, Which they cannot deny.
The 4 Bears never saw a White Man hungry, but what he gave him
to eat, Drink, and a Buffalo skin to sleep on, in time of Need. I was
always ready to die for them, Which they cannot deny. I have done
every thing that a red Skin could do for them, and how they have

repaid it! With ingratitude! I have Never Called a White Man a Dog, but to day, I do Pronounce them to be a set of Black harted Dogs, they have deceived Me, them that I always considered as Brothers, has turned Out to be My Worst enemies. I have been in Many Battles, and often Wounded, but the Wounds of My enemies I exhalt in, but to day I am Wounded, and by Whom, by those same White Dogs that I have always Considered, and treated as Brothers. I do not fear *Death* my friends. You know it, but to *die* with my face rotten, that even the Wolves will shrink with horror at seeing Me, and say to themselves, that is the 4 Bears the Friend of the Whites—

Listen well what I have to say, as it will be the last time you will hear Me. think of your Wives, Children, Brothers, Sisters, Friends, and in fact all that you hold dear, are all Dead, or Dying, with their faces all rotten, caused by those dogs the whites, think of all that My friends, and rise all together and Not leave one of them alive. The 4 Bears will act his Part. (Chardon, 124–25)

The fur frontier had the most powerful effect of all the frontier experiences—perhaps because it was the first, perhaps because it was re-experienced from the Atlantic to the Pacific over several hundred years. The fur trapper as explorer amassed vast knowledge about geography, animals and plants, and about the Native Americans. Personified by John Jacob Astor, the fur industry was the first example of a successful American monopoly. It forever and irrevocably changed both the European and the Native American through experiential, linguistic, mercantile, and epidemiological influences. It was, on occasion, an instrument of national will for France, Spain, Great Britain, and the United States. And it implanted in our national psyche the attitude of exploitation rather than conservation of nature.

George Caleb Bingham. *Daniel Boone Escorting Settlers through the Cumberland Gap*, 1851–52. Oil on canvas, 36½ × 50¼". Washington University Gallery of Art, St. Louis. Gift of Nathaniel Phillips, 1890. Bingham idealizes and romanticizes Boone's role in bringing settlers to the trans-Appalachian West. Light portions of this painting create a halo effect around these people, who, in the nineteenth century, were often thought of as bringing "civilization" into the darkness.

3

Life on the Explorers' Frontier

The Atlantic seaboard had been inhabited by various frontier types: the fur trader, the fisherman, the hunter, the cattle-raiser, the miner, and the pioneer farmer. Each of them utilized—often exploited—the land; all of them, as well as educators, the military, and the clergy, co-existed (sometimes harmoniously, sometimes not) with their predecessors on the land, the Native Americans. With Daniel Boone's opening of the first good wagon route through the Appalachians in 1769, settlers began pouring into the Ohio Valley, ignoring government regulations and dispossessing the Indians who moved like an unwilling vanguard ahead of them. By the end of the eighteenth century the flood had reached the Mississippi, the next major geographical barrier after the Appalachians. The United States was no longer a narrow strip along the Atlantic; it now stretched one-third of the way across the continent.

In 1801 President Thomas Jefferson learned that Spain had secretly ceded Louisiana—most of the land between the Mississippi River and the Rocky Mountains—to France. Acutely conscious of the need for a port at the mouth of the Mississippi if America were to prosper in international trade, Jefferson instructed Robert R. Livingstone, U.S. minister to Paris, to negotiate for such a port or for permanent trading rights in New Orleans; subsequently he sent James Monroe to join Livingstone and provided them with a $2 million appropriation and an option to go as high as $10 million to buy New Orleans.

Although Napoleon had acquired Louisiana with the hope of building a North American empire, he became embroiled in a slave revolt in Haiti led by Toussaint l'Ouverture. That military action (which some call his Vietnam because so many of his troops were destroyed while fighting guerrilla insurgents), coupled with the threat of war with England, convinced him to abandon his American imperial plans. Thus, instead of discussing the purchase of New Orleans, Napoleon offered to sell all of Louisiana to the United States.

The agreed-upon price was $15 million, or approximately four cents per acre for about 828,000 square miles including today's states of Louisiana, Arkansas, Oklahoma, Missouri, Kansas, Colorado, Nebraska, Iowa, Minnesota, North and South Dakota, Wyoming, and part of Montana. Despite Federalist opposition on the grounds that U.S. law made no provision for buying foreign territory, the Senate approved the purchase on October 20, 1803, and in 1804 a territorial government was established. By bold vision and equally bold, though not strictly constitutional, diplomacy, Thomas Jefferson doubled the size of the United States and laid the foundation for it to become a continental nation. He now needed more information on this newly acquired real estate.

Jefferson had long been interested in the trans-Mississippi West. He had proposed three prior explorations: in 1783 he'd put the proposition to Revolutionary War hero General George Rogers Clark; three years later he encouraged John Ledyard, a civilian, to walk across Siberia and thence east from the Pacific; and in 1792, as vice president of the American Philosophical Society, he'd urged funding for an expedition by André Michaux, a French botanist. For various reasons, none of these proposals succeeded.

THOMAS JEFFERSON'S CORPS OF DISCOVERY

Now Jefferson chose his private secretary, Army captain Meriwether Lewis, to lead the expedition. Lewis chose as co-commander of the expedition William Clark, a fellow Virginian whose judgment he trusted implicitly, having served under him in the army. In addition, Clark's skills complemented Lewis's. Whereas Lewis knew the rudiments of botany, geology, and ethnology, Clark was a better terrestrial surveyor, a better mapmaker, and a better waterman than Lewis; moreover, he had already experienced command and "had a way with enlisted men" (Ambrose, 97).

In his instructions to Meriwether Lewis, Jefferson clearly outlined his expectations: "The object . . . is to explore the Missouri River & such principle streams of it, as, by it's course and communication with the waters of the Pacific Ocean, may offer the most direct & practicable water communication across this continent, for the purposes of commerce." The topography of the route was to be carefully recorded: rapids and islands, mouths of rivers, possible portages where boats could be carried over short stretches of land bypassing waterfalls. Observations of the latitude and longitude of all such significant landmarks "are to be taken with great pains & accuracy . . . [and] entered distinctly & intelligibly for others as well as yourself." The raw data was to be forwarded to the war office for final computation. Jefferson cautioned Lewis to make "several copies" of such observations, as well as of all his notes. One copy, he suggested, should "be written on the paper of the birch, as less liable from damp than common paper" (DeVoto, ed. *Journals of Lewis and Clark* 481–483).

In addition, Lewis was to take notes on the land and the plants and animals it produced, especially those not common to the United States; on mineral resources, especially metals, limestone, coal, salt, and mineral waters; and on climate, including temperature, prevailing winds, presence of frost, snow, lightning, or hail, and the dates specific plants begin to bloom or particular animals or birds appear. Lewis as naturalist was to be a pathfinder for the economic development of Louisiana.

The journals engagingly and clearly present such information. For example, on April 10, 1805, a few days beyond Fort Mandan, Lewis observes that the quality of beaver taken by three French traders traveling close to them is "the best I have ever seen." And at Fort Clatsop on January 7, 1806, he pens a detailed description of the beaver and its habits and includes a recipe for "beaver bate" to lure the animal to a trap—a mixture of castoreum from the beaver's preputial glands, plus cinnamon, nutmeg, and cloves, all pulverized and mixed with "ardent spirits" until it is of the consistency of table mustard. The passage is typical of Lewis's detailed observation and his ability to make the unfamiliar clear to his audience.

Jefferson, with an eye to trade with the Indians along the route, charged Lewis with finding out as much as possible about them: the names of individual nations, their population, and the extent of the lands in which they lived; their languages, traditions, laws, and customs; their relationship with nearby tribes; their methods of agriculture, hunting, and fishing; their tools and weapons for war and peace; the "moral and physical circumstances" differentiating them from "the tribes we know"; and, with a view toward ultimately bringing these Indians into a U.S. trade orbit, the "articles of commerce they need or furnish." Lewis and Clark were to be ethnologists in the service of trade. Moreover, they were to observe the "state of religion, morality, and information" among these tribes in order to better "enable those who endeavor to civilize & instruct them, to adapt their measures to the existing notions & practices of those on whom they are to operate" (DeVoto, ed. *Journals of Lewis and Clark* 483). It was clear that subsequent to the return of the Corps of Discovery, others—missionaries, teachers, Indian agents—would attempt to assimilate the Native Americans into Euro-American culture; equally clear was

Jefferson's belief that the Indian, unlike the black, *could* be assimilated. Much of the knowledge to be gathered was, thus, not simply to facilitate trade but to encourage fundamental cultural change. Such knowledge, correctly utilized, would allow agents of the Great Father to meet his new dependents where they were.

With a view to the future, Jefferson was adamant on yet another point: members of the expedition were to be as "friendly and conciliatory" toward the Indians as possible. They were to assure the tribes along the route that the expedition's purpose was innocent, peaceful, even benevolent. As demonstration of his benevolence, Jefferson instructed the captains to take along "some matter of the kinepox" with which to inoculate the Indians against the ravages of smallpox. (Ironically, within thirty-three years smallpox would bring virtual extinction to the very Mandans with whom the expedition wintered over 1804–1805.) The captains were to consult with Indian leaders about locations most convenient for "mutual emporiums" and to determine which trade goods they preferred.

Although ideally the expedition was to achieve multiple goals, Jefferson's priorities were clear. If ever they were threatened by a superior force, if ever their passage was blocked, if ever meetings threatened to degenerate into confrontation, conflict, or combat, "you must decline it's further pursuit, and return. [I]n the loss of yourselves, we should lose also the information you have acquired." Lewis was given the freedom—and the responsibility—to assess possible danger and to retreat from it if need be. "We wish you to err on the side of your safety & bring back your party safe, even if it be with less information," admonished Jefferson (DeVoto, ed. *Journals of Lewis and Clark* 485).

If, perchance, when they reached the Pacific there was a trade ship at the Columbia, Lewis should "send two of your trusty people back by sea" with a copy of the notes. And if Lewis believed the return trip overland for the remaining members of the expedition was too hazardous, he was authorized to return all of them by sea. To this end, Jefferson not only communicated the general purpose of the expedition to the ambassadors from France, Spain, and Great Britain, but he also provided Lewis and Clark with open letters of credit authorizing them to purchase anything they needed—clothes, provisions, transportation—and guaranteeing the provider full payment from the U.S. government (DeVoto, ed. *Journals of Lewis and Clark* 485–86).

Not only suppliers were to be treated fairly. Members of the expedition, to be discharged at their request upon their return to the United States, were to be provided full back pay for the duration of their absence; moreover, Jefferson would recommend that each receive a "soldier's portion of land"—a grant of land identical to the bonus given Revolutionary War veterans—320 acres (DeVoto, ed. *Journals of Lewis and Clark* 486).

This was, indeed, a military expedition. Under the co-command of Captains Lewis and Clark as they left St. Louis were twenty-eight enlisted men; a detachment of seven additional soldiers under the command of Corporal Warfington who were to accompany them as far as the Mandan villages and then return with notes and specimens gathered to that point; two interpreters; Clark's slave, York; a number of St. Louis boatmen; and Lewis's dog, a black Newfoundland named Seaman. (An especially important later addition was Sacajawea, wife of interpreter Toussaint Charbonneau. Without her help in acquiring horses, the expedition might have failed to cross the Rockies.) The enlisted men were an elite group. There had been many volunteers, motivated in part by the opportunity for adventure and in part by the promise of land. Lewis and Clark selected them for their physical strength, their ability to shoot and hunt, and their character. But even as they were sworn into the Corps of Discovery, they were not yet an elite, cohesive unit. First it was necessary to subordinate the individual to the group and to strengthen each man's responsibility to the ultimate mission.

To achieve this, there were, early on, several instances when strict military discipline—and punishment—had to be applied. During the rather boring winter camp at Wood River in 1803, after huts were built and alterations to the keelboat completed, there was little to do. Ammunition was limited; thus, target practice, which the men enjoyed, was held only once a day. Moreover the women at the nearby settlement were nearly all married, so there was no avenue for entertainment there. Consequently the young men frequently drank, and fought, and drank some more. But when such unruliness passed from fights within the ranks to threatening sergeants (as occurred when John Shields opposed an order and wanted to return to Kentucky, or when John Colter disobeyed orders and loaded his gun, threatening to shoot Sergeant Ordway), something had to be done. Shields and Colter were put on trial for mutiny on March 29, 1804. They asked forgiveness and promised to "doe better in the future"; the captains relented and accepted the two into the permanent party (Ambrose, 130). But the Corps had not yet meshed as an elite force; it was still a critical mass of youthful energy, ready to achieve great things or explode into mutinous irresponsibility.

Discipline

On May 17, 1804 (the group had embarked on May 14), Privates Warner and Hall were sentenced to twenty-five lashes for having gone AWOL; Collins aggravated his punishment for the same offense to fifty lashes by insubordination. On July 12, Private Willard was tried for sleeping on watch; he received 100 lashes each day for four days though it was a mild punishment for what in the field was usually a capital offense. On August 4, Private Reed deserted, ostensibly to go back for a knife he'd left at the prior campsite. (That this excuse was originally considered plausible reveals how conscious the captains were that they were on an expedition of uncertain length and certain hazards with no chance of resupply; every weapon, even a knife, was essential.) When Reed had not shown up by the next day, four men were sent to bring him back and, if he would not surrender peaceably, to shoot him. On August 18 he was tried. He confessed that he "Deserted & stold a public Rifle Shotpouch Powder & Ball" and asked for mercy. Thus, they "only Sentenced him to run the Gantlet four times through the Party & that each man with 9 switches Should punish him and for him not to be considered in future as one of the Party" (DeVoto, *Journals* 20).

Significantly, "the evening was closed with an extra gill of whiskey and a dance." Although this in part was to seal the diplomacy with the Oto chiefs there in camp, one can hypothesize that it was also to raise the morale of the enlisted men whose major duty that day had been to administer punishment to one of their own. The last corporal punishment occurred on October 14 when John Newman was court-martialed for insubordination, received seventy-five lashes, and was ordered discharged from the permanent company. At that time the expedition was among the Arikaras, and the harsh punishment "alarmed the Indian Chief verry much," so much that he "cried aloud." Clark explained the reason for the punishment; the chief admitted that for some offenses he sometimes punished men by death, but that "his nation never whiped even their Children, from their burth" (*Journals* 51).

Though Lewis and Clark imposed military discipline when necessary, that alone could not have forged the men into a unit capable of carrying out Jefferson's ambitious charge. There were, in addition, the shared hardships and hazards; each difficulty overcome bound them together. In addition, though Lewis and Clark bore officer rank, issued orders, and demanded obedience, they too shared the rigors. Capable woodsmen and watermen, physically powerful, able to think on their feet, courageous, they did not ask their men to do what they were unable or unwilling to do. Both men hunted for food; Lewis occasionally helped pole the keelboat and cooked for the men; both captains took their turns standing watch; and both men treated diseases and injuries, returning the men to health and vigor so they could continue with the demands of the expedition. Moreover, between the Marias River and the Great Falls of the Missouri, Lewis saved Private Windsor's life. As they were passing along the face of a bluff, the thawing mud of the buffalo trail an "impassable grease," Lewis slipped and nearly fell down a ninety-foot precipice, saving himself only with his espontoon (a pike-like weapon). Struggling up to a spot where he could stand "with tolerable safety," he heard Windsor cry out, "God, God, Captain, what shall I do?" He too had slipped and was lying on his belly, his right leg and arm hanging over the chasm, and scrabbling desperately with his left for some purchase on the bluff. Not yet recovered from his own narrow escape, Lewis talked the man to safety: use your knife to dig a hole in the bluff in which to put your right foot; take off your wet moccasins that are more slippery than bare feet; crawl slowly forward on your hands and knees, keeping your rifle in one hand and knife in the other. Lewis thus saved the man who, trustingly, had called out to him.

Consequently the men willingly followed Lewis and Clark. The fact that they endured more pain, worked through more hardships, achieved more than any of the men thought they could, and never protested decisions, even when they disagreed with them, attests to the captains' leadership. The expedition was now a "tough, superbly disciplined family" (Ambrose, 293).

From the first, the conditions they met required all the strength the men could muster. Traveling upstream on the **Traveling** Missouri against the current in their keelboat and two pi- **Conditions** rogues was exhausting and dangerous. The Missouri is an alluvial river with constantly collapsing banks; thus, it was a minefield of submerged tree branches, snags and sawyers, and, at times, sandbars that not only impeded movement upstream but threatened damage to the little craft. Several decades before steam engines were utilized on the river, power was provided mostly by the men—rowing, poling, or towing the boats—though two horses had been purchased for use in towing when conditions of the banks made it possible. Sometimes sails were rigged when the winds were right, but a sudden gust or change of direction could capsize the boats. Some of the men could not swim. When, on the upper Missouri, they came upon impassable stretches or waterfalls, they had to portage around them—that is, unload the canoes, carry them and their contents around the unnavigable spot, and then reload them. Often the land route first had to be discovered, and it was sometimes long. Around the Great Falls of the Missouri, for example, the distance was eighteen and one-quarter miles over ground that was comparatively level but carpeted with cactus. By then the party's only footwear was moccasins; for protection they sewed double soles of parfleche (buffalo rawhide) as did the Plains Indians, but still their feet were repeatedly and viciously lacerated. To facilitate hauling the canoes and baggage, they constructed "truck frames," first of cottonwood and then, when they broke, of the tougher willow. Wheels were made by cutting slices of the trunks. Even after applying mechanical science to lessen human labor, this portage was exhausting. Clark wrote:

the men has to haul with all their strength wate & art, . . . notwithstanding the coolness of the air [drenched] in high presperation and every halt, those not employed in reparing the course, are asleep in a moment, maney limping from the soreness of their feet some become fa[i]nt for a few moments, but no man complains, all go chearfully on. [T]o state the fatigues of this party would take up more of this journal that other notes which I find scarcely time to set down. (*Journals* 147–48)

When they ran out of the Missouri, they rode and led Indian horses fortuitously supplied by Sacajawea's people; without them the expedition would have been at risk because, unable to carry enough across the mountains, they would have had to cache (or bury) even more of their stores of food, ammunition, lead, and trade goods. Once across the mountains they made dugouts in which they descended the Columbia, sometimes daring to run the rapids, much to the astonishment of Indians watching them from the banks. At the mouth of the Columbia, "the Seas roled and tossed the Canoes in such a manner . . . that several of our party were seasick" (*Journals* 280).

Along the route, going and coming back, they endured winds so severe that one was labeled a "hurricane," flash floods, frost in May, hail seven inches in diameter, eleven days of ceaseless rain at Fort Clatsop on the Pacific, snow in the Bitterroot Mountains so deep in June 1806 that they were delayed five weeks on their return.

Clothing Their clothes wore out. Hunters sent out for game below the Teton River complained that the alkali and other "mineral substances" ate through their moccasins (*Journals* 31). As early as June 1805 uniforms were in tatters and everyone was wearing elkskin shirts and breeches. By the time they were in view of the Pacific, Clark purchased two beaver skins from which to make a robe "as the robe I have is rotten and good for nothing" (*Journals* 229). Life during the rainy season at Fort Clatsop was even more miserable because nearly half the men's leather clothes had rotted. Wrote Clark: "if we have cold weather before we can kill & Dress skins for clothing, the bulk of the party will Suffer verry much" (*Journals* 284). On August 8, 1806, as they arrived back at the mouth of the Yellowstone River, Lewis wrote that since they left the west side of the Rockies, they had not had time to dress skins and make clothes; thus, most of the men were "extreemly bare" (*Journals* 443). It is thus no surprise that as they approached St. Louis in September 1806 and met up with the trader Auguste Choteau, "several of the party exchanged leather for linen shirts and beaver for corse hats" (*Journals* 471).

Food and Drink The men consumed an enormous number of calories towing the keelboat, dragging equipment on portages, scouring the countryside for game, climbing mountains, wrestling, dancing—even just staying warm. Their appetites were enormous. A man could eat as much as nine pounds of meat a day along with whatever fruits he could find—raspberries, currants, grapes, watercresses, wild onions, and artichokes—and still feel hungry.

Lewis had laid in a supply of rations at Camp Wood during the winter of 1803–1804: "4,175 complete rations at $.14 each; 5,555 rations of flour at $.04 each; 100 gallons of whiskey at $1.28 each; 20 gallons of whiskey at $1 each; 4,000 rations of salt pork at $.04 each; plus ground corn" (Ambrose, 133–34). In addition, he had earlier requisitioned a supply of portable soup, a mixture of beans and mixed vegetables that could be reconstituted on the trail. Lewis was so enthusiastic about this soup, which "forms one of the most essential articles in the preparation" for the expedition, that he spent $289.50 on 193 pounds of the stuff, an amount higher than that for any other category of provisions and as much as he'd originally estimated for his scientific instruments, arms, and ammunition (Ambrose, 86). The reviews from the men were, at best, mixed (*Journals* 241).

As the expedition set out up the Missouri, a daily routine was established. Lewis divided the men into three squads, or "messes," and each evening Sergeant Ordway distributed the day's provisions. These were to be cooked immediately with a portion to be reserved for the next day, as no cooking was allowed during the day. The basic menu was on a three-day cycle: hominy and lard on day one, saltpork and flour on the second, and pork and cornmeal on the third (Ambrose, 145). In part to conserve such purchased supplies and in part because the men preferred fresh meat to cold hominy and lard, hunting parties went out every day. Some meat they preserved; Clark records on June 5, 1804, that they "jerked the [deer] meat" killed the day before (*Journals* 6).

Jefferson had asked the captains to learn what they could of the indigenous plants and animals along the route. Granted, they collected specimens of new animals, such as the prairie dog, but they also ate their way through a wide variety of species. Clark shoots beaver, "the flesh of those animals the party is fond of eating" (*Journals* 104); they catch catfish—"verry fat, a quart of Oile Came out of the surpolous [surplus] fat of one of those fish" (*Journals* 14). As they approach the Continental Divide, trout are plentiful; once they reach the Columbia, salmon too, though many men got sick from dried salmon traded by the Indians. (It was probably incompletely dried, thus containing bacteria.) They eat ducks, geese, brants—even a swan or two. When they kill a grizzly bear, always a formidable opponent, they "divided him among the party" for fresh meat but also boil "the oil and pout it in a cask for future uce; the oil is as hard as hogs lard when cool" (*Journals* 105). From bear's oil and dried meat they made a kind of pemmican (155). Occasionally there were treats: Lewis, assigning himself the duty of cook, boiled dried buffalo meat and "made each man large suet dumpling" (149). At the Great

Falls of the Missouri, Lewis is almost euphoric: "My fare is really sumptuous this evening; buffalo's humps, tongues, and marrowbones, fine trout parched meal pepper and salt, and a good appetite; the last is not ... the least of the luxuries" (138).

Later Lewis describes in some detail Charbonneau's *boudin (poudingue) blanc* (white gut pudding), which "we esteem one of the greatest delacies [delicacies] of the forest." Charbonneau takes about six feet of the lower part of the large intestine of a buffalo, and with his thumb and fingers squeezes out "what ... is not good to eat," though some of the flavor remains. He then stuffs it with a mixture of the hump meat and kidney suet, to which is added salt, pepper, and flour. When the ends are tied, "it is then baptised in the Missouri with two dips and a flirt, and bobbed into the kettle; from whence after it be well boiled it is taken and fried with bears oil untill it become brown, when it is ready to esswage the pangs of a keen appetite ... such as travelers in the wilderness are seldom at a loss for" (*Journals* 107–8).

Food would not always be so ample, however, a fact of which Lewis was acutely aware. Past the Three Forks of the Missouri he notes, on June 31, 1805: "when we have plenty of fresh meat I find it impossible to make the men take any care of it, or use it with the least frugallity, Tho' I expect that necessity will shortly teach them this art" (173). In the mountains game becomes scarce. On September 6, Clark notes, "nothing to eat but berries, our flour out, and but little corn" (235). They purchase fish and dogs from the Nez Percé, though of the latter Clark writes, "all the Party have greatly the advantage of me in as much as they relish the flesh of the dogs" (246). They also purchase horses from the Nez Percé, primarily as transportation, but, as Clark added, to "Eate if necessary" (232). It soon was. The journals starting on September 14, 1905, repeatedly have entries saying, "we were compelled to kill a Colt for our men & Selves for want of meat." The first time seemed unique; they named the spot Colt Killed Creek. Descending the Columbia they traded for more dogs, dried fish, camas roots, and acorns (259).

After a miserable winter at Fort Clatsop—no trading ship was there from which they could requisition supplies—the return trip began, rife with food shortages. Once again they ate horses when necessary, but while crossing the Bitterroot Mountains even the horses went hungry, for the snow was still deep and often crusty from partial thaws. Roots seemed the only food until the salmon should come upstream to spawn. One creek was christened Hungry Creek. Things grew so desperate that on May 21, 1806, the remaining trade goods were divided among the men so they could bargain individually with Indians.

Such privations potentially threatened the mission. The expedition had so little food that despite the services the Nez Percé had rendered during the previous year, in addition to caring for the horses over the winter, the captains were unable to reward them. Clark wrote: "their object I believe is the expectation of being fed by us . . . however *kind as they have been* we must disappoint them at this moment as it is necessary that we should use all frugallaty as well as employ every exertion to provide meat for our journey" (*Journals* 401). Hardly an enviable position for men whose charge was to bring word of the power of the Great Father and to convince the Indians of the advantages accruing from an alliance with the United States!

Lewis ordered the hunters out to "kill some . . . meat for these people whom I was unwilling to leave without giving them a good supply of provision after their having been so obliging as to conduct us through those tremendious mountains" (*Journals* 419). However, this hunt was not successful. By June 29 their bear's oil was exhausted and they were reduced to "roots alone without salt" (413). Fortunately, by July 11 they came upon a huge herd—they estimated 10,000—of buffalo within a two-mile circle. They killed eleven animals; Lewis notes that the hump and the tongue will feed four men for one day (427). Nonetheless, pressing hard, almost desperate to get home before another winter set in, by September 18 the party, only 150 miles above St. Louis, was subsisting on pappaws (custard apples) (417). Their enthusiastic reception on September 21 by the citizens of St. Charles—who, like most of the rest of the country had given them up for dead—made it worthwhile. Four days later in St. Louis, they enjoyed "in the evening a dinner & Ball" (478).

Despite the fact that the trip to the Pacific and back was arduous and often dangerous, the Corps of Discovery maintained morale by celebrating—sometimes spontaneously, sometimes on special holidays. At a place they named **Entertainment** Independence Creek, they celebrated in 1804 the first Fourth of July west of the Mississippi. At sunrise and at sunset they fired the swivel gun mounted aboard the keelboat. Though the day was somewhat marred when Joseph Field was bitten by a rattlesnake, Captain Lewis treated him with a poultice of Peruvian bark, which drew out the poison. That evening an extra gill of whiskey was issued to all hands. (The usual daily ration was one gill. Lewis had bought all the whiskey that could be carried without sacrificing other important supplies, but it was not enough to last the trip, even when watered down.) The last of it was poured to celebrate July 4, 1805, a sad moment indeed, though while they were descending the Columbia one of the party, J. Collins, improvised and presented them with "verry good *beer* made of the Pa-shi-to-quar-mash [camass] bread" that had repeatedly gotten wet and had thus gone moldy (*Journals* 260). In the interim the captains occasionally issued an extra ration to maintain morale. For example, on the evening of Reed's court martial, August 18, which was also Lewis's birthday, "the evening was closed with an extra gill of whiskey and a Dance untill 11 o Clock" (*Journals* 20).

Lewis was conscious of the need for entertainment. On April 26, 1805, when they had reached the junction of the Yellowstone River, he writes: "much pleased at having arrived at this long wished for spot, . . . in order to add in some measure to the general pleasure . . . [of] our little community, we ordered a dram to be issued to each person; this soon produced the fiddle, and they spent the evening with much hilarity, singing & dancing, and seemed as perfectly to forget their past toils as they appeared regardless of those to come" (*Journals* 101). On Christmas Day, 1804, the cannon was fired three times as the flag was raised and everyone was served a ration of rum. Some men went out to hunt while others spent the day dancing. Though they were now at Fort Mandan, "the Savages did not Trouble us as we had requested them not to come as it was a Great medician [medicine] day with us," wrote Sergeant Ordway (*Journals* 74).

The second Christmas, at Fort Clatsop, was far more bleak. At sunrise the soldiers woke the captains with a rifle volley and song. Then they exchanged presents. Clark received a pair of moccasins that one private had made and a woven basket from another; Sacajawea gave him two dozen white weasel tails; and Lewis gave him a vest, underdrawers, and socks. The captains, though keeping some tobacco for future trade with the Indians, distributed half of it among the men who smoked; the non-smokers each got a handkerchief (Ambrose, 314). Aside from that, the day, like most of their stay on the Pacific, was miserable. Clark wrote: "We would have Spent this day the nativity of Christ in feasting, had we any thing either to raise our Sperits or even gratify our appetites, our Diner concisted of pore Elk, So much Spoiled that we eate it thro' mear necessity, Some Spoiled pounded fish and a few roots" (Ambrose, 314).

Although the Corps of Discovery celebrated Christmas 1804 alone, they shared that winter's New Year's celebrations with the Mandans. They visited one of the villages where they entertained their hosts with Private Cruzatte's fiddle-playing. One soldier danced on his hands, but the central attraction was York, Clark's slave, who especially fascinated the Indians. They were astonished that so "large a man should be so active"; moreover, they were suspicious of his color, and some of them tried to rub off the black (Ambrose, 194–95).

Several days later the Mandans invited the garrison to join them for the buffalo dance. Held in the communal earthen lodge, the dance began to the music of rattles and drums. The old men, dressed in their best, ceremoniously arrived and seated themselves in a circle. Soon the young men, accompanied by their wives, filed in and took their seats in an outer circle behind the elders. Following a smoking ceremony the young men,

Charles M. Russell, *York*. Watercolor, 1908. Courtesy of the Montana Historical Society, Gift of the Artist. During the winter of 1804–5 at Fort Mandan, members of the Corps of Discovery exchanged many social visits with their Mandan hosts. In this watercolor, which provides good detail of the interior of a Mandan lodge, a Mandan chief, fascinated with York's black skin, tries to rub off its color.

one by one, offered their young wives, who presented themselves naked to the old men. As Clark then described the ceremony, "the Girl then takes the Old man (who verry often can Screcely [scarcely] walk) and leads him to a Convenient place for the business, after which they return to the lodge." The purpose of the ceremony, Clark notes, "is to cause the buffalow to Come near So that They may kill them." Because the buffalo migrated great distances during the winter in search of grass, the Mandan held the buffalo dance to attract them. Moreover, the Mandan believed "that power—in this case, the hunting abilities of the old men— could be transferred from one man to another through sexual relations with the same woman." The Americans, thought by the Mandans to have "great good luck and big medicine," benefited. They too were offered young women, and many participated in the ceremony with extraordinary zeal. Four days later the Mandan had a good buffalo hunt (Ambrose, 195; *Journals* 76).

Although the relations with the Mandans were most prolonged, Lewis and Clark also record social activities with other tribes along the route. While among the Nez Percé, they enjoyed watching and occasionally participating in horse races; "several of [these Nez Percé horses, wrote Clark] would be thought swift horses in the atlantic states" (*Journals* 390). This was high praise from a Virginian. In addition, Clark records the men whiling away the time before they could cross the Bitterroot Mountains by holding "foot races . . . [between] the men of our party" and the Indians, "after which our party devided and played at prisoners base untill night." After dark there was fiddle music and dancing (*Journals* 400).

Always there were women. Recreational sex was far from rare on the expedition. Sergeant Gass called the Arikara women "the best looking Indians I have ever seen," and Sergeant Ordway agreed: "some of their women are very handsome and clean" (Ambrose, 180). Clark observed that "a curious custom with the Souix [*sic*] as well as the rickeres is to give handsom squars [squaws] to those whom they wish to Show some acknowledgments." Though such attention was rebuffed in their towns, two Arikara women followed the Corps to their next campsite and "pursisted in their civilities" (*Journals* 51). An old Chinook woman appeared at a Pacific campsite near Cape Disappointment with six of her daughters and nieces; "she was selling their favors." Of this, Clark observed, "Those people appear to view Sensuality as a Necessary evil. . . . The young females are fond of the attention of our men" (Ambrose, 310). At Fort Clatsop a young chief, Cuscatah, trying to sweeten a trade deal, offered each captain a young woman, "which we . . . declined excepting . . . which displeased them . . . the female[s] . . . appeared to be highly disgusted at our refuseing of their favors" (Ambrose, 314).

The result of all this social intercourse was venereal dis- **Health and**
ease, so common among the men that it was rarely men- **Disease**
tioned. At Fort Mandan, Clark wrote: "Generally helthy
except Venerials Complaints which is verry Common
amongst the natives and the men Catch it from them" (*Journals* 90). On
the return trip Lewis notes, "Goodrich and McNeal are both very unwell
with the pox which they contracted last winter from the Chinook
women" (*Journals* 417). Nearly all the men, at one time or another, suffered from " 'brakings out, or irruptions of the Skin' probably caused by
venereal disease" (Ambrose, 292).

The treatment was standard: ingesting mercury. Lewis routinely ad-
ministered pills of mercurous chloride to the men (Ambrose, 197). However, there were dangerous side effects of the treatment. Ambrose notes
that the phrase "mad as a hatter" referred to hatmakers who used mercury in their work and became slightly crazy from breathing in the fumes
(197). And Gary Moulton suggests that the mercury treatment may have
contributed to the surprisingly high proportion of men of the Corps who
died young (Ambrose, 320n).

Though Lewis may not have been correct when he wrote about curing
men of venereal disease "by the uce of mercury" (*Journals* 315), the men
remained surprisingly healthy during the two-year trek. Only one, Sergeant Floyd, died, apparently of infection following a burst appendix
(*Journals* 21).

There were, of course, many less serious problems. Mosquitoes and
gnats swarmed over the men, compelling "us to brush them off or have
our eyes filled with them" (*Journals* 154). While descending the Columbia
the men were covered with fleas, apparently from straw at an Indian
camp: "every man . . . was obliged to strip naked . . . [to brush] the flees
off their legs and bodies" (*Journals* 263). In July 1804 extreme heat, coupled with exertion, affected most of the party; one case of sunstroke was
recorded (*Journals* 9). In October 1804 many men, including Clark, complained of rheumatism; this was not surprising given the cold, damp
conditions. The pain and spasms were treated by applying a hot stone
wrapped in flannel (*Journals* 53, 55). Several suffered from toothache;
most, from boils, which Lewis calls "tumors," some of which were enormous. Clark lanced one that discharged half a pint of pus (*Journals* 13).

There are several references to becoming sick from the food: choke-
cherries and red haws produced digestive disorders, as did tainted dried
salmon. Dysentery—a "lax and heaviness in the stomach," as Clark put
it, and which he attributed to the water—was treated by Glauber's salts
(*Journals* 174). Clark describes being "taken verry unwell with a pain in
the bowels & Stomach, which is certainly the effects of my diet." The
previous night, with nothing to eat but dried fish and roots, he and Lewis

were in agony: the meal "Swelled us in Such a manner that we were Scercely able to breath for Several hours" (*Journals* 242–43). Descending the Columbia, several men suffered from the purgative effects of drinking salt water (*Journals* 281).

Moreover, many suffered from "feet so mangled and bruised with the stones and rough ground over which they passed barefoot, that they can scarcely walk or stand" (*Journals* 127). Winter brought special hazards— snowblindness from sun reflected off the snow, and numerous cases of frostbite; Clark even writes of York's frostbitten penis (*Journals* 72). Both on the Columbia and on the last stages of the return trip on the Missouri, men complain of sore eyes. Clark describes the problem: "their eyes inflamed and Swelled in Such a manner as to render them extreamly painful, particularly when exposed to the light" and suggests its cause: "I am willing to believe it may be owing to the reflection of the sun on the water" (*Journals* 475). Chuinard, however, suggests that venereal disease may also have been a factor (Ambrose, 223; Chuinard, 158, 279). And, from being frequently wet, the men often suffered from colds and influenza.

Accidents There were, in addition, accidents. While constructing Fort Mandan, several men cut themselves with axes (*Journals* 64).

While taking down the mast on the keelboat, Sergeant Pryor dislocated his shoulder; it took four tries before it was popped back into place (*Journals* 69). On the return through the Bitterroots, John Potts "cut one of the large veins on the inner side of his leg" and John Colter's horse fell on him, the two rolling over and over among the rocks. The potentially most disastrous, however, was Private Cruzatte's shooting Captain Lewis in the buttocks while they were out hunting. Seeing movement and thinking it was an elk, Cruzatte fired, hitting Lewis. This is the captain's account:

> I was in the act of firing on the Elk ... when a ball struck my left thye about an inch below my hip joint, missing the bone it passed through the left thye and cut the thickness of the bullet across the hinder part ... ; the stroke was very severe; I instantly supposed that Cruzatte had shot me in mistake for an Elk, as I was dressed in brown leather and he cannot see very well; under this impression I called out to him damn you, you have shot me, and looked toward the place the ball had come, seeing nothing I called Cruzatte several times as loud as I could but received no answer. I was now preswaded [persuaded] that it was an Indian that had shot me as the report of the gun did not appear to be more than 40 paces from me and Cruzatte appeared to be out of hearing of me. (*Journals* 445)

Lewis hobbled back to the keelboat, where Sergeant Gass helped him out of his clothes and Lewis treated himself by inserting rolls of lint into his wound to keep it open and let it heal from the inside out. In addition he made a poultice from Peruvian bark, which, he believed the next day, had lessened potential inflammation. Nonetheless, the "pain I experienced excited a high fever and I had a verry uncomfortable night" (*Journals* 446).

The accident occurred on August 11, 1806. On August 19, Clark wrote that the wounds were healing but hoped that Lewis would be able to walk in eight to ten days. He had, in the meantime, spent much of his time lying face down. On September 9, Clark wrote: "My worthy friend Cap. Lewis has entirely recovered. his wounds are heeled up and he can walk and even run as well as ever he could [although] the parts are yet tender" (*Journals* 471).

This accidental shooting was one of several potentially pivotal moments on the expedition. Recall the time Lewis almost fell over the cliff (*Journals* 130); another time, the command tent was moved only moments before a large tree that would have "crushed [us] to attoms" crashed down on the original spot (112). Another time Lewis seriously underestimated the hostility of the Blackfeet and let down his guard; the result was a shootout that caused the only two Indian deaths by white bullets and that nearly killed Lewis: "Being bearheaded I felt the wind of his [the Indian Lewis had shot in the belly] bullet very distinctly" (*Journals* 437–40). Each incident could have changed the history of the American West. Each could have delayed a realistic rather than a mythological understanding of the West. For although Lewis and Clark failed to find the Northwest Passage (they could not do the impossible), they added immeasurably to the nation's knowledge of its newly acquired territory and the land beyond. According to Herman J. Viola,

the expedition achieved all of its scientific objectives. Lewis and Clark compiled exhaustive and accurate information about the regions they visited, laboriously recording observations about flora and fauna, native inhabitants, and natural resources and climate. They determined the true course of the Upper Missouri and its major tributaries, proved that a navigable waterway did not connect the Mississippi and Columbia rivers, and made the first real contributions to understanding the topography of the Far West.... In addition to their maps of western topography, the explorers returned with incredible amounts of scientific information. They discovered and described hundreds of species of fish, reptiles, mammals, birds, plants, and trees. Among mammals alone, they are credited with discovering the pronghorn antelope, bighorn sheep, mountain beaver, prairie dog, mountain goat, grizzly bear, coyote, mule deer, and various species of rabbits, squirrels, foxes and wolves. (*Exploring* 20, 22)

After a four-month, 4,000-mile trip, one prairie dog and one magpie were among the survivors of living specimens they sent to Jefferson. These creatures, Jefferson was informed by a servant at the executive mansion, had been placed in the room "where Monsieur receives his callers" (Viola, *Exploring* 22).

Interactions with the American Indians
In addition, Lewis and Clark accomplished most of Jefferson's instructions relative to the tribes along the way. They had significant encounters with the Oto, Yankton Sioux, Teton Sioux, Arikara, Mandans, Hidatsa, Blackfeet, Shoshone, Nez Percé, Flatheads, Walla Walla, Yakima, and Chinook. To all they brought the standard message: that the Indians had a new father who desired that they live in peace with one another, who would protect them, and who was desirous of establishing trade with them. Especially with the Teton Sioux, from whom the captains expected trouble, they took a firm stance. When negotiations broke down (in part due to inadequate translation) and young warriors seized the cable of the keelboat, denied them the right to proceed, demanded trade goods and threatened to take them by force, insulted the captains by bumping into them while pretending drunkenness, and ultimately brandished bows and arrows, Lewis and Clark responded by ordering the swivel gun as well as all rifles trained on them. Though preferring more moderate speech, Clark told them that "we were not Squaws but warriors" and that "we were Sent by their great father the president of the United States and if they misused us that he or Captain Lewis could by writing to him have them all destroyed as it were in a moment" (Ordway's entry, *Journals* 37).

Though the Tetons were not won over and still provided a threat to the return journey, Bernard DeVoto believes that "the moral of the episode was that a new breed of white men had come to the Upper Missouri [who, unlike some prior traders] could not be scared or bullied. The moral was flashed along the Indian underground faster than the expedition could travel" (DeVoto, *Journals* 34). Thus, DeVoto suggests, upstream tribes were likely to be more solicitous. This policy of peace through strength seems to have worked. Only when Lewis and Clark truly let down their guard—as they did with the Blackfeet—did members of the expedition get into real trouble. (The hostility of the Blackfeet, the only tribe that suffered casualties from the Corps of Discovery, would continue to be a serious consideration for subsequent fur traders on the Upper Missouri.)

However, most relations with the Indians were far more harmonious. The presence of Sacajawea, the teenage wife of translator Toussaint Charbonneau, of course did no harm. A woman traveling with the expedition signaled more meaningfully than words that its purpose was peace, not war. In her own right she was a useful translator, and the fortuitous reunion with her brother Cameahwait (by then chief of the Shoshone, from whom she had earlier been abducted) virtually assured a successful though difficult passage across the Continental Divide. Cameahwait provided not only instruction on the geography of the country but also the horses necessary to traverse it.

Though the captains rarely refer to Sacajawea by name, usually calling her "the Indian woman," the medical care they gave her during the birth of her son and the subsequent complications created a bond that became more important than that of her being the interpreter's wife. Likewise, there are numerous accounts of the captains providing medical care to tribes they met; their care was so successful that the gratitude was at times embarrassing. As Clark notes, "those . . . cures have raised my reputation and given those nativs an exolted oppinion of my skill as a phy[si]cian." Recognizing his limitations, he verbalizes his policy: "We take care to give them no article which can possibly injure them, and in maney cases can administer & give such medicine & sirgical aid as will effectually restore [their health] in simple cases" (*Journals* 372–73). (Remember Jefferson's suggestion that they take along kinepox to inoculate against smallpox.)

The captains were assiduous in learning what they could about future U.S. trading partners. They compiled vocabularies of different tribes and took copious notes on hunting methods, religious practices, and manifestations of grief (e.g., among the Gros Ventres this involved chopping off a finger at the second joint). They exchanged gifts—peace medals, metal axes, robes, and food. In an especially telling incident after Lewis had given the chief of the Nez Percé a peace medal, "he insisted on exchanging names with me according to their custom . . . and I was called Yo-me-kol-lick which interpreted is the *white bear skin folded*" (*Journals* 415). It was a significant tribute to be named for the grizzly bear.

An extension of such cross-cultural exchange also fulfilled another Jeffersonian charge—to encourage influential chiefs to visit Washington. The reasons for such delegations were mixed. Although Jefferson was aware that the presence of tribal leaders in Washington might ensure the expedition's safety, in a more significant vein their visit would be an opportunity to demonstrate the power of the United States and to reveal American customs, religion, architecture, and politics.

On May 19, 1804, Pierre Chouteau, a St. Louis businessman, set off for Washington with some mineral specimens, the first map produced by the expedition, a horned toad—and some Osage chiefs. They arrived in Washington in July and met with Jefferson. All told, delegates from about a dozen tribes, including the Pawnee, Mandan, Osage, and Arikara, visited Washington as a direct result of contact with Lewis and Clark (Viola, *Diplomats* 24). As they met each tribe, Lewis and Clark encouraged delegations to visit the Great Father (Jefferson). Although some bureaucrats objected to the costs of such visits and suggested that money could be saved by having the Indians camp along the way to avoid "tavern rates," Jefferson staunchly supported such expenditures to woo the Indians. As he explained to Congress, "good relations with the tribes on the Missouri were 'indispensable to the policy of governing those Indians by commerce rather than by arms,' and the cost of the former was much less than the cost of the latter" (Ambrose, 336). Speaking with delegation members, Jefferson emphasized the nation's peaceful goal—to establish commerce. He admonished them: "On your return tell your people that I take them all by the hand, that I become their father hereafter [and] that they shall know our nation only as friends and benefactors" (Viola, *Diplomats* 25). Thus began the practice—which would continue into the twentieth century—of bringing Indian delegations to Washington.

On balance, the Lewis and Clark expedition successfully accomplished what it had set out to do. Jefferson knew that others would have to complete the work begun by the Corps of Discovery. Explaining the intent of the expedition, he wrote, even before Lewis and Clark had returned, "the work we are now doing is, I trust, done for posterity, in such a way that they need not repeat it. . . . We shall delineate with correctness the great arteries of this great country: those who come after us will extend the ramifications as they become acquainted with them, and fill up the canvass we begin" (Viola, *Exploring* 25–26). And so they did: military expeditions, naturalists, painters, and railroad surveys crisscrossed the West, adding to the store of knowledge, promoting the doctrine of manifest destiny, and linking the continent through technology. But, as Herman J. Viola succinctly noted, "No other 19th-century expedition to the Far West would be so free of blunders" (*Exploring* 20).

OTHER EXPEDITIONS

Among those who followed Lewis and Clark was Lieutenant Zebulon Montgomery Pike, who neither climbed nor named Pike's Peak. However, his name would be memorialized in the motto of a nation restless to go west; "Pike's Peak or bust" was scrawled on many a covered wagon.

Having returned a party of Osage Indians, previously captured by the Potawatomi, to their village, Pike and his men set out in September 1806 to explore the southern Great Plains and to explore the source of the Arkansas River. He found the land to be inhospitable and worthless for agriculture, going so far as to predict it would become the American

Sahara. However, this could be an advantage, he felt, for the region could become a buffer between Spanish and American territory, a region that "if used without waste [could] feed all the savages in the United States territory one century" and that could "also serve as a barrier to Westward expansion because it could force American citizens 'so prone to rambling' to 'limit their extent on the west, to the borders of the Missouri and Mississippi.' " In this way the myth of the Great American Desert was born (Viola, *Exploring* 30), which would persist until after the Civil War and which was resurrected during the Dust Bowl of the 1930s.

Stephen H. Long, of the army's topographical engineers, led five expeditions into the trans-Mississippi West from 1816 to 1823, covering roughly 26,000 miles. Perhaps his greatest contribution was convincing the War Department that scientific data gathering was as important as military mapping and surveying. Thus, scientific professionals were enlisted in exploring the West, an activity that had been the province of enthusiastic amateurs in Jefferson's day. However, after two decades of government-sponsored exploration the fever cooled in the halls of Congress, perhaps due to the unpromising reports of Pike and Long. For most of the rest of the next two decades the region was explored—informally but thoroughly—by fur traders and mountain men. Among them was John Colter of the Lewis and Clark expedition, who had decided to remain behind. Seeking new trapping areas for his employer, Manuel Lisa of the Missouri Fur Company, he explored the Tetons, crossed the Continental Divide, and was probably the first white man to see what is now Yellowstone National Park.

THE PATHFINDER AND THE GREENHORN: JOHN CHARLES FRÉMONT AND CHARLES PREUSS

Between 1842 and 1853, Colonel John Charles Frémont led five expeditions across the West. Nicknamed "The Pathfinder," he probably covered more territory than any other explorer of his day.

He employed mountain men, among them Kit Carson, Thomas "Broken Hand" Fitzpatrick, and Joseph Walker, as expedition guides. On his way to the Pacific in 1843–44 he essentially followed the established emigrant route. In 1843, 900 settlers arrived in Oregon, augmented the next year by 1,200 more (Milner, O'Connor, and Sandweiss, 164). Thus, Frémont was hardly venturing into the unknown as Lewis and Clark had done. Indeed, he frequently writes in his journal of sage brush crushed by wagon wheels, of finding a "broad plainly beaten trail" (Frémont, *Exploring Expedition* 150), of a remarkable depletion of game, especially buffalo ("an occasional buffalo skull and a few wild antelope were all that remained of the abundance which had covered the country with animal life"), and its impact on the "miserably poor" Indians who "drew aside their blankets, showing me their lean and bony figures" (143). He describes the Hudson's Bay Company operation at Vancouver and its intricate overland network to Montreal (193–95). He regrets missing Dr. Marcus Whitman, absent from his missionary establishment at Walla Walla, but "an abundant supply of excellent potatoes" from the mission garden "furnished [the expedition] a grateful substitute for bread" (Frémont, *Exploring Expedition* 182–83).

Although Frémont rarely forged new trails, his expeditions were far from insignificant. Especially because of the presence of German cartographer Charles Preuss, they collected significant scientific data. On the 1843–44 expedition they carried scientific instruments including "One refracting telescope by Frauenhofer . . . , Two sextants, by Troughton, One pocket chronometer, No. 837, by Goffe, Falmouth . . . One cistern barometer, by Frye & Shaw, New York, [and] Six thermometers and a number of small compasses" (*Exploring Expedition* 106). When necessary, Frémont could and did improvise repairs to these fine instruments. He once replaced the broken glass of a barometer with a powder horn of transparent elkhorn:

> This I boiled and stretched on a piece of wood to the requisite diameter, and scraped it very thin in order to increase to the utmost its transparency. I then secured it firmly in its place on the instrument, with strong glue made from a buffalo, and filled it with mercury, properly heated. A piece of skin, which had covered one of the vials, furnished a good pocket, which was well secured with strong thread and glue, and then the brass cover was screwed to its place. The instrument was left some time to dry; and when I reversed it, a few hours after, I had the satisfaction to find it in perfect order. (*Exploring Expedition* 63)

He constantly described geological formations, recorded temperatures of the air and streams, and collected botanical and fossil specimens; meteorological and astronomical observations were part of the daily regimen, and when clouds interfered with such sighting, Frémont estimated the height of mountains by the temperature at which water would boil. He was apparently the first explorer to carry the daguerreotype into the field to take pictures of the land. Moreover, Frémont and his men were the first to conduct a boat exploration of the Great Salt Lake (*Exploring Expedition* 152–59) and to identify and describe the Great Basin (275–77). Frémont frequently did chemical analysis of the soil, determining, for example, the percentage of silica, alumina, lime, magnesia, oxide of iron, phosphate of lime, and decomposed vegetable matter (294); such data supplemented descriptions ("the soil of the level prairie which sweeps directly up to the foot of the surrounding mountain, appears to be very rich, producing flax spontaneously and luxuriantly ... [as well as] strong, green and vigorous grass" [179]). Such descriptions provided eastern readers an antidote to the myth of the Great American Desert and encouraged farmers to move into the plains. In addition, especially on the 1843–44 expedition, Frémont compiled tables of daily and cumulative distances (291–94). Of these and the related narratives, the historian Allan Nevins observed: "Can we wonder that ... Joseph Ware's *The Emigrant's Guide to California* (1849), much used in gold rush days, was largely founded on Frémont's narratives, reproducing whole sentences verbatim?" (Nevins, 20).

Perhaps equally important, Frémont's reports on his expeditions excited America's imagination. Unlike the Lewis and Clark journals, which languished for years before publication, Congress ordered 10,000 copies of the combined reports of the 1842 and the 1843–44 expeditions; they appeared expeditiously in 1845. Though the original title, *Report of the Exploring Expedition to the Rocky Mountains in the Year 1842, and to Oregon and North California in the Years 1843–44*, was cumbersome, the writing was often vivid. Frémont was a good storyteller, providing real-life adventures that later dime novelists would be hard-pressed to equal. In one, Kit Carson and Alexander Godey, in pursuit of stolen horses, crept to within thirty yards of a Mojave Indian camp; then, however, horses whinnied and alerted the Indians, who greatly outnumbered the two Americans. Carson and Godey gave a war shout and charged the camp. Let Frémont take the narrative from there:

> The Indians received them with a flight of arrows ... one of which passed through Godey's shirt collar, barely missing his neck; our men fired their rifles [with] ... a steady aim, and rushed in. Two Indians were stretched on the ground, fatally pierced with bullets; the rest fled, except a lad that was captured. Then scalps of the fallen were instantly stripped off; but in the process, one of them, who had two balls through his body, sprung to his feet, the blood streaming from his skinned head, and uttering a hideous howl. An old squaw, possibly his mother, stopped and looked back from the mountain side she was climbing, threatening and lamenting. The frightfull spectacle appalled the stout hearts of our men; but they did what humanity required, and quickly terminated the agonies of the gory savage. (*Exploring Expedition* 263)

In preparing his reports for publication, Frémont was lucky in having his wife, Jesse, as collaborator with him. She wrote and polished what he dictated. Once revealing the fact that he got nosebleeds from the strain of writing, Jesse wryly observed, "The horseback life, the sleep in open air, had unfitted Mr. Frémont for the indoor work of writing" (qtd. in *Exploring Expedition* xi).

In contrast are the private diaries of Charles Preuss, cartographer and artist on the first, second, and fourth Frémont expeditions to the Far West. Written for his wife rather than for publication, they reveal a man so different from Frémont that one wonders why, after the first expedition, Preuss signed on for two more. Preuss's motive seems simple: rather than a zest for adventure, ambition for public office, or love of public acclaim, he went along to support his wife and family, to whom he makes repeated homesick references.

The Preuss diaries provide primary documentation of points not resolved or left unmentioned in Frémont's reports. For instance, it is Preuss who records the fact that Frémont took a daguerreotype camera with him—the first explorer to do so—to record what artists had previously been hired to do. (One remembers Charles Bodmer traveling with Maximilian von Wied.) And, despite having little admiration for Frémont, he resolves the question of blame for the disastrous fourth expedition when, lost in the snows of the Sangre de Cristo Mountains, the party divided, some in search of a route to Taos, others prolonging their long death by cannibalism. Preuss absolves Frémont and lays the blame squarely on the mountain man Old Bill Williams, who, he says, was not a competent guide despite his assurances to the contrary. (Most trappers declared that it was impossible to cross these mountains during the winter.)

Equally interesting, the diaries provide very human insights into the feelings of a greenhorn on the frontier. Preuss, essentially a city man, hated almost everything about the first expedition and used his diaries to vent his emotions in a way that otherwise would have been impossible in the macho society of *voyageurs*, soldiers, and mountain men with whom he traveled. He whines; he sneers; he remains generally unimpressed with his companions or the country through which they travel. Of the "eternal prairies and grass" almost never broken by trees, a terrain that Frémont loves, Preuss writes, "To me it is as if someone would prefer a book with blank pages to a good story. The ocean has, after all, its storms and icebergs, the beautiful sunrise and sunset. But the prairie?" (Preuss, 5). Because they've been en route for only a week, the cartographer perhaps has not yet learned to see the beauty of life on the prairie.

He begins to learn new skills—like washing his own shirt—and congratulates himself. "Turned out a little better than the first time" (Preuss, 7). A few days later it seems to be too much effort: "I have decided to imitate one of our hunters by keeping my shirt on my body until it falls off. To wash I have no time, no desire, and no skill. Lice and fleas we shall get from the Indians anyway" (9). He finds a solution: "I was lucky to engage one of the men to do my laundry. One must take *such* a journey in order to enjoy thoroughly many a comfort to which one pays no attention in ordinary life" (13).

However, he begins to adapt or at least to demonstrate some wry humor. By the time they return to Fort Laramie, everyone's clothes are torn, and Preuss has to wear two pairs of trousers "so that one can cover the holes in the other" (59). At the fort he has an Indian woman make him a pair of leather pants. Though he can now "hang a blanket around myself" in lieu of his tattered coat, to go "without pants, only a rag over the delicate parts, like the Indians—no, no, that would be carrying the joke too far" (62). In one of his last entries from the first expedition, although Preuss still likes almost nothing about the trip, he recognizes that he has changed. "I wonder how I shall behave when I get back into civilized countries" (75).

In the meantime, hoot owls keep him awake all night (6); in the mountains he has difficulty keeping warm at night because "the best spots were already taken by others," and he is kept awake by the cold, by the smoke from the fire, and then by becoming "frightened because a burning piece of wood fell close to my feet (40–41). Even when he slept in a tent, he complains: "One blanket underneath, another blanket on top; damned hard" (3).

He is appalled by the "dirty cooking" (3), finds a pigeon "tough," refuses to eat raw liver (5), traps a large turtle "which is being prepared for soup tonight, if our cook, the rascal, will only know how to fix it." Apparently the cook didn't, for on the following day Preuss wrote of a prairie hen someone had shot, "If the cook cannot prepare it any better than the turtle, let him gulp it down himself" (8–9). Everyone else looked forward to arriving in buffalo country, anticipating good meat. Of his first taste, Preuss wrote,

> The fire crackles and the pots are steaming. An entire rib-side is placed on sticks, which are pounded into the ground, obscuring the view. The marrowbone laid upon the coals spreads its stench through the neighborhood. I am summoned, and the often discussed buffalo feed starts. We start with bouillon, which is, of course, not skimmed off. If one could eliminate the dirt, it would be a delicate meat broth. The marrow was too raw and too fat for my taste, the ribs likewise too raw. However, I am willing to agree ... with the admirers of buffalo meat ... that it would taste better than our beef if it were prepared like the latter. (17)

A month later Preuss has grown to like buffalo meat, though he still complains about the cook. Buffalo meat "should be better prepared. My teeth are often quite sore, and the meat is often so carelessly roasted on a wooden spit that one's mouth drips with red blood" (49–50). Several weeks later still, his stomach has adapted to the frontier, although his interpersonal skills have not. "A polecat! Last night a stinker was killed, and we ate it this morning for breakfast. I never thought that such a foul-smelling beast could taste so good. During the attack it squirted right into Badeau's face; the fellow still smells of it" (59).

As they start from Chotteau's Landing, Frémont gives Preuss a gentle horse; the "unaccustomed effort" of riding, however, "made me quite stiff" (3). Frémont seems to take pity on the greenhorn cartographer; "[he] gave orders that one of the men had to saddle, groom and feed my horse" (4). One can imagine the man's response! After a long, forty-mile ride on July 5, Preuss is so "worn out . . . I could hardly stand up" (19). By July 20, Frémont realizes that Preuss cannot do his work of sketching while on horseback and so "has given orders to prepare a seat for me on one of the carts" (29). At the end of August he whines,

> Traveling in this rattle trap does not please me very much. If it were not too demanding, I should like to ride horseback one day and in the cart the next day. But Frémont is now riding my mare, and I don't like to say anything. . . . I have bruised my nose in the cart because of the bumpy road. One more month of these tribulations—then, I hope, it will be over. (Preuss, 58)

Apparently oblivious to the special considerations Frémont gave him, Preuss frequently confides to his diary his disdain for the commander. As early as the third day he notes he's "annoyed by that childish Frémont" and calls him a "foolish lieutenant" (3). He denigrates Frémont's ability to make astronomical calculations (8, 65), comes close to calling him a liar when Frémont returns from a buffalo hunt with "not even the tongue" despite claiming he shot an animal (17); scorns Frémont's Fourth of July treat as "miserable" red wine (18), and blames his "negligence" for forgetting Preuss's mosquito net (13)!

He mocks Frémont's efforts with the daguerreotype:

> Yesterday afternoon [August 2, 1842] and this morning Frémont set up his daguerreotype to photograph the rocks; he spoiled five plates that way. Not a thing was to be seen on them. That's the way it is with these Americans. They know everything, they can do everything, and when they are put to a test, they fail miserably. . . . Frémont wasted the morning with his machine. (Preuss, 32–33)

Preuss also questions Frémont's scientific knowledge:

That fellow knows nothing about mineralogy or botany. Yet he collects every trifle in order to have it interpreted later in Washington and to brag about it in his report. (35)

The antagonism may have become mutual and increasingly petty, though not directly or openly expressed: "There was such a hurry this morning [August 22, 1842] that Frémont became angry when my horse urinated. He whipped its tail when it had only half relieved nature" (50).

Beneath the vitriol one can discern pathos in some of Preuss's entries. Always he is the outsider, the other. He feels isolated, taking pleasure only in reading. He is alone among a company of men. To his diary—and thus to his wife, vicariously—he admits what he cannot say to any of his companions:

The dreariest and most miserable aspect of this journey is that there is no human being with whom I can converse. . . . I should be satisfied if I had only a single German comrade. We just move silently ahead, one after the other, as if it were a funeral procession. How different such an expedition would be in Germany. To be sure, it doubtless weighs so much on me because I am the only foreigner. Yet an American would feel much more comfortable in Germany, provided he could speak German and were socially inclined. (48)

On the first expedition, Preuss muses: "Alas, I shall probably never become an American, no matter how well I may fare in this country. I shall long for Germany as long as I live" (34).

Yet he does change. Perhaps unintentionally, perhaps as a result of his culturally imposed isolation, and certainly anachronistically, Preuss illustrates a part of Frederick Jackson Turner's frontier thesis: that the frontier is "the line of most rapid and effective Americanization. The wilderness masters the colonist," finding him "a European in dress, industries, tools, modes of travel, and thought" (George Rogers Taylor, 5). If he is to survive the environment, he must adapt.

In his diary entries of the first expedition, Preuss rails against the conditions and yet slowly begins to adapt. In the entries for the second and fourth expeditions the tone has changed; he whines much less, indeed has become almost matter-of-fact. He is no longer the greenhorn. He can now find his way when separated from the group; he can make himself a shirt by cutting two holes in an antelope skin and tying it in the back (90); he can bite off part of an ant's nest or catch frogs, pull off their legs, and chew them to survive (117–18). Though not as skilled as the mountain men, he has learned to track. Most of all, his attitude has changed with his acquisition of skills. "Everything will be all right if I only keep a stiff upper lip" (118).

Preuss's legacy, thus, may not only be exquisite and precise maps of the American West or insights into the day-by-day chemistry on an expedition of exploration, but also a highly subjective case history confirming essential elements of the Turner thesis.

GEORGE CATLIN, "PICTORIAL HISTORIAN"

George Catlin provides a final illustration of the explorers' life. When he set off in 1830 from Pennsylvania, abandoning his second career, his parents, and his new wife to spend the better part of eight years "amongst the wildest tribes of Indians in North America," he passionately followed a conviction so strongly held that it was nearly an obsession: he felt that the decline of the Native American was inevitable as the frontier moved westward, and that those people and their culture must be recorded before they either became extinct or inexorably changed. Thus, he set off to become a "pictorial historian" of their way of life.

He first became interested in Indians as a child, in part from listening to his mother's stories of being captured by Indians during the Wyoming, Pennsylvania, Massacre of 1778. Acquiescing to his father's desires, he studied law and practiced until, falling in love with painting, he sold all his belongings (including his law library, though he kept his rifle and fishing tackle) and moved to Philadelphia in 1823 to pursue a career painting portraits and miniatures. A year later he was elected to the Pennsylvania Academy of Art and, in a few more years, had twelve of his paintings and drawings (including a full-length portrait of Governor DeWitt Clinton of New York) on exhibit at the American Academy of Fine Arts. Despite this success he was restless and dissatisfied.

His future revealed itself when a delegation of Indians from the Far West stopped in Philadelphia on their way to Washington. Fascinated with these "noble and dignified . . . Indians . . . in all their classic beauty . . . wrapped in their picturesque robes, with their brows plumed with quills of the war-eagle" (Catlin, vol. 1, 2), Catlin knew his destiny and surmised theirs. Convinced that civilization and its concomitant evils of "whiskey, the small-pox and the bayonet" (4) would not only continue the decimation of the Indian population but also destroy their cultures, Catlin saw the need for immediately recording a "literal and graphic delineation of the living manners, customs, and character of an interesting race of people, who are rapidly passing away from the face of the earth" (3). He vowed that "nothing short of the loss of my life shall prevent me from visiting their country, and of becoming their historian" (2).

Not able to go west immediately, Catlin began painting portraits on the Iroquois reservation in New York, among them one of the Seneca orator Red Jacket. These, however, were reservation Indians whose lifestyle and culture had made major compromises with "civilization." So in the spring of 1830 he left for St. Louis, hub of the fur trade, where he met General William Clark, now superintendent of Indian Affairs for the western tribes. Having shown him the portfolio of his Indian paintings, Catlin got support from the co-leader of the Lewis and Clark expedition.

Clark answered his questions, allowed him to set up an easel in his headquarters to paint leaders who had come in on tribal business, introduced him to a number of Indian agents, and took him along to a treaty council at Prairie du Chien between the United States and the Sauk and Fox, Iowa, Missouri, and Sioux. Thankful for such opportunities but wanting to go further west where Indian culture was still relatively untouched, Catlin was aboard the steamboat *Yellowstone* on her maiden voyage to Ft. Union in 1832.

Unlike Lewis and Clark, whose report was to include far more than the native tribes, and unlike Frémont, who was motivated at least in part by self-aggrandizement, Catlin's entire being was subsumed by his drive to record Indian cultures in their waning days. He visited forty-eight different tribes, painted (in oil) 310 portraits of Indians "in their native dress" and 200 other oil paintings of Indian religious ceremonies, games, buffalo hunts, housing and dances, as well as landscapes. Moreover, he collected artifacts—a "wigwam," robes, headdresses, moccasins, rattles, and weapons.

His goal was to capture Indian culture as it was, not as it would soon be with the influence of the trading post, the army, or the missionary. His goal, furthermore, was to correct misperceptions and to defuse prejudices toward the Indians. To this end he opened the North American Indian Gallery in 1837, and in 1841 he published *Letters and Notes on the Manners, Customs, and Conditions of the North American Indians.* These two volumes are filled with detailed character sketches, anthropological field notes, narratives of buffalo hunts, and descriptions of religious ceremonies.

Because of Catlin's obsession to reveal the Native American as uncorrupted and unchanged by white civilization, as "honest, hospitable, faithful, brave, warlike, cruel, revengeful, relentless—yet honorable, contemplative and religious being[s]," Catlin's *Letters and Notes* reveal far less about *his* life on the frontier than do the journals of Lewis and Clark, Frémont, or Preuss. As a corollary, they reveal far more of the life of the Native Americans.

The portraits, in words and paintings, are so detailed that one is tempted to wonder how a former lawyer from Pennsylvania could have achieved them. First, he was far more adept at hunting and fishing than might be expected. Moreover, he was a good enough horseman that on one occasion while visiting the Minataries, he participated in a horse race; one of the rules, he discovered after laying his bet, was that both horses and riders were to race totally naked (Catlin, 197–198). On this instance he had no translator nearby to provide explanation; usually he did. Catlin unabashedly made use of translators—Indian agents, traders, and *voyageurs*—whenever he could; the dozens of languages of the tribes he visited would otherwise have made his mission impossible.

Ba'Tiste, a free trapper, accompanied him during much of his time on the Plains. Perhaps equally crucial was gaining the trust of the Indians he wanted to paint. Plains Indians utilized painting as a means of recording their history (the winter counts of the Sioux, for example, painted on a buffalo hide recorded the year's most significant event) or as a means of decoration and personal honor (as when acts of heroism were painted on their robes—equivalents, perhaps, to campaign ribbons and medals for the modern U.S. military). However, they were completely unfamiliar with portrait painting.

While he was among the Mandans, Catlin induced two of the principal chiefs to come to his lodge to be painted; no one else was allowed inside, nor did the chiefs look at the works in progress. When Catlin finished the portraits the chiefs instantly recognized their likenesses, pressing their hands over their mouths in astonishment. "Then they walked up to me in the most gentle manner, taking me in turn by the hand, with a firm grip; with head and eyes inclined downward, and in a tone as little above a whisper—pronounced the words 'te-ho-pe-nee Wash-ee!' and walked off. . . . At that moment I was Christened with a new and great name— . . . 'great *medicine white man*' " (Catlin, vol. 1, 106).

Catlin had earlier learned that "medicine" among the Indians meant "mystery," the inexplicable. A "medicine man" thus had power and inspired awe and sometimes fear. After the chiefs told the tribe about the paintings, a curious crowd gathered. The portraits were held up over the door of the lodge so all could see.

> The likenesses were instantly recognized, and many of the gaping multitude commenced yelping; some were stamping off in the jarring dance—others were singing, and others were crying—hundreds covered their mouths with their hands and were mute; some, indignant, drove their spears frightfully into the ground, and some threw a reddened arrow at the sun and went home to their wigwams. (Catlin, vol. 1, 107)

The crowds pronounced Catlin "the greatest medicine man in the world" because he had "made living beings." Viewing the portraits, they could see the chiefs laugh a little and smile, but most awesome, they could see their eyes move, following the observer. (This effect is often noted about good portraits, but to the Mandans it was magical.) The technique inspired awe. It also inspired fear, for some (especially the squaws) felt that if the painter had put some life into the portrait, he must have taken it away from the subject. Such a man was dangerous; his "*medicine* too great for the Mandans," for if he could thus create life, he could take it away if he chose. Furthermore, some believed, "bad luck would come to those I painted. . . . I [would] . . . take a part of the existence of those whom I painted, and carry it home with me amongst white people, and that when they died they would never sleep quiet in their graves" (Catlin, vol. 1, 108).

The situation was volatile. Even if no physical harm resulted, such attitudes would effectively block any other Mandans from sitting for Catlin, thereby denying him his purpose. He was, however, invited to their council meeting, where he explained that his medicine—painting—could be learned by any of them with practice, that his intentions were entirely friendly, and that in his country "brave men never allowed their squaws to frighten them with their foolish whims" (vol. 1, 108). The upshot was that Catlin was invited to a feast and presented with a medicine man's rattle and "magical wand . . . strung with the claws of the grizzly bear, with hoofs of the antelope—with ermine—with wild sage and bat's wings—and perfumed withal with the *choice* and *savory* odor of the pole-cat—a dog was sacrificed and hung by the legs over my wigwam, and I was therefore and thereby initiated" into the society of medicine men (vol. 1, 109). Catlin had achieved the entrée necessary to continue his life's work.

George Catlin was nothing if not realistic. He recognized the inexorable, almost predestined reality of manifest destiny. He knew what the British government had not known when issuing the Proclamation of 1763: it was impossible to bottle up the force, already released, of the movement west of white settlers. He recognized, too, the inevitability of cultural change among the Indian nations. Indeed, his purpose—to paint Indians as they were before they had undergone further change—was predicated on this fact. Nor was he a millenialist, like the practitioners of the Ghost Dance in the 1890s who believed that with faith and virtue such changes could be reversed. Rather, he argued for the benevolent intervention of the government and of missionary organizations to make inevitable change as positive as possible.

Throughout his work is an implicit recognition of a continuum among Native Americans, from the most noble to the most decadent. Where an individual Indian was on the continuum depended, to a great degree, on his contact with white civilization.

Catlin would not have accepted Frederick Jackson Turner's definition of the frontier as the "meeting point between savagery and civilization." Indeed, he saw the frontier more as the low point of a U—the highest points being the Euro-American society of the East, from which he came, and the as yet relatively untainted civilization of some of the western tribes. To reach the classic West, still virginal and pure, from the East,

> one is obliged to descend from the light and glow of civilized atmosphere, through the different grades of civilization, which gradually sink to the most deplorable conditions along the extreme frontier; thence through the most pitiable misery and wretchedness of savage degradation; where the genius of natural liberty and independence have been blasted and destroyed by the contaminating vices and dissipations introduced by the immoral part of *civilized* society. Through this dark and sunken vale of wretchedness one hurries, as through a pestilence, until he gradually rises again into the proud and chivalrous pale of savage society in its state of original nature beyond reach of civilized contamination. Here he finds much to fix his enthusiasm upon, and much to admire. (Catlin, vol. 1, 60)

It is at the frontier, this nadir of civilization—both white and red—where the stereotyped "epithet of 'poor, naked, and drunken savage' can be . . . applied" (Catlin, vol. 1, 60).

The unfortunate effects of civilization on the Native American are also explored by Catlin in his examination of Wi-Jun-Jon (Pigeon's Egg Head or The Light), an Assiniboine warrior selected by Major Sanford to represent his nation in a delegation to Washington in 1832. Catlin, in St. Louis when the delegation arrived en route to the nation's capital, painted him then.

> In his nature's uncowering pride he stood a perfect model. . . . [Though he had not wanted to have his picture painted because of the medicine] yet he stood unmoved and unflinching amid the struggles of mysteries that were hovering about him, foreboding ills of every kind, and misfortunes that were to happen to him in consequence. . . . He was dressed in his native costume, which was classic and exceedingly beautiful; his leggings and shirt were of the mountain-goat skin, richly garnished with quills of the porcupine, and fringed with locks of scalps taken from his enemies' heads. Over these floated his long hair in plaits, that fell nearly to the ground; his head was decked with the war-eagle's plumes—his robe was of the skin of a young buffalo bull, richly garnished and emblazoned with the battles of his life; his quiver and bow were slung, and his shield, of the skin of the bull's neck. (Catlin, vol. 2, 196)

George Catlin, *Pigeon's Egg Head (The Light) going to and returning from Washington*. Oil on canvas, 1837–39. 29 × 24" (73.6 × 60.9 cm). 1985.66.474. National Museum of American Art, Smithsonian Institution, Gift of Mrs. Joseph Harrison, Jr. The Light, an Assiniboine chief, visited Washington in January 1832. In these two portraits, Catlin expressed his dismay at the transformation of a noble warrior to a pompous poseur.

Months later, almost too coincidentally, Catlin was the only passenger aboard the *Yellowstone* except for American Fur Company employees and Major Sanford with the returning delegation. They had spent the winter months in the standard whirlwind tour of forts and harbors, military weapons and balloons, and huge cities with tall buildings, all culminating in an audience with the Great Father. And now, here was Wi-Jun-Jon:

> He had exchanged in Washington his beautiful . . . and classic costume [for a full military uniform.] . . . It was broadcloth, of the finest blue, trimmed with lace of gold; on his shoulders were mounted two immense epaulettes; his neck was strangled with a shining black stock, and his feet were pinioned in a pair of water-proof boots, with high heels, which made him "step like a yoked hog." . . . On his head was a high-crowned beaver hat, with a broad silver lace band, surmounted by a huge red feather . . . ; his coat collar stiff with lace, came higher than his ear. . . . A large silver medal was suspended from his neck by a blue ribbon, and across his right shoulder passed a wide belt, supporting . . . a broad sword. . . . On his hands he had drawn a pair of white kid gloves, and in them held, a blue umbrella in one, and a large fan in the other. . . . [H]e was strutting and whistling Yankee Doodle about the deck of the steamer. (Catlin, vol. 2, 196–197)

Wi-Jun-Jon had become a fop, his native dignity disguised by his new finery. Moreover, from beneath the tails of his military greatcoat one can see two poorly hidden bottles of whiskey. Wi-Jun-Jon had been seduced by the worst of white civilization. Worse yet, he had lost the respect of his tribe, for as he tried to relate the unimaginable truth of what he'd seen—ships with seventy-four guns, immense cities, the great council house in Washington, people ascending into the air as if by magic, suspended beneath a large round bladder (the balloon)—his former friends wrote him off as a liar and an impostor. "He has been . . . among the whites, who are great liars, and all he has learned is to come home and tell great lies" (Catlin, vol. 2, 197). He was disgraced; his earlier leadership potential was dissipated. Yet it was rumored that along with his fancy new clothes he had acquired special magical powers which would protect him from ordinary lead bullets. Thus, when he broke his umbrella over the head of a particularly obnoxious heckler, the man melted down the handle of an iron pot, molded it into a bullet, and blew off the top of Wi-Jun-Jon's head (Viola, *Diplomats* 89–91; Catlin, vol. 2, 197–200). In contrast to the disgrace of Wi-Jun-Jon, Catlin almost idealizes the Mandans in general and their second chief, Mah-to-toh-pa (Four Bears), in particular. "No set of men that I ever associated with have better hearts than the Mandans, and none are quicker to embrace and welcome a white man than they are . . . no man in any country will keep his word and guard his honor more closely" (Catlin, vol. 1, 182).

Of Mah-to-toh-pa he writes:

> [This] most popular man in the nation [is] free, generous, elegant and gentlemanly in his deportment—handsome, brave and valiant; wearing a robe on his back, with the history of his battles emblazoned on it; which would fill a book [by] themselves. . . . This, readers, is the most extra-ordinary man, perhaps, who lives at this day, in the atmosphere of Nature's noblemen. (Catlin, vol. 1, 92)

This most-loved leader of the Mandans, after explaining much of his culture to Catlin, allowed him to witness what few white men ever had: the four-day annual religious ceremony and initiation ordeal culminating in applicants being suspended from skewers that pierced their bodies. Four Bears then invited him to a feast, at the conclusion of which he presented the white painter with the robe on which he'd sat, "explaining to me by signs that the paintings which were on it were representations of the battles of his life, where he had fought and killed with his own hand fourteen of his enemies; that he had been two weeks engaged in painting it for me, and that he had invited me here on this occasion to present it to me" (Catlin, vol. 2, 116–17). The reciprocal friendship and respect are clear.

It is thus especially poignant to read Catlin's account of the extinction of the Mandans, caused by smallpox accidentally introduced to the tribe. He was not present; the news was brought to him in New York by the fur trader Kenneth McKenzie. Catlin was so in shock that he "dreads" to write of it. Yet he *must* write of the last days of his great good friend, Mah-to-toh-pa:

> This fine fellow sat in his wigwam and watched every one of his family die around him, his wives and his little children, and after he had recovered from the disease himself; when he walked out, around the village, and wept over the final destruction of his tribe; his braves and warriors, whose sinewy arms alone he could depend on for a continuance of their existence, all laid low; when he came back to his lodge, where he covered his whole family in a pile, with a number of robes, and wrapping another around himself, went out upon a hill at a little distance, where he laid several days despite all the solicitations of the Traders, resolved to *starve* himself to death. He remained there till the sixth day, when he had just strength enough to creep back to the village, when he entered the

George Catlin, *Four Bears, Second Chief, in Full Dress*. Oil on canvas, 1832. 29 × 24" (73.7 × 60.9 cm). 1985.66.128. National Museum of American Art, Smithsonian Institution, Gift of Mrs. Joseph Harrison, Jr. Catlin described Four Bears (Mah-to-toh-pah) as "one of Nature's noblemen" (Catlin, vol. 1, 92). Not long after Catlin painted him, Mah-to-toh-pah and most of the Mandan succumbed to smallpox.

horrid gloom of his own wigwam, and laying his body alongside of the group of his family, drew his robe over him and died. (Catlin, vol. 2, 258)

Although he was not an explorer like Meriwether Lewis, William Clark, or John C. Frémont, George Catlin was in many ways a forerunner. He was an advocate of cultural integrity, if not autonomy, a century before the civil rights movement. His proposal to establish on the Great Plains a national park "containing man and beast, in all the . . . freshness of their nature's beauty" (Catlin, vol. 1, 262) antedated by decades the establishment of Yellowstone, our first national park, in 1872. Like others such as Karl Bodmer, Alfred Jacob Miller, and John Mix Stanley, he painted Native American life for present and future perusal in the nation's art galleries and museums. Like future scholars of the Bureau of American Ethnology, he went to the Indians not to modify their culture but to record it. And forty-six years before Buffalo Bill's Wild West Show, Catlin's Indian Gallery popularized the American West, providing Easterners and Europeans access to and appreciation of Native American culture amid a relatively unchanged physical environment. As he anticipated others' work, George Catlin was an explorer not of land but of culture.

"The Miner," the frontispiece from the book *The Buckeye Rovers in the Gold Rush: An Edition of Two Diaries,* edited by H. Lee Scamehorn, Edwin P. Banks, and Jamie Lytle-Webb (Ohio University Press/Swallow Press, 1989). Reprinted with the permission of Ohio University Press/Swallow Press, Athens.

4

Life on the Miners' Frontier: The New Eldorado

The name *California* first appeared in print in a romantic novel published in Seville, Spain, in 1510: *Las Servas de Esplandián* written by Garcí Ordóñez de Montalvo. It recounts the adventures of a youth, Esplandián, who during his travels arrives at a place "on the right hand of the Indies ... an island called California very near to the Terrestrial Paradise." Ruled by Calafia, an Amazon queen, "the island everywhere abounds with gold and precious stones and upon it no other metal is found" (Hart, 398; Holliday, 25). Fully 338 years later, real gold in literally fabulous amounts was discovered in California, drawing adventurous youths from around the world. In the meantime, however, California languished as a sleepy, flea-infested province of Spain and Mexico.

Descriptions by early Spanish explorers were hardly promising. California displayed a "bleak coast"; its "primitive natives" knew nothing about gold. After 1602 California, still printed on Spanish maps as an island, seemed unworthy of exploration—until the Russians challenged Spain by expanding their fur-trading operations southward from Alaska. In response, in 1769–70 a Spanish expedition built missions and presidios (fortified settlements) at San Diego and Monterey; a handful of priests and soldiers were to colonize California for Spain. Ironically, this occurred at the same time England's colonies on the eastern seaboard were inaugurating their struggle for freedom.

Spain's hold on California was tenuous, in part because it seemed to offer so little to potential settlers that only the poorest, most miserable would go voluntarily. Their numbers were augmented only by "idle, undesirable people"—convicts from Mexican jails. Indeed, Father Junipero Serra, father-general of the Franciscan padres, pleaded with the Spanish vice-regal government "not to look upon California and its missions . . . as exile. Being sent to our missions should not be a form of punishment, nor should our missions be filled with worthless people who serve no purpose but to commit evil deeds" (qtd. in Holliday, 26–27). Moreover, there was increasing political unrest. For more than a decade following 1808, Spain's colonies were in revolt. Mexico achieved independence in 1821.

During the Mexican period (1822–46) the California missions were secularized and their lands were transferred to approximately 800 families who established a pastoral California. Cattle ranching dominated the economy. Some of the ranchos were enormous—up to 250,000 acres. And many of the former mission Indians provided cheap labor; one rancho, for example, utilized 600 Indians as house servants and field hands (Holliday, 27).

Most of the land-owning families lived along the coast and in the coastal valleys. Sparse population (2,000 non-Indians in 1810; 6,000 by 1840) meant that the settlements did not have to move inland. Thus, there was little reason to explore or to settle territory that would eventually bear a bonanza of gold. Richard Henry Dana, who arrived in California aboard a ship in the hide trade, penned vivid descriptions of California ranch life in *Two Years before the Mast* (1840). The ranchers depended on trade with foreigners for necessities as well as luxuries, from boots and shoes, coffee and agricultural implements, to wines, tobacco, mirrors, and jewelry, paying for them with "California banknotes"—cowhides. As many as 40,000–50,000 hides, cleaned and dried, were regularly packed into the hold of a single ship for the voyage around Cape Horn to Boston.

In addition to lessening the provincial isolation of the Californios, this trade brought Britishers and Yankees to California, some of whom (sea captains or sailors or shipping agents) received land grants, swore allegiance to Mexico, adopted Catholicism, married into prominent local families, and prospered. By 1849 such foreigners numbered 380 (Holliday, 27).

In addition, other Americans were starting to trickle in from the East. They came along routes discovered by Jedediah Smith, who as a co-owner of the Rocky Mountain Fur Company had trapped beaver in the San Joaquin Valley in 1826 and had in 1827 become the first white man to cross the Sierras. Many of the newcomers were farmers rather than ranchers; they settled along the Sacramento and San Joaquin Rivers and generally retained their Protestant religion and had little to do with either the Californios or the Mexican government at Monterey. Indeed, they viewed both with some disdain as "miserable people who sleep and smoke and hum some tune of Castilian laziness, while surrounding Nature is inviting them to the noblest and richest rewards of honorable toil" (Holliday, 30).

Fearful that they might be expelled by the Mexican government from land they occupied without title, and encouraged by the presence of John C. Frémont and his topographical engineers, a number of these Americans seized Sonoma and declared it their capital, proclaiming California an independent republic. Their flag of rebellion—made of unbleached muslin with a brown star and a brown grizzly bear drawn in blackberry juice atop a red flannel stripe—spawned the nickname Bear Flag Republic. The Republic was short-lived, however, lasting only from June 10 to July 9, 1846. Anticipating a declaration of war between the United States and Mexico, Commodore John Drake Sloat sailed the flagship *Savannah* into Monterey harbor on July 7, 1846, landed 250 men, raised the American flag, and announced American occupation. The U.S. possession of California was subsequently cemented by the treaty of peace signed on February 2, 1848 (Hart, 33).

Among those Americans who arrived in California, two were especially important: Sam Brannan and John Augustus Sutter. Brannan arrived on July 31, 1846, leading 238 Mormon men, women, and children who sailed aboard the *Brooklyn* from New York City to Yerba Buena (later San Francisco), hoping to escape religious persecution in the United States. Much to their disappointment, California had just been seized by the United States. Brannan consequently sent some of his men inland to the Sacramento Valley, where they settled near Sutter's ranch. Brannan, who had published a religious paper in New York, established California's first newspaper, the *California Star*, and California's first flour mill. Always an entrepreneur, Brannan invested heavily in real estate and established a store at Sutter's Fort.

THE DISCOVERY OF GOLD

Prior to landing at Monterey in 1829, Sutter had seen much of the world. Born in Germany and raised in Switzerland, he had arrived in New York City, gone with traders from St. Louis to Santa Fe, and then traveled overland to Oregon before sailing to Honolulu and Sitka. Arriving finally in California, he became a Mexican citizen and received the largest possible land grant—eleven leagues, or 48,400 acres—at the junction of the Sacramento and American rivers. On this rancho he used Indians as labor, planted wheat, vineyards, and orchards, and established a European-style barony called Nueva Helvetia; his trading fort here was the western terminus for many American emigrants' travel. However, unexpected disaster struck as he was building a sawmill on the American River. It was here, on January 24, 1848, that his partner, James Marshall, discovered gold. Marshall described the moment: "My eye was caught by something shining in the bottom of the ditch. . . . I reached my hand down and picked it up; it made my heart thump, for I was certain that it was gold. The piece was about half the size and shape of a pea. Then I saw another" (qtd. in Holliday, 33).

Sutter's workmen deserted shortly after the discovery, ironically beginning his decline to poverty while his mill remained unfinished, hides prepared for trade rotted, and squatters destroyed his property. By 1852 he was bankrupt.

The outside world at first greeted the discovery of gold with some skepticism. Indeed, the two San Francisco weeklies, the *Californian* and the *Star*, gave only casual mention. But on May 12, Sam Brannan returned to the City from Coloma holding aloft a quinine bottle filled with gold dust and shouting, "Gold! Gold! Gold from the American River," thereby exciting among many a "very violent attack of the gold fever" (Holliday, 35).

What Edward Kemble, editor of Brannan's paper, had originally called "a sham . . . got up to guzzle the gullible" (Rice, Bullough, and Orsi, 177) had so profound an effect that on May 29 the *Californian* observed:

> The whole country from San Francisco to Los Angeles and from the seashore to the base of the Sierra Nevada resounds to the sordid cry of gold, gold! GOLD! while the field is left half planted, the house half built and everything neglected but the manufacture of shovels and pick-axes. (qtd. in Holliday, 35)

San Francisco was soon nearly deserted. By mid-June, wrote Thomas O. Larkin, U.S. consul in San Francisco, only 200 people remained in the city, three-quarters of the population having stampeded to the gold fields; stores were closed, business suspended, doctors and lawyers boarded up their windows, outbound ships in San Francisco Bay were deserted by their crews, and newspapers suspended publication. Even the naval commander recognized the inevitable: "To send troops out here would be needless, for they would immediately desert" (Holliday, 35–36; Rice, Bullough, and Orsi, 177).

As people rushed to the mines, Sam Brannan grossed $36,000 at his store near Sutter's Fort between May 1 and July 10. This was the first example of a general pattern: during the gold rush, those who profited were usually not the miners but those who provided the miners with goods and services.

As luck—or irony—would have it, all this was a U.S. bonanza. Marshall's discovery occurred on January 24, 1848; the Treaty of Guadalupe Hidalgo was signed on February 2, 1848, setting the Rio Grande as the border with Mexico and ceding to the United States territory constituting the present states of California, Nevada, Utah, Arizona, and parts of Wyoming and Colorado. In the stroke of a pen the United States had become a nation stretching from sea to sea, instantly acquiring natural wealth that had remained undiscovered throughout centuries of Spanish and Mexican rule. Some Protestant ministers proclaimed from their pulpits that "the discovery [was] the work of God, who had hidden the gold so long as Popery—the Catholics—held sway over California" (Holliday, 25)! Certainly it was a stroke of luck. Equally certain, it meant that nothing would ever again be the same in California:

> In one astonishing year the place would be transformed from obscurity to world prominence, from an agricultural frontier that attracted 400 settlers in 1848 to a mining frontier that lured 90,000 impatient men in 1849; from a society of neighbors and families to one of strangers and transients; from an ox-cart economy based on hides and tallow to a complex economy based on gold mining; from Catholic to Protestant, from Latin to Anglo-Saxon. The impact of the new California would be profound on the nation it had so recently joined. (Holliday, 26)

The gold rush of 1848 added about 600 to the non-Indian population of California. Few came from "the States" until 1849 because many people originally discounted what they'd heard as mere rumors (Rice, Bullough, and Orsi, 178).

However, what had first been perceived as rumor was soon verified. In mid-September 1848 the New Orleans *Daily Picayune* published an interview with Navy Lieutenant Edward F. Beale, who was carrying to Washington dispatches confirming the discovery of gold—as well as samples of that gold. On December 5, President Polk announced to Congress: "The accounts of the abundance of gold in . . . [California] are of such extraordinary character as would scarcely command belief were they not corroborated by authentic reports of officers in the public service" (Holliday, 48). On December 7, 1848, Lieutenant Lucien Loeser arrived with a dispatch from Richard B. Mason, California's military governor—and 220 ounces of pure gold. Mason called the gold strike so rich that it could finance the Mexican War "a hundred times over" (Rice, Bullough, and Orsi, 178). Of even greater impact were personal accounts of success in the gold fields. These letters, sent to friends and relatives, were eagerly published by newspapers. To Easterners who had lived frugally, such stories of instant success fueled the desire to rush to California.

the news generated "California frenzy" in the East. Horace Greely's *New York Tribune* observed on January 30, 1849, that

The Discovery's Effects in the East

> the ordinary course of business seems for the time to be changed. The bakers of sea-bread keep their ovens hot day and night . . . ; manufacturers of India rubber goods, Gutta percha, oil cloth, etc. have very large demands to supply; the makers of rifles, pistols

and bowie knives can scarcely furnish as many of the articles as called for.... In fact, goods of every description sell ... at present, and articles which have long been unsaleable are packed up and sent away.... Boxes, barrels and bales crowd the sidewalks, and hundreds of drays convey to the wharves the freight now being stored away in seventy vessels [bound] for the Gold Regions. (Rice, Bullough, and Orsi, 178–79)

Inventors announced patented mining machinery—the "hydro-centrifugal Chrysolyte or California Gold Finder" and the "Archimedes Gold Washing Machine." Imaginative dreamers—or con men—announced an "aerial locomotive" that could carry 50 to 100 passengers safely from New York to California in three days at a cost of only $200. Shipowners announced sailing dates for almost anything that would float—schooners, old whaling ships, brigs, and steamers (Holliday, 50).

On January 11, 1849, the *New York Herald* tried to assess this California fever:

The spirit of emigration which is carrying off thousands to California ... increases and expands every day. All classes of our citizens seem to be under the influence of this extraordinary mania.... What will this general and overwhelming spirit of emigration lead to? Will it be the beginning of a new empire in the West, a revolution in the commercial highways of the world, a depopulation of the old States for the new republic on the shores of the Pacific?

Look at the advertising columns of the *Herald*.... Men of property and means are advertising their possessions for sale, in order to furnish them with means to reach that golden land. Every city and town is forming societies to cross the Isthmus or to double Cape Horn....

Poets, philosophers, lawyers, brokers, bankers, merchants, farmers, clergymen—all are feeling the impulse and are preparing to go and dig for gold and swell the number of adventurers to the new El Dorado.

The spirit which has thus been awakened in this country by the discovery of the gold mines in California ... exceeds everything in the history of commercial adventure (Holliday, 48–49)

THE ROUTES TO CALIFORNIA

Eyewitness accounts stirred excitement back east about California, which was "then but a blotch of yellow on the schoolboy's map of 1847" (Mulford, *Story* 5). When old sea captains arrived in New England whaling villages with word that "them stories about finding gold in Californy was all true" (Mulford, *Story* 5), gold fever struck. On the eastern seaboard people rushed to ports, even braving outbreaks of cholera. One adventurous young man wrote to his sister: "We think nothing of it. California fever has actually frightened it off" (Buck, 31).

What the April 28, 1849, edition of the *New York Tribune* headlined as "The Great Migration" saw thousands of Americans joining fortune-hunters from around the world to swell the population of once-sleepy California. In December 1849, senators and representatives-elect from California prepared and forwarded to the U.S. Senate a "Memorial" requesting admission of California into the Union as a state. Central to the argument was the dramatic increase in population. From April 12 to December 31, 1849, the arrivals by sea numbered 29,069; by way of Santa Fe, about 8,000; from Mexico, 6,000–8,000; and overland, an estimated 30,000. These figures did not include the 3,000 sailors who deserted from ships arriving at San Francisco. Though the California lawmakers rounded off the numbers, choosing to underestimate rather than to overestimate, they informed the U.S. Senate that California's population had surged from 26,000 on January 1, 1849, to 107,069 a year later (Read, 4).

Most of the gold-seekers had wildly fanciful impressions of California. Even those who formed companies and established formal constitutions and bylaws cited as their purpose "mining and trading with the Indians," who were "expected to give stores of gold and furs in exchange for gilt watches, brass chains, and glass beads." Optimism and Yankee inventiveness thrived. "The companies bought safes, in which to keep their gold, and also strange and complex gold-washing machines . . . invented by Yankees who never saw and never were to see a gold mine." Moreover, they were often completely unprepared for the physical realities of California. "The Sacramento River was reported as abounding in alligators. Colored prints represented the adventurer pursued by these reptiles. The general opinion was that it was a fearfully hot country full of snakes" (Mulford, *Story* 7).

People believed that wealth would be easily obtained. Some who could not go themselves invested in those who could, paying half the cost of their transportation and outfit, expecting in return half the gold the emigrants dug. Such people saw California as a get-rich-quick scheme rather than as a new home. "Five years at most was to be given to rifling California of her treasures, and then that country was to be thrown aside like a used-up newspaper and the rich adventurers would spend the remainder of their days in wealth, peace, and prosperity in their Eastern homes" (Mulford, *Story* 7). Few were psychologically or physically prepared for what they would endure. Of a group leaving from his New England whaling village, Prentice Mulford wrote: "What an innocent, unsophisticated, inexperienced lot [they were]. Not one of them could bake his own bread, turn a flapjack, re-seat his trousers, or wash his shirt" (*Story* 9). They would learn. Their first lessons would be taught en route, whether by land or by sea.

During 1849 as many as 40,000 reached California by sea
The Route or by land-sea routes. The greatest volume of travelers was
by Ship around Cape Horn, or through the Straits of Magellan. This
route, about 17,000 miles in length and five months in duration, was longer and more hazardous—but cheaper—than mixed land-sea routes. About half of those rounding the Horn went as individuals; the other half organized into joint stock companies, many of which bought their own ships and planned to sell them and the cargo in San Francisco to provide money for their mining expenses.

From December 7, 1848, to February 8, 1849, 136 ships cleared Atlantic ports for California. Most of them were "small, poorly manned, and poorly equipped to carry passengers." Some were whaling ships hastily converted to carry passengers rather than oil and blubber. These averaged 300 tons with a crew of fifteen. Most were sailing vessels that could make eight or nine knots per hour under the trade winds; they were vulnerable to dangerous gales called "williwaws" by the sailors and to maddening calms, especially near the equator. Moreover, in order to catch the best winds they often had to run far out into the Atlantic and Pacific, measurably increasing the length of the journey. Dangerous conditions at Cape Horn and in the Straits of Magellan so frightened passengers that some demanded a voyage around Africa instead. Steamships were less dependent on winds, but only a dozen reached California during 1849; some of these, like the *California*, the *Panama*, and the *Oregon*, were intended to remain in the Pacific on the Panama–San Francisco run. And even though their technology meant less dependence on the winds, it also occasioned new mechanical problems: bilge pumps failed, pipes burst, and time was spent refueling along the way. At the beginning of the gold rush only a few clipper ships, swift greyhounds of the sea, had yet been built. Of the 775 ships that sailed for California in 1849, most were small and slow (Pomfret, 1–10).

To passengers who endured the average five months aboard ship, hardships were many—crowded conditions, poor food, and stale water; emotions ranged "from ennui to terror"; and omnipresent complaints sometimes escalated into near rebellion. First-person accounts from logs and diaries give a good sense of life aboard ships on the Cape route.

One of the first trials was seasickness, which struck almost as soon as the ship was out of sight of land. James L. Tyson, a doctor, describes victims of this malady: "The pale faces, sad and dejected, vinegar-like visages of most of the passengers told but too plainly the tale, that a heavy sea and stiff breeze were exacting their accustomed dues from fresh water sailors, and oblations, powerful, heaving, and running over,

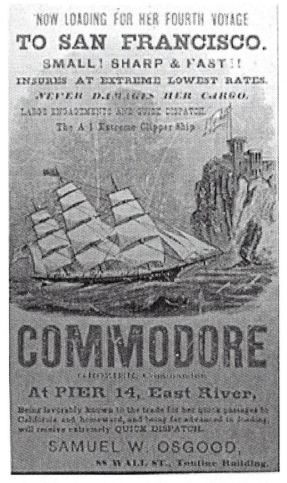

NOW LOADING FOR HER FOURTH VOYAGE
TO SAN FRANCISCO.
SMALL! SHARP & FAST!!
INSURES AT EXTREME LOWEST RATES.

At PIER 14, East River,

SAMUEL W. OSGOOD,

Trade card: The Clipper Ship "Commodore." Reproduced courtesy of the Museum of the City of New York. Despite seasickness, storms, stale water, and awful food, over 25,000 gold-seekers took sea routes in 1849.

were poured out at the shrine of Neptune!" Those who were not nauseous found the sight "ludicrous in the extreme." But often, as they were "laughing and talking most joyously at the misfortune of another," yet another wave would strike the ship and a new group would join those already vomiting over the rail (Tyson, 6–7).

Charles Ellis, a passenger on the *North Bend*, was more empathetic.

"Some of us are green enough to require salting"—an allusion to mid-nineteenth century methods of preserving meats from putrefaction (Pomfret, 19). Captain Cleveland Forbes of the steamer *California* noted on the fourth day out of New York that even the third mate was very seasick (Pomfret, 183). John N. Stone, passenger on the *Robert Bowne*, remembered with some cynicism that a severe gale at the Cape made it impossible to stand on deck without "clinging" to something. Many sailors took to their bunks, apparently sick. Stone suggests, however, that they'd simply learned there were good sailors among the passengers who wouldn't let the ship sink, and chose to let them suffer the effects of the elements (Pomfret, 121). Indeed, to offset boredom many passengers took a hand in running the ships.

Even on the most modern of ships, design problems sometimes intensified discomforts for all aboard. Captain Forbes writes of the *California* that the bath was inconvenient and the water closets were in the wrong place; the "Ladies cabin" was constantly flooded and the steward's pantry was always "afloat" from leaking pipes. Moreover, the engineers' rooms were too hot—up to 120° Fahrenheit (Pomfret, 186).

Besides seasickness, other problems plagued seamen and passengers alike. Captain Higgins of the *North Bend* was observed "in drawers [underpants] & slippers holding his hand to his face, the victim of a violent attack of the toothache" (Pomfret, 78). Few California-bound ships carried medical personnel on staff, so unless competent doctors had been bitten by the gold bug, passengers and crew were on their own for up to five months. One might speculate whether Captain Higgins's toothache was related to diet aboard ship, which could cause scurvy. Those going ashore often regretted it. Mr. Baird, the chief engineering officer of the *California*, went ashore at Rio and "drank too much grog & is now suffering the consequences" (Pomfret, 204). More serious was cholera, so feared that many ships were put in quarantine or not allowed to land at all at usual ports of call. And among the passengers that the *California* was to pick up at Panama, many suffered from dysentery "which proceeded from eating too much fruit & drinking Brandy on the fruit which is rank poison" (Pomfret, 223). There were mental aberrations as well, perhaps caused by the long, claustrophobic voyage. At least one passenger, a previously harmless Irishman, suddenly became a raving maniac, imagined himself to be the captain, and began issuing orders to the crew until, after trying to throw the mate overboard, it became necessary for everyone's safety to put him in irons (Pomfret, 114–15).

Food and Drink on Board Ship. The quality and quantity of food aboard ship varied greatly, usually in direct correlation to the competence and integrity of the captain. Prentice Mulford remembered that there was plenty to eat. "We relished our 'lobscouse,' hard tack, salt junk, beans, codfish, potatoes and [a special treat] Sunday's and Thursday's duff [a boiled plum pudding]. . . . Lobscouse is a preparation of hard bread, first soaked and then stewed with shredded salt beef. It looks somewhat like rations for a delicate bear" (*Story* 29). On most ships there were stock pens for chickens and pigs, which were slaughtered when needed (though sometimes they washed overboard in a storm, seriously compromising the supply of fresh, not salted, meat for the rest of the voyage). Aboard the *North Bend* a "sumptuous" dinner consisted of tongue pickled in vinegar, served with fried pork and potatoes, pickles, pepper sauce, and pancakes (Pomfret, 19). For variety there were creatures of the sea. Some tried fried porpoise, observing that it tasted like moose meat or beef liver (Pomfret, 17). Others tried sea birds, stewed or baked, although they were oily from feeding on fish (Pomfret, 40). These menus quickly grew monotonous; moreover, fresh fruits and vegetables were noticeably missing.

Even on the best voyages, ships' supplies ran out. Sometimes the captain would purchase goods from passengers who had carried private supplies for just such emergencies. Other captains hoarded foodstuffs, planning to sell them for vast profits in San Francisco.

John N. Stone recounted such behavior on the part of Captain Cameron of the *Robert Bowne*. This "idiotic old knave" had ordered the best goods stowed so they couldn't be reached until the ship was unloaded in San Francisco. Thus, the passengers were deprived of butter and sugar during most of the voyage. The beef, bread, and pork that were edible were stowed beyond reach; the passengers were compelled to eat " 'old horse' (beef as dry and tasteless as a piece of oak wood), pork frequently yellow and tainted—sometimes even very offensive to the smell; and old navy bread that was both mouldy and wormy." To make matters worse, the waiters were not supplied with dishcloths and toweling, but used their shirts and vests, "reeking with grease and filth," to wash dishes in cold salt water. The passengers' tin plates thus acquired a coating of dirt "thicker than three coats of varnish (Pomfret, 117–18). Even worse were the "black navy bread, probably 5 years old . . . full of blue mold and worms an inch long" and the "pea soup, of which every pea in it had contained a black bug; and bugs and all had been boiled up together" (Pomfret, 123, 155). No wonder that one night the storeroom was broken into and a box of raisins taken. The captain offered a twenty-dollar reward for the capture of the thief (Pomfret, 116). Even the tea and coffee were awful. Served in "empty oyster cans" and tin cups, it was made from the sweepings of ships' holds after the cargo had been offloaded, and it was prepared with water that had stood in a cask for years, "the smell of which would have made a landsman vomit" (Pomfret, 126).

Prentice Mulford, aboard the *Wizard*, noted that the beverages aboard ship "would have been pitched into the gutter" (*Story* 30) had they been served on shore. Nevertheless, he drank the coffee for it was better than the gallon of rusty, brackish water that was served daily. The "fresh water" was kept below in an iron tank, and as the deck leaked "a small portion of the Atlantic had slightly salted it. It resembled chocolate to the eye, but not to the palate" (*Story* 30). Of the food aboard the *Wizard* Mulford concluded: "We soon learned . . . how well we had lived at home. Our sea fare of hard tack and salt junk taught us how to appreciate . . . the broiled steaks, hot cakes, and buttered toast of home tables" (*Story* 28).

Danger on Board Ship. In addition to such run-of-the-mill discomfort, the emigrants were aware of real dangers. The *Gulf Stream* sailed from New York City on the last of January 1849 with over a hundred passengers and, four days out, foundered with all hands but one perishing (Pomfret, 40). Strong winds and currents often threatened to smash ships in the narrow passages of the Straits of Magellan. Cries of "man overboard!" were heard; during calm seas the person was simply hauled in, the very frightened recipient of a saltwater bath (Pomfret, 27). The outcome was not always so successful. James Tyson describes the death throes of a sailor who was washed from a bowsprit by a monster wave. "Awful . . . and harrowing [it was] . . . to look upon a human being in the last agonies, straining every muscle to sustain himself, with his eyeballs nearly starting from their sockets." By the time the ship could turn to rescue him, "I saw his cap for a moment float past on the top of a wave, but . . . the strong man had perished . . . to rise no more" (Tyson, 8–9).

Profiles of the Passengers on Board Ship. Who were the passengers who braved the vicissitudes of the Cape? Captain Forbes's comment about the "Ladies small cabin" aside, most who chose to sail around the Cape were men. Franklin Buck commented on the absence of women amid the general exodus to California. "The worst feature of the business is: There are no females going out. Everything else that you can think of is going, but the ladies hang back. What are we going to do? Society is bad, you know, composed all together of either sex. The women must follow the men shortly. . . . Think what rich husbands they could get!" (Buck, 32). (In contrast, some women, like Mary Jane Megquier, crossed the Isthmus of Panama, and a great many, comparatively speaking, went on overland routes to California.) But men—aboard ship and in the mines—would have to adapt to a predominantly masculine society.

These men represented a wide cross-section of backgrounds, characters, and professions. Charles H. Ellis wrote that in his company "we have several carpenters, one mason, one painter, one shoemaker, one saddler & trunk maker, one coach maker, two or three paper makers, one doctor and a dentist." Regardless of their backgrounds, their "all-absorbing object is *Gold, Gold* . . . and all to a man is provided with necessary implements for mining" (Pomfret, 23). Ellis and his son kept the invoice for goods purchased for their voyage.

Invoice
Supplies Purchased by C. H. & H. Ellis from Aspinwall & Bro.

½ Bbl Pork $18	$18.00
½ Sack Flour $8	8.00
1 bbl Pilot Bread, 100 at 10 cents	10.00
20 lbs Beans, 5 cents	1.00
1 lb Pepper	1.00
1 Box Salt	.38
1 lb Saleratus	.62
2 Shovels	2.00
2 Wash Pans	4.50
1 lb Powder	1.00
6 lbs Tobacco	2.25
1 Bag	.50
	$49.25
14 lbs Sugar, 50 cents	7.00
	$56.25
1 Case Whiskey	7.00
	$63.25

Source: John E. Pomfret, ed., *California Gold Rush Voyages, 1848–1849: Three Original Narratives* (San Marino, CA: Huntington Library, 1954), 96.

Their ship, the *North Bend*, was small, carrying 12 officers and men and 32 passengers. Yet there was great heterogeneity. The captain was from Maine; other officers were from Norway, New Orleans, and Salem, Massachusetts; the stewards and the cook were African Americans, or "coloreds" as Ellis identified them. Seamen were from Sicily and Scotland, in addition to New England. Passengers, mostly from New England, also included one from London and two from Ireland; their ages ranged from 19 to 40.

On the much larger *Robert Bowne* (32 officers and men and 167 passengers), passengers' ages ranged from 10 to 62, with most in their twenties and thirties. They were mostly skilled craftsmen or small merchants. Because the cost of transportation and equipment ranged from $750 to $1,000 (Rice, Bullough, and Orsi, 181), few laborers could go; laborers' wages in 1848 were $1 per day. Among the passengers were 24 farmers, 9 carpenters, 8 shoemakers, 8 tailors, 8 clerks, 7 merchants, 6 jewelers, 4 grocers and machinists, 3 gunsmiths, butchers, millers, brass foundrymen, mechanics, house joiners, and blacksmiths; 2 masons, painters, coachmen, storekeepers, and bookkeepers; and 1 of each of the following:

caulker, silversmith, druggist, paper maker, "segar" maker, teacher, marble cutter, assayer, iron rail worker, brick layer, bookbinder, printer, compositor, nurseryman, stone cutter, canal boatman, dock builder, cooper, cotton weaver, harness maker, whip maker, lawyer, cabinet maker, confectioner, locksmith, wagon maker, rope maker, glass cutter, physician, cook, and baker. One person simply described himself as a "gentleman"; another, as "nondescript." There were four identified only as laborers. One young boy (a runaway?) was identified only as a "lad." Seven boys accompanied their fathers. Of the lot, there were two women, wives of a brass foundryman and a hotel keeper.

Entertainment while on Board Ship. How did such a diverse group of people spend the time cooped up aboard ship? Many simply enjoyed observing nature. There are journal entries about dolphins, porpoises, butterflies, whales, cape pigeons, squids, turtles, sharks, and albatrosses. Chores consumed some time: catching rainwater in barrels and taking turns at the washtub, though Prentice Mulford describes the lazy man's method—tying a shirt to a line and trailing it behind the ship. (Those utilizing this method, however, had to learn how to use a needle to mend their clothes.) Some—out of necessity or boredom—took on sailors' jobs, standing night watch, reefing sails, helping cut and gather wood and get fresh water while on shore. Often, as the ship's crew grew "more & more helpless every day with lame hands [and] lame arms," passengers had to pitch in "or we shall never reach our . . . destination." Most passengers, however, felt such work was not their responsibility (Pomfret, 107).

Before sailing, Frank Buck bought fifty-eight books for $9.44 and a B.[ack] G.[ammon] board and one dozen packs of cards. "We have 24 rifles, powder and shot, harpoons, fishing tackle, and a sail boat . . . to amuse ourselves on our long voyage," he wrote (Buck, 30–31). He also planned to study Spanish—"to exchange my French for Spanish and learn that on the voyage" (29–30).

Music was also an important diversion, with passengers taking the initiative in arranging the program. Some recall waltzing on the cabin roof; others, the pleasure of exchanging musical numbers with the few ships they passed. Occasionally there were opportunities to visit other emigrants; passengers from the *Olivia* and the *Boston*, for example, visited the *Robert Bowne* while in harbor in the Straits of Magellan.

Once again aboard ship, many passengers spent time studying; subjects mentioned in journals include French, Spanish, and astronomy. Lectures were presented on phrenology, astronomy, and medical issues such as the "evil effects" of mercury and bloodletting (Pomfret, 125). Especially as the voyages wore on, seemingly interminably, the audiences became less receptive and the critiques more brutal.

Ellis noted that "some of the passengers are exercising their ingenuity at the invention and construction of machines for washing gold. Several plans have been exhibited, many of which will no doubt answer the purpose." But he realized that although they were becoming seasoned travelers, they were novices at mining; "it is impossible for us [to decide which inventions will work] until we arrive at the scene of our labours" (Pomfret, 75). Others discovered that the wood found ashore at Port Famine in the Straits of Magellan was easy to work; they passed the time making "small boxes, letter stamps, and other toys which serve as a memento of the voyage" (Pomfret, 87). Even amid tedium, many passengers recognized the momentous nature of the voyage and the adventure that would follow.

All was not serious, however. Passengers sat around in the evening "cracking nuts & jokes" (23). Others "played a rub at whist" (28). Once into the Pacific, life became more relaxed. Passengers resumed old habits of lounging around the decks in shirtsleeves and slippers, writing, reading, learning to make different kinds of knots, smoking, telling stories, and, inevitably, talking about what great things they were going to do when they got to San Francisco (Pomfret, 72).

Sundays were usually spent singing sacred music accompanied by musical instruments (Pomfret, 26). Often such hymn sings were followed by a promenade on deck (28). On board the *Robert Bowne* a passenger read the Episcopal service and lectured on the subject "Is God a Being?" (119). Nationalism was high; thus, the Fourth of July, "one of the greatest days in America," was celebrated aboard most ships. (Many had hoped to be in San Francisco to celebrate.) Aboard the *North Bend* many shaved for the first time since leaving Boston. The steward killed the last pig and "made us an excellent pie for our 4th of July dinner" (Pomfret, 91–92). Aboard the *Robert Bowne* the "73rd anniversary of American Independence [was not] forgotten by Americans amidst the perils of the sea." At daybreak the holiday was greeted by passengers firing off guns and pistols. At 11:00 A.M. everyone assembled on deck to participate in a formal program including prayer, "Hail Columbia" sung by a passenger, the reading of the Declaration of Independence, an oration, thirteen toasts, and the benediction, all followed by "Yankee Doodle" on the bugle played by another passenger (Pomfret, 147).

Despite attempts at entertainment, life grew more tense as anticipation of arrival in San Francisco increased, only to be frustrated by Pacific calms or winds that blew ships far to the west. Aboard the *California* the problem was compounded. When it arrived at Panama, 700 ticketholders who had crossed the Isthmus vied for its 250 berths. The result, wrote Captain Forbes, was a "ship filled to cramnation . . . & everyone looking out for himself with peculiar aptness" (Pomfret, 223).

Forbes, a competent and upright man, was appalled at the passengers' behavior. Though there were many decent people, both in cabin and steerage, "we have also many of the scum of creation, Black legs, gamblers, thieves, rummers & Drunkards, and if we make the trip without difficulty & great loss to the ship by their pilfering and waste, I will be much surprised" (224). Although Forbes hoped for the best, his worst fears were realized. Many were loudly discontented with the ship's crowded conditions, but not one of them was willing to be left behind. Many trashed the ship, which was completing its maiden voyage. Forbes, again, was appalled:

> It is heart rendering to see them abuse the furnature. Handsome cushions & Mattresses are brought on deck [in part to provide resting spots anywhere but in the crowded belowdecks] and laid on the wet & coal dust and are spat upon & trodden upon by those one might expect the worse conduct from, but all seem to be bound to California with the idea that low conduct & uncouth deportment is necessary to make them appear of importance. (224)

Conventions of society began to break down as everyone looked out for himself. Not even ministers were immune. Forbes described one of these "Rev. Devines" at mealtime: "While saying grace [he] was hauling a dish of green peas towards his plate and in conclusion emptied the whole on his plate," looking for more and devouring his meal as if his life depended on it (Pomfret, 226). Such behavior abated a bit as the weather turned worse. Forbes observed: "Many of the Passengers are sea sick which makes them more quiet" (225).

Passengers' behavior was so bad, on the whole, after Panama, that Forbes swore that he would not command the ship again for $10,000. Nor did passengers who had endured the trip around South America want to repeat it. Charles Ellis wrote, in no uncertain terms, "One thing is certain, if ever I am permitted to visit America again . . . I shall take some different rout than crossing the Atlantic & Pacific" (Pomfret, 76). What he could not yet know was that the long confinement, lack of exercise, poor diet, and exposure often meant that emigrants to California coming via the Cape arrived in poor condition for the arduous work of mining. Those coming overland or by mixed land-sea routes—if they survived—generally acquired a resilient toughness during the journey.

The Land-Sea Routes
While many fortune-seekers chose the Cape route, others chose the quicker land-sea routes across Mexico or Panama. In 1847 Congress subsidized the United States Mail and Pacific Mail companies to provide steamship service between the coasts, with an intervening trek across land, usually through Panama. In 1855 a railway across the Isthmus was completed, reducing to three hours this two- to four-day trip.

Some, like William Perkins, had intended to cross the Isthmus, but when his boat sprang a leak he opted to cross Mexico to Mazatlan and catch a steamer from there to San Francisco. Others, like Daniel Woods, had originally planned the Mexican route.

William Perkins was elected captain of his company when it was organized at Fort Brown, Texas, where they bought wagons, harness, and mules after having gotten passports from the Mexican consul. For the next "two hundred leagues," he wrote, "we had two enemies to guard against, the Indians and the cholera" (Perkins, 77). Though they saw entire households perish from the disease, only one of their party died of it. And though the Indians were "on their annual excursion of pillage and bloodshed at the expense of the defenseless Mexicans," ravaging haciendas and mutilating corpses, Perkins boasted of not losing a single animal to them.

Obstacles along the Mexico Route. The Treaty of Guadalupe Hidalgo, signed on February 2, 1848, ended the war with Mexico. Consequently, Perkins and his company found many Mexicans "in an exasperated state of mind" toward Americans; they avoided conflicts by "uniform good behavior" (77).

Religious custom provided an even greater challenge. Perkins's company arrived in the town of Saltillo on the morning of Good Friday. It was Mexican custom to forbid any travel in the street with horses or carriages until after Easter. The prohibition was "strictly enforced, and foreigners have been stoned by the populace" or arrested for violating it. Perkins sought, but could not gain, permission to travel through town; not wanting to delay their travel for three days but realizing the danger of a confrontation with the Mexicans, Perkins put his wagons in the middle of his troops and entered town with rifles unslung and carried across the pommels of the men's saddles. People scowled; some swore; the plaza was full of townspeople ready to block their way. Perkins "ordered a momentary halt, directed every man to dismount and take off his hat, and then we proceeded slowly through the *plaza* and past the cathedral, each man with his rifle in one hand and in the other his hat and the reins of his bridle." It worked. "The natives . . . taken by surprise, and pleased with our simple act of devotion and consideration for their religious feelings, were quite disarmed of their anger" (78). Indeed, some cheered, little girls offered flowers, and handsome women "smiled graciously" (78).

From there on, the obstacles were mainly the Mexican terrain and climate: over the Cordilleras at least ten thousand feet high, over roads so steep that mules had to make prodigious leaps up the slippery rock faces. Descending the opposite slope they came to a tropical paradise, the road winding through groves of bananas, coconuts, and date trees. Cacti twenty-five feet high with flowers as big as dinner plates lined their passage. In this paradise they ate corn tortillas, wild honey, and meat from wild game and armadillos. Their morning alarm clock was the chattering of myriads of gorgeously plumed parrots (Perkins, 78–80).

Daniel Woods's journal echoes these experiences, though it tends to emphasize hardships. While they shot deer and alligators, they became victims of mosquitoes, ticks, fleas, and jiggers; Woods devised a bag made of cotton into which he crawled at night, pulling it up around his head to avoid these pests. His company, always on guard against guerrillas and robbers, never dispensed with a night guard; rumors of revolution kept them on edge, as did roadside crosses marking murder sites. Across the desert the dust and sand were suffocating, and in the mountains Woods experienced a "painful giddiness" when lying down at night and rising in the morning. His comments on the facilities for travelers are scathing. At the *meson* the traveler had to spread his own bedding on a floor that seems never to have been swept (29). Even worse, one morning he noticed "a number of *tarantulas*—the venomous black spider of the tropics—hanging upon the wall of our room" (30). Woods is not too fond of food in the *fondas*: soup with red pepper, "rice with thin Indian cakes," squash fried in lard. Though he seems to like dessert, custard made of rice or chocolate, he calls *pulque*, a drink made of the maguey cactus, "a most hateful species of whiskey." The cross-cultural impact of prior travelers across Mexico was evident when, trying his Spanish, he addressed a well-dressed and beautiful "signorita" and was greeted in return with "a terrible oath, and a most obscene expression in English" (32). At first shocked and confused, Woods realized that this apparently genteel woman had been the victim of American soldiers who, in the guise of teaching her English, made her think such obscenities were polite greetings.

This experience, as well as other cross-cultural exchanges—political, religious, or culinary—suggest one of the major impacts of the gold rush on Americans: they became less provincial and more sophisticated. These fortune-seekers were perhaps the first large group of Americans to be placed on the world stage.

Obstacles along the Isthmus of Panama Route. A few Americans crossed Mexico to the Pacific; far more crossed the Isthmus of Panama. Indeed, the Isthmus route was the shortest and quickest route to California. Bayard Taylor, a journalist for the *New York Tribune* who was assigned to report on California during the gold rush, spent only fifty-one days en route from New York City to the Golden Gate. A typical journey would entail boarding a steamer in New York or New Orleans, with the port city of Chagres, Panama, as the destination. Passengers would there disembark and scramble for canoes or flatboats to carry their goods as far upriver as Gorgona, from which they continued cross-country to Panama City, where they again boarded a steamer, now bound for San Francisco. The *California* and its sister ships, the *Panama* and the *Oregon*, had been sent to the Pacific by the U.S. Mail Steam Line; however, during the first years of the gold rush there were simply too few ships in the Pacific to accommodate all those clamoring for passage. The wait for a ship to San Francisco was both exasperating and boring. One stranded fellow fumed, "I get more tired of Panama every day. . . . I should like to see an earthquake or a revolution" (Holliday, 417).

During the time the *California* was en route around the Horn (October 6, 1848, to January 17, 1849), at least seventeen ships disgorged their passengers at Chagres. Their eagerness to reach the gold fields, intensified by the arduous trip across Panama, made them furious when, having arrived at their Pacific port, they could not get immediate passage to California. As the Isthmus route was the most crowded, much tension developed through almost constant competition—for porters, mules, and lodging. Moreover, since the Isthmus route was the most expensive, requiring an outlay of cash for steamer tickets and expenses across land, travelers wanted to reach the mines as quickly as possible to recoup their expenses. In addition, many had purchased what they thought were tickets from Panama to San Francisco, but when—as in the case of the *California*—seventy Peruvian passengers were picked up en route, the Americans were outraged. The extra expenses incurred by a prolonged stay at Panama City did little to help their tempers or their wallets.

The travelers across Panama were a heterogeneous group. For example, when the *Falcon* left New York on December 1, 1848, it carried 29 passengers, most of them government employees and missionaries. But when it left New Orleans, the next port of call, it carried an additional 193 passengers, including approximately 100 "Southern backwoodsmen, carrying pans, pots, axes and whatever kind of equipment they thought necessary for digging gold." Unfortunately, the *Falcon* had berths for only 100 additional people. When Captain Notestein threatened to use force to remove some of the extra people, "the backwoodsmen spat tobacco juice on deck and brandished their revolvers." Notestein had additional bunks put in the hold and in the dining room (Perez-Venero, 462). Bayard Taylor corroborates the description of these passengers, who, to New Yorkers, were a new breed of Americans, "tall, gaunt Mississipians and Arkansans, Missouri squatters who had pulled up their stakes yet another time," and an "ominous number of professed gamblers."

Such people became a stock figure in nineteenth century American humor as the Pike, who was stereotyped as a "loutish, ignorant, distrustful, but acquisitive backwoodsman" (Hart, 329). In *Home and Abroad* Taylor described the Pike as "the Anglo-Saxon relapsed into semi-barbarism. He is long, lathy and sallow; he expectorates vehemently; he takes naturally to whiskey; he has the 'shakes' his life long at home, though he generally manages to get rid of them in California; he has little respect for the rights of others; he distrusts men in 'store clothes,' but venerates the memory of Andrew Jackson" (qtd. in Hart, 329). Each one of them "carried arms enough for a small company" and spent his time dozing on deck or going into the forecabin for drinks (Taylor, 8). The Pike appears in at least two folk songs of the period. One begins,

> My name is Joe Bowers
> And I've got a brother Ike
> I come from old Missouri
> Yes, all the way from Pike

and continues, depending on the variation, with increasing ribaldry. A more appealing folkloric version of the Pike appears in the gold rush song "Sweet Betsy from Pike."

Not only did travelers meet people the likes of which they'd never met before, but the trip itself offered new experiences, which were not always pleasant. These began at Chagres, the main port on the Caribbean side of Panama.

Stopovers. It is clear that Panama adapted quickly to the influx of foreigners, if one considers the various descriptions of Chagres. Mary Jane Megquier, traveling with her doctor husband, was the first American woman to cross the Isthmus. She found the people of Chagres "a simple, inoffensive people—cleanly in their person and dress" who "understand perfectly the getting of dimes from the Americans" (Megquier, 19). Some helped unload baggage from the steamers; others owned canoes that would carry the baggage upriver; at least one other collected admission to a "fine old castle built of stone by the baccaniers [*sic*]," which, surrounded by a moat and ancient guns, commanded the harbor. Americans were already rushing to it like tourists. Frank Marryat, however, observed that the only souvenir Americans were likely to take with them from Chagres was an especially "malignant fever." He described the town:

> It is composed of about fifty huts, each of which raises its head from the midst of its own private malaria, occasioned by the heaps of filth and offal, which putrefying under the rays of a vertical sun, choke up the very doorway. On the thresholds of the doors, in the huts themselves—fish, bullock's heads, hides, and carrion are strewed all in a state of decomposition; whilst in the rear is the jungle, and a lake of stagnant water, with a delicate bordering of greasy blue mud. (Marryat, 2)

Though Megquier was fascinated by the town, she was somewhat dubious about the bill of fare at the Crescent City Hotel at the edge of the village: "beef and fish by the yard[,] stewed Monkeys and Iguanas . . . my appetite has not been quite sharp enough to relish those yet" (Megquier, 19).

Originally hotels were merely tents, but by the end of 1849 Chagres had four frame hotels, two stories tall with porches around each floor. The "bedrooms" were large, barracks-like rooms filled with cots at $4 per night or hammocks at $2. If the hotels were crowded, women guests slept in the same room as the men, separated by screens made of palm leaves or blankets. Because of the nearby swamp, eating places in Chagres were overrun by cockroaches. In one inn, a Forty-Niner ordering coffee learned there was no coffee grinder. Glancing out the window he discovered a native girl squatting on the ground, chewing the coffee beans and spitting them into the pot! The man chose to forego his morning caffeine (Perez-Venero 464–66).

Alejandro Perez-Venero argues that because everyone passing through Chagres had money, the town soon took on the flavor of the wildest of frontier towns. Bars, gambling houses, and entrepreneurial women enticed travelers to part with their money. Drinks in the bars cost one dollar and up, about seven times the cost in New York City. Travelers were gouged in some bars by "dance hostesses" who kept half the price of the drink. When they were offered a drink, the "hostesses" ordered a Blue Moon—only colored water—though the customer paid the full price of the drink. At the gambling houses travelers could drop their money at roulette, blackjack, casino poker, faro, or craps. One of the busiest brothels was the House of All Nations, run by a French couple and staffed with women including mademoiselles from New Orleans and even some girls from Paris. Because there were neither banks nor law enforcement in Chagres, many prostitutes had large quantities of money in their rooms. Thus, many carried guns even while entertaining. One visitor commented, "Disconcerting as hell. All the time she kept one hand on her blasted six shooter!" The general high spirits of Chagres were dampened somewhat, for one could die of malaria, cholera, yellow fever, typhoid—or gunshot wounds. And because Chagres had no cemetery, the dead were simply dropped into the Chagres River (Perez-Venero 462–67).

Heading upriver to the interior was also challenging. Except for the "muddy coffee with hard bread" that she had for both breakfast and dinner on the first day, Mary Jane Megquier seemed to enjoy herself, perched atop carpet bags in a 22-foot canoe paddled by two natives. When her party stopped for the night, she was the only woman among some one hundred men. Consequently, the natives who had prepared their meal—"it was rich seeing us eat soup with our fingers"—offered her their hut for the night. However, her rest was constantly interrupted, for since "a white lady was such a rare sight," they kept coming in all night to look at her (Megquier, 20).

James Tyson was less fortunate. He and three other men slept crammed together, along with their luggage, in one canoe, pestered all night by fleas. The next night they slept ashore, having "built up a huge fire on the sand, to keep off the prowling wild beasts and venomous serpents" (Tyson, 20). Marryat too spent his first night in his canoe, exhausted by the sights: the luxuriant tropical vegetation woven into an almost impassable mass along the river, a "well bleached sycamore tree, half thrown across the river," an "ants' nest, about the size of a bee hive, . . . glorious water lilies" and, close by, "floats an alligator who has been dead some time, and hasn't kept well, and on top of him two black cormorants, which having evidently over-eaten, are shot on the spot and die lazily" (Marryat, 2–3).

Bayard Taylor had to pay $15 for canoe passage upriver from Chagres. Startling him, but indicating the influence of Forty-Niners on Panamanian culture, his boatman Juan "struck up 'Oh Susanna!' " though he mangled the words (Taylor, *El Dorado* 13). Taylor got along well with his boatmen but observed that other travelers, "blustering fellows, with their belts stuck full of pistols and bowie knives, which they draw on occasion but take good care not to use, have brought reproach upon [the U.S.] by their silly conduct" (18). The boatmen resent their pusillanimous abuse and now refuse to serve anyone who treats them badly. "If the Americans are good, then we are good; if they abuse us, we are bad," said Ambrosio, another boatman, "We are black, but *muchas cabelleras* [very much gentlemen]." Just short of Gorgona, Taylor encountered yet another victim of the nineteenth century version of the ugly American, a priest named Padre Dutares who "had frequently been cheated by Americans and was therefore cautious." By common courtesy, Taylor and his companions overcame his suspicions and received "a splendid supper of fowls, eggs, rice boiled in cocoa milk, and chocolate, with baked plantains for bread" (19).

From Gorgona, the trip was made by mules or tough little mustangs over trails so precipitous that sometimes the animal would plant its feet at the top and slide down, or so narrow that to prevent contusions against the walls of the crevice the riders took their feet out of the stirrups and balanced them on their mules' necks. During rainy season the mud in places came up to the animal's belly. Riders were often thrown off when their mounts lost their footing. If the trip was hard on the riders, it was often fatal to the horses. Mary Jane Megquier's party counted fifty-two dead horses on a 24-mile stretch of road. She attributed it to the fact that muleteers bought them cheaply—for $8 or $10—and fed them "on the tops of sugar cane once a day." For the women on this portion of the trail, conventions of polite behavior often had to be abandoned. Some had started with side-saddles but learned that on treacherous terrain it was safer, though less ladylike, to ride astride like a man. Megquier noted that she made herself "a double gown of red calico, a tunic and trousers" for crossing the Isthmus (8). She and others recommended that women adopt the new fashion—bloomers. In September 1850 a Mrs. Gillingham faced up to the difficulties of the Gorgona–Panama City route. "Having neglected to provide herself with a Bloomer costume, she had either to ride a mule attired in her usual dress . . . or submit to the novel mode of riding on the back of a nude native, lashed in a chair. She adopted the latter mode of conveyance" (Holliday, 432).

Life in Panama City. Arrival in Panama City was the end of the trail, but many travelers had to wait there for days or weeks for a ship to San Francisco. Their frustration grew with their time in port, California being so near yet so far away.

Bayard Taylor notes that the city was "already half American" when he arrived in late summer of 1849. "The native boys whistled Yankee Doodle through the streets and Señoritas of the pure Castilian blood sang Ethiopian melodies [from] Virginia to their guitars" (Taylor, 26–27). Because when he arrived there were nearly three hundred passengers competing for only fifty-two steamer tickets, a lottery was held to select the lucky ones to leave Panama. Those remaining simply had to adapt to—or endure—local conditions for a while longer.

A Panamanian newspaper founded in 1849 by an American advertised the American Hotel, the French Hotel, and the Oregon Hotel, plus many bars and restaurants owned by Americans. Mary Jane Megquier remarked that when she arrived in April 1849 it was rumored that 2,000 Americans were in town, "filling every nook and cranny" (13). Thus, she endured her hotel despite the fact that stones and bricks were falling out of crumbling mortar, "leaving holes for the cats, dogs, [and] rats which are trooping through our room every night but they take a bee line from one hole to another not stopping to make our acquaintance" (12). Because of the tremendous demand, prices were high: flour at $50 per barrel; codfish at 25 cents per pound, and ham at 50 cents per pound (Megquier, 13). Across the patio she saw "gentlemen I presume that never was in a kitchen" sweating over an "old stove about two thirds of the time to keep soul and body together" (18). Even before they reached the mines, the fortune-seekers were learning to fend for themselves.

James Tyson was somewhat shocked by Panamanians who went to Mass on Sunday morning and to cock fights in the afternoon. Even more preposterous was the sight of a local priest *"dressed in his canonical robes and three-cornered hat, playing cards!"* (28). Doctor that he was, Tyson gave others advice on eating and drinking. At his hotel "fish, flesh, and fowl" were served, and the only "vegetables" were "rice boiled in fat, and fresh rolls" (31). Nonetheless, he warned travelers against indulging in the "lucious fruits," saying that eating fruit and drinking copious quantities of water brought on Panama fever, which sometimes led to death. The fact that he blamed the fruit is interesting because elsewhere he noted that water of the streams was full of decayed vegetable matter. Instead of drinking water in Panama, Dr. Tyson recommended "a glass of claret or ale"; brandy, however, should not be consumed, for "the blood already fired by the fierce rays of an equatorial sun, can not long endure the accumulated heat and fatal disease will almost necessarily be the result" (Tyson, 31).

Despite these somewhat fanciful diagnoses, disease was a real threat in Panama City. Bayard Taylor expressed his relief at boarding his ship, for cholera had "carried off one-fourth of the native population" and created "havoc" among the Americans (30). In such an environment Mary Jane Megquier's doctor husband did "nearly business enough to pay our expenses which is $18 per week" (Megquier, 23). These threats to health, the frustrating delays, the daily depletion of money saved for the trip, and the crowded conditions meant that travelers leapt at almost any chance to leave Panama City. Though many argued later, from experience, that only a steamer provided suitable transportation in the Pacific, very few waited; most took the first available sailing ship. Some even set off for San Francisco in canoes!

Between 1848 and 1869 about 375,000 people used the Panama route (Perez-Venero, 469), materially and culturally changing the Isthmus and, in turn, being changed by their experiences. For the most part their goal was the mines. Thus, most did not stay long in San Francisco. The majority of gold-seekers took the overland routes from Independence or St. Joseph, Missouri, even though they were longer and more arduous.

Overland Travel   In part, their choice was a simple matter of logistics. General Persifor F. Smith, who had traveled on the *California*'s maiden voyage, had seen for himself the chaos of those stranded in Panama City clamoring for passage. In a report to Washington dated October 7, 1849, he wrote, "The route by the Isthmus is too expensive and too insignificant for the number of travelers. The steamers can bring with propriety not three hundred [emigrants] a month, while the emigration by land, if divided throughout the year, would average three thousand a month" (qtd. in Read, 3).

Although a portion of these travelers went by the Santa Fe–Gila route, the majority followed routes forged during the height of the fur trade: along the Platte to Fort Laramie, through South Pass, and then either north to Fort Hall or south to Salt Lake City. In June 1849 the St. Joseph *Adventure* passed on the observations of a "Mountain Trader in the employ of Mr. Jos. Robidoux" returning from Fort Laramie: "In some places there were several teams abreast, generally going forward without accident or detention. . . . There are probably on the route, beyond Fort Kearney, not less than fifty or sixty thousand oxen, mules, and horses" (Read, 4). Major Osborne Cross of the Mounted Riflemen reported that by June 1, 1849, over 4,000 wagons, 20,000 persons, and 50,000 animals had passed Fort Kearney. In November 1849 the "Report of the Chief Engineer" emphasized the importance of Forts Kearney and Laramie; in the preceding eighteen months "nearly 8,000 wagons, 30,000 people, and 80,000 draught animals have passed along this thoroughfare on the way to California, Oregon, and Salt Lake" (Read, 2–3). The Buckeye Rovers, a group from Athens, Ohio, counted 50, 100—even 600—wagons seen or passed per day. The year 1850 saw no lessening of the flood. One emigrant reported that by May 21, fully 2,754 wagons, averaging 4.5 men to the wagon and including "seventy-six ladies," had passed Fort Kearney. He had traveled hard that day—30 miles—and had passed between 400 and 500 wagons; another reported that he had passed "at least two thousand" wagons between St. Joseph and Fort Kearney (Wyman, *California* 107–9). It is thus no surprise that Bayard Taylor, who had come via Panama, would write of the overlanders: "This California Crusade will more than equal the great military expedition of the Middle Ages in magnitude, peril and adventure. The amount of suffering which must have been endured in the savage mountain passes and herbless deserts of the interior cannot be told in words" (47).

As far as Fort Hall or Salt Lake City, the route was fairly straightforward; even beyond those points the Forty-Niners who followed sound advice had only to endure—not discover—the trail. Between 1849 and 1851 at least three dozen guidebooks for travel to the gold fields appeared in the United States (Perez-Venero, 465). Not all were equally reliable. Although many accurately recounted distances and obstacles and offered valuable advice, some were written by people cashing in on gold fever who had never made the trip themselves. As one emigrant observed in a letter back home, "The distance across the great Sublette Cutoff is much greater than the books tell you. Ware says it is 35 miles, but it has been measured by Roadmasters [devices like odometers], and found to be 53 miles to the first ferry, and 56 miles to the lower one" (Wyman, *California* 94). Joseph E. Ware, author of *The Emigrant's Guide to California*, while warning emigrants to travel light, gave bad advice to greenhorns who were desperate for specifics—that their wagon loads should not exceed 2,500 pounds, an excessive weight (Scamehorn, 175). The wisest early travelers hired experienced guides, many of them former mountain men.

However, as their numbers grew ever more vast, some emigrants sought less-traveled routes in the hope of making better time or finding more grass; occasionally such travelers, in dangerously small groups of a wagon or two, were down to their last mouthfuls of water. Some perished.

Obstacles for Overland Travelers. The overland travelers were at the mercy of nature, geography, and climate. They had a narrow window of opportunity to complete their travel, starting late enough that the new spring grass would be high enough to feed their animals, but not so late that they would be trapped in the Sierra Nevada snows. Nearly all were familiar with the disastrous 1846 experience of the Donner Party, which had elected to take the untried Hastings cutoff; its progress over deserts and mountains was slow—at one point making only thirty-six miles in twenty-one days—until, in early November, the party was blocked at the pass that was later named for them. Because of the snow, relief parties could not reach them until mid-February, by which time some of the survivors had been reduced to eating the flesh of the dead in order to survive (Hart, 116–17).

Though this awareness may have hastened subsequent emigrants' travel, it did little to ease it. Whereas water early on was described as "sweet," it soon grew more and more alkaline. One of the Buckeye Rovers noted that while one was in view of the Rockies it was dangerous to drink any water except from the Platte River. "Saw a pond encrusted with Salaratus . . . white as snow. We constantly watch that none of our cattle drink from any slough or run. It is thought that the air contains alkali to such a degree that emigrants will not use milk in this neighborhood." The next day, "we crossed a small stream that we were aware to be poisonous. I washed my hands and face; it felt like lye" (Scamehorn, 26).

Finding good and plentiful grass was equally crucial. An emigrant noted early in May 1850 that because of the cool, dry spring, there was little or no grass; his group had left St. Joseph with twenty-five bushels of grain per team of oxen and, not yet having reached Fort Kearney, had only ten bushels per team left (Wyman, *California* 106). Another remarked on 21 May that there was so little grass the animals could barely subsist. Why? "A number of persons" early in the season had "set fire to the prairie 'to see it burn,' never dreaming of the injury they were inflicting upon those coming behind them" (Wyman, *California* 107). Others' motives were more sinister. Bayard Taylor was told of one man who with unbelievable "malice and cruelty" set fire to the meadows of dry grass, simply to retard the progress of those "who were behind and might else overtake him." He received peremptory justice, as some of those mounted their fastest horses, caught up with him, and "shot him from the saddle as he rode" (Taylor, *El Dorado*, vol. 2, 39). Sarah Royce, less dramatic but no less desperate, described how her group kept their oxen from starving for one more day while crossing the desert. In Salt

Lake City they had filled their mattress tick with a little fresh hay—not too much in order to keep the load light. They subsequently emptied the mattress for the starving animals (Royce, 42). During the desert stretch, the combination of heavy sand and little grass or water weakened many animals, which simply dropped in their tracks. William B. Royall wrote to those back home: "Thousands of putrid carcasses of horses, mules and oxen lay along the track and [by] now they have been forced to make a new one" (Wyman, *California* 70).

After plains and deserts, the final obstacle was the mountains. Climbing them was bad enough, but getting down was even worse. Some emigrants unhitched the oxen and lowered their wagons with ropes. Others left one yoke of oxen hitched, locked all the wagon wheels, and then cut a bushy pine tree to drag behind the wagon; the combined resistance usually prevented wagon, oxen, and earthly goods from plummeting down the mountainside (Taylor, *El Dorado*, vol. 2, 41).

C. R. School wrote to his father back in Missouri, describing all he had experienced but knowing his experiences were nearly unbelievable. His "toil and privations," truly told, would seem like the "grossest fiction." He vowed never to travel overland again "while there is one vessel on old ocean" (Wyman, *California*, 73–74). His overland trip had lasted from May 1 to September 8, 1849, by no means the longest journey. Nothing could induce him to repeat it. Yet thousands more were behind him on the trail, and more yet would follow in successive years.

Transportation of Overland Travelers. They came by every imaginable mode of transportation, in light wagons pulled by several oxen and two cows, brought along for the milk; by prairie schooners that "looked tall as houses . . . having deep beds, with projecting backs and high tops" (Royce, 3, 54). Early on, women and children rode in the wagons; later, as the animals grew exhausted, the women walked. They carried their babies, which after a while became exhausting. One woman describes her solution: "I got tired packing the babies so I took a long sack and fixed it so it could be fastened on the ox. A hole was cut on each side like a pair of saddlebags and a baby was placed in each end. The little fellows would ride thus and sleep half their time" (Read, 14–15).

Some walked from the outset, some with packs on their backs, some guiding draft animals, and a few with barnyard cows packing household goods. "M.M.G." wrote of a 60-year-old who had walked from Maine "with his rifle on his shoulder and his faithful dog by his side," believing he could make it from Fort Kearney "on twenty-five meals"; his goal was to gain a dowry for his favorite daughter and thus "enable her to marry an editor, lawyer, or statesman" (Wyman, *California* 47–48). A "lean and stalwart Scotsman" was observed pushing a wheelbarrow at the rate of twenty-five to thirty miles a day (Wyman, *California* 95). So many people were en route that "Cheyenne," a self-proclaimed humorist, observed that "the Indians begin to talk of emigrating to the East" (Wyman, *California* 111).

Disease and Accidents on the Overland Trail. Though Easterners at first expected dangers from Indians, disease and accidents were truly deadly. Cholera was the most lethal. Indeed, in 1849 there was such a severe national cholera epidemic that President Zachary Taylor declared August 3 a national day of prayer: "At a season when the Providence of God has manifested itself in the visitation of a fearful pestilence which is spreading its ravages throughout the land, it is fitting that a People whose reliance has ever been in His Protection should humble themselves before His throne, and, while acknowledging past transgressions, ask a continuance of Divine Mercy" (qtd. in McLear, 178).

Prayer was perhaps the only hope, for it was not until 1893 that Robert Koch isolated the bacterial cause, *Vibrio cholerae asiatica*, which enters the body through the mouth and causes an infection in the intestine. Death results (often within a few hours of the first signs of illness) from dehydration caused by diarrhea and vomiting. At the time, people thought it was caused by everything from "evening mists" to a "lack of electricity in the victim's system." Because many believed that filth, either physical or moral, was a cause, families often hid the cause of death from friends and neighbors. Thus, many deaths attributed to "miscellaneous causes" were probably caused by cholera. Among the patent medicine treatments were Captain Paynter's Cure for Asiatic Cholera and Dally's and Connell's Magic Pain Extractor (Holliday, 58).

In 1849, St. Louis was struck especially hard by the epidemic. It was thought to have been brought by German "immigrants who came up from New Orleans as steerage passengers—filthy, dirty, and corrupt from all manner of disease. *We* [italics added] have no fears" (Holliday, 71). Not only does this Forty-Niner's observation reveal the xenophobia present long before the Foreign Miner's Tax was conceived, but it demonstrates the failure to recognize a major public health issue. St. Louis at the time had no sewer system, and rainwater, human waste, garbage, and animal manure formed "stagnant pools of yellow-green water" that created "an atmosphere of chills and fever [that] seemed to envelop the town" (McLear, 172). Crowded conditions and ignorance of sanitation on the week-long to ten-day boat trip upriver from St. Louis to Independence, a major "jumping-off" point for the gold fields, provided an excellent breeding ground for the disease. Aboard the *Monroe* cholera swept through the 300 passengers, killing 53; the panicked survivors deserted the boat in Jefferson City (Holliday, 89). Nor did the disease disappear on the early stages of the overland trail. Men in a rush toward gold left campsites littered with trash, rotting food, and—worse—clothing and bedding fouled by dying patients. The disease was further spread by flies, contaminated water, human excrement left unburied, and contact with cholera patients who had been abandoned by their frightened traveling companions. The number of graves mentioned in travelers' diaries suggests that at least 1,500 died of the disease east of Fort Laramie (Holliday, 115). One doctor traveling with a group from Chicago recommended "a dose of laudanum with pepper, camphor, musk, ammonia, peppermint or other stimulant. . . . The medicine is aided by friction, mustard plasters and other external applications" (Holliday, 96). No matter what the treatment, the disease was prevalent until emigrants reached the Black Hills. There, probably because of the higher altitude, pure water, and less congested conditions, it disappeared.

Though cholera was the worst, it was by no means the only disease affecting the overland travelers. "Much sickness in your camp?" became a common greeting (Scamehorn, 7). People worried about smallpox as well as cholera; indeed, some companies told Indians whom they met that smallpox was rampant among them, a ruse they felt would keep away Indian depredations. In addition, many contracted "mountain fever" and believed "the mountain air is too pure for their lungs, giving coughs and in some cases fever" (Scamehorn, 40). It was, instead, probably the tick-borne infection known as Colorado tick fever or Rocky Mountain spotted fever. The travelers also fell victim to "land scurvy," probably due to a shortage of fresh fruits and vegetables. Sore lips from exposure to wind and sun were a general complaint. One of the Buckeye Rovers wrote, "would advise those coming this route to bring court plaster for lips, nose, and perhaps ears; mine sore" (Scamehorn, 16). Mosquitoes ate people alive; rain drenched them; the sun burned them.

Travelers' diaries also record accidents. A wagon fell off a makeshift bridge; its passengers leapt out at the last minute, receiving only scratches where otherwise they would have been crushed (Bruff, 11). A father and son were killed in their sleep by a tree that fell on them in a storm; the mother continued the journey with her other children (Read, 11). A 9-year-old "colored boy" driving a team was run over by a heavy wagon, one wheel passing over his face and the other over his chest, but he was "expected to recover" (Scamehorn, 36). People were bitten by rattlesnakes, though not as many as one might expect. On June 22, six or eight men drowned trying to cross the Platte, which was ten to fifteen feet deep with a rapid current; before the diarist completed his entry, another man drowned. "It seems a little like a battlefield," wrote the appalled Ohioan (Scamehorn, 24). "If one of these frail boats oversets [at makeshift ferries], all on board are lost. Not one in a thousand can save his life by swimming, no matter how expert a swimmer. The water is cold, being formed from the melting snows, and the current rolls, boils, and rushes along with a tremendous velocity," wrote another (Holliday, 188).

In some locations, enterprising Mormons provided a ferry service at the rate of $4 per wagon. One of the Buckeye Rovers was cognizant of the irony: "While others are chasing wealth, they are catching it, no dream" (Scamehorn, 39).

Finally, when virtually everyone set out onto the Plains armed with rifles, pistols, and fowling pieces in anticipation of hunting and as a protection against Indians whom they expected to be hostile, it is no wonder that east of the Rockies the number of emigrants wounded or killed by other emigrants far exceeded those killed by Indians (Holliday, 115). An army officer at Fort Kearney referred to emigrants as "walking arsenals" and commented wryly, "Arms of all kinds must be scarce in the States, after such a drain as the emigrants have made upon them" (Holliday, 138). A Mr. Steadman's gun "burst, breaking lock, stock, and barrel. Happily none hurt" (Scamehorn, 15). Others were not so lucky. One man threw a bundle of clothes out of his wagon; on landing it hit his gun, which discharged, shattering his knee and ending his dream of gold (Holliday, 133). A Mr. Gilmore accidentally shot himself through the leg while putting a cap on his pistol (Scamehorn, 17). Another man pulled his shotgun out of his wagon muzzle-first and shot himself in the foot (Scamehorn, 41). Yet another went to check on his picketed mules late at night and, when he didn't identify himself quickly enough, was shot dead within a few yards of the camp (Wyman, *California* 64).

From disease and accident, the way west was marked by a succession of graves. Some burials were formal. J. Goldsborough Bruff described the interment of the first casualty among his company. While his grave was being dug about 400 yards from the trail, they sewed this cholera victim in a blue blanket and prepared a bier of his tent poles. Then, in clean clothes and uniforms, they marched "two by two" in a funeral procession to the measured time of a dirge played by a "key bugle, flute, violin, and accordion." His body, covered by the Stars and Stripes, was lowered into the grave with bridle reins. An "elderly gentleman" read the funeral service, and a firing party in uniform fired a salvo over the grave, which was marked by head and footstones carved by Bruff. Its letters were filled in with "blacking from the hub of a wheel" (Bruff, 32–33). Most funerals were not nearly so formal or most graves so permanent. As one of the Buckeye Rovers recalled, "a majority of the dead interred last year have been dug up by the wolves; naked skulls and torn clothes [are] the only monuments of the departed" (Scamehorn, 127).

Psychological Stress. In addition to physical dangers, most of the emigrants experienced psychological stress as well. Most were fairly provincial and had not previously ventured far from their homes. Many suffered from homesickness, especially on birthdays or wedding anniversaries. Journal entries on such days are surprisingly sentimental: "My Birthday! Thirty-one years since the light first dawned on these eyes and

I was folded in a parent's arms. Now for the first time absent on the return of this day. My breast heaves with emotion . . . !" (Scamehorn, 31–32). As the journey wore on, prolonged living in close proximity to other men often resulted in suppressed or smoldering anger that was easily ignited by insignificant events into quarreling, fighting, and stabbings. One traveler later recalled, "If there is anything that tries a man's patience and brings out his combativeness . . . it is a trip across the plains. . . . If there is any inclination to shirk or do any little mean trick or the slightest tendency to hoggishness, it will soon develop" (Holliday, 146). Even their ambivalence toward the trip resulted in depression. Just before leaving Independence, William Swain wrote, "I confess that I had the blues when I found I had the prospect of being one hundred days on the plains. I had a mind to start home. But upon reflection, I think that duty to myself and *family* and relatives will not permit me to look back" (Holliday, 97).

The psychological stresses were even greater for the relatively few women on the overland trail. A good many of them had become widows en route—from disease or accident. Unable to turn back they forged ahead, taking on the unfamiliar responsibility of being a single parent, and being unable for the children's sake to reach closure through mourning. Bruff described the plight of one German immigrant woman whose husband, for some unknown reason, had "gone back some distance." Her son is sick in their wagon; with no one to watch over them, her oxen have wandered off; she is "sitting on the wagon-tongue, weeping." Bruff realistically assesses her future: "This poor woman sees hard times indeed; the son will probably die, the Indians or emmigrants [sic], some of whom are little better than the savages . . . will carry off their oxen, and finally the husband take care of himself" (Bruff, 56–57).

Even a woman whose future is far less bleak is suddenly shocked by the reality of the experience. Sarah Royce, traveling with her husband, had "for months anticipated" setting out, rather looking forward to "camping out" for the first time in her life. What she noticed, as night was coming on at the end of their first day, was that "no house was within sight." Intellectually, of course, she knew that there would be none. But now, "seeing night come on without house or home to shelter us and our baby-girl"—and the recognition that it would be this way for many weeks—was "a chilling prospect . . . there was a terrible shrinking from it in my heart." Outwardly brave, she "kept it all to myself," but the "oppressive sense of homelessness, and an instinct of watchfulness, kept me awake" (Royce, 4).

Joint Stock Companies. To ease the difficulties of the journey, many emigrants banded together in joint stock companies. Some were founded at the jumping-off places; others were organized near the gold-seekers' homes. Thus, many names—such as the Wolverine Rangers, the Buckeye

Rovers, or the Washington City and California Mining Association—reflected the group's starting point. Though motivated by personal ambition, most emigrants recognized the advisability of traveling with others for security. Greenhorns—city men, even farmers who knew nothing of the terrain through which they would pass—would profit from others' experience. Often former mountain men were hired on as guides for the early parties.

The joint stock companies were also business partnerships, with members pooling their funds to buy wagons, stock, and mining equipment. Often people staying at home invested in the companies, providing necessary cash to those starting out in the expectation of a share of the profits. At meetings held before leaving, formal Articles of Association and Agreement were drafted and published in the local paper like any other legal notice.

The Articles of the Wolverine Rangers serve as an example of these documents. Their purpose was specifically stated; the undersigned agreed to join "for the purpose of mutual safety and advantage in prosecuting an overland route to California from Independence on the Missouri River, and after arriving at the place of destination." Each man had to pay a nonrefundable $10 fee at the time of signing; $75 more was due before leaving—though, if necessary, the Board of Directors could levy additional requests as long as the amount was equal for each member. The Board, elected by the members, included a captain, lieutenant, secretary, treasurer, and steward, each to serve specified three- or six-month terms, each to fulfill specific responsibilities. The captain, for example, was "to conduct and command the expedition, pursuant to the orders and suggestions of the Board of Directors—and to preserve order and decorum on the members." Recognizing that they knew little about the frontier, the Wolverine Rangers agreed to select an agent whose job it would be to find the best sources and prices for supplies; two members of the company, bonded, were then to go, with company funds, to assist the agent in purchases. Once the Wolverines reached the gold regions, any member could, on two weeks' notice to the directors, resign from the Company and receive his portion of its current value. Until then, each member "binds himself" to fulfill "upon his honor" his duties to the association—"to be orderly, temperate and faithful—obedient to the will of the majority, properly expressed—and to stand by and relieve, so far as in his power, any member in peril or distress." The Articles could be amended, or others added, by a two-thirds vote.

If a member were to die, his share of the value of the company property would be kept for his next of kin or some other person appropriately designated. For the purpose of the trip, "each member shall provide himself with a good rifle, 3 lbs. powder, 10 lbs. lead, and a good hatchet, and such other things as he may deem desirable, or useful." The roster of sixty-four members and officers, including a blacksmith, three saddlers, two "local preachers," farmers, tobacconists, one physician, one "daguerrean," one lighthouse keeper, and one (!) miner was published in the Marshall [Michigan] *Statesman* on April 11, 1849, one week before the Wolverines' departure (Holliday, 461–65).

Perhaps most significant, these Articles reflect a democratic organization. The power lay ultimately in the members, though specific responsibilities were delegated to elected representatives. Thus, it may be seen as a precursor of the pragmatic ad hoc governments that grew up in the mining camps. Its very democracy, too, lead to a more harmonious trip than was experienced by groups run in a more autocratic, quasi-military fashion, such as J. Goldsborough Bruff's group, which seemed full of dissension almost from the start.

Regardless of his style, the decisions a leader of an overland company had to make—whether to lay over a day near good grass or to push ahead, how to punish a man who fell asleep on guard duty, how to quell disagreements before they grew into destructive dissatisfaction—were taxing. One company leader later wrote: "To be the leader of an emigrant train through the wilderness is one of the most unenviable distinctions. . . . Some may think the children of Israel in the wilderness were a clamorous set, but they were nothing more than what folks are now" (Holliday, 147).

A Typical Day on the Overland Journey. Life on the journey west from Independence or St. Joseph was long and slow and tiresome. The Buckeye Rovers, for example, recorded for their first month the following daily (*not* hourly) mileages: 11, 25, 20, 15, 22, 15, 15, 16, 25, 15, 15, 22, 15, 25, 15, 20, 5, 3, 12, 12, 22, 20, 19, 15, 22, and 20. (Distances were measured by counting the revolutions of the odometer, or roadometer, a wheel of known circumference.) Most people today commute further one way to work than the Rovers' average 16.96 miles.

The day started at daybreak or earlier, with wheels rolling by 6:00 A.M. Prompt starts were essential for the group's success. Mothers learned it was preferable—to prevent delays—to let their children continue to sleep for a few hours after the wagons were under way (Read, 9). Often wagons that delayed the group's start were required to take a position at the rear of the line, a significant punishment given the dusty conditions. (Normally wagons took turns, day by day, in the lead.) Across the desert, starts were as early as 2:00 A.M., though sometimes the wagons kept rolling all night and stopped during the heat of the day.

Even on ordinary days, emigrants faced much physical labor. Driving the teams—oxen or mules—took patience, delicate fingers, and strong wrists, especially at the outset when the animals were less used to harness. (Back in the jumping-off towns, the demand far exceeded the supply of well-broken draft animals.) Many companies could not afford to buy well-broken mules, so that became the first task. Bruff writes, "Next to exposure to bad weather, the mule-breaking job comes hard on the 'boys.'—Most of them knew as much about mules, when they arrived here, as the mules did about them" (Bruff, 570 n.27). Next the animals were branded for later identification. On the trip, care of the animals was an ongoing, crucial responsibility. Wise companies gave them, rather than the emigrants, priority when water was in short supply. Men daily scouted for good grass and water; in fact, stopping sites were often determined by their availability. When grass was unexpectedly plentiful, men would scythe and gather it for future use. As more and more wagons were on the road, this became increasingly difficult. When there was grass at a stop, the animals had to be picketed so they could graze. Night watches were set to protect them against the feared Indians—or the more dangerous "white Indians," who, having lost their own animals, preyed on those of others. In addition, the animals had to be shod repeatedly en route; lameness could be deadly to emigrants depending on them.

The wagons, too, demanded care. Axles broke and had to be repaired. Wheels shrank from their spokes in the hot, dry air and required refitting. Sometimes wagons proved to be excessively long—and thus heavy—and were shortened; chosen for their capaciousness and comfort, their very size put unnecessary demands on the teams. When the companies came to rivers, animals had to be swum across and rafts constructed to ferry the wagons. Sometimes makeshift bridges were constructed.

Nearly everyone overloaded wagons at Independence or St. Joseph with all kinds of useless articles. Wagons, whimsically named "Red Rover" or "The Pirate" or "The Ass," were crammed full with necessities and follies ranging from extra axles and blacksmith's anvils to rocking chairs and featherbeds, to intricate gold-washing machinery and even "underwater diving suits and bells" that greenhorns were convinced would be useful when working the California river bottoms. When the load became too great for the exhausted animals, travelers jettisoned the wagons' contents. Banks wrote, just past Fort Laramie:

> The waste of provisions on this road is truly wonderful. Some three thousand pounds of iron in one place. Wagons worth seventy-five to one hundred dollars broken up, chains and harness, saddles, and large quantities of tolerable good clothing. Piles of bacon and in one place some three hundred pounds of good flour, pilot bread in large quantities. Anything that impedes our progress, not necessary to life, is cast away as worthless. Many are changing their mode of travel from wagons to pack saddles. Costly trunks torn to pieces. Wagon tires and every kind of irons literally strewed along the

J. Goldsborough Bruff, *On the Plains, Preparing to Feed (Buffalo-chip Fuel)*. This item is reproduced by permission of The Huntington Library, San Marino, California, HM 8044 #16.

road. Gold ahead! Men seem reckless to all save that. (Scamehorn, 290–21)

Sarah Royce recalled that at one roadside dump she found a "little book, bound in cloth and illustrated with a number of small engravings" titled "Little Ella"; she put it in her pocket, thinking her young daughter would enjoy it (Royce, 55). Others, however, combed such travelers' litter for more mercantile reasons: Mormons from Salt Lake City and teamsters from the jumping-off towns scavenged such sites, planning to sell the goods to the next wave of ignorant emigrants.

Food, Drink, and Cooking on the Overland Trail. Other chores included hunting to supplement purchased food supplies and gathering fuel supplies—wood where it was available and buffalo chips where it was not. Those who had cook's duty had chip collecting as first chore each night, providing much amusement to their friends as they "jump[ed] from the wagon, gunny bag in hand, and made a grand rush for the largest and driest chips." It took an average of five bushels of chips to cook supper and breakfast for twelve persons. The fuel contributed to the atmosphere. "The chips burn well when dry but if damp or wet are smoky and almost fireproof," wrote one. Added another, "They emit a delicate perfume" (Holliday, 150–51).

For a predominantly male population, cooking itself was a chore. The cook often walked ahead to the campsite in order to have supper ready when the rest arrived. Some Wolverine Rangers complained about their cook, a Mr. Bailey, who did not have supper ready even though "he had been . . . here since three o'clock." These hungry campers were perhaps oblivious to the cook's chores. After traveling as far that day as the rest of the company, the cook fetched water for coffee, however far a stream was from camp; collected fuel and made it burn, even in a downpour; and put aside his own exhaustion long enough to feed his companions, who could rest after picketing their animals (Holliday, 128). To compensate for all this extra work, cooks were excused from night guard duty.

One man, writing to his sister in Kentucky, saw something of the humor of his situation—as well as a new appreciation of women:

> You would be amused to see us . . . cooking and washing—but never washing our hands. . . . I feel [I need] advice from you . . . in biscuit-making and . . . brewing coffee. . . . I have always been inclined to deride the vocation of ladies until now. But I must confess it is the most irksome I have ever tried. . . . I wish you could take supper with me, that you might judge the hardness and durability of our biscuits. I must at some time send you a recipe for making this lasting sort. (Holliday, 97–98)

No matter who did the cooking, food was hardly what it had been at home. William Swain cites a day's menu when they were living "tolerably well." For breakfast: meat fried in batter, boiled beans, pancakes, pilot bread [ship biscuit], and coffee. For dinner: tea, rice, meat, and pilot bread (Holliday, 104). When the wagons had been lightened to ease up on the oxen and mules, food too was jettisoned; thus, later on the trail, food supplies often ran perilously short. By the time they reached the Humboldt, "many companies subsisted on rancid bacon with the grease fried out by the hot sun, musty flour, a few pinoles, some sacks of pilot bread broken and crushed and well coated with alkali, and a little coffee without sugar" (Holliday, 229). Bayard Taylor notes that it was not unusual for such emigrants "to kill a quantity of rattlesnakes, with which the mountains abounded, and have a dish of them fried, for supper" (Taylor, *El Dorado*, vol. 2, 39). John Edwin Banks recalled his delight on finding gooseberries and wild peas, which, with venison from the abundant deer in the Sierra Nevada, provided their first fresh food for most of the trip (Scamehorn, 89).

Entertainment along the Overland Trail. Although the trek was long and difficult, emigrants took opportunities to break the tedium. Because so many were on the trail at once, people could visit over evening campfires with those from other companies. This, too, lessened provinciality as people from Vermont sang with those from New Jersey and people from Ohio swapped stories with those from Washington City.

Mrs. Margaret Catherine Haun, one of a party from Clinton, Iowa, describes how, during the day, "we womenfolk" visited from wagon to wagon, making "congenial friends" with whom to walk "ever westward," telling of loved ones left back in "the States," sharing dreams for the future, and even "whispering a little friendly gossip of emigrant life." In the evening "tatting, knitting, crocheting, exchanging receipts for cooking beans or dried apples or swopping food for the sake of variety kept us in practice of feminine occupations and diversions." She notes that although most went early to bed, an hour or so around the campfire was relaxing. "The menfolk lolling and guessing, or maybe betting, how many miles we had covered during the day. We listened to readings, story-telling, music and songs and the day often ended in laughter and merrymaking" (Read, 9).

Arriving at settlements and forts such as Salt Lake City and Forts Kearney and Laramie broke the monotony and provided opportunities to reprovision and to post letters for home. Like tourists ever since, the emigrants' first views of natural landmarks such as Chimney Rock or Scotts Bluff or the Rockies themselves left them in awe. And, like tourists since, passing gold-seekers left their names, slogans, and graffiti carved and daubed in tar on Independence Rock. Arriving at such landmarks also gave travelers a sense of progress. In addition, other types of people they met helped break the monotony. They met wagons loaded with furs coming east; these too gave them opportunities to send mail home. Some met—and were horrified by—"Frenchmen married to squaws" (Scamehorn, 42). There were soldiers moving to new postings in Oregon, and deserters from Fort Laramie seduced by the news of gold.

But even more horrifying were those returnees from California who had spent time in the mines, had "seen the tail of the elephant and can't bear to look any further"; they knew firsthand that life in California was "not as flattering as we had heard." ("Seeing the elephant" was a universal expression during the gold rush years, symbolizing the dream to dig great riches in the new land. It originated from the experience of going to a circus and not being favorably impressed with the much-touted elephant. Both en route and in the mines, unexpected difficulties beset the Forty-Niners. As a result the phrase "to see the elephant" took on the meaning of facing up to difficulties, of enduring the worst possible ordeals, and somehow surviving. In short, it came to mean facing the truth rather than maintaining illusions.) But the westward emigrants were not to be dissuaded. "Our motto is 'Go ahead.' I don't think there is one man in our company today who would sell his interest for $500" (Scamehorn, 87; Holliday, 131–32). To those who had not yet seen the elephant, the returnees were, quite simply, failures.

Also breaking the monotony were days set apart for celebration and meditation. Many companies had written into their articles of incorporation mandatory stops for Sunday. This was not, however, a day of true rest. "The men were generally busy mending wagons, harness yokes, shoeing the animals etc. and the women washed clothes, boiled a big mess of beans, to be warmed over for several meals, or perhaps mended clothes. . . . If we had devotional services the minister-pro-tem stood in the center of the corral while we kept on with our work" (Read, 9).

In contrast, the Fourth of July was marked almost universally by patriotic celebration. Most companies, heavily armed, used the Fourth as an excuse to fire their guns. The Buckeye Rovers fired a gun for every state in the Union and one for California and the gold diggings. In the excitement, one of the Rovers shot off his thumb. Many companies were reaching the Rockies around the Fourth. One made punch and cooled it with a lump of snow from a snowbank. Another made ice cream and flavored it with wild peppermint (Holliday, 149). Another company, after a thirteen-gun salute at sunrise, slept in. This luxury was followed by a formal ceremony: a prayer, a reading of the Declaration of Independence, an oration, and music including "Hail Columbia" and "The Star-Spangled Banner." Dinner included "ham, beans, boiled and baked, biscuits, john cake, apple pie, sweet cake, rice pudding, pickle vinegar, pepper sauce and mustard, coffee, sugar and milk." After the dinner, the toasting began. "The boys had raked and scraped together all the brandy they could, and they toasted, hurrayed, and drank till reason was out and brandy was in." Later the boys danced by moonlight (Holliday, 67–68). Many suffered hangovers on July 5.

Women and Children on the Overland Route. Perhaps aware of such behavior among all-male companies, Mrs. Haun wrote that the presence of women and children tended to provide a "good influence," reducing aggression and encouraging better care of the teams as well as better sanitation and cleanliness and more regular and better-cooked meals. The results, she argued, were fewer accidents and less sickness and waste. However, she may simply have been a fairly straight-laced, conventional woman.

Certainly that was true in matters of dress, for she always "wore a dark woolen dress. . . . Never worked without an apron and a three-cornered shoulder kerchief, . . . I presented a comfortable, neat appearance" (Read, 9). This woman, so concerned with "feminine occupations and diversions," would have been shocked at the advice given by T. H. Jefferson in his *Accompaniment to the Map of the Emigrant Road from Independence, Missouri, to San Francisco, California.* Recommending that abandoning wagons and crossing the Sierra Nevada on pack and saddle animals would be wise, he suggested that "side saddles should be discarded—women should wear hunting frocks, loose pantaloons, men's hats and shoes, and ride the same as men" (Read, 7).

Adapting on the Overland Route. On the overland route, many learned to adapt to new conditions. Carrying with them conventions of past lives, they improvised, redefined their expectations, and endured. Because of the hardships they'd experienced, many of the overlanders were better prepared to face the unknowns of California than were those who had gone by sea. Many travelers reflected on their experiences en route.

D. H. Moss, writing to his relatives, swore: "I don't think I will ever be caught on the plains again if there is any other safe chance of getting to the States" (Scamehorn, 64). Dame Shirley—Mrs. Louisa Amelia Knapp Smith Clappe—who had come to California with her husband via the Cape, held a romanticized view of the overland trip: lying down "under starry skies," rising upon "dewy mornings," seeing something "new and wonderful," "enchanting" every day—until she saw the women arriving after crossing the Sierra Nevada.

> The poor women arrive, looking as haggard as so many Endorean witches; burnt to the color of a hazel-nut, with their hair cut short, and its gloss entirely destroyed by the alkali, whole plains of which they are compelled to cross on the way. You will hardly find a family that has not left some beloved one buried upon the plains. And they are fearful funerals, those. A person dies; and they stop just long enough to dig his grave and lay him in it, as decently as circumstances will permit, and the long train hurries onward, leaving its healthy companions of yesterday, perhaps, in this boundless city of the dead. On this hazardous journey, they dare not linger. (Clappe [Shirley], 181)

In contrast, however, is the recollection of Sarah Royce—she who had been so unnerved by her first night on the road at seeing no signs of human habitation. In mid-October, with weather so cold that "water froze in our pans not very far from the fire," she'd forged ahead of her group, sometimes tugging the pack mule up the steepest places, eager for her first glimpse of California. As she looked down from the last mountain, the Sacramento Valley seemed to send up a "smile of welcome." Writing years later, Royce remembered the moment:

> California, land of sunny skies—that was my first look into your smiling face. I loved you from that moment, for you seemed to welcome me with a loving look into rest and safety. However brave a face I might have put on most of the time, I knew my coward heart was yearning all the while for a home-nest and a welcome into it, and you seemed to promise me both. (Royce, 72–73)

THE MINERS

For most, however, the promise was gold. Whether they'd arrived by ship in San Francisco or by pack train over the mountains, all wanted to get to the gold regions as soon as possible. There the gold-seekers, most of whom had no prior knowledge of mining, had to learn how to find and extract the gold. Some had phenomenal success; others barely scraped by; still others quickly realized that fortune lay not in mining but in supplying the miners with goods and services. This varied society, constantly improvising, experimenting, finding ad hoc solutions to conditions as they found them, in the space of a few years brought change—in California and in themselves—that was irrevocable.

Who were these miners? Most were young, under 30 years of age. Over 90 percent were male. "A grey beard was almost as rare as a petticoat," wrote one contemporary. Almost 25 percent were foreign born, a fact that Dame Shirley affirms:

> You will hear in the same day, almost at the same time, the lofty melody of the Spanish language, the piquant polish of the French . . . the silver, changing clearness of the Italians, the harsh gangle of the German, the hissing precision of the English, the liquid sweetness of the Kanaka, and the sleep-inspiring languor of the East Indian. To complete the catalogue, there is the *native* Indian, with his guttural vocabulary of twenty words! . . . I fancy them a living polyglot of the languages, a perambulatory picture gallery, illustrative of national variety in form and feature. (Clappe [Shirley], 109)

Although some, like Sarah Royce and her husband, stayed to establish prominent California families, many did not see California as a permanent residence but rather as a place to exploit before returning home. Because of the cost ($750–$1,000 for transportation and equipment when an eastern workman could expect $1 per day), few of the first gold-seekers were of the laboring class. Lawyers, teachers, and doctors were represented among them, as were farmers, sailors, merchants, blacksmiths, and tanners; there were, however, few ministers. Dame Shirley wrote of a distinguished-looking man, an "accomplished monte-dealer and horse-jockey" who was rumored to have been a minister in the States (Clappe [Shirley], 124).

Despite their relative scarcity, it was the "poor workman . . . one accustomed to manual labor [who] has a better chance of wealth than one who has hitherto been ashamed to dig," argued "V.J.F." in a letter home. He continued, "The carpet knights and silken striplings, who are perhaps leaving their mother's sides for the first time, are scarcely capable of sustaining the hardships, privations, and exposure—the digging, delving, and washing, by which the precious metal is obtained. It requires a greater sacrifice not only of the comforts but also of the necessities of life, than is generally imagined" (Wyman, *California* 29–30). Daniel Woods recalls with astonishment one of these misfits:

He seemed to have just turned out of Broadway, or to have been turned out of a bandbox. He was exquisite, even to the white kid gloves, eye-glass, and Cologne water, with dancing pumps, and a small gold box suspended about his neck by a gold chain, in which to put his gold. With his dirk-knife, elegantly chased, he would go into a hole already dug, and spend an hour in scraping the dirt from the rocks, which he washed with great care, putting the few scales in the gold box around his neck. He had been transplanted from some greenhouse to these rough mountains and soon faded away and died. (Woods, 177)

Leonard Kip, reminiscing about his 1849 experiences, recalled that less than half those who came to the mines stayed; the majority sought some other livelihood in the cities. Those who stayed did so for a variety of reasons. Kip identified four classes that made up the majority of miners. There were those for whom mining provided the excitement of gambling; they believed, despite the probabilities, they they would strike it rich. There were those who were happy to be working for themselves rather than for an employer; being their own masters compensated for low pay. There were others whose "vicious temperament" attracted them to a life in which, without fear of punishment, they could "drink, fight, and gamble, and indeed, do anything except steal and murder." And there were those who, lured to California by "specious hopes," remained, trapped in the mines by their failure (Holliday, 176).

Nearly all these men were amateurs who had to learn mining techniques in the field. Under the most favorable conditions, with abundant surface deposits, gold was easily recovered by using spoons, knives, and shovels to scoop paydirt from riverbanks and riverbeds. However, after the first flush, mining techniques grew ever more complicated, initially requiring the collaboration of three to five men; then, as greater mechanization was applied, the investment of significant capital became necessary.

The most common form of mining during the gold rush was placer mining, in which the gold, found mixed with gravel and dirt, was shaken free. The simplest implement for this method of extrication was a pan (or *batea*, as the Mexicans called it); thus, the method is known as panning. E. Gould Buffum, who spent six months in the gold fields in 1849–50, describes this process:

Mining Techniques

The process of pan-washing is the simplest mode of separating the golden particles from the earth with which it is amalgamated. A common-sized tin pan is filled with the soil containing the gold. This is taken to the nearest water and sunk until the water overspreads the surface of the pan. The earth is then thoroughly mixed with water and the stones taken out with the hand. A half rotary motion is given to the pan with both hands; and, as it is filled, it is lifted from the water, and the loose light dirt which rises to the surface washed out, until the bottom of the pan is nearly reached. The gold being heavier than the earth, sinks by its own weight to the bottom, and is there found at the close of the washing, mixed with a heavy black sand. This is placed in a cup or another pan till the day's labor is finished, when the whole is dried before the fire and the sand carefully blown away. (Buffum, 72)

A slightly more sophisticated mechanism for separating gold was the cradle. John Edwin Banks describes its use:

The cradle is shaped much as its name would indicate; usual length four to five feet, breadth at the bottom twelve inches, the top eighteen, a box placed on top and in the back occupying one third its length. The box contains a screen to prevent large stones or lumps of earth from passing through. Just below this is an apron, or cloth, sloping towards the back of the cradle so that the earth and water must pass through its whole length. The bottom of the cradle is divided by two or three bars to prevent the gold from washing out, which, being much heavier than any of its neighbors, is caught here. The cradle is placed on legs over the stream; the operator seats himself on the left, using his right hand to dash in water while he rocks with the other. The screen is made of zinc, sheet iron, tin, or sticks, the meshes one-fourth to one-half an inch in diameter. With one of these a man will wash from twelve to twenty bushels of earth per day, having one or two men in the meantime to dig and carry it to him. The last washing must be carefully performed in a pan. (qtd. in Scamehorn, 92–93)

Most diarists note that the cradle allowed three to five men to work cooperatively. Usually one shoveled dirt into the cradle, a second poured in water, a third rocked, while two others brought dirt to the river's edge. Prentice Mulford, describing his first trial-and-error efforts at using a borrowed cradle by himself, wryly demonstrates the need for partners:

I had no teacher [in the use of the cradle], and was obliged to become acquainted with all its peculiarities by myself. First I set it on a dead level. As it had no "fall" the sand would not run out. But the hardest work of all was to dip and pour the water from the dipper [onto] the gravel in the sieve with one hand and rock the cradle with the other. There was a constant tendency on the part of the hand and arm employed in pouring to go through the

"Daguerreotype of flume in the bed of a river, late 1850." Reproduced courtesy of The Bancroft Library. 1905.16242 (85). Late 1850 daguerreotype of a flume, probably in Feather or Yuba River mines. The whirling paddle wheels turned by the force of the flume powered pumps that removed water from claims in deep parts of the river bed.

motion of rocking and *vice versa*. . . . I seemed cut up into two individuals, between whom existed a troublesome and perplexing difference of opinion as to their respective duties and functions. Such a conflict, to all intents and purposes, of two different minds inside of and acting on one body, shook it up fearfully and tore it all to pieces. I was as a house divided against itself and could not stand. However, at last the physical and mental elements thus warring with each other inside of me made up their differences, and the left hand rocked the cradle peacefully while the right hand poured harmoniously, and the result was about $1.50 a day. Soon after I found my first mining partner. (Mulford, *Story* 95–96)

As more miners swarmed into the fields (it is estimated that in 1852, 100,000 were actively engaged in mining), it became increasingly harder to find gold along the riverbanks. Thus, the rivers themselves were turned out of their courses. Knowing that gold lay in alluvial deposits, miners constructed dams and dug new channels into which the rivers were turned.

Buffum noted that in one spring and summer fifteen different points on the North Fork of the American River had been so diverted. To dam a space of approximately thirty feet took two weeks of back-breaking labor in digging, moving dirt, and wrestling rocks. Such labor was not always rewarded, for in some locations little or no gold was found. He estimates, however, that an average for productive locations was $50 per day per man (Buffum, 78–79). Banks, however, tells of his group laboring for three months with nothing to show for it.

To provide water for the washing process, some companies built intricate aqueduct-like sluices. But water—or lack thereof, because rivers had been diverted—sometimes caused trouble. Those working downstream no longer had necessary water. Banks tells of one instance in which downstream miners came up to a place where a dam had been constructed, threatening to destroy it. Those who had worked so long on it replied they'd defend the dam with their lives. They did so, shooting thirteen men caught in the act of tearing down the dam. He tells of another location where two "gentlemen" agreed to settle the dispute over water by a duel. Their hands shook so badly that no one was hurt. And that, wrote Banks, "is one of the last evidences of civilization being in these parts" (qtd. in Scamehorn, 135). Despite several meetings held among the miners in his location, the "end result is to get water *if you can*" (qtd. in Scamehorn, 156).

Though offering no legal solution to such squabbles, Buffum foresaw the necessity of combining capital and labor. "As yet no scientific apparatus has been introduced, and severe manual labor has produced . . . golden results. When steam and money are united for the purpose, I doubt not that the whole waters of the North and Middle Forks will be turned from their channels, and immense canals dug through the mountains to bear them off" (Buffum, 79). The time of the individual miner working with primitive tools was drawing to a close.

One successful combination of capital and science was hydraulic mining, by which a powerful stream of water from a large hose was directed against hillsides to reach the gold buried there. Devised in 1853 by Edward E. Matteson of Connecticut, this method opened new sources after placer mining had exhausted the gold from riverbeds. An article from the Sacramento *Weekly Union* in 1854 described the process by which 120 feet of hillside were washed away to reveal bedrock:

With a perpendicular column of water 120 feet high, in a strong hose . . . , ten men who own the claim are enabled to run off hundreds of tons of dirt daily. So great is the force employed, that two men with the pipes, by directing streams of water against the base of a high bank, will . . . cause immense slides of earth, which often bring with them large trees and heavy boulders. To carry off these immense masses of dirt, they have constructed two sluices. . . . After these immense masses of earth are undermined and brought down by streams forced from the pipes, those same streams are turned upon the tons of fallen earth, and it melts away before them, and is carried away through the sluices with almost as much rapidity as if it were a bank of snow. No such labor-saving power has ever [before] been introduced to assist the miner in his operations. (Rice, Bullough, and Orsi, 183)

However efficient this technique, it ravaged the terrain and was prohibited in 1884 because of the pollution it caused. (Hart, 200; Rice, Bullough, and Orsi, 182).

Yet another method of mining that combined science and capital—quartz, hard rock, or lode mining—involved sinking shafts and bringing ore to the surface. Early on, such ore was crushed by the *arrastra* introduced by Mexican miners. A mule dragged grinding stones through a circular rock-lined trough to pulverize gold-bearing quartz. (Later, steam power and stamping machines accomplished the task.) Next, mercury or quicksilver was used to separate the gold from the pulverized rock. Bayard Taylor observed that quicksilver might well be used by individual miners. Mixing quicksilver with some of the sand left after panning or rocking would create an amalgam. The quicksilver could be evaporated by heating the amalgam in a retort. The result: gold that had previously been unobtainable. The human consequences, as we shall see later, were less golden.

Earnings   The total annual value of gold extracted at the height of the gold rush was phenomenal, even stated in mid-nineteeth century dollars (Rice, Bullough, and Orsi, 185):

1848	$245,000
1849	$10,151,360
1850	$41,273,106
1851	$75,938,232
1852	$81,294,700
1853	$67,613,487
1854	$69,433,931
1855	$55,485,395

The figures, of course, would be much higher converted into 1998 dollars.

With a combination of hard work and luck, people made fabulous sums during the early years. Robert and Charles Springer wrote home in September 1849: "We have worked eight days and have made $16,000. . . . A man that will half work can make a great fortune in three years" (Wyman, *California* 78–79). Rumor or hearsay sometimes exaggerated the sum. "I was told," wrote "Mifflin" in October 1849, "that a friend of mine has started for St. Louis . . . with $100,000 worth of dust, and that Col. Fremont took $90,000 to San Francisco the other day" (Wyman, *California* 82). William Swain garnered an ounce—worth $16—on his first day in the diggings, $35 on the second, and $92 on the third. "I picked up a lump worth $51 which cost me no more labor than stooping down to pick it up." He readily admitted that such days' profits were not common but that they "set the tone and character to the affairs of California," causing an inflation in the costs of provisions, merchandise, and labor. "The merchant," he wrote, "when told that men find from $16 to $100 a day, very readily concludes they can easily pay $1 for a pound of potatoes or $2 for a pound of dried apples . . . [which] in the state of New York [cost] half a cent for the former and four cents for the latter" (Holliday, 331).

Wages also were inflated. So many men were rushing to the mines that in San Francisco few workmen could be had at any price. In Sacramento in August 1849, "common workmen are worth from $10 to $16 a day and scarce at that" (Wyman, *California* 77). At Sutter's Fort in January 1850, "a good cook in a public house gets from $200 to $300 per month; a boy of eighteen years of age, in the Masonic and Odd Fellows' Hospital, gets $150 per month" (Wyman, *California* 88). But costs also rose. Board on the Feather River in September 1849 "is worth $10 a day, and rough at that" (Wyman, *California* 78). John Edwin Banks, starting to make planks for constructing a dam, was conscious of costs: "Got two axes ground; one dollar each for the use of a grindstone, two dollars for the use of a cross-cut saw per day, also two dollars for the use of a broad-axe per day, and sixteen dollars if it is injured. This is one way to make money" (qtd. in Scamehorn, 123).

Moreover, despite hard work most miners were not consistently lucky. Prentice Mulford noted that with all the delays caused by weather and construction problems, the claim from which he had anticipated great riches "settled down to an average of two and a half to three dollars per day" (*Story* 104). Writing to her sister, Dame Shirley tried to correct the impression she'd left in an earlier letter describing a "lucky strike" in which a man gleaned $256 from a single "basin of gold." "Such luck is as rare as the winning of a hundred thousand dollar prize in a lottery. We are acquainted with many here whose gains have *never* amounted to much more than 'wages'; that is, from six to eight dollars a day. And a 'claim' which yields a man a steady income of ten dollars *per diem*, is considered as very valuable" (Clappe [Shirley], 76). This is corroborated by a miner who scrupulously recorded what he and his partner made in September and October 1849. Daily totals equaled: $23.00, $37.00, $28.00, $23.00, $22.00, $24.00, $28.00, $26.50, $20.00, $28.00, $21.50, $64.00, $36.00, $50.00, $24.00, $24.00, $51.00, $35.00, $20.00, $21.00, $35.00, $20.00, $28.99, $24.00, $32.99, $24.00, $1.50, $20.00, $32.50, $30.50, $24.00, and $20.00 (Wyman, *California* 84–85).

These figures, it should be remembered, are for 1849; as more entered the mines, the average daily wage fell. Historians have computed the average daily wages for white miners (see below; Rice, Bullough, and Orsi, 186); generally nonwhite miners, especially Chinese, were relegated to areas already worked over and thus had lower yields.

1848	$20
1849	$16
1850	$10
1851	$8
1852	$6
1853–55	$5

Granted, such daily income sounded attractive to workers back in "the States" who were taking home $1 to $1.25 a day. But the disappointment when the dream didn't pan out was bitter. As early as August 10, 1850, O. H. Chapman wrote from Weavertown, telling his family back in Ohio of his safe arrival. Already he realized the prospects of success were "sadly humbugged." He had heard rumors that on the larger streams "every foot of ground is occupied by claims" and there were thus thousands who couldn't even get the chance to dig (Scamehorn, 189 n.12).

Hardships of Mining

Though most did not experience the bonanza they'd expected, they either wouldn't or couldn't go home immediately. Some simply did not have the cost of transportation. Others couldn't face having failed in an adventure everyone had expected to be profitable. So they stayed, enduring much hardship. It is worth looking at the conditions of their everyday life.

First and foremost, mining demanded hard physical work in extremely uncomfortable conditions. After the first "lucky strikes," finding "color" required hours of attacking rock with pickaxes, bending and hoisting water (which weighs eight pounds per gallon) into the cradle, excavating boulders from riverbeds, and moving them to build dams. Just to get to their claim, miners had to hike up and down precipitous mountainsides.

Separating the gold from sand, dirt, or gravel usually meant standing in the river, frigid from melting snows, while the sun beat down. One could be wet from icy streams below the waist and from sweat above. And, after a day of such backbreaking labor, the miner returned to his cabin or tent to cook his dinner, bake bread for the next day, and then fall into his blankets on the ground, still in his clothes that were clammy from the day's work. He did remove his boots, often using them as a pillow. During his sleep he was frequently pestered by fleas or mosquitoes and often so overrun with rats that cats became welcome companions. Indeed, William Perkins was once offered one ounce of gold dust for every pound his cat weighed, so eager were other miners to have a mouser (Perkins, 166).

In 1851 Dame Shirley tried her hand at mining-for-a-day. Her description of being a "mineress" is unintentionally ironic. To get her sister a souvenir—$3.25 worth of gold dust—"I wet my feet, tore my dress, spoiled a pair of new gloves, nearly froze my fingers, got an awful headache, took cold, and lost a valuable breastpin" (Clappe [Shirley], 76). Prentice Mulford knew the pain of unexpectedly hitting a boulder with his pick, the vibrations traveling "like a shock along the iron, up the handle, and into one's arm and 'crazy bone'" (*Story* 108). He knew firsthand how debilitating such work was—it quickly made a man look ten years older than he was. "You can't keep up this sort of thing—digging, tugging, lifting, wet to the skin day after day, summer and winter, with no interval of rest, but a steady drag twelve months of the year—without paying for it. There's dissipation of muscle as well as in the use of whiskey" (*Story* 113). Another miner advised friends at home, "The work here is very hard. $1 a day in New York is better than $10 here" (Wyman, *California* 75). Bayard Taylor likewise tried to disabuse those who thought gold mining was an easy way to gain a fortune. "If anyone expects to dig treasures out of the earth, in California, without severe labor, he is wofully [sic] mistaken. Of all classes of men, those who pave streets and quarry limestone are best adapted for gold diggers" (Taylor, 87). Something of the desperation of those "lawyers, doctors, clergymen, farmers, soldiers [and] deserters" who have flocked to the gold fields was captured by Daniel B. Woods:

This morning, notwithstanding the rain, we were again at our work. We *must* work. In sunshine and rain, in warm and cold, in sickness and health, successful or not, early and late, it is work, *work* WORK! *Work or perish!* [We work] not for *gold*, but for *bread*. . . . Cheerful words are seldom heard, more seldom the boisterous shout and laugh which indicate success, and which, when heard, sink to a lower ebb the spirits of the unsuccessful. We have [today] made 50 cents each. (Woods, 103)

On sites often named for the first person who worked them (Owesley's Bar, for example) or for notable events (Murderer's, Rattlesnake, Rich, or Condemned Bars, for example), miners' clothing was simple: a pair of heavy pants, often corduroy, tucked into heavy rubber boots; a flannel shirt, usually red or blue; a heavy leather belt into which a Colt's revolver was stuck; and a shapeless hat. There was no one to dress for, and the work quickly tore and snagged clothes. This necessitated yet another chore: the miner had to learn how to wield a needle to patch his clothes. Although many wore the same clothing day after day, James L. Tyson, a doctor/miner, recommended a change of "under clothing" and socks for health's sake.

Meals necessary to sustain the miner's physical activity were filling but not necessarily nutritious; moreover, food was quite expensive in part because it had to be packed in at a cost of from 50 cents to 60 cents per pound. Staples **Food and Drink for the Miners** included flour, salt, jerked meat, bacon, and coffee. For variety there were sometimes dried apples, stewed; boiled potatoes, sliced and fried in lard; mince pie made of "salt beef previously soaked to freshness, dried apples, molasses, and vinegar in lieu of cider" (Mulford, *Story* 115–16). Milk was a luxury costing more than whiskey, though some ambitious miners invested in a cow or two to fill this need. One such entrepreneur, however, returned from mining to discover his cow had eaten his tent and his sweat-soaked change of clothes in its need for salt. Prentice Mulford recalls buying an entire sack of rice for variety— and economy. He did not know, however, that "rice swells amazingly." His first pot "swelled up, forced off the lid, and oozed over. Then I shoveled rice by the spoonful into everything empty which I could find in the cabin. Even the washbasin was full of half-boiled rice. Still it kept on. I saw then that I had put in too much—far too much." After repeated experiments with this astonishing grain, and a "gradually decreased appetite for rice," Mulford calculated that it would take "seven years on that Bar ere I could eat all the rice in that sack" (*Story* 184). Though told with self-deprecating humor, the incident reveals the difficulties many of the miners found in learning to live without women. Fresh fruits and vegetables, except for potatoes and occasional onions at 90 cents per pound, were virtually unheard of in the mines. In Dry Diggingsville in October 1849, a cabbage cost $1 (Wyman, *California*, 145).

Food prices generally were higher in the mines than in the cities. John Banks traveled from his claim to Coloma to buy potatoes at 75 cents per pound; in the mountains they would have cost $1.50 (Scamehorn, 109) During the winter of 1849–50 when communication with Sacramento was cut off by the rains, prices rose in the mines. Flour and pork cost from $1.00 to $1.50 per pound, and other things in proportion (Wyman, *California* 88). Even in reasonably good weather, freight costs increased

"Bringing lunch to gold diggers in Auburn Ravine, 1852." Reproduced courtesy of the California History Room, California State Library, Sacramento, California. While few women actually mined, many ran boarding houses, took in laundry, and baked. They worked hard and often amassed small fortunes—thus illustrating the larger truth that it was not the miners themselves, but those who supplied their goods and services, who made the expected bonanza.

prices enormously. J. D. Stevenson wrote to his son-in-law in New York that a barrel of flour costing $12 in San Francisco would cost $12 more in freight to Sutter's Fort and $125 more to the nearest mine, thus costing $152 per barrel in the mountains (Wyman, *California* 144). E. Gould Buffum cited prices in the mines during the winter of 1849–50:

> Flour was selling at one dollar per pound, dried beef at two dollars, sugar at a dollar, coffee seventy-five cents, molasses four dollars per gallon, pork two dollars per pound, miserable New England rum at fifty cents per glass or eight dollars per bottle and tobacco at two dollars per pound. At these prices, the trader and transporter realized a greater profit from the miner's labour than the miner himself. (Buffum, 96)

The consequences of such a diet soon became clear. J. D. Stevenson noticed that many men "who came into the town with long purses of the precious metal are broken in health and constitution." He had heard that scurvy had broken out and expected more of it due to lack of fresh vegetables (Wyman, *California* 144–45). Buffum was among the victims of "land scurvy" and describes his own symptoms: swelling and severe pain in his legs, which he at first thought was rheumatism; swelling and bleeding of his gums; increased swelling in his legs, which eventually "turned completely black" and left him unable to work. He treated himself with boiled sprouts from beans apparently spilled from a teamster's pack, and a "decoction of the bark of the Spruce tree." Recovering enough to get into Coloma, he lived on a vegetable diet—at $3 per pound for potatoes—and recovered (Buffum, 97–99).

Health and Disease of the Miners

Many miners had arrived sick or weakened from their overland journey. Many complained of colds, rheumatism, and arthritis—not surprising, considering the time spent in icy streams. Diarrhea is often mentioned, as are dysentery, typhoid, and, occasionally, cholera. Poison oak grew lushly through most of the mining region, as many were to discover; William Perkins swelled up twenty-four hours after contact, his hands and feet and face so severely swollen that he was blinded for three days (Perkins, 93–94). John Banks fainted one night, the only time in his life; the reason is unclear, though it may have been from exhaustion or possibly from "fantish" (rancid) rice. He narrowly missed smashing his head against his fireplace. One of the more bizarre deaths was recorded by William Perkins—that of a young Canadian who died after eating fresh pork. It turned out that people had set out arsenic to kill rats, and the pig had consumed the dead rats. The meat, nonetheless, was sold by "unprincipled vagabond dealers ... who richly deserve lynching" (Perkins, 302). And, of course, when miners used quicksilver, they suffered from mercury poisoning. Prentice Mulford describes the results of heating the mercury/gold amalgam to evaporate the mercury:

> The [mercury] covered walls, tables, and chairs with a fine, frost-like coating, and on rubbing one's finger over any surface a little globule of quicksilver would roll up before it. Then we went to Chinese Camp and gave the doctor about half our individual week's dividends to get the mercury out of us. Three weeks of sore mouths and loosened teeth followed this ... exposure. It was through such experiences as these that we became in California practical mineralogists. (Mulford, *Story* 104)

Besides disease, there were accidents aplenty. William Perkins blamed most accidents, including falling into water-filled pits and drowning, on drunkenness (117). As on the overland journey, guns accidentally discharged. People were swept away by streams suddenly flooded by winter rains or melting snow. Snakes, including rattlesnakes, came into campsites, especially in dry seasons; Banks recalls killing one that "was among our dishes" (qtd. in Scamehorn, 123). Grizzly bears still abounded in the mountains. One broke a man's arm so badly that it had to be amputated (Scamehorn, 125). Many accidents occurred during construction of dams or diverting of rivers; rocks loosely piled up fell, crushing and bruising men in their way, and sometimes breaking bones. Banks tells of a man who died from taking too much opium (qtd. in Scamehorn, 126–27).

There were far from adequate physicians present to care for those laid low by disease or accident, though Dame Shirley's husband was one of them. Some doctors clearly sought to cash in on the bonanza. "A physician's fee," reports Banks, is "an ounce of gold, no matter how short the distance may be." And most were young and inexperienced (qtd. in Scamehorn, 93). Although one man who broke his leg was amazed at the generosity of his fellow miners, who, in twenty-four hours, collected $200 for his care, a "Mr. McMeans" opened a hospital in Salmon Falls and required $12 in advance—or securities—before admitting a patient (Scamehorn, 136). In Sonora, however, a public subscription raised money for a hospital where "the sick of all nations are tended by nurses and a good physician" (Perkins, 116). Banks told of a Dr. Swan, "famed, if not for his skill, certainly for heavy charges." He charged six ounces of gold to ride five miles to a patient; his total bill was nearly $400, of which the young man could pay only $289 because he continued to be sick for months after his treatment and thus could not work. Nonetheless, the doctor sued him for payment. A jury of miners, however, determined that the doctor should return $89 to the patient and pay court costs of nearly $200 (qtd. in Scamehorn, 139). William B. Royall had similar complaints: "Physicians are all making fortunes in this country; they will hardly look at a man's tongue for less than an ounce of gold! I have known Doctors, although they are scarcely worthy of the title (for the most of them here are quacks), charge a patient as much as one hundred dollars for one visit and prescription" (Wyman, *California* 158).

The doctor, however, could sometimes be the victim. James L. Tyson treated a man who "had been on a drunken frolic, and whooping and yelling as such characters are apt to do . . . had fallen and dislocated his lower jaw." Tyson popped it back in place, much to the man's delight. Though he left with many thanks and promised to return in the afternoon to settle his bill, Tyson "never saw him afterward" (Tyson, 71–72). Tyson noted that some people, "either from inability or disinclination to pay for medical attention," chose to treat themselves. They frequently died, "or they were walking shadows for months, with impaired intellects, and rarely recovered their accustomed vigor." Though he may not have been entirely objective about those who tried home remedies, Dr. Tyson's assessment of the ravages of mining on general health was clear: "I never saw more broken-down constitutions than I witnessed during my stay in California, and few who work in the mines, ever carry home their usual full health" (Tyson, 80).

In addition to deaths from disease and accidents, there were suicides committed by men disillusioned by poverty after months of hard work. Men who had come to California with high hopes of striking it rich grew despondent as they returned to Stockton or Sacramento or San Francisco with the hope of earning just enough to pay their way back home. Some attempted to work their way home as firemen or stewards on the steamships. Those who found no such escape became truly despondent. One contemporary source, clearly exaggerating, claimed that suicides caused by disappointment were as numerous as deaths resulting from natural causes (Wyman, *California* 85). Daniel Woods records twelve suicides in October 1849, enough to concern the congregation at the tent chapel in San Francisco. He cites the case of a young man who went to the outskirts of the city, meticulously removed his tie, took his razor from its case, and carefully cut his throat (Woods, 72). John Banks described another suicide attempt. A man who had been sick for several weeks and despairing of regaining health gashed his throat three times with a butcher knife. Though he cut deep into his windpipe, he was too weak to cut his jugular and languished for several days before he died (qtd. in Scamehorn, 145).

Of course, there were also deaths caused by casual recreational violence. With the prevalence of knives and guns carried on miners' persons, it was not unlikely that a fight, often caused by drunkenness, escalated from fists to more lethal weapons. However, early on, there was little actual crime despite literal **Crime and Justice** lawlessness. Perhaps because everyone harbored the hope of finding vast wealth, there appeared to be little need to steal. People safely left their tools on site, and there are numerous accounts of miners leaving sacks of gold dust unattended—and unmolested—in their tents as they were at work all day digging for more.

A pragmatic ad hoc democracy tailored rules to local conditions. Staking claims illustrates this process. Where gold deposits were especially rich, claims might be as small as ten feet square. In other localities a miner might be required to stand in the center of his "dig" and heave his pick as far as he could to establish the corner boundaries of his claim. His name having been recorded, the miner would leave his pick and shovel to mark his claim; in one locale if he had not returned by the first of June, when water would have subsided enough to work the claim, any other man could take his place (Scamehorn, 116). Near the town of

Eldorado a company could claim as much of the stream as it could drain (Scamehorn, 124). Committees elected in each camp or mining district made up the rules, applying solid common sense. Many such rules established by local committees were so sound that they later were incorporated into the California mining codes and water laws.

However, with the influx of thousands of miners from all over the United States and the world came some with checkered pasts. Such fugitives from the law elsewhere were the subjects of a contemporary ballad:

> What was your name in the States?
> Was it Johnson or Thompson or Bates?
> Did you murder your wife and flee for your life?
> O, what was your name in the States?   (qtd. in Rice, Bullough,
>   and Orsi, 185)

Crime, when it did occur, was dealt with swiftly and decisively. W. B. Royall outlined legal principles succinctly: "The best of law prevails; the law of honor. A man may set his gold in the street, and no one dare touch it, for death is inevitably the reward of the rogue" (qtd. in Wyman, *California* 177). There were no jails; moreover, while wanting to enforce justice or at least deter further crime, miners wanted to get back to their claims as soon as possible. J. Goldsborough Bruff remembers one man who stole two bags of gold dust and was sentenced to have his head shaved, his ears cropped, and then to be whipped with a gun-cleaning rod before being banished from town (Bruff, 313). In other locations lashes were laid on with riatas (or lariats); a quick exodus was encouraged by promising an additional fifty lashes on the bare back each day the miscreant stayed in town (Bruff, 450–53). Bayard Taylor justifies the punishment one man received for stealing ninety-eight pounds of gold: he received 100 lashes, had his head shaved, and had both ears cut off.

> It may conflict with popular ideas of morality but, nevertheless, this extreme course appeared to have produced good results. In fact, in a country without not only bolts and bars, but any effective system of law and government, this Spartan severity of discipline seemed to be the only security against the most frightful disorder. The result was that, except for some petty acts of larceny, thefts were rare. . . . [T]he risk was so great that such plunder could not be carried on to any extent. (Taylor, 92–93)

When the crime was murder, capital punishment—by hanging or shooting—was employed. Usually people were executed after a trial by a jury hastily assembled from among the miners. In other instances criminals underwent "Judge Lynch's Court"—arrest, a voice vote from the citizenry, sometimes a mob, and almost immediate stringing up. One of the most extreme examples of lynch law occurred in Dry Diggings. There, five miners who spoke only Spanish or French were caught stealing and were immediately flogged. Two of them were accused of previous theft and murder and—without proof of guilt—were hung. For years afterwards, Dry Diggings was called Hangtown.

Especially as anti-foreign sentiments grew, non-Americans were the victims of harsh punishment that was intended, in part, as a deterrent to crime. Sometimes bandits took on the status of folk-hero. Joaquin Murietta was one such character, though there is uncertainty as to whether he was actually only one man or a composite of many. At any rate, Frank Marryat described the grotesque end of "a famous Mexican robber, Joaquin Carillo." With much effort and loss of life, he had finally been caught in 1851 and decapitated:

> When I left San Francisco his head was to be seen by the curious preserved in spirits of wine; and however revolting such a spectacle may be, it is a punishment that one would think would deter the reflective from crime. Fancy one's features distorted by the convulsive throes of violent death, staring whitened and ghastly from a glass bottle, turned from with horror by the gaping crowd, and then deposited, for all ages, growing more hideous with each year on the shelves of a surgical museum! (Marryat, 183)

Life—and death—in the mines was often brutal, always hard. But on occasions miners did find relaxation **Entertainment** and entertainment. Winter was a slack time in the mines because of snow and rain. Some miners thus went into nearby towns or even to San Francisco; others waited out the time in their mountain cabins. Those who stayed entertained themselves or simply relaxed from the back-breaking labor. They slept in, played cards, washed their clothes, read, and speculated on their next year's success. Miners were hungry for news from the East, so old copies of newspapers were read assiduously, even when they were months old. Those who could not afford candles (at $4 a pound) by which to read would build a small brush fire, and as one miner kept the fire going, his partner would read aloud (Woods, 103). Though Bayard Taylor claims never to have seen miners read, other diarists make repeated references to books. And despite the primitive life many led, most readers preferred good books to trash. John Banks recalls reading "several romances," only one of which, *Trapper's Bride*, was good.

For many who came overland, books had been one of the first items jettisoned because of their weight. Many of the novels Banks saw on the trail or in California "were written by depraved minds." But on the shelves of his cabin he had "quite a number" of good things to read: mostly medical books and magazines, *Knickerbocker's* and *Blackwoods* and the *Edinburgh Review*, an old copy of a biography of great men, Lyell's *Geology*, two books of philosophy, and "an English work entitled *Dialogues of Devils*," which "comes far short of *Paradise Lost*" (qtd. in Scamehorn, 105, 152). Prentice Mulford remembered that as early as 1854 or 1855 the "boys" at Hawkin's Bar pooled their money and sent down to San Francisco for books to establish a library including geology books and a full set of American encyclopedias: "heavy and nutritious mental food rising into the lighter desserts of poetry and novels "(*Story* 92). He described one miner who read as he ate; he "devoured beef and lard, bacon and beans and encyclopedias, Humboldt's 'Cosmos' and dried apples, novels and physical nourishment at . . . the same time" (*Story* 92, 181).

However, not all miners were readers, nor were books everywhere available. Consequently, many miners enjoyed other activities in the mining towns. High on the list were drinking and gambling. Lacking any other home or social circle, they frequented tavern tents where, according to J. D. Stevenson, "cards are the only books to be found." Though miners might be cautious at first, as more liquor was consumed and stakes raised, many left to sleep on the ground and awaken "with aching heads and empty purses" (Wyman, *California* 175). However, whether in the mining camps or in Sacramento or San Francisco, the saloon was often the "best house" in town, offering miners what might have been their only aesthetic experience. The saloon was built of wood when surrounding businesses were still of canvas; often the decor included gilt-framed mirrors and paintings; musicians frequently added to the ambience with instruments including piano, flute, violin, cello, and trumpet; and in Sacramento "Ethiopian melodists . . . nightly call upon 'Susanna!' and entreat to be carried back to Old Virginny" (Taylor, *El Dorado*, vol. 2, 29). One miner recalled that nearly everyone drank, and that of one hundred people passing his cabin, "twenty or thirty go reeling." Much behavior seemed predicated on a single goal: to make money. Another miner, somewhat shocked, wrote of a doctor who "keeps a trading post, sells whiskey, etc. through the week, drinks brandy freely and preaches on Sunday. Who cares? Not the Devil!" (Holliday, 336).

Since mining itself was so often a matter of luck, it is not surprising that games of chance were popular. The most commonly played game was monte, though dealers were also adept at euchre, faro, grab, and vingt-et-un. Professional gamblers followed miners to every new strike.

Their diggings are in the pockets of the miners and not in the pockets of the [river] bars. . . . They offer the simple and foolish as good a chance to lose the results of months of labor and privation in an hour as is done in the more showy and magnificent halls in the city.... Generally a few days spent in one place is sufficient to drain the font of the gambling miner's stream, and when all have 'come down with the dust' who will pay tribute to folly, the gambler rolls up his blanket, shoulders his pile, and climbs to another bar. (Holliday, 336)

In San Francisco and Sacramento, "from good authority we are told that there are several Methodist ministers . . . now dealing monte . . . for the purpose of gain" (Holliday, 336). Repeatedly, the gold rush allowed people to redefine themselves.

Moreover, the saloons and gambling houses allowed miners to enjoy the presence of women, who were decidedly scarce in California. About the attractions of one gambling house, one miner wrote that in addition to a "splendidly" stocked bar and a band of musicians, "abandoned women visit these places openly. I saw one the other evening sitting quietly at the monte table, dressed in white pants, blue coat, and cloth cap, curls dangling over her cheeks, cigar in her mouth and a glass of punch at her side. She handled a pile of doubloons with her blue kid gloved hands, and bet most boldly" (Wyman, *California*, 176). William Perkins reflected on all such activities: "The want of respectable female society, rational amusements, and books, has aided greatly to demoralization of many whose natural character would have kept them aloof from temptation had there been any other means but the gambling houses and drinking saloons, to have assisted them in whiling away the hours not devoted to labor" (Perkins, 290).

Though less frequently noted, there was other recreation. One man mentioned going pistol shooting in the cemetery (Perkins, 296). Another forked out $2 to spend an evening in a leaking tent to watch a "circus," apparently consisting mostly of juggling and acrobatics (Scamehorn, 158). Several mentioned attending a bull and bear fight, in which the two animals were tethered just within reach of each other and gored, gouged, scratched, and bit each other (Marryat, 131; Perkins, 273ff). In areas where there were large numbers of Mexican miners, bullfights were held. Dancing was popular. In the camps, men often had to dance with men, one wearing a handkerchief to designate himself as the "woman." In the towns, surprisingly elaborate balls were organized. William Perkins describes one in Sonora to which fifty invitations were issued:

The music was a piano, a violincello, a harp, a violin, and a couple of guitars; the dances, all those fashionable in the old world. . . . There was also plenty of singing in French and spanish; and the supper was something really wonderful for the mountains. Ices, creams, blancmange, pastry, cold ham and fowls, pheasant pies, quail pasties. . . . And then the wines! . . . Cargoes of the richest wines produced in France and the Mediterranean were sent to San Francisco in the first excitement of the gold fever. . . . For some months we had been purchasing exquisite champagnes, clarets, Burgundies, sherries, even Lachrymachristi. . . . At the supper, two dozen of claret, three dozen of champagne, and one dozen of Burgundy were consumed; a very moderate quantity. . . . It was broad daylight when the "women folks" were taken home, and we addressed ourselves to our daily duties, very well satisfied with our first Ball in California, and quite proved that our half savage life had not made us forget the steps of the Mazurka and Polka. (Perkins, 244–45)

Dame Shirley, with her rather tart tongue, told of the hazards of such a ball. Though on the evening of the ball at Indian Bar everyone behaved well, men nonetheless expectorated; as a result, "there was some danger of being swept away in a flood of tobacco juice." However, since the floor was uneven the juice collected in puddles, which dancers could usually avoid, "merely running the risk of falling prostrate upon the wet boards in the midst of a gallopade" (Clappe [Shirley], 186–87).

Homesickness Despite such occasional respites from hard work, many miners were ravaged by homesickness. Separated from family and friends, some even literally dreamed of home. This malady seemed to affect the successful as well as the failed miners. C. R. Scholl wrote that within twelve months most wished "a thousand times" to be home. E. R. Pratt wrote to his brother, "Although I am making money here, yet I am one of the most unhappy human beings on earth, and shall continue to be till I return to my family. I suppose you know that I always had a roving disposition; you may depend I am cured of it; when I get home, I shall stay there" (Wyman, *California* 81, 128). Such moroseness usually intensified on holidays, which brought memories of home. The Fourth of July, so often celebrated during the optimistic trip overland, was a lonesome day in the mines; even worse were birthdays, wedding anniversaries, and Christmas.

Homesickness was worsened by infrequent delivery of mail from home. Despite arranging with expressmen to bring mail from San Francisco to the mines at $2 to $2.50 per letter, many men went months between. Some grew so impatient they could stand it no longer. Daniel Woods rode for five days on an obstreperous mule to San Francisco— only to learn from the postmaster that his letters had just been forwarded to the mines (Woods, 70). The arrival of mail usually broke the "corroding" sense of despair. A young miner from Wisconsin wrote to his wife, "If you could have seen us when we received our letters, you would have laughed ... perhaps called us fools—such hoorahing, jumping, yelling and screaming. . . . You will take good care and write often when I tell you I live upon your letters, with a small sprinkling of pork and bread" (Holliday, 310). However, the arrival of bad news was devastating; physicians regularly withheld from their patients news of the deaths of loved ones.

In addition to the distances involved, it seems apparent that poor mail delivery was due in part to the U.S. Post Office Department failing to prepare adequately for the influx of population to California and the consequent demand for mail services. Because of the cost of overland transportation, most mail was sent by steamboats, making their arrival an eagerly anticipated event in San Francisco. When three regularly scheduled steamboats arrived with no mail during the summer of 1849, a public protest meeting was called. Finally, on the last day of October the *Panama* arrived with thirty-seven mailbags. Bayard Taylor, in the city at the time, volunteered to help the clerks sort the 45,000 letters and "bushels of newspapers." The job took over "forty-four hours of steady labor," during which time the post office was literally under siege. People pounded on the door and windows; some tried to sneak in when clerks opened the door to get a bucket of water; some tried to bribe the clerks to get their mail first. To avoid a riot when the mail was finally ready, patrons were ordered to form lines. It took a person at the end of the longest line six hours to reach the window! Some people near the front of the line sold their places for $10 or $25 and, doing so daily, made a good living. Others did too. Vendors of pies, cakes, and newspapers set up shop in front of the post office, and others carried cans of coffee to patrons waiting in line (Taylor, *El Dorado*, vol. 2, 208–13).

Of course, another cause of homesickness was the absence of women. The harbormaster at San Francisco **Women on the** in 1850 counted 35,333 men arriving as opposed to **Mining Frontier** 1,248 women. For the overland emigrants that year, the count at Fort Laramie was 39,560 men, 2,421 women, and 609 children. Most women arriving by sea stayed in San Francisco or settled in Sacramento; few went to the mines. In September 1849 a miner in Yuba City reported glumly that in the town of 2,000 there were only about a dozen women (Holliday, 354). Sarah Royce reported that the first time she attended church in San Francisco, there were only six or eight women in the whole congregation (Royce, 103). At church—and in the mining camps where she and her husband lived for several months—she was treated with extreme courtesy. Once men were cutting wood on the mountain above her home, and she heard one warn, "Look out not to let any sticks roll that way, there's a woman and child in that tent." On another occasion a young miner stopped at her tent on his way to work and asked if he could speak to her daughter Mary, "about the size of a little sister I left at home" (Royce, 80). Many women who were widowed on the overland trip but had continued on had multiple proposals of marriage soon after their arrival. John Banks, reflecting on this scarcity of women, remembered the early myth: "The Amazons got along well enough without men; Californians are trying the opposite experiment. For my part, I pronounce it a complete failure" (qtd. in Scamehorn, 130).

Though respectable women were treated with respect, a good living could be made by their fallen sisters. Like so many other commodities in California, their value reflected economic laws of supply and demand. When there were few other women, prostitutes were in demand. Some writers reflected outrage, but their censure in no way affected the business. A shocked John Banks, reflecting on the moral decadence of miners "whose only love is gold," forecast a "far more awful state of society" in the next five years. "Abandoned women seem necessary to make men fiends. These are arriving by thousands and spreading through the mines. In San Francisco fifty to one hundred dollars will buy one. Gambling is now mated" (qtd. in Scamehorn, 121). Some of these prostitutes donned men's clothes to ride horseback from camp to camp. "One celebrated character of this kind said she had made $50,000 and regretted that she had not double the capacity for increasing her gains" (Holliday, 355). But William Perkins clucks his tongue at women working in the gambling houses in Sonora, these "forms of angels in the employ of Hell." He muses, "It is terrible! and enough to make a gambler foreswear his unholy trade. And to think that these lost women were once innocent children—once the joy and pride of happy mothers—pure virtuous girls—many of them once happy wives!" Perkins, however, remains pragmatic: "But I am talking flat treason against our only polka partners. It won't do. We must lay aside some strait-laced ideas and accommodate ourselves, as best we may, to this extraordinary scene we find ourselves actors in" (Perkins, 260). Not only did the gold-seekers sometimes redefine themselves, but they allowed social conventions to mutate.

This may be seen in variations on the institution of marriage. In Sonora, Perkins reports, some "adventuresses" attach themselves to men on a semi-permanent basis, paying a "nominal tribute to virtue by giving out that they are married." Perkins questions why anyone needs to know the truth. Instead, as in so many other aspects of gold rush society, "each one strives to cover the nakedness of reality with the mantle of illusion" (Perkins, 218). Franklin A. Buck, however, could not ignore reality. He was called in 1859 to serve on a jury in a divorce court that had all the salacious details of a modern soap opera, details so embarrassing that one woman witness asked that the courtroom be closed before she'd testify. The couple, originally from Tiffin, Ohio, quarreled over her flirting with other men. The husband came to his claim one morning and announced that the "d——d bitch had gone." The wife admitted leaving, commenting on the *"qualifications* of her husband" and his inability to satisfy her; and a best friend of the wife testified that though she had seen her lying on a bed with a young man hugging her, she "didn't think there was 'anything improper' going on or she should have stopped it at once, of course" (Buck, 176–77).

Most women, however, maintained moral and social conventions. At the same time, many found ways to profit in California's booming economy. Some took in washing, a tremendous boon to men who had been sending shirts to Hawaii. Women could thus earn $50–$60 a day; at cooking, $30 a day (Holliday, 355). Others took in boarders. In October 1849 one woman from Maine wrote home that ten boarders brought in $189 a week, or $75 clear after expenses had been paid. She admitted, "I have to work mighty hard," baking all her bread in a Dutch oven and doing the rest of her cooking at a small fireplace. She also took in ironing, "making seven dollars in as many hours." However, she had absolutely no social life. "I have not been in the street since I began to keep [a boarding] house." She recognized that she'd been caught up in the mercenary drive of many Forty-Niners; "It is nothing but gold, gold . . . and I want to get my part" (Wyman, 147–48). Another woman seemed almost ebullient despite her hard work:

> I have made about $18,000 worth of pies—about one third of this has been clear profit. One year I dragged my own wood off the mountain and chopped it, and I have never had so much as a child to take a step for me in this country. $11,000 I baked in one little iron skillet, a considerable portion by a campfire, without the shelter of a tree from the broiling sun. But now I have a good many "Robinson Crusoe" comforts about me. . . . I bake about 1,200 pies per month and clear $200. . . . I intend to leave off work the coming spring, and give my business to my sister-in-law. Not that I am rich, but I need little, and have none to toil for but myself. (Wyman, *California* 149)

The experiences of these women illustrate a larger truth, that it was not the miners themselves but rather those who supplied goods and services to them who made the expected bonanza. This was especially true during 1849 before competition drove prices down. That first year witnessed enormous inflation: a boiled egg cost 75 cents. A steam engine bought for $2,000 in the East sold for $15,000. A farmer cleared $25,000 selling vegetables (Holliday, 303). Aside from the saloon keepers, boarding house operators, bakers, entertainers, prostitutes, laundresses, and gamblers, many became merchants and storekeepers; some repaired boots and shoes; some hired themselves out as day laborers to help build banks, stores, and houses in burgeoning cities such as San Francisco.

Some river captains and crews transported miners and their supplies from San Francisco to Sacramento; others operated ferries and toll bridges. Some auctioned horses and mules; others packed goods to the mines on these animals. Some delivered scarce milk or fresh meat. Others delivered even scarcer letters and, equally important, established express companies, bonded and guaranteed to carry gold dust safely to the East. As the demand for lumber increased to build flumes and dams, some went into lumbering or became sawmill operators. Some drove stage coaches. Recognizing miners' hunger for news, some established newspapers. In some localities with a larger-than-usual number of young people, some became teachers, though such men had to face jealous suitors who were upset that the schoolteacher could spend up to six hours per day with much-sought-after young women. Especially as the towns and cities grew, some speculated in real estate.

Moreover, as people realized that money could make money, many stopped sending their earnings East but rather invested it in the local economy, garnering interest that was at times as high as 10 percent per month; others loaned money to temporarily out-of-luck miners or, more frequently, for development of commercial enterprises. The economy, driven by gold and the rapid influx of emigrants, was in ferment, establishing California (especially San Francisco) as a prime commercial center to rival even New York. It is worth noting that at least two major U.S. companies—Wells Fargo and Levi Strauss—had their origins in providing goods and services to the Forty-Niners.

EFFECTS OF THE GOLD RUSH

Affecting as it did so many aspects of American society, from transportation to banking, from a sense of geography to a sense of morality, from entertainment to law, how should the gold rush experience be assessed?

First, it made the United States a more cosmopolitan, less provincial nation. New England sea captains, Missouri farmers, and Ohio tradesmen joined with Georgia miners, southern slaves, and Pennsylvania schoolteachers in the first truly national experience since the Revolution. Moreover, they shared the experience with people from all around the world, of many races and religions, some with strange languages and stranger customs. Though this exposure to diversity did not always ennoble—there were instances of rampant bigotry and legalized exclusionism, as in the Foreign Miner's Tax—it did broaden people's awareness.

Previously, as the frontier had advanced incrementally across the Appalachians into Kentucky and Tennessee and then inched toward the Mississippi and on up the Missouri, it had offered escape and hope for a new start on cheap land to people already inured to hardship. California offered hardships aplenty, but almost from the outset it also offered business opportunities for investors and entrepreneurs. It was, thus, the first American frontier that welcomed city folk, a frontier that quickly passed from the rough and primitive to the urbane and sophisticated.

By leapfrogging over half the continent to establish a populous economic center on the Pacific, the gold frontier accelerated the demands for better transportation and communication networks and more efficient implementation of government services. In the meantime, it required an ad hoc participatory democracy that demonstrated, despite its excesses, that law best evolves from social needs rather than from imposition by distant governments.

The gold rush gave people extraordinary freedom to redefine themselves, to test their previous beliefs, to become someone new, free from family tradition or social expectation. An extraordinary number transplanted old values to the new land. But perhaps because of the seemingly mythical opportunities that California offered, it legitimized material goals as well as moral expectations. In addition, material success achieved by those women who did come inaugurated a redefinition of gender relations and, perhaps, a weakening of traditional patterns of domestic life.

More quickly than other frontiers, the California gold frontier fused capital and technology to achieve economic goals, a central example of which is hydraulic mining. In this sense it also accelerated the exploitation, even destruction, of natural resources that in general marked the movement of Americans west. In short, more so than other frontiers, the gold frontier created or encouraged traits such as independence, restlessness, materialism, gender equality, and a pragmatic democracy. Collectively these defined California as America's America, a place to try, once again, to achieve the American dream.

Cowboys on the range. Reproduced from the collections of the Library of Congress. This photo suggests something of the immensity of the Plains and the cattle industry that exploited its grasslands.

5

Life on the Land: Alien Exotics—Cowboys and Settlers

For over two centuries the advance of the American frontier westward was generally into contiguous territory. But when missionaries arrived in Oregon in 1834 to preach to the Indians, their letters home told of opportunities to harvest crops and lumber as well as souls; by 1846 some 8,000 emigrants from the United States had trickled into Oregon. The 1849 California gold rush changed San Francisco from a sleepy backwater port to an international metropolis in a matter of months; the trickle had turned to a flood. For all practical purposes, the westward migration literally jumped over most of the land between the Mississippi River and the Rocky Mountains. Indeed, as late as 1870 most of the Great Plains and the Rockies had a population of less than two people per square mile. (It should be noted that during the nineteenth century, census figures referred to non-Indian population.)

Admittedly, fur traders and trappers had exploited the beaver and bison and had funneled furs and hides to metropolitan St. Louis. But permanent settlers were few, in part because prior to the Civil War the South opposed homesteading in these areas, and in part because of the myth of the Great American Desert. But gradually discoveries of gold and silver drew miners eastward from California to rapidly established interior urban centers. Moreover, the U.S. population tripled from almost 4 million at the first census in 1790 to over 12.8 million in 1830, increasing pressure to move west. That population growth, coupled with patterns of land exploitation rather than conservation—some boasted of "wearing out two or three farms in a lifetime" (Carnes and Garraty, 42)—had, by

1870, increased population in the first tier of states west of the Mississippi to 18–45 people per square mile, burgeoning in some locales to as many as 90 (Carnes and Garraty, 48).

The Great Plains is a vast region, roughly centered on the 100th meridian and stretching from the Gulf of Mexico to the Canadian border. Its climate is varied, with a mean annual average air temperature ranging from a high of 70°–75°F to a low of 35°–40°F. In the northern plains, winters are frequently marked by heavy snowfall, even blizzards, with temperatures dropping to 40, 50, or even 60° below zero. Those who work on the land—cowboys or farmers—must endure harsh extremes. Although the temperature range is wide, normal annual precipitation for the entire region is only 16–32 inches, compared to 32–48 inches for the regions east of the Mississippi.

For the area roughly between the 93rd and 103rd meridian, the natural vegetation on the plains, from Oklahoma north to the Dakotas, was tall grass. Fingers of this prairie grass extended eastward into Indiana. To the west of the prairies, extending to the Rockies, the natural groundcover was short grass. In Texas the vegetation was mixed: mesquite and creosote bush as well as grasses. Extending into the grasslands of the region along rivercourses were forests of oak, hickory, chestnut, and yellow poplar. Thus, in contrast to the eastern woodlands where land had to be cleared before it could be farmed, most of the Great Plains was ready for the plow; conversely, lumber for housing, fencing, or fuel was in short supply. (Indians of the Great Plains would make annual trips into the Rockies to secure straight poles for lodges and travois. Traditional Mandan shelter near their Missouri River gardens was sod- or earth-covered structures, shored up by cottonwood frames; during hunting season, the buffalo-hide teepee served as shelter [Carnes and Garraty, 34].)

The land was ideally suited for grazing. One trail boss, driving a herd north from Texas in 1871, stopped in amazement to watch a "mixed herd of thousands of buffaloes, horses, elk, deer, antelope, wolves, and cattle" crossing the trail, "a peaceable kingdom on the plains" (Forbis, 161). King was the buffalo, upon whom the Plains Indians were dependent. They used virtually every portion of the animal: meat was eaten fresh, dried in the sun or over smoky fires, pounded and mixed with fruits into pemmican; hides provided clothing, shelter, and during the heyday of the fur trade, articles of trade; horns were shaped into cups and sewing utensils; hooves were boiled into glue; and sinews served as thread.

Although it's impossible to know with certainty how many buffalo roamed the Great Plains after they had disappeared from east of the Mississippi in the late eighteenth century, the numbers probably peaked at 25 million animals. These were divided into the southern herd (below the Platte River), estimated at 6–7 million in the mid-nineteenth century,

Buffalo running toward the camera. Reproduced courtesy of the Western History Collections, University of Oklahoma Library. Thousands of buffalo once roamed the Plains. The overarching image of the nineteenth century frontier experience, buffalo illustrate the symbiotic social, religious, and economic relationship between the land and the Native Americans—a symbiosis subsequently destroyed by hunters providing meat for railroad crews and army forts, and by homesteaders who plowed the grasslands.

and the northern herd, which was somewhat smaller. Before the Civil War these herds existed in a generally comfortable symbiosis with the land, though suffering from cyclical droughts when they had to compete with Indian horse herds and wild mustangs for sparse grasses. Predators, primarily wolves, thinned the herds; and, as they came in contact with cattle being driven across the plains to Oregon, many contracted brucellosis. (This nineteenth century introduction of disease is interesting in contrast to late twentieth century ranchers' fears of their cattle contracting the disease from Yellowstone Park buffalo herds.) In the 1830s and 1840s the first commercial killing occurred as Indians traded robes for use in the East and in Europe. These hunts, however, were usually seasonal; animals were only taken when their fleece was plush. In addition, there was no profit in killing more animals than Indian women could process into robes.

However, pressures on the buffalo herds increased. Eastern Indians, removed to west of the Mississippi, created an additional demand for subsistence. The coming of the railroads marked the beginning of the

end for the buffaloes. Initially many were killed to feed railroad construction crews; trains, however, also brought sportsmen to the Plains,
men who killed for fun, not meat; in addition, the railroads provided
cheap transportation east for hides. When, in 1871, a New York tannery
developed a process that could turn the hides into good leather, buffalo
could profitably be killed year-round; the fleece was no longer the primary raw material. (Much of the leather was used to produce the belts
driving the increasingly industrialized East.) By 1874 some 15 million
buffalo had been slaughtered in the Plains.

Hunting the buffalo was easy and profitable. Because the buffalo has
very poor eyesight, a favorite method of the hide hunter armed with a
Sharp's rifle and skinning knife was to approach from downwind and
fire away at the herd; unless they caught his scent, one after another
could be dropped while others continued grazing, oblivious to those
dying around them. Because a single hunter could kill up to 100 before
the herd stampeded, skilled hunters could take 2,500–3,000 animals in a
season. One group of 16 hunters reportedly killed 28,000 animals in only
a few months in 1873 (White, *It's Your Misfortune* 219). Receiving $2.50
per hide and 25 cents per tongue, a man could earn hundreds of dollars
in a few weeks; a professional buffalo hunter could garner $8,000–$10,000
a season (Bartlett, 35).

Despite their earnings, the buffalo hunters had an unenviable social
position on the plains and were scorned by many cowboys. Teddy Blue
explained:

> Cowpunchers and buffalo hunters didn't mix much, and never
> would have even if the buffalo hunters hadn't went out of the pic-
> ture when they did. The buffalo hunters was a rough lot—they had
> to be, to lead the life they had. That buffalo slaughter was a dirty
> business. [He goes on to describe how skinners would follow after
> the hunters, loading skins in wagons; often, however, they would
> simply leave carcasses to rot.] Riding the range you would find lots
> of skeletons with pieces of hide still sticking to them. It was all
> waste.
>
> All this slaughter was a put-up job on the part of the government,
> to control the Indians by getting rid of their food supply. . . . [I]t
> was a low-down dirty way of doing the business, and the cow-
> punchers as a rule had some sympathy with the Indians. . . . The
> buffalo hunters didn't wash, and looked like animals. They dressed
> in strong, heavy, warm clothes and never changed them. You
> would see three or four of them walk up to a bar, reach down inside
> their clothes and see who could catch the first louse for the drinks.
> They were lousy and proud of it. (Abbott and Smith, 120–21)

Killing Buffalo for Pleasure. Reproduced from the collections of the Library of Congress. Beginning with the 1870s, many buffalo were killed by professional hunters for their hides, which were converted to machine belts for industrial plants. The meat was usually left to rot. Moreover, with the advent of the railroad came tourists, many of whom engaged in recreational hunting.

When a bill passed Congress in 1874 to curb buffalo hunting, President Grant refused to sign it, for, as Blue suggests, exterminating the buffalo had become part of national policy. Among others, General Sherman suggested that killing off the buffalo was an effective means of starving the Indians into submission (Bartlett, 34). Between 1872 and 1874, hide hunters took an estimated 4,374,000 buffalo. Most of the meat was left to rot. An English tourist along the Arkansas River in 1873 reported that "for some thirty or forty miles along the north bank . . . there was a continual line of putrescent carcasses, so that the air was rendered pestilential and offensive to the last degree" (White, *It's Your Misfortune* 219). Moreover, many hides were wasted, some because hunters did not know how to skin the beasts, others because too many were killed at once. Contemporary sources suggest that three to five buffalo were killed in 1872 for each hide that reached market (White, *It's Your Misfortune* 219). Only a few years later, all that was to be seen of the once seemingly limitless herds were piles of bones, collected by wandering scavengers and sold to be turned into everything from fertilizer to bone china (Forbis, 161). By 1883 the buffalo had been hunted virtually to extinction. The demise of the buffalo marked the end of an ecological era.

DEVELOPING THE PLAINS

The historian Alfred W. Crosby noted that because of similarities in climate between Europe and North America, European flora and fauna could live and thrive here "if the competition is not too stiff" (*Ecological Imperialism* 7). Once the buffalo was gone, the Plains became prime real estate for new occupants, primarily cattle. The introduction of European "exotics" began with the importation of sheep, pigs, cattle, and horses as well as cats, goats, donkeys, and mules—and, coincidentally, rats— by Columbus on his second voyage in 1493. In the Caribbean, an "irrevocable" transformation of flora and fauna had occurred by 1550; elsewhere the change spread with European settlers and, in the case of horses and some pathogens, ahead of them. By 1845, close to 300,000 cattle were roaming loose in Texas; some were truly wild descendants of the criollos, introduced by the Spanish, and some were abandoned by Mexicans after the Texas war (Forbis, 50). On the northern plains, traders who had bought exhausted cattle and oxen from overland emigrants discovered that cattle could winter on the plains. Cattle and, in some locations, sheep replaced the buffalo on northern and southern plains. Initially they thrived on the lush grasslands. But long before the homesteaders' plows turned the sod, these animals—and their human exploiters—began to impact the natural vegetation. Sheep (whom John Muir, the pioneer environmentalist, called "hoofed locusts") tore and shredded range grass, resulting in occasional armed opposition from cattlemen.

However, the damage caused by sheep was multiplied by overgrazing cattle.

There were 7.5 million head of cattle grazing lands north of Texas by the mid-1880s, driven by the cattlemen's conviction that apparently limitless grasslands would feed all the cattle required by the constantly increasing demand of American consumers for beef (White, *It's Your Misfortune* 223). These forces, made worse by cyclical droughts, led to a decline of gramma and buffalo grasses, the chief cover crops of the Plains. Of course, the drought cycles had occurred when the buffalo was king of the Plains; however, excess buffalo simply starved or, weakened, were pulled down by predators. An equilibrium between animal and plant life was thus maintained. Industrial ranching destroyed this equilibrium, and European exotic plants took root. "Usually," notes Crosby, "such invasions are ... successful only if the original ecology of the area has been shattered—as, for instance, by widespread overgrazing" (*Columbian Exchange* 112). On the Great Plains the Russian thistle, the tumbling tumbleweed of cowboy songs, became so common that today most people think of it as native.

The groundcover, already assaulted by the cattle and sheep industries, was further destroyed by the homesteaders' plows and the introduction of crops such as wheat into the Plains. One consequence of the destruction of the native groundcover was erosion. By the end of the 1930s virtually the entire Great Plains region suffered from moderate to severe sheet erosion and slight to severe wind erosion, or a combination of severe wind and water damage. Though the damage was not confined to the Plains (elsewhere Americans practiced strip mining, clear-cutting of timber, and one-crop planting that exhausted the soil), by the 1980s a thousand tons per square mile were swept away by wind and water across the nation. Incredibly, experts note that the "Mississippi River alone deposited 15 tons of sediment a second into the Gulf of Mexico" (Carnes and Garraty, 17). The economic and human consequences were vividly dramatized by John Steinbeck in his novel of the Dust Bowl, *The Grapes of Wrath*.

"Pioneering," writes historian Patricia Nelson Limerick, "involved [the] ... process of introducing new variables into an already complicated setting" (*Legacy* 157). The Native American world was an intricately structured, usually respectful interrelationship between human and beast. The Okanogan creation legend reads, in part:

The earth was once a human being. ... Earth is alive yet, but she has been changed. The soil is her flesh, the rocks are her bones, the wind is her breath, trees and grass are her hair. She lives spread out, and we live on her. When she moves, we have an earthquake. ... The ancients were people, yet also animals. ... All had the gift of speech, as well as greater powers. . . . Besides the Ancients, real people and real animals lived on the earth at that time. Old One made the people out of the last balls of mud he took from the earth. . . . They were so ignorant that they were the most helpless of all the creatures Old One had made. (Erdoes and Ortiz, 14)

Parts of the Kiowa legend "The Buffalo Go" are also instructive:

The buffalo were the life of the Kiowas. Most of all, the buffalo were part of the Kiowa religion. . . . [W]hen the white man wanted to build railroads, or when they wanted to farm and raise cattle, the buffalo still protected the Kiowas. . . . [Then] there was war between the buffalo and the white men. . . . The white men built forts . . . hired hunters to do nothing but kill the buffalo. . . . [Finally there was but one surviving buffalo herd, which entered an opening in Mount Scott.] Inside Mount Scott, the world was green and fresh. . . . The rivers ran clear, not red. The wild plums were in blossom, chasing the redbuds up the inside slopes. Into this world of beauty the buffalo walked, never to be seen again. (Erdoes and Ortiz, 490)

As long as the hunters killed animals in an appropriate manner, ritually honoring the animals and killing them only to satisfy their needs, it was believed the animals would return. Thus, when the buffalo disappeared from the Plains, the Sioux believed they had gone underground because the whites had killed them disrespectfully (Milner, O'Connor, and Sandweiss, 245). Such beliefs explain in part the Indian wars discussed in Chapter 6 as well as the messianic belief in the Ghost Dance at the end of the nineteenth century. In contrast, for those in the cattle and sheep industries, animals were not at all anthropomorphized. They were simply commodities produced to meet market demands. By turning the sod and turning the Plains to farmland, homesteaders supplanted animals, whose traits—and the values they symbolized—became either icons (as in the American eagle, or the buffalo minted onto the buffalo nickel) or attractions of popular entertainment, whether in zoos or Wild West shows. Ironically, by the time of the 1918 publication of Willa Cather's *My Antonia*, the plow, a major factor of ecological change, had itself become a symbol of an idealized, happier, pre-industrial America.

What was life like in that brief half-century on the Great Plains frontier of the cowboy and the homesteader?

THE COWBOY

The cowboy is, without doubt, the most recognizable of American frontier heroes.

Ever since Owen Wister's prototypical cowboy novel, *The Virginian*, the mythic cowboy has been the epitome of valued American traits: physically competent but emotionally reserved; tempered strength that can erupt in action to protect a woman or enforce justice; virtuous, though not prissy; hardworking yet able to enjoy practical jokes; a man among men, yet attractive to women, in part because of his very aloofness. In a post-frontier era, argues William A. Savage Jr., "the cowboy hero is . . . evocative of a significant period in the American past. . . . [H]is myth . . . suggests to Americans what they might have been and what they might yet become. The cowboy speaks directly to the American's need to get through the day" (*Cowboy Hero* 38). Like heroes of storytellers from time immemorial, the cowboy hero simultaneously serves as an escape from daily tedium and as a role model for what might be. Unlike Cody or Custer or Carson, few are remembered by name; few participated in a single significant event—such as the battle of the Little Big Horn, which was amply documented. Instead, the cowboy's very anonymity may make him a mythic Everyman.

Although in American popular culture the cowboy is central to our imagination, in reality he was, according to some historians, little more than a hardworking, often seasonal employee in a complex, far-reaching web of historical, economic, technological, and industrial forces. Despite Owen Wister's portrayals of the cowboy as a white Anglo-Saxon, the cowboys through the years have been Mexican, Native American, African American; moreover, immigrants from England, Scotland, and Germany found themselves in the saddle. Though the word *cowboy* was originally applied to Tory guerrillas of the Revolutionary War, Charlie Siringo, himself a cowboy, says that it first came into popular use during the opening two years of the Civil War when Texas boys not old enough to enlist in the Confederate army "tried to hold the family cattle on the home range and keep the calves branded." Because of their youth they were called cow*boys* (Sawey, 21–22).

In the 1850s, Texas ranchers had begun to market the Texas longhorn, a new breed descended from the Spanish **The Cattle** criollo, to which had been introduced other genetic strains **Market** including the English shorthorn. The Civil War interrupted development of the Texas cattle industry. Not only did many of the ranch hands find themselves in the Army of the Confederacy, but the war made it difficult to get their cattle to market. Thus, by the end of the war a large number of longhorns—some estimate as many as five million—roamed free in Texas.

The longhorn is an extremely tough, resilient animal, able to travel great distances with little water; moreover, it can protect itself against predators with horns measuring up to five feet from tip to tip. However, it is not an ideal beef animal, reaching its full weight of 1,000 pounds only after eight to ten years. It has often been described as "eight pounds of hamburger on 800 pounds of bone and horn." At the end of the Civil War these longhorns were a glut on the Texas market, selling at only $3–$6 a head. In contrast, a good-quality steer sold in New York for $80; in Illinois, for $40; and in Kansas, for $38 (Milner, O'Connor, and Sandweiss, 255). Clearly it made good business sense to move Texas cattle north and east to more lucrative markets.

There was, however, one major—though tiny—problem. The Texas cattle carried a small tick that transmitted splenic fever, commonly known as Texas or Spanish fever, to which the longhorns were generally resistant. However, on the trail north the ticks dropped off and found new hosts, devastating dairy herds, breeding stock, and oxen that lacked resistance. Tick fever was the first cause of trouble between farmers and cowboys on the Plains. Because of the tick, Missouri had banned Texas cattle as early as 1851; in 1867 Kansas established a quarantine line east of which the cowboys could not drive their herds.

It was discovered, however, that cold northern winters killed the tick. Thus, cattle could be driven north to fatten for a winter or two, after which they were ready for market—and tick-free, thus welcome in the eastern markets. Nearly simultaneous results of the tick problem and its solution were the creation of cattle towns and an infusion of entrepreneurial capital into the cattle business.

The first of the cowtowns was Abilene, established in 1867 by Joseph McCoy at the juncture of the Kansas Pacific Railroad and the Chisholm Trail. In that year an estimated 35,000 cattle came up the Chisholm Trail; over twenty years, the number reached two million (Milner, O'Connor, and Sandweiss, 255). Each summer the herds moved north to Abilene and other towns such as Wichita, Ellsworth, and Dodge City; the towns and the trails that fed them moved progressively west as farmers and their quarantines moved into the region.

The longhorn, however, still did not produce prime beef—and beef was what the American public now wanted. Pork had been supplanted as the meat of choice as cookbooks and magazines began to describe pork as "difficult to digest, unwholesome and unhealthy"; beef became a "health food" (Milner, O'Connor, and Sandweiss, 256). But consumers wanted nicely marbled beef. Cattlemen thus began importing purebred Hereford and Shorthorn bulls to the Plains to improve the longhorn stock.

In 1871 Dr. Hiram Latham, a public relations man for the Union Pacific Railroad, published a booster pamphlet entitled *Trans-Missouri Stock Raising* that unabashedly sought investors in the western cattle business. He argued in part that if the United States was to be competitive in international markets, it must furnish its laborers with cheap food, including beef. Land in the West was cheap and animals fattened well there, Latham and other such boosters argued, guaranteeing immense profits. Newspaper stories promising 40 percent annual returns brought a flood of investors and the formation of new cattle companies on the northern plains. In 1883 alone, twenty new companies were organized with a capitalization of $12 million (White, *It's Your Misfortune*, 223). Baron Walter von Richthofen, the uncle of the Red Baron of World War I fame, published *Cattle Raising on the Plains of North America* in which he projected that from an initial herd of 100 cows one could, in ten years, have a herd of 2,856, assuming four out of five had calves every year and that heifers starting calving at 2 years of age (Forbis, 62). Such optimism now sounds unbelievable. Nonetheless, eastern investors included William Rockefeller; Marshall Field of Chicago; August Busch, the brewer; James Gordon Bennett, editor of the *New York Herald*; and Theodore Roosevelt.

To achieve great profits, production costs also had to be controlled. With the introduction of railroad refrigerator cars, pioneered by Gustavus Swift, shippers no longer had to pay freight on live animals; a dressed carcass cost half as much to ship as did a live animal. By the 1880s refrigerated beef was less expensive in the East than fresh beef; between 1883 and 1889 the price of prime cuts dropped 40 percent (Milner, O'Connor, and Sandweiss, 256). Beef became mass produced, with a few packing houses such as Swift and Armour dominating the market.

There thus grew up a dichotomy between the cattleman—the investor, the entrepreneur, the businessman—and the cowboy, his employee. Though he was essential to the enterprise, the cowboy usually received from $25 to $40 a **Cowboys' Earnings** month plus room and board (Milner, O'Connor, and Sandweiss, 261–62). Teddy Blue describes receiving 25 cents per head for running a herd of beef in the last open range in Montana during 1878; he notes that he made $125 a month, "big money for a boy in those days when the usual wages ran as low as ten dollars" (Abbott and Smith, 34). A transplanted Englishman, Frank Collinson, recalled earning $14 a month on his first job in Medina County, Texas, in 1872 (Collinson, 8). Charles A. Siringo noted that the greenhorn who wanted to be a cowboy might at first have to work only for his "chuck" (i.e., his board), but this was worth it to "acquire all the knowledge and information possible on the art of running cattle." Starting wages, he remembered, were from $15 to $40 a month, depending on latitude. On northern ranges the wages were higher, but so were expenses; cowboys needed warmer clothing and bedding during the long, severe winters. He continued:

After you have mastered the cow business thoroughly—that is, learned not to dread getting in mud up to your ears, jumping your horse into a swollen stream when the water is freezing, nor running your horse at full speed, trying to stop a stampeded herd, on a dark night, when your course has to be guided by the sound of the frightened steer's hoofs—you command *good* wages, which will be from $25 to $60 per month. (Siringo, *Texas Cow Boy* 340)

On the debit side, the cowboy's equipment required an initial outlay of funds that could range considerably. A "fancy" outfit might cost $500: saddle, $100; saddle blanket, $50; quirt and riata, $25; a pearl-handled Colt's .45, $50; a Winchester rifle, $75; Angora goat chaps, $25; and a Spanish pony, $25. However, a "serviceable" outfit could be bought for $82: pony, $25; leggings, $5; saddle, $25; saddle blankets, $5; spurs, bridle, and stake rope, $5; and Colt's .45, $12 (Sawey, 28–29).

In the early Texas cattle industry, it was the custom for cowboys who assisted at branding to receive a portion of the cattle in return. Cowboys could also acquire mavericks (motherless calves whose owners could not be determined). Thus, some cowboys could take the first steps toward becoming cattlemen. However, on the northern plains the mavericks were declared the property of the stock raisers' associations and auctioned off. Thus "mavericking—a way to begin a career of enterprise—became rustling—a way to begin a career of crime" (Milner, O'Connor, and Sandweiss, 265).

Often the cowboy was laid off during the winter months, for ranch owners could get by with a skeleton staff and did not want to pay idle hands. During this time, especially on the northern plains, cowboys would take odd jobs around saloons or livery stables, trap or hunt wolves, mine, or simply ride the chuck line—that is, ride from ranch to ranch, staying at each until their welcome wore out. But at roundup, ranches needed a full complement of help.

The Roundup The roundup was the product of the open range. Before barbed wire, cattle put out to graze cared nothing for the niceties of land ownership. They drifted to the best grass and water, with herds from different ranches mingling. Thus, at least annually it was necessary for ranchers to organize a roundup. On many of the large spreads, this was a major undertaking. The Prairie Cattle Company, Limited, one of the largest, grazed 156,000 cattle over five million acres. On such a spread, opined an old cowhand, roundup was equivalent to "a farmer in Massachusetts turning a cow out to graze and finding her months later in Delaware" (Forbis, 47). Roundups were usually held twice a year. At the spring, or general, roundup, the cowboys' principal job was to collect the owner's cattle and brand new calves; the fall roundup focused on selecting beeves for market.

On the northern plains, especially in Montana and Wyoming where corporate ranching had produced vast herds, the roundup was a cooperative venture of many ranches, each providing its outfit or crew and its own chuck wagon, which was the center of a moving operation. An old-time rancher recalls roundups in the heyday of the open range:

In the old days on the roundups each outfit had its own mess wagon with from 30 to 50 men. Each man rode from 7 to 11 horses, part circle horses, part cutting horses, and a night horse. We had breakfast at 3:30 A.M. our horses saddled and on the circle at 4 A.M. some [circles] were 15 M[iles] some 40 M. you would roundup from 3,000 to 10,000 on each ride. you had dinner when the last man was in, sometimes 9 A.M. sometimes 4 P.M., then changed horses and worked the herd, cut out the beef and cattle that had drifted from their home range and kept them under herd until you reached their home range where they were turned loose. you also branded all calves in the same brand their mother carried. it made no difference whether the owner had a representative there or not.

supper was at 6 P.M. Then you saddled your night horse, went to the herd you were holding, and relieved the herders. They were through for the day. you got the herd bedded down at 8 P.M., left two men to guard them, and went to bed. the guard was changed every two hours so sometime during the night your sleep was broken and you smoked cigarettes and sung to the cattle for a couple of hours. this was the procedure followed every day and Sunday too. it was never too hot or too cold, rain or snow, to interfere with the work. (Brown and Felton, 173–74)

After an early breakfast of sowbelly, hot biscuits, and coffee, the cowboys roped their horses, saddled up, and set off to scour the range for cattle. Few dallied at breakfast; it was considered a disgrace to be the last one ready to go when there was work to be done (Brown and Felton, 174). They usually rode in a half-circle along a diameter marked by the route of the chuck wagon from its morning position to a predetermined afternoon position. There the outfit would have dinner, the main meal of the day. Traditionally a rancher killed one of his beeves for the outfits working on his land. The cook would barbecue this fresh beef, having already prepared a variety of pies and puddings, all of which was washed down with coffee. Then came the afternoon's work.

The cowboys would mount their cutting ponies to separate individual cows and their calves from the main herd. Usually these animals were cut in a strict order, those from the outfit with the most cattle—usually those of that day's home range—selected first. One by one the calves were roped, dragged to the branding fire, and thrown on their side. Roping was considered by many to be the most dangerous job on roundup, for a rope carelessly snubbed around the saddle horn could nip off a cowboy's thumb or finger. The cowboy who threw the calf would sit on its neck while another pushed its top hind leg forward, stretching its hide taut for the branding iron and, if it was a young bull, exposing its scrotum in preparation for castration.

The calf was marked with the same brand its mother wore; the cows usually stayed close to their calves, sometimes attempting to protect them but always identifying them by proximity. The branding iron, heated only to a dull red so it would not burn below the outer layer of skin, marked the calf with one of 4,000 registered brands. Since all brands (except those that represented a unique design, such as Teddy Roosevelt's Elkhorn) were made up of combinations of letters, numbers, short dashes or bars, circles or portions of circles, a brand for a cow and a calf could be relatively quickly assembled on the spot. On average, 300 calves could be branded in an afternoon.

While the calf was down it was usually also earmarked—its ears cropped or notched on the end, top or bottom. Generally it was easier on the range to make quick identifications from earmarks than from brands. If the calf was a young bull it was now castrated, both to make it more gentle and to encourage more rapid weight gain. For every hundred heifers, eight promising young bulls were left uncastrated as breeding stock. One cowboy kept a tally book as each calf was branded; as an additional check, the bulls' scrota and heifers' ear notches were thrown into separate buckets to be counted at the end of the day's work.

Several other processes were completed during roundup. Because the long horns were dangerous, cowboys used special clippers or even axes and saws to remove them. In addition, any necessary doctoring was done now, though some maladies had to be treated by cowboys riding range during the summer.

Riding Range On the range, blowflies frequently laid their eggs in open wounds, such as fresh brands or castrations. These eggs developed into screw worms—¾ inch maggots that caused great pain and sometimes death to the animal. To daub the wound and kill the blowflies, cowboys carried bottles of a carbolic acid–axle grease mixture. For a mange-like disease, the standard treatment was to douse the cow with kerosene—and to hope it didn't wander too close to a campfire (Forbis, 83).

Other summer chores included dragging cows from bogholes in which they'd gotten stuck while trying to avoid the blowflies, plowing firebreaks, moving cattle from one range to another to avoid overgrazing, and fighting grass fires. Charlie Siringo recalls a curious firefighting method: one of the larger animals was killed and its carcass split in half; ropes attached, the wet carcass was then dragged slowly along the blaze, putting out most of the flames; the remainder were beaten out with wet saddle blankets (Sawey, 58–59).

The introduction of barbed wire and windmills in some ways made life easier but also created new chores. Men were assigned ten to fifteen miles of fenceline to repair the wire and to reset "deadmen"—these were buried boulders used to keep the fence taut, but they were often washed out by heavy rains. Moreover, the wire created more veterinary calls. Will S. James notes that "the cattle never having any experience with it, would run full tilt into it, and many of them got badly hurt, and when one got a scratch sufficient to draw blood, the worms would take hold of it." Despite his strong disapproval of any sort of lawlessness, he understood others' outrage: "The man who had horses cut up and killed by the wire, often felt like cutting down all of it, and in many instances did" (James, 108–9). Standard windmills were thirty-two feet high, some higher, so the job of scrambling up the ladder to grease the gears was not without danger; the whirling vanes could knock a cowboy off, plunging to earth from the equivalent of a three-story building. And, as the cattle business became more modern and some land was put into cultivation—wheat, corn, melons, but mostly hay—the cowboy found himself doing an increased amount of farm labor.

The cowboy on the long drive north from Texas faced additional hardships. The central rationale for the long drive was that the calf survival rate was better in the comparatively warmer Texas climate, whereas cattle fattened better for market on the grasses of the northern plains. Moreover, even before cowtowns were established at the junctions between trail and railroad, there were beef markets in the North—army posts, mining communities, and Indian reservations; early on, longhorns were the basis of seed herds on the northern ranches. **Driving Cattle North**

When Joseph McCoy established Abilene, Kansas, in 1867, the heyday of the long drive began. Between 1867 and 1887 the number totaled 5.5 million animals (Forbis, 21). The year 1871 saw the greatest number— 600,000—driven north in one year. Over half of these remained unsold; others, driven onto overgrazed land, died during the harsh winter of 1871–72. The ranchers' plight was made worse by the Panic of 1873 during which banks refused to extend credit and many young, thin cattle had to be sent east before they were ready for market, thus further depressing their price. The glorious dreams of men such as Baron von Richthofen had turned to nightmares. By 1875 the long drive sent only 150,000 north from Texas, the end of the first boom in the cattle business (Milner, O'Connor, and Sandweiss, 260).

To the cowboys driving cattle north, weather and working conditions had greater immediacy than did macro-economics. George Deffield recorded his impressions of one long drive from Texas to Iowa in 1866:

Upset our wagon in River & lost Many of our cooking utencils . . . was on my Horse the whole night & it raining hard . . . Lost my Knife. . . . There was one of our party Drowned to day . . . & several narrow escapes. . . . Horses *all* give out & Men refused to do anything. . . . Awful night . . . not having a bite to eat for 60 hours . . .

Frederic Remington, *Fixing a Break in the Wire Fence.* Reproduced courtesy of the
Denver Public Library, Western History Collection. Although life on the ranch
was generally more comfortable than life on the cattle drive, it demanded
different skills. Repairing barbed wire fences was a common chore, necessitated
by posts dislodged by the freeze-thaw cycle of northern Plains winters.

> *Tired.* . . . Indians very troublesome. . . . Oh! what a night—Thunder
> Lightning & rain—we followed our Beeves *all* night as they wan-
> dered about. . . . Hands all Growling & Swearing—every thing is
> wet & cold . . . Have *not* got the *Blues* but am in *Hel of a fix.* . . . My
> back is Blistered badly. . . . Flies was worse than I ever saw them.
> . . . One man down with Boils & one with Ague. . . . Found a Hu-
> man skeleton on the Prairie to day." (qtd. in Forbis, 17)

The long drive continued from early spring to late fall, the herds ranging in size from 300 to 3,000 head, though the largest, in 1859, was 15,000.
Generally the cowboy-to-cow ratio was between 1:250 and 1:400 (Richard
Harding Davis in Savage, *Cowboy Life* 102; Forbis, 136, 142). A day's drive
was usually no more than ten to fifteen miles, for if the cattle were to
arrive in good condition they had to be allowed to graze along the way.
On occasion, in order to reach water the drive might be as long as twenty
miles. For the cowboy this meant a long day in the saddle, keeping the
herd together and rounding up the stragglers. (Most cattle had been
given a temporary trail brand on their flank for identification en route;
some outfits also cropped the tails of trail herds [Fletcher, 15].) Cowboys
took up positions at point (in front of the herd), on the flank, and to the

rear; these positions were alternated so that the worst job in the rear, eating dust, was shared by all.

When the herds reached rivers, swimming the cattle across was not easy. Though they might initially plunge into the water to slake their thirst, once in the river (especially when it was swollen from heavy rains) they often panicked, milling around in circles and even climbing atop one another's backs, with the lowest animals being in real danger of drowning. For cowboys, many of whom did not swim themselves, getting these animals out was dangerous work. Other steers drowned in sinkholes or became mired in quicksand. They had to be roped and pulled out. The experience sometimes left them unable to travel. Baylis John Fletcher recalls one instance of a "trail hospital" where crippled and disabled cattle were cut out of the herd and left with a solitary herder until they were able to travel again (Fletcher, 48–49).

There were other hazards and discomforts on the long drive. Hail was sometimes as large as quail eggs, capable of beating birds and rabbits to death. In May 1874, seventy-eight horses from one outfit froze to death in an unseasonable Texas blizzard. As the herds crossed the Red River they passed out of Texas law into The Nations—Indian Territory—where Indians might beg or even rustle cattle. In 1881 the Crows of Montana asked $1 a head for a drive to cross their tribal lands; when the figure was refused, they stampeded the herd. The event was captured in a Charles Russell painting (Forbis, 10–11). The Indians, however, were generally less of a hazard than homesteaders who were angry at herds that trampled their fields. By Kansas law, a plowed furrow around a field was the legal equivalent of a fence; any loose stock crossing it was considered to be trespassing, and the owner of the herd was liable for damage. A latter-day trail boss described the drive as "one continual row from start to finish" with homesteaders (Brown and Felton, 162). By 1882 farmers, angry at crop destruction and fearful of tick fever, were so adamant that virtually all of Kansas was off-limits to trail herds. The cowboys' response was the slogan, "Bend 'em west, boys. Nothing in Kansas anyhow except the three suns—sunflowers, sunshine, and those sons of bitches" (Forbis, 157).

The most common cause of cowboys' deaths was being dragged by a horse (Forbis, 29–30); many others, however, also met death from pneumonia, tuberculosis, and being struck by lightning. Yet cowboys probably feared the stampede most (Fletcher, 49). Almost anything could spook a herd, especially at night: a coyote's howl, a cowboy lighting a cigarette, a sudden rumble of thunder. Fletcher remembers trailing a herd through Victoria, Texas. A woman, fearful that the cattle would trample her roses, waved her bonnet at them, starting a panic; before they were gotten under control, they'd smashed most of the yard fences in town (16).

Usually, though, stampedes happened on the trail at night after the cattle had been bedded down. The single best way to stop them was to ride with the herd until you'd caught up with the leaders and then turn them in circles, gradually diminishing in size until the cattle could be gentled into sleep again. For night guard duty cowboys picked their quietest, gentlest, most sure-footed horses. Even so, accidents happened—most likely a hoof plunging into a prairie dog hole. The result could be fatal. Teddy Blue describes such an accident:

> [T]hat night it come up an awful storm. It took all four of us to hold the cattle and we didn't hold them, and when morning come there was one man missing. We went back to look for him, and we found him among the prairie dog holes, beside his horse. The horse's ribs was scraped bare of hide, and all the rest of horse and man was mashed into the ground as flat as a pancake. The only thing you could recognize was his six-shooter. We tried to think it was the lightning hit him, and that was what we wrote his folks. ... But we couldn't really believe it ourselves. ... I'm afraid his horse stepped into one of them holes and they both went down before the stampede. ... The awful part ... was that we had milled them cattle over him all night, not knowing he was there. ... After that, orders were given to sing when you were running with a stampede, so others would know where you were as long as they heard you singing, and if they didn't hear you, they would figure that something had happened. (Abbott and Smith, 43–44)

Though in this passage the cowboys were told to sing to locate each other, singing was soon seen to be an effective way of soothing the cattle at night and thus preventing stampedes. One cowboy, riding around the herd clockwise, would sing one verse; his partner, riding in the opposite direction, would sing the next from the opposite side of the herd (Abbott and Smith, 260–62). The worst thing a man could do on night guard was to fall asleep. Singing helped some here too, but a number of cowboys tell of rubbing tobacco juice in their eyes, with the resulting pain preventing sleep.

A string of good horses was essential to the cowboy. Most were relatively small (12 to 14 hands in height and weighing from 700 to 900 pounds) mustangs or mustangs interbred with U.S. Cavalry thoroughbreds. Often they roamed grasslands for about four years; breaking them to saddle and bridle took an average of four to six days, though a good cutting horse took longer and a good horse for night guard required a quiet temperament. One of a cowboy's most expensive purchases was his saddle, often the equivalent of a month's pay. This was not, however, an extravagance, for a good rider in a good saddle could ride for fifteen hours and seventy miles and end with a healthy horse, whereas a poor rider in a bad saddle could make a horse sore in an hour. Each cowboy was expected to keep his horse's feet in good condition by trimming the hooves and shoeing when necessary. Their tails were kept thinned out and short by pulling out hair by hand until it reached only to the hock; a "long-tailed horse was the mark of a farmer or a town gambler" (Brown and Felton, 137). How a man treated his horse was a measure of character. Not all were kind or caring, but those who were earned respect. Teddy Blue notes that it was a deadly insult to ride a cowboy's horse without his permission (Abbott and Smith, 32).

The center of the cowboys' world, whether on roundup or on the trail, was the chuck wagon. Though cowboys weren't unduly picky as long as their food was clean and reasonably well cooked, no outfit kept a poor cook because **The Chuck Wagon** bad food eventually made for a grouchy crew. A good cook was prized, and often only the foreman received higher wages. Around his chuck wagon, the cook—often called "Miss Sallie" or "Cookie"—was king, though his working hours were long, sometimes leading to extreme crankiness and bizarre idiosyncrasies. A common saying on the range was that "only a fool argues with a skunk, a mule, or a cook" (Brown and Felton, 139). One cook was discovered stirring a pot of navy beans with his Colt's .45, then cleaning the barrel of beans by firing at a nearby rock. Asked why he did this, he replied that he was checking to see if the beans were soft enough to eat (Brown and Felton, 148).

The cook's day began early, for breakfast was usually over by 3:30 A.M. Before that, he'd built his fire and prepared a hearty breakfast of hot bread or biscuits, meat, stewed dry fruit, and coffee for the cowboys whom he sometimes woke by banging lids of dutch ovens together, cymbal-like. As they set off to care for the cattle, he washed their tin plates and cups (though cowboys were expected to scrape their own plates clean and deposit them in the communal "wreckpan"), made bread, packed up the chuck wagon, and now working as a teamster, drove it to the site selected for dinner. Along the way as they reached creeks, cowboys or the cook's helper gathered brush or broken branches for the cookfire. Elsewhere they picked up "prairie coal," that is, dried cow or buffalo manure; this they did wearing gloves, for scorpions often lived under the chips (Forbis, 155).

Most of the daily menu was prepared in dutch ovens: baked beans, roast beef, boiled potatoes, short ribs with onions; bread was often mixed up in the dishpan. "Son of a bitch stew" was made of marrow from beef bones, sautéed in hot grease, then boiled with peppers and potatoes. Desserts might include more stewed fruit, spice cake made without eggs or butter, pies, or "moonshine"—rice and raisins simmered **The Cowboy's Food and Drink** until done. More simply, it might mean "lick"—molasses or Karo syrup dripped over canned tomatoes and leftover biscuits, or straight-from-the-can yellow cling peaches in syrup. Pickles were a real treat in a diet noticeably lacking in fresh vegetables and depending heavily on "prairie strawberries"—beans. Charlie Siringo remembered often skipping the noon meal when work was especially pressing. One of his favorite meals was calf ribs broiled by the campfire and a large dutch oven full of loin, sweetbread, and heart, all smothered in flour gravy. Often forks and knives were not used, being replaced by the cowboys' pocket knives or bowie knives (Sawey, 29).

Coffee was a staple for the cowboy. Green coffee beans bought in 100-pound sacks from the Arbuckle Company were parched in dutch ovens; preferred were roasted beans, more expensive, bought in 30-pound cans from the Oriental Tea Company of Boston. The coffee grinder was usually side-mounted to the chuck wagon. Most cowboys did not drink their coffee straight. Because white sugar was rarely available, granulated brown sugar was used, unless "Cookie" was angry and the coffee was sweetened with molasses. The granulated brown sugar often became so hard in its barrel that it had to be chipped free and then run through a meat grinder before it could be used. On the range the coffee was often brewed with water collected from bogs, where streams had been dammed up for cattle to drink. When, on occasion, an animal had become stuck and died in the bog, the cook's helper would "pull bog"— that is, wade into the muck and pull out the animal. Nonetheless, they "without flinching, drank . . . and enjoyed it" (Luchetti, *Home* 92).

On most outfits, liquor was forbidden in camp. However, "camp" was defined as 100 feet from the fire. On only one occasion in his whole career did Teddy Blue see this rule broken—and then the cowboys went out into the sagebrush to consume a bottle of whiskey. The fact that it happened even once was surprising, for "drinking and cattle didn't mix"; it was far too dangerous (Abbott and Smith, 115).

Shelter for the Cowboy On the trail, only the cook could take shelter under the chuck wagon. The cowboys slept on the ground, often surrounding their bedrolls with lariats, which was thought to ward off snakes. They had, for a bed, a large tarp (about 7' by 16'), which when folded could serve as top and bottom covers; sometimes a quilt was added for comfort. In spring near prairie bogs where mosquitoes were thick, they often pulled the tarp up over their heads. The tarp did little, however, to keep out rainwater pouring over the prairies after a sudden storm, so the cowboy would often wake up in a soggy quilt and soaked to the skin.

However uncomfortable it might be, the cowboy's bed was his private place, containing his "tobacco sacks, cigarette paper, buckskin and leather, a marlinspike, perhaps a picture of the cowboy's girl, some old letters, magazines, shirts, underwear, socks, a clean suit, an extra pair of boots, soiled clothes, a spare cinch and a rope" (Forbis, 132).

Life on the ranches was considerably more comfortable. Even line camps established for cowboys riding the imaginary lines of the ranch looking for drifting cattle provided a reasonably comfortable home. Frank Collinson describes one: **Life on the Ranch**

> My home was a dugout . . . constructed by digging into a bank near water, with logs on the side for support. The top was covered with poles, mud, and soil and suspended by a ridge-pole. The average dugout was about ten by twelve feet, and two or three men could live comfortably in one. They were warm in winter and cool in summer. There was a fireplace in them with a chimney, dug down. I lived in [such] prairie homes half of my life—and spent my happiest days in them. (Collinson, 121–22)

The bunkhouse on the ranch was a more permanent structure. Sometimes built in the "saddlebag plan," it was two structures—the bunkhouse and the cookhouse/mess hall connected by a "dogtrot," or breezeway. More often the bunkhouse was simply a separate building made of cottonwood logs, daubed with mud or even cow manure to keep out the winds. The bunkhouse was usually cold in winter and hot in summer, when it was also so infested with lice and bedbugs that cowboys slept outside. Charlie Siringo remembered that he and his bunkmates made a rule that anyone picking off a "grayback"—a louse—and throwing it on the floor without killing it must pay a fine of 10 cents to go into the kitty for buying literature (Forbis, 81). Mostly the bunkhouses smelled: a "composite of sweaty men, dry cow manure, the licorice in chewing tobacco plugs, old work boots and the smoke from lamps that were burning coal oil or perhaps even tallow rendered from the generous supply of skunks that scavenged around the ranches" (Forbis, 81). The interior decor was untidy—"clothes hung on the floor so they wouldn't fall down and get lost." The floor was sometimes wood, but more often packed dirt. Bunks were covered with quilts, buffalo robes, or wolfskins. The walls were sometimes whitewashed and sometimes papered with old magazines, newspapers, or mail-order catalogues.

Boredom, broken by work, dominated life in the bunkhouses. Cowboys who were literate (and many were, having received good educations) read everything from novels and farm journals to labels on tomato cans or the "wallpaper" itself. Poker was popular, even though on some ranches card playing and gambling of every description were strictly forbidden; **Entertainment for Cowboys** dominoes were also popular. Music helped while away the evenings; many cowboys played banjos, mouth organs, fiddles, Jews harps, or guitars. Sometimes cowboys held kangaroo courts, the "accused" being ineptly defended from trivial or trumped-up charges, and the punishment being outrageously humiliating, such as being tossed in a horse trough.

On special occasions such as Christmas or the Fourth of July, the ranch owner and his wife might invite hands to dinner or even to a dance. But usually (especially on smaller ranches, where the only women present were the wives of the owner and the foreman) some of the cowboys were "heifer-branded" and wore frilly aprons to indicate they were the "women" at the dance. (The ratio of men to women in cattle country was 10:1, with most reputable women being already married.) The cowboy historian Ramon Adams once described line duty as living the "life of a buck nun" (Forbis, 62). Charlie Siringo described courting two girls from New York, "the only young ladies in the neighborhood." When he abruptly proposed in the "Texas way" by asking one "how she would like to jump into double harness and trot through life with me," she blacked his eye with a roasting ear she had been cleaning for dinner (Siringo, *Texas Cow Boy* 81). This was probably one of the less violent confrontations between cowboys and homesteaders.

The Cowtowns For most cowboys, life on the long drive or on the ranch was a life of social deprivation. The cowtowns were their outlet. El Paso, Ellsworth, Dodge City, Miles City, Fort Griffin, and dozens of others were established, like Abilene before them, at the juncture of the cattle trails and the railroads. They brought more than a convenient means of getting animals to the Chicago packinghouses and eastern markets. Teddy Blue remembered El Paso in 1880 as a "wide-open town. The railroad was coming and always ahead of it there comes these tent saloons and honky-tonks, a whole army of them" (Abbott and Smith, 57). He remembered Forsyth, Nebraska, in 1883, just before the Northern Pacific was completed through Montana, as having one store, two saloons, a barber shop, a livery stable, and a boarded-up hotel—the buffalo hunters who had provided it business were now gone. The only women were the storekeeper's wife and a "fat old haybag who had been scalped by Indians at the mouth of the Musselshell a few years before and was laying with the barber" (Abbott and Smith, 92). Frank Collinson remembered Dodge City in June 1874 merely as a typical western "rag town" with lots of semi-permanent canvas structures (Collinson, 38). When they were first founded the cowtowns were rough, raw, and dusty, with as many as 30,000 cows at a time overwhelming 500 residents. Pens were built near the railroads—Abilene's, for example, could handle 120,000 head per year—and the cowboys' last responsibility with their charges was to urge the cattle up

Shipping beef to Chicago. Reproduced courtesy of the Montana Historical Society, Helena.

chutes into cattle cars. This they sometimes did by prodding them along, the origin of the word *cowpoke.*

Most cowtowns quickly took on an almost frenetic pace. Collinson called Fort Griffin, Texas, of the mid-1870s "the wildest and most colorful of all"—and he'd seen them all, from Dodge City, Kansas, to Ogallala, Nebraska.

The buffalo hunters and the skinners, fresh from a woman-less country farther to the west, flocked to Fort Griffin for a fling, their pockets bulging with money. Hardened surveyors and their assistants rode into town with compass and chain after locating countless sections of previously unappropriated land. Bullwhackers and sunburned, bewhiskered soldiers just returned from the indescribable hardships of a Staked Plain campaign . . . filled the barbershops for shaves and haircuts and hot baths in the tin tubs in the rear. Black sheep from prominent families elsewhere flocked to Fort Griffin to forget the past and begin life anew. Questionable women stayed in their shoddy rooms by day, but came boldly out at night when fiddles begun to play, flitting about the saloons, dance halls, and gambling dens like bright fireflies. Honest ranchmen and merchants and their loyal wives established homes and brought the first culture and permanence to the raw, untamed town. They all mingled together, those Fort Griffinites, the good and the bad, in one common herd, and left their marks, for good or bad, on the Clear Fork town. (Collinson, 84–85)

Dodge City in 1884 was the busiest trailhead town with nineteen saloons, a "lush" casino, and a seasonal population of two thousand. There a beef broker could "seal a $20,000 deal on a handshake," and the cowboy, released briefly from his work, could get a bath, a woman, and a "bottle of Kansas sheep dip"—whiskey (Forbis, 172–73).

In most cowtowns, saloons outnumbered other establishments by as much as two to one. There and in gambling houses the cowboys played poker, keno, faro, and monte, often encouraged by bar girls or "soiled doves" (prostitutes like Squirrel Tooth Annie of Dodge City, who carried a pet squirrel and eventually quit her profession to get married). Another especially colorful lady of the night was Connie the Cowboy Queen, who wore a $250 dress embroidered with the brands of every ranch from the Yellowstone to the Platte (Forbis, 123). Dusty streets, sometimes lined with wooden sidewalks, were bordered with the town's business establishments—dry goods and grocery stores, photography studios, theaters, sometimes a roller-skating rink or bowling alley, billiard parlors and pool halls, dancehalls, barber shops and hotels.

Into such towns the cowboys swarmed when they were paid off. Generally the tone was live and let live—literally—and as long as the cowboys respected the town's etiquette, they were left alone. After all, they brought an influx of money. Alfred Henry Lewis remembered that there were only four things a cowboy must not do: he must not insult a woman; he must not shoot his pistol in a store or bar-room; he must not ride his pony into those places; and he must not ride his pony on the sidewalks (*Wolfville Nights* 15).

Sometimes, however, there was too much temptation. Charlie Siringo remembered one Fourth of July in Dodge City when he and a buddy got drunk in the Lone Star Dance Hall, then run by Bat Masterson; they picked a fight with some old-time buffalo hunters to "prove the superiority of the cowboy class." Siringo's friend was stabbed, but the two buddies eluded the law. He later wrote: "This incident illustrates what fools some young cowboys were after long drives up the Chisholm Trail and after filling their hides full of the poison liquors manufactured to put the red-shirted Irish rail-road builders to sleep, so that the toughs could 'roll' them and get their 'wads.' Instead of putting a cowboy to sleep it stirred up the devil in his make-up, and made him a wide-awake hyena" (*Lone Star Cowboy* 64–65). Besides the usual horseplay and too much liquor, Teddy Blue suggests another reason trail hands often had trouble with the law in cowtowns. Most of the Texas cowboys had served in the Confederate army, and most of the marshals were Northerners. Though "down home one Texas ranger could arrest the lot of them . . . up north you'd have to kill them first" (Abbott and Smith, 28).

There was a schizophrenic quality to these cowtowns. On the one hand, many were, at least at first, populated largely by profiteering seasonal operators—representatives of northern meat packers and midwestern feedlot owners, gamblers from Mississippi riverboats, and prostitutes who went back to Memphis, St. Louis, or New Orleans when the cowboys returned to ranch or trail. Consequently Theodore Roosevelt, who generally admired and respected the cowboy, called cowtowns "wretched [places] in which drinking and gambling are the only recognized forms of amusement, and where pleasure and vice are considered synonymous terms" (Roosevelt, 92). In an official publication of the National Livestock Association, the cowtowns were described as products of existing conditions. "Civilization was pushing its way . . . [west] with the irresistible force . . . of glaciers . . . [and, like glaciers], shoving ahead a morainic mass—a conglomeration of human debris" (National Livestock Association [NLA], 551). Abilene in 1870 was perceived by some as "the wickedest and most God-forsaken place on the continent" (NLA, 507). With a permanent population of five hundred, it had thirty-two licensed saloons (NLA, 508).

Such observations reflected the positions of increasing numbers of permanent residents—grangers, doctors, lawyers, ministers, and teachers; to many of them, cowboys were no longer welcome. Although the wide-open towns had brought a temporary infusion of money, good money was beginning to be made in land speculation and construction. Thus, city governments began to pass ordinances forbidding the bearing of firearms within town limits and appointing marshals and deputies to deal with those who did. Reformers began to levy fines on prostitution and gambling, though cynics felt these were less to curtail sin than to raise local revenue. Nonetheless, changes were in the wind. When one newspaper editor wrote, "people who have money to invest go where they are protected by law" (Forbis, 186), there was the clear suggestion that one era—that of the trail drive and the open range—was closing and a new one—that of farmers and entrepreneurs—was opening. Whether one attributes the change to the completion of more and more branch lines of the railroads, or to the increasing use of barbed wire, or to the disastrous winter of 1886–87 in which thousands of cattle died frozen on the northern plains, "the life that surrounded [the cattle trails] could not endure. The homes of thousands of settlers have pre-empted the grazing grounds. Railroads are ten times more numerous than were the trails, and like the cavalier, the troubadour, the Puritan, and the 'Forty-Niner,' the cowboy and his attendant life have become but figures in history" (Harger, 742).

THE SETTLERS

With the movement of farmers and settlers across the Mississippi and Missouri River barriers into the vast open lands of the Great Plains came a profoundly significant change in the relationship between man and the land. The desire actually to own land, to have certified legal title to it, was a primary factor sounding the death knell not only to Native American occupation of the land but also to the lifestyles of earlier frontiersmen.

The cultural difference was most pronounced with the Native Americans. For the Indian, the man-land "connection was intimate, organic, even religious. Many Native American creation myths had Indians emerging from the earth, as from the womb. The earth, then, is the Mother, the source of life, to be respected and cherished. Certainly one could not possess her; especially emphatically, one could not sell her" (Jones, *Christopher Columbus* 94). For the fur trappers, there was no sense of ownership of the land itself. Forts might be built; businesses established, licensed, and sold; the natural environment exploited; but both traders and trappers were essentially transients. Whereas nations might be concerned with political control of a region, for most individuals the issue of land ownership was simply irrelevant. And whereas on the frontier individual ranchers often sought control of water sources, the concept of land ownership was often very loosely interpreted, with cattlemen making use of more land than they owned. Moreover, because the public domain was government land (i.e., nobody's land), it was everyone's land. With the coming of the settler all this changed, and boundaries, whether they were simply plowed strips or barbed wire, defined attitudes as well as ownership.

Acquiring Land   The farmers' settlement of the Great Plains was a nineteenth century manifestation of two complementary truths that had been evident since colonial days: land hunger, and a recognition that population increased the value of land. British colonies, as well as proprietors such as William Penn, gave away land to attract settlers. Virginia adopted the headright system, which gave land to those who "paid their own way to America or who completed an indenture." By the time of the Revolution most Americans felt there should be easy access to land—that it should be cheap or even free to those wanting to establish family farms (Foner and Garraty, 877). Under the Articles of Confederation and then the Constitution, land not included in the original thirteen states became public domain owned by the national government. The Land Ordinance of 1785 provided for surveying and selling this public land; it established the rectangular system of surveying into townships six miles square, sections a mile square—or 640 acres, and quarter-sections of 160 acres.

In the nineteenth century two laws specifically addressed western settlement. The Pre-Emption Act of 1841, recognizing the fact that many people had simply gone to the frontier prior to government surveys and claimed land by virtue of their presence, assured squatters that they would have first chance to purchase 160 acres at $1.25 an acre. This, however, meant a significant cash outlay for people who had little savings. For example, when Howard Ruede decided in 1877 to leave home in Bethlehem, Pennsylvania, for a new life in Kansas, he went to the bank and withdrew his entire life savings—$75; of this, railroad tickets cost him $23.05 (Ruede, 3). Consequently there was a growing demand for the government to give land free to those who would live on it and cultivate it. This—coupled with the belief that farmers were "more democratic, honest, hardworking, independent, virtuous, and patriotic than city residents" (Foner and Garraty, 878), and thus, that to increase the number of farmers would benefit the nation—led eventually to the Homestead Act of 1862. In 1865 President Andrew Johnson said that "the lands in the hands of industrious settlers, whose labor creates wealth and contributes to the public resources, are worth more to the United States than if they had been reserved . . . for future purchasers" (Fite, 16).

The law guaranteed qualified individuals 160 acres of land as long as they built a residence and lived on the land for at least five years; the cost was minimal—a filing fee of $19. If a person could not or did not want to live on the land for the full five years, it was possible after six months to pay the government $1.25 per acre in cash, a process known as commutation. This stipulation meant, in fact, that the democratic intent of the law could be violated, and speculators or even "professional squatters" acquired land for resale. Such squatters had no intention of developing a homestead. Instead they'd stake a claim—often the best land or a good mill site—sell it, move, stake another claim, and so achieve profit (Dick, 32–34). This, of course, directly violated the provision of the law that required applicants for homesteads to swear the land was for "his or her exclusive use" (Fite, 17).

Other provisions of the law caused creative personal adaptations. Men or women over age 21 could stake claims, but a husband and wife could not do so simultaneously. Thus, Elinore Stewart was careful that her fiancé, Clyde, had already gained title to his homestead before she agreed to marry him (Stewart, *Letters* 133–34). The stipulation that "anyone who is the head of a family" could claim land led to marriages among 19- and 20-year-olds hungry for land; some young women adopted children to meet this clause. Though each person could claim only 160 acres, sometimes several members of the same family staked out adjoining claims, in fact doubling the family property. Hamlin Garland describes how his grandfather and father then built a double house across the line between their two farms, fulfilling the legal requirements but also providing companionship in a land in which loneliness could be lethal (*Son* 248).

Staking the claim was often haphazard. Garland notes that he and his friends measured the distance from township lines by "counting the revolutions of our wagon wheels" and then laid out their boundaries with "pocket compass and a couple of laths" (*Son* 304). They then marked their claims with "straddle-bugs"—three boards "set together in tripod form" and used as a sign of occupancy. Because lumber was scarce and it was difficult to immediately build a shanty, the straddle-bugs "took the place of 'improvements' and were fully respected. No one could honorably jump these claims within thirty days and no one did"(*Son* 303).

Though Garland honestly meant to establish residence, as the law required, others did not, and a number of scams were employed. The government land offices usually required that a residence at least twelve feet square be constructed. Some clever scoundrels got witnesses to swear that a house was "twelve by fourteen"; in reality, some of these were whittled with a penknife and measured twelve by fourteen *inches*. In Nebraska an enterprising scam artist built a small house on wheels, which he towed from place to place with a team of oxen; charging $5 a day, he enabled many an unscrupulous man to "swear that he had a bona fide residence on his claim" (Dick, 35).

Although much land was acquired directly from the federal government at nominal cost, it could be purchased from other sources. Between 1850 and 1871 the railroads received 175,350,000 acres from the public domain as subsidies for construction of transcontinental and branch lines (Foner and Garraty, 879). Many states were granted two sections in each township for support of common schools; and in the Morrill Land Act of 1862 states were given 30,000 acres of land for each congressman and senator as endowment for agricultural and mechanical colleges. Land grants and land controlled by railroads in Kansas, for example, amounted to 10,340,512 acres—or about one-fifth of the state. And in Nebraska, while 1,471,761 acres were acquired between 1863 and 1872 under the Homestead Act, "land granted to railroads and . . . bought with agricultural college scrip and with soldiers' bounty land warrants amounted to 9,435,796 acres" (Fite, 17). The process was intensified as railroads and local communities, territories, and states actively advertised in the East and even in Europe to attract settlers.

A House "Twelve by Fourteen." From Albert D. Richardson, *Beyond the Mississippi* (Hartford, CT: N.p., 1867). Sometimes land ordinances were unfortunately vague. While one criterion for claiming land was building a 12 × 14 house, the dimensions were not always stipulated as feet— one preemption fraud was to construct a "house" of 12 × 14 *inches*.

A Bona Fide Residence. From Albert D. Richardson, *Beyond the Mississippi* (Hartford, CT: N.p., 1867). Some created a "service industry" aiding fraudulent land speculators. They constructed a legal-sized house, on wheels, and pulled it from location to location.

Hardships for the Settlers

No matter how potential settlers acquired the land, and no matter how they got there—by steamboats, trains, farm wagons, stage coaches, or on foot—many were in for a rude awakening. Though establishing a farm in the grasslands initially seemed easier than it had been in the woodland East where trees had to be girdled, cut, and burned and stumps grubbed out before land could be plowed, the environment of the Great Plains was far from hospitable. This was, after all, a region that George Catlin had pronounced "almost one entire plain of grass, which is and ever must be, useless to cultivating man" (qtd. in Dick, 164).

The climate itself was a trial. Howard Ruede remembered that August in Kansas produced temperatures of 108°F in the shade and 128°F in the sun (Ruede, 140). Hamlin Garland recalled summer in Dakota Territory as "ominous":

> The winds were hot and dry and the grass, baked on the stem, had become as inflammable as hay. The birds were silent. The sky, absolutely cloudless, began to scare us with its light. The sun rose through the dusty air, sinister with flare of horizontal heat. The little gardens . . . withered, and many of the women began to complain bitterly of the loneliness, and lack of shade. The tiny cabins were like ovens at mid-day. (*Son* 308)

Winter was equally formidable. Garland observed, "No one knows what winter means until he has lived through one in a pine-board shanty on a Dakota plain with only buffalo bones for fuel" (*Son* 309). Grace Fairchild remembered a cow breaking the ice and stepping into a water hole one winter; one back leg froze and "the next spring her leg dropped off." Her husband fashioned a wooden leg, but after the cow kicked out and the leg hit him in the head, they fattened her and butchered her in the fall. "We couldn't tell any difference between a three-legged cow and a four-legged one when the steaks were on the table" (Wyman, *Frontier Woman* 23). The winter of 1885–86 was especially hard. According to a South Dakota folk saying, "It was so cold that when he died they just sharpened his feet and drove him into the ground" (Wyman, *Frontier Woman* 115). Elinore Stewart remembered such extremes in Wyoming: "They have just three seasons here, winter and July and August" (6).

Though there were summer droughts, when the rains came they turned the soil to a thick, viscous gumbo. Many settlers recall it clinging to wagon wheels until it was eight to ten inches thick before it fell off of its own weight. Later, graded gravel roads made travel easier, but the soil was unchanged. As settlers said, "If you stick to this country when it's dry, it will stick to you when it is wet" (Nelson, 40).

Across the open plains the wind was omnipresent and often nerve-wracking. Mary Clark wrote to her parents from her South Dakota claim:

> The wind was too fierce. Really it was something awful and it hardly ever goes down. It actually blows the feathers off the chickens' backs. . . . I can't put up many pictures and things for everytime the door opens they all blow off the wall. . . . It's so funny—we noticed how terrible loud everyone talks out here and now we find ourselves just shouting away at the top of our voices. We discovered it must be the wind and unless you yell you can't be heard at all. (Nelson, 37)

If a windstorm hit on washday, everyone rushed outside to get the clothes before they blew away. Buckets, pails, and lightweight tools might be blown for miles if they didn't first catch on fences.

The same winds, blowing over sun-baked land, produced dust storms, clouds of soil hundreds of feet high that blotted out the sun, filled the house with dust, almost smothered cattle in the stable, exposed the roots of young wheat, causing it to wither and die, and sent homesteaders into "dull despairing rage" (Garland, *Son* 128).

Bad as summer winds were, winter blizzards were worse. The Ammons sisters, returning from school, saw a blizzard coming "like white smoke," and before they got home they could not see their hands before their faces (Nelson, 35). With the thermometer at $-30°F$ and the snow blowing at 80 miles per hour, it seemed as if the sun had been "wholly blotted out and that the world would never again be warm" (Garland, *Son* 110). Homesteaders rigged ropes between house and barn so they wouldn't get lost going to feed the animals. Dr. Bessie Rehwinkel, returning from a house call, was caught in a sudden Wyoming snow storm. Driving blindly, her horses becoming more exhausted by the minute, she recalled, "My whole body was becoming numb, and I began to feel an almost irresistible drowsiness creeping upon me." Finally, miraculously, she saw a light through the gloom, and "covered from head to foot with an icy sheet of snow which had frozen into a crust so that I had become a human icicle," she was welcomed into that very house she had left three hours earlier (Rehwinkel, 76–77). Another winter wanderer was not so lucky. Lost in a storm he killed his horse, ripped him open, and crawled into the body cavity to stay warm. He was found several days later, frozen into his equine tomb (Dick, 222).

One of the most terrifying natural disasters was the prairie fire, which might be caused by a lightning strike, a spark from a train, or human carelessness. It was simultaneously horrifying and awesome. "The sky is pierced with tall pyramids of flame, or covered with writhing, leaping, lurid serpents, or transformed into a broad ocean lit up by a blazing sunset. Now a whole valance of fire slides off into the prairie, and then opening its great devouring jaws closes in upon the deadened grass" (Dick, 216). Such a fire could roar across the plains destroying homes, barns, haystacks, even whole settlements in its path. It was the unwritten law that whenever a fire broke out, every able-bodied person must pitch in to fight it, plowing firebreaks, setting backfires, and slapping tongues of flame with wet rags. To be the cause of such a fire not only was embarrassing but also brought legal penalties. A settler convicted of carelessness with fire could receive six months in jail and a thousand-dollar fine (Nelson, 38).

Settlers were also pestered by native critters. Mosquitoes were so bad during summer that some farmers would build a fire at the door and let the wind blow smoke into the house; eyes smarting from the smoke were, to most people, preferable to the welts raised by the voracious insects (Ruede, 89). Flies mercilessly attacked cows in their stalls—and the women or children milking them. During August and September when men were in the field cutting oats or hay, crickets ate coats or hats left beside the haystack, gnawed pitchfork handles, and devoured any leather straps left lying about (Garland, *Son* 209). On occasion cinch bugs, small, "evil-smelling" insects, devoured the wheat crops at harvest time, bringing financial disaster to farmers (Garland, *Son* 215).

Probably the most destructive insects were grasshoppers, which thrived on hot, dry conditions. In 1866 they darkened the sky in a column 150 by 100 miles wide; they were so numerous that they stopped horseraces in Fort Scott, Kansas, covering the track up to three inches deep. In 1874 grasshoppers ravaged crops from the Dakotas to Texas. They came in such large numbers that their weight broke tree limbs and mashed corn stalks and potato plants. One settler reported that his chickens and turkeys gorged themselves on hoppers; their meat subsequently had the flavor of grasshoppers. Men had to tie strings around their pantslegs to keep the insects from crawling up their legs. Women attempting to protect their gardens by covering them with bedsheets watched in horror as the grasshoppers simply ate through the bedclothes. Creek water was so stained with grasshopper excrement that it was the color of coffee. And near Kearney, Nebraska, grasshoppers were so thick on the Union Pacific lines that trains were stopped. Section hands were called out to shovel the insects off the tracks, which were so oily and greasy that the wheels spun (Dick, 202–6). One intriguing byproduct of the grasshopper invasions were inventions for dealing with them— among them the "grasshopper dozier," a long pan made of tin and sheet iron and filled with kerosene. It was pushed through the fields; grasshoppers fell in and died, their carcasses dumped in the fields in mounds five feet high (Dick, 211).

Another hazard, the rattlesnake, was mentioned so often by diarists as to be commonplace. Miriam Davis Colt remembered seeing rattlers crawling or hanging over sills near her front door. At night she'd hear "peculiar noises" under the floor, which at first she thought were rats. Instead they were snakes, and her husband kept a stout hickory stick near their bed to drive the snakes away (Colt, 104). Mollie Sanford, in her bare feet, heard the tell-tale sound, killed a snake, and hung its eleven rattles on a tree as a trophy (Sanford, 40). The snakes did not fear people but slithered into homes, barns, and cellars. Children playing in the yard were their most frequent victims, though adults and livestock also died of snakebite. Nearly everyone carried a hoe to kill any rattlers they might encounter (Nelson, 38–39). Sometimes they actually invaded the house. One young boy awoke in the night complaining that his brother, sleeping in the same bed, was pinching him; the parents quieted the boys, and in the morning one was dead—of snakebite (Bartlett, 218).

It was no wonder, with all these natural disasters and herpetological and entomological plagues, that Grace Fairchild "questioned in my own mind how a sane man could [drag] his family into such a . . . country" (Wyman, *Frontier Woman* 13). Indeed, faced with such disasters some homesteaders who could afford it left the country, the sides of their wagons emblazoned with bleakly humorous slogans such as "From Sodom, where it rains grasshoppers, fire and destruction" (Dick, 206).

Although the farming frontier of the Great Plains may have fulfilled, for some, the dream of owning property, it was neither an adventure nor an idealized acting out of the Jeffersonian concept of the yeoman farmer. Although there were variations in both the scope and methods of farming—most **The Settlers' Work** notably the large-scale, nearly industrialized bonanza wheat farms of the Red River Valley or the irrigated farms around Salt Lake City—most farms on the Plains were small, labor-intensive operations in which men, women, and children struggled against nature to eke out a marginal existence. For most families, 160 acres was more than enough land to farm. Work could be brutal with little power other than human and few mechanical contrivances. A man often had to walk miles to borrow a neighbor's team of oxen to plow his fields; after an exhausting day he'd return the animals and face another long walk home. They'd cut grain with cradles, dig wells with broken-handled picks, hoe corn, and lacking grindstones, chop whatever wood was available with dull axes. A sense of the homesteader's hardships is reflected in Garland's dedication to *Main-Travelled Roads*:

To My Father and Mother

Whose half-century pilgrimage on the main-travelled road of life
has brought them only toil and deprivation, this book of stories is
dedicated by a son to whom every day brings a deepening sense
of his parents' silent heroism.

Work was hard, almost as inexorable as the cycle of seasons that it
followed. All work tested animal and human endurance. One of the most
difficult jobs was breaking the sod for the first time. The ordinary breaking plow turned a strip of sod twenty to thirty-three inches wide; to
accomplish this, one needed a yoke of six oxen. (Most farmers preferred
oxen to horses for their strength.) However, many farmers had no team
at all, or only a couple of animals, so they either had to borrow a neighbor's team, hire the work done (which was rarely possible for cash-
strapped newcomers), or do the work with what they had. Sometimes
the first-year settlers only planted sod corn, gashing the sod with an ax
and then dropping in seed corn. This was, however, only a temporary
measure, postponing the almost epic struggle of man and beast against
sod unbroken since pre-history. Hamlin Garland remembers a "giant"
neighbor bracing himself for the shock of the plow, pulled by four straining horses; his father sat on the beam to add weight and keep the coulter
in the ground. "These contests had the quality of a wrestling match, but
the men always won" (*Son* 104).

The work exacted its toll. Oscar Micheaux learned from experience that
gummy soil was best tilled with plows that made a slanting cut; his made
a square cut, causing roots and grass to collect on the plowshare, requiring frequent stops to clean it. He was not used to driving horses,
nor could he keep the plow in the ground at first. He later wrote, "I
hopped, skipped and jumped across the prairie, and that plow began
hitting and missing, mostly missing. . . . I sat down and gave up to a fit
of the blues; for it looked bad, mighty bad for me." Eventually he mastered the technique, and by the end of the summer he'd broken more
than 120 acres. (Most homesteaders broke only a few acres at a time,
planted them, and then tackled a few more. Micheaux, however, being
the only black in his part of South Dakota, wanted to prove he was the
equal of white farmers.) However, he paid for the accomplishment: "As
it had taken a fourteen hundred mile walk to follow the plow in breaking
the one hundred and twenty acres, I was about 'all in' physically when
it was done" (Nelson, 51–52). It was not for nothing that Willa Cather
invested the plow with an almost epic significance in her novel of Nebraska, *My Antonia.*

Usually after the land was plowed it had to be dragged or harrowed,
breaking up clods and pulverizing the soil prior to planting. Garland

Solomon D. Butcher, "John Curry sod house near West Union, Custer County, Nebraska, 1886." Reproduced courtesy of the Solomon D. Butcher Collection, Nebraska State Historical Society. While to modern readers sod houses look only slightly better than shacks, they were a huge improvement over the dugout. However, sod houses did have their disadvantages: vermin set up housekeeping in the sod, and muddy water dripped from the roof after an especially heavy rainfall.

remembers that "dragging is even more wearisome than plowing, . . . for you have no handles to assist you and your heels sinking deep into the soft loam bring such unwonted strain upon the tendons of your legs that you can scarcely limp home to supper" (*Son* 100). Once the crop was in, the war of weeds began. Howard Ruede describes day after day hoeing corn, his blue shirt bleaching to red across his back from sun and sweat (87, 106–7).

In the early years the harvesting of wheat, rye, and oats, as well as cutting hay, was done with a sickle. The harvester would grasp the stalks in his left hand and, with his right, draw the sickle close to where the bunched stalks were held. Consequently most harvesters bore one or more scars on their left hands from the sickle coming too close. Periodically the harvester would stop, hang the sickle on his belt, and bind the sheaves. Using such techniques a man could harvest, on average, three-quarters of an acre a day. The work was easier and more efficient with a scythe or cradle, but it was not until the arrival of horse-drawn McCormick reapers, which could cut fifteen acres a day, that the farmer was freed from back-breaking labor.

Generally neighbors would move from farm to farm (especially during harvesting and threshing seasons), helping each other and eliminating the need to hire help. In addition men would often exchange labor, using a monetary value to determine the length of services provided. For example, Howard Ruede cut wood for neighbors at the rate of $1 per cord; rather than paying him in cash, one neighbor planted potatoes for him and another agreed to break an acre of sod for every three cords of wood. On another occasion he worked at the sorghum mill at the rate of one gallon of molasses per day; he then made a deal with another neighbor to plant his wheat in exchange for molasses. Oftentimes no cash at all was involved in these transactions. People did whatever work was required. Ruede dug cellars, plowed, shelled corn, and stripped sorghum at the mill. With skills he thought he'd abandoned back in Pennsylvania, he set type for the town newspaper and, when the editor was gone, published it himself. For this he was sometimes paid in cash, though at no set rate (Ruede, 66–67, 157, 40, 69).

Men with carpentry or painting skills could work in the burgeoning new towns; there too they could find jobs in livery stables, saloons, stores, or pool halls. Some families made a little money selling farm surplus in town. Many women made butter, kept chickens for eggs, spun flax or wool for sale. Keturah Penton Belknap recorded in her journal the prices she and her family received in Iowa in the 1840s: 12.5 cents a pound for butter, 6.5 cents a dozen for eggs, fresh pork for 5 cents a pound; corn at 12.5 cents a bushel unshucked, and, for their wheat, $3 a barrel after having had it ground, buying barrels, and hauling it sixty miles to Keokuk. At the end of one year, she noted rather proudly, they had $20 in silver to "put in the box" (Luchetti and Olwell, 136).

It is clear that on the homesteaders' frontier everyone worked and work was not gender-specific. Though milking cows was often considered women's work, men did that chore too; conversely, when more help was needed in the fields, women pitched in. Women, however, were generally in charge of the house and the children. They tended the garden, nursed the sick, taught the children before a school was organized, sewed and repaired the family's clothing, cooked and baked—often without benefit of a stove. Washday was often a nightmare. Before a good well was dug on the claim, women saved a little water every day for the week's washing. Miriam Davis Colt recalls going "to the spring five times today; three times is my usual number," making "five miles travel for me [on foot] to bring sixty quarts of water" (Colt, 106).

Women's Roles as Settlers

Many women also had to make their own soap. Priscilla Merriman Evans describes her technique: "[I] took an ox and a gunny sack and went out into the field where the dead cattle had been dragged [after the disastrous winter of 1885–86] and I broke up all the bones I could carry home. I boiled them in saleratus and lime, and it made a little jelly-like soap" (qtd. in Luchetti and Olwell, 167). Miriam Davis Colt wondered what her mother back east would think of her white clothes in this land of little soap or water. All she could say was that they were "clean for brown—but . . . awful dirty for white." She and her family stopped wearing nightclothes, she said, once they got to Kansas, "because I could not bear to have them take on the brown color" (Colt, 135–36).

When the first labor-saving devices—the sewing machine and the washing machine—became available, women who could afford them were ecstatic. The sewing machine was driven by human power, with the woman working a treadle with her feet. The washing machine was essentially a small tub with a hand-turned paddle for agitating the clothes; its primary advantage was that the children could be assigned the task of operating it, freeing their mother from the drudgery of scrubbing the clothes on a washboard.

Though some women took their unremitting labor in stride—Mollie Sanford said, "I can put my hand to almost anything" (Sanford, 58)—some historians suggest that the hymns they sang may have reflected their hopelessness, their exhaustion, and their yearning for release as much as they did their religiosity:

> When at last life's day is ending,
> As the ev'ning draweth nigh
> And the sun is slowly wending
> Down behind the western sky.

'Twill be sweet to think of pleasures
That shall never know decay,
In that home of joy and splendor,
Just beyond life's twilight gray

Chorus:
Rest, sweet rest, and joy and gladness,
Comes when toil, when toil is o'er,
Sweetest resting comes when toil is o'er.
'Twill be joy and rest eternal
On the other shore. (qtd. in Bartlett, 354)

Death, to some, might be preferable to unending labor. Hamlin Garland, remembering his mother, confirmed this: "I doubt if the women—any of them—got out into the fields or meadows long enough to enjoy the birds and the breezes. Even on Sunday as they rode away to church, they were too tired to react to the beauties of the landscape" (*Son* 138–39).

Children's Roles as Settlers   Children, too, were expected to work. Garland remembers trying to be a "good little soldier" and live up to the expectations of his father, a Civil War veteran. Early on he and his brother had the responsibilities of grown men. They chopped and stacked wood, hunted cattle that had wandered off, harrowed and cross-harrowed the fields until "tears of rebellious rage" creased the dust on their faces. At age 10 he had been taught to handle bundles of thoroughly dried barley shocks; at age 14 he was one of five men on a crew binding straw after the reaper had passed (149–51). Kept out of school during October and November, he first plowed and then husked corn. His father was not unkind, giving him the freedom to do what he wanted and go where he liked on Sunday as long as he was back in time for milking.

His experiences were not unique. Other children, some as young as age 4 or 6, had chores: to carry in enough fuel—wood or cow chips—each night to last the next day, to bring in water from the barrel outside, to fill kerosene lamps. For recreation, many had to make do and use their imaginations because toys weren't available. Elinore Stewart remembers her daughter calling a block of wood her "dear baby," a spoke from a wagon wheel "little Margaret," and a barrel stave "bad little Johnny" (Stewart, *Letters* 13–14).

Sometimes children worked off their homestead. Parents controlled their children's labor, and a father could generally claim his son's wages until he was 21 years old (Schob, 174). In 1858, 14-year-old Frank O'Brien was hired out to work on a farm seven miles away; having walked there, he found his quarters to be in the attic, which he shared with seed corn, dried pumpkins, and fieldmice. His work included washing dishes, helping with the threshing, churning butter, turning the grindstone as his employer sharpened tools, and cleaning the hay mow (Schob, 189–90). Farmers, especially widowers, often advertised for hired girls; because of the disproportionate male-female ratio, many girls found themselves married early.

Children's work was not always voluntary. On at least one occasion a farmer, with too many mouths to feed, agreed to indenture two of his children to another man looking for "draft animals." The agreement was that the employer would buy them each a pair of shoes if they worked out. Their mother, who had not originally been consulted, so harassed her husband that a week later they rescued the children, sick, terrified, bewildered, and maltreated (Schlissel, Gibbons, and Hampsten, 221–23). Given the often brutal hardship of work on the frontier and given such treatment of children, it is not surprising that tired animals were also sometimes mistreated. Mollie Sanford told of one man, angered because his horse was balky, who after piling hay around him literally set a fire under the animal, then left him in agony until Mollie's father shot him (Sanford, 66).

Although breaking the sod and getting the first crop in were the first order of priority, making a homestead habitable required finding water, building a home, and fencing the property. Good water close to the house was not only **The Homestead** a convenience to eliminate the labor of carrying buckets great distances for washing, cooking, and watering the garden; it was also a matter of health, as there were numerous instances of people getting diarrhea or worms from questionable water sources. Finding a good water source was the first problem. Folk wisdom advised that one should observe the surface of the land just before sunrise; green spots in the grass suggested water below. If spiders were present in such locations, the odds were even more favorable. Many homesteaders engaged professional water witchers who ranged over the land with a forked stick (preferably of witch hazel, peach, or willow); the stick dipped from its horizontal position to point to an underground water source. After the well was dug in such a location, farmers' wives brought up the water with a bucket and windlass. As time went on, hand pumps or windmills made the chore easier.

On most of the Plains, wood was too valuable to be used for fencing. Consequently hedges were planted, the most successful of which was the osage orange. Only gradually, as farmers became more successful, did barbed wire make its appearance.

The first home for most farmers was either a tar-paper shack or a dugout. Most were small, only large enough to meet government requirements of a ten-foot by twelve-foot structure. The Ammons sisters, who had purchased a relinquished claim and were happy there was already a house on it, were horrified to discover it was a shack resembling a "none too substantial packing-box tossed haphazardly on the prairie" (Nelson, 27). Such shacks were easy to build, requiring minimal materials: some cheap lumber for framing, a couple of rolls of tar paper, and some nails. They were flimsy, however, and if not anchored down might fly away in a high wind. To keep them warmer in winter, settlers often lined them with red or blue building paper, the color indicating the quality. The inferior red paper was thinner, costing $3 a roll, whereas the blue was twice as expensive. Said one settler, "Blue paper on the walls was as much a sign of class on the frontier as blue blood in Boston" (Nelson, 28). As further winter insulation, farmers often banked these structures with manure from the barn. Grace Fairchild noted that "when the smell got too bad in the spring, we knew it was time to take the insulation away" (Wyman, *Frontier Woman* 16). During the summer the tar-paper shacks were unbearably hot, as the black exterior absorbed the sun's rays.

The dugout was generally more comfortable. The homesteader excavated an embankment to create a space approximately fourteen feet square and then added a front wall of sod bricks. The cost was minimal (Bartlett, 216):

one window	$1.25
18 feet of lumber for a door	.54
one latch and pair of hinges	.50
one stovepipe joint to go through the roof	.30
3 pounds of nails	.19
	$2.78

Although there were some disadvantages, as when a cow or horse crashed through the roof, the dugouts were usually warm in winter and cool in summer. Priscilla Merriman Evans described the interior of a dugout owned by Stephen Markham, a former Mormon bishop:

There was a large fireplace in one end with bars, hooks, frying pans, and bake ovens where they did the cooking for the large family [of three wives and seven children]; and boiled, fried, baked, and heated their water for washing. There was a long table in one corner, and pole bedsteads fastened to the walls in the three other corners. They were laced back and forth with rawhide cut in strips and made a nice springy bed. There were three trundle beds, made like shallow boxes, with wooden wheels, which rolled under the mother's bed in the daytime to utilize space. There was a dirt roof, and the dirt floor was kept hard and smooth by sprinkling and sweeping. The bed ticks were filled with straw. (Luchetti and Olwell, 166)

Cattlemen often scornfully referred to homesteaders living in such dugouts as "nesters" or "scissorbills" (Bartlett, 215).

Some people built an above-ground addition to the dugout, using its walls as a foundation for a sod house, or soddy. Most started from scratch. Often neighbors would gather for a house-raising bee and erect a house in a day. First the sod was cut—2 ½" was an ideal thickness—in strips 12" wide; these were then cut into 18" lengths with a spade. The best time for breaking sod for a house was when the ground was soaked from rain or snow. Like large, flat bricks, the sod was laid layer after layer in the desired dimensions, though " 'seven feet to the square' is the rule, as the wall is likely to settle a good deal, especially if the sod is very wet when laid" (Ruede, 28–29). Generally the door and windows were set in place first, and the sod walls built around them. Forks of a tree were then placed at each end of the house and a ridgepole laid between them. Rails of any available material—sorghum stalks, willow switches—were then laid from the ridge pole to the walls. Atop them, more sod was placed for the roof. Howard Ruede spent $10.05 for such a soddy and a year's supply of firewood in Kansas in 1877. Sometimes an especially heavy rainfall would leak through the roof, muddying clothes hung from the wall or even dripping onto the beds, thus adding to the housewife's chores. Many diarists remember various sorts of vermin (especially fleas, mice, and bedbugs) that infested these houses. One woman recalled helping her grandmother take down the canvas tacked over their ceiling each spring and fall to get rid of dirt and vermin that had fallen from the roof (Myres, 153–54). The problem with bugs was minimized when settlers plastered interior walls with a mixture of clay, water, and ashes (Bartlett, 218).

In most areas of the Plains frontier a frame or brick house was seen as a status symbol, indicating that the farmer had achieved a degree of success. The social stratification was even more apparent in town. However, in part because the margin between success and failure was so narrow for farmers in this region, depending largely on vagaries of climate, there was in the country a kind of "pure democracy" (Garland, *Son* 171). Though a family might live in a shack, no one looked down on them. As Howard Ruede notes, "A man in rags is as much respected as if he was dressed in broadcloth, provided he shows himself a man" (Ruede, 13).

Homesteaders' Clothing

On the homesteaders' frontier, most clothing was more utilitarian than fashionable, though new clothes brought a lift to the spirits. Keturah Penton Belknap remembered spinning flax all winter in her spare time and weaving a piece of linen to sell. With the money she got a "new calico dress for Sunday," a pair of new shoes, and material for an everyday dress. "It was cotton warp colored blue and copper and filled with paler blue filling, so it was striped one way and almost as nice as gingham" (Luchetti and Olwell, 136). Her plan was to make one new dress each year so she always had one "for nice"; with a "clean check apron I would be alright"(138). Priscilla Merriman Evans learned to weave different shades of gray by varying the proportions of black and white wool, though when making skirts she always added a row of bright colors—red, blue, green—halfway up the skirt. She learned to use madder, indigo, logwood, copperas, and other roots to provide color. And, with their simple patterns, "when our dresses wore thin in front, they would be turned back to front and upside down and have a new lease on life" (Luchetti and Olwell, 168). Elinore Stewart remembers sewing underwear out of sugar and flour sacks, petticoats from the larger ones and "drawers" from the smaller (90). Howard Ruede bought overalls for $1.25; when they sprouted holes, he patched them himself with whatever was at hand, often using a variety of colors and fabrics, even feed sacks, so that sometimes his backside was adorned with a feed mill slogan. He took to wearing no socks or underwear, and on one occasion mentions that he is writing a letter clad only in his shirt and cap (147). Despite all his mending, his favorite coat is "ripping fast . . . one pocket entirely out." Moreover, "my shoes are well ventilated at the toes" (99). He notes that prairie grass is awfully hard on shoe leather. He later bought two pairs for $2.25, a 25-cent discount for buying several. Despite the danger from rattlesnakes and the toughness of the grass, many took to going barefoot. Hamlin Garland mentions burning his bare feet while trying to put out a prairie fire.

Boys wore long pants, not celebrating the transition from boyhood to adulthood, as did their eastern cousins, by changing from short pants to long. Perhaps because children did adult work, "even my eight year old brother looked like a miniature man with his full-length overalls, high-topped boots and real suspenders" (Garland, *Son* 93). In summer, work clothes generally consisted of a "straw hat, a hickory shirt, and a pair of brown denim overalls." But since their best suit (they only had one) was made of "blizzard weight" wool, they endured "tortures" in their Sunday best, replete with starched shirts and paper collars (177). On the farm they wore cavalry boots; only when they moved to town did shoes become an option. One of Garland's fondest boyhood memories was getting new boots—his had red tops with a golden moon in the center—even though his father insisted they be a size too large so they'd last longer (91).

Although some young women attempted to keep up with fashion, replacing their worn-out hoops with grapevines (Sanford, 76), many also adopted more practical expedients. Mollie Sanford found her skirts an impediment when searching for a strayed cow and thus went out in an "old suit of Father's clothes" (53). And Miriam Davis Colt, tired of having the hems of her dresses burned by cooking fires and frayed by grass, adopted bloomers; in them, she also rode a horse astride instead of sidesaddle (Colt, 49, 110).

Food, too, was functional—to fuel the body with enough calories for an arduous day's work. Hamlin Garland describes harvest work punctuated by meals—breakfast of flapjacks, sausages, and coffee; a midmorning lunch of milk, cheese, and "fresh fried-cakes, brought to the fields" by his **Food and Drink for the Settlers** sister; a noon dinner of boiled beef and potatoes and supper at six. Clearly while the men sweated all day long in the fields, the women broiled over the kitchen stove. The Garlands were lucky, however, for many families lived on the edge of starvation, especially in bad crop years.

With no refrigerators or even ice boxes, food had to be preserved. Fruits were gathered fully ripe and placed in handy containers—barrels, tubs, or jars—and covered with pure spring water; the scum that formed on the surface fuctioned like the paraffin of later jam makers. Everything that could be dried, was—green beans, corn, rhubarb, berries, even pumpkins. Home canning was not common on the frontier, so fresh tomatoes were placed in barrels of strong brine and kept submerged by weighted boards. Some fruits were preserved by boiling sweets, though sugar was rare and was usually replaced by molasses or honey. Molasses, Ruede notes in a reflection on frontier grammar, "is a plural noun" as in "I ain't ate so many molasses this year as I did last" (148, 152). The importance of some sort of preservative is evident in his comment about ham: "I have a hard time with the meat flies and have taken thousands of eggs off of the ham. I have no dark or smoky place to keep it in, and they get inside of the paper in which it is wrapped" (53). By late in the century, canned goods made their way onto the Plains. One observer noted that "Bachelors' huts were always surrounded [by a rusting pile of cans]; where there was a woman to do the cooking, there were fewer cans." Most farm wives considered using canned goods as unthrifty. One, apparently oblivious to the dangers of botulism, scoffed at a neighbor's wastefulness because "she discarded any canned goods that were not perfect" (Nelson, 186 n.2).

For poor farmers who could not give up their coffee fix, there were coffee substitutes: parched barley, rye, or wheat; okra seeds; dried carrots; or "coffee essence"—a mixture of squash and pumpkin baked very dark and put in the pot and boiled for fifteen minutes (Dick, 272). The poor also found meals monotonous. The *Nebraska Farmer* of January 1862 printed thirty-three different ways of cooking corn (Dick, 270–71). Children subject to such a diet containing few fresh fruits and vegetables sometimes developed scurvy (Dick, 275).

Health and Diseases of the Settlers	Though there were some frontier doctors (Bessie Rehwinkel's career is one example), they were as scarce as ministers or teachers at first. Despite their absence neither disease, accidents nor death took a holiday. Diarists mention almost routinely everything from the common cold, rheumatism, diarrhea, and the mysterious fever and ague to smallpox, scarlet fever, pneumonia, and consumption. Several mention children with worms; one recalls a neighbor hooking a finger into a child's rectum to remove them. For measles Grace Fairchild applied a flaxseed poultice to her daughter's back, an onion poultice to her chest, and a hot-water bottle to her feet "until the measles broke out" (Wyman, *Frontier Woman* 10). Others tried turpentine and sugar to prevent worms, and they thickened eggwhites in vinegar as a cough syrup (Luchetti and Olwell, 27). Folk remedies suggested rubbing fresh peach leaves on the head for baldness, and eating a handful of sumac leaves twice a week for bed-wetting (Bartlett, 366). Howard Ruede liked to use skunk fat, which was "good for all kinds of sores, rheumatism, etc., and for greasing boots" (170).

People also suffered greatly from toothache. Mollie Dorsey was "piled up in bed with a swollen jaw, my face decorated with a poultice" (Sanford, 159). There are few references to preventive medicine or dentistry, although Miriam Davis Colt remembered one woman who "mopped" her teeth with a little swab, "first dipped into her snuff box" (Colt, 150).

In areas of contact with Native Americans, some settlers adopted Indian medicine. Mollie Dorsey Sanford tried a version of the sweat lodge to treat herself for chills and fever when quinine failed to work: "I went for three successive mornings and jumped into the creek [it was November and icy], would then wrap myself in a blanket, rush up to the house, pile into bed and take a sweat" (Sanford, 59).

Some families had copies of popular "medical" books such as Dr. Richard Carter's *Valuable Vegetable Prescriptions for the Cure of All Nervous and Putrid Disorders*. One such book sold over 100,000 copies in its first decade in print (Bartlett, 365). Others resorted to patent medicines. Garland remembers garish almanacs—merely small, badly printed patent medicine pamphlets with a loop of string by which they could be hung by the kitchen stove for reference. Such pamphlets were given for free, but the products they advertised—"Harley's Bitters" or "Allen's Cherry Pectoral"—always seemed to cost a dollar a bottle. In a land of hard work and little accessible entertainment, the traveling medicine show (despite its "90 proof" quackery) was a hit for farmers come to town.

Accidents also took their toll. There are frequent references to ax cuts. While one man was cutting wood, the ax slipped and cut his good kneecap. "It was with difficulty that he crawled home," his wife reported.

"He was very weak from loss of blood" (Luchetti and Olwell, 166). Howard Ruede seems almost accident prone. He narrowly missed cutting off his foot with an ax, which glanced from a log and took a slice out of his shoe (65). He hit himself in the head with a pick while digging a dugout and "bled like a stuck pig. . . . It made my head ache, and I did no more this afternoon for fear I would bleed again" (191–92). While hauling sand for the construction of a schoolhouse he was stepped on by his ox but had to walk six miles home—"pretty painful . . . [for] when an ox is pulling hard his tread is pretty heavy, I assure you" (220). Grace Fairchild had an accident with a shotgun and blew her thumb "back over my hand"; she pulled her thumb back in place, tried to tape shut a three-inch gash, and, when that didn't work, got a needle and thread and sewed it up (Wyman, *Frontier Woman* 80).

The matter-of-fact tone with which people describe accidents is echoed in Elinore Stewart's account of a neighbor woman treating her hired man. He'd mashed his fingernail and neglected to take care of it; gangrene set in. She sat him down and told him one could tell whether there was danger of blood poisoning if the patient put his hand on a block of wood and stared at the sun. As he did so, she "chopped off the black, swollen finger," gave the man morphine and whiskey for shock, and, with a razor, laid open the green streak running up his arm, immersed the whole arm in a solution of bichloride of mercury, and then dressed the wounds with absorbent cotton soaked in olive oil and carbolic acid (Stewart 221–22).

The illnesses were not only physical. Repeatedly homesteaders mentioned feeling dwarfed by the immensity of the Plains. This sense of insignificance, coupled with brutally hard work, poverty, and loneliness, made many declare, like Maggie Brown, "I would give 5 years of my life if I had never seen this state [Colorado]" (Schlissel, Gibbons, and Hampsten, 107). Men were not exempt from this depression. Howard Ruede wrote, "If there is anything I hate, it is to have to work alone—without a human being or animal in sight" (134). Occasionally this loneliness blossomed into full-blown insanity, as is described in Ole Rolvaag's novel, *Giants in the Earth*. The character Beret grew "more sober . . . more locked up" within herself, while a "heavy heart lay all the time" in her bosom (qtd. in Myres, 169). Grace Fairchild describes "one of our neighbors [who] lost his mind, and his wife kept him busy carrying . . . coal from one side of the basement to another, day after day" (Wyman, *Frontier Woman* 3).

When death came, the neighbors pitched in, closing the eyes of the deceased, washing and clothing the body, folding its arms and holding them in place until rigor mortis set in. Where no lumber was available, bodies were buried wrapped in a sheet or blanket. Sometimes floors or furniture were cannibalized to make a coffin, which was then blackened with soot or lamp-

Death on the Frontier

black to make it presentable. The burial usually took place the day following the death; there was no embalming. If friends sat up with the corpse overnight, they kept a cloth moistened with vinegar on its face to delay mortification. Usually, unless there was a circuit-riding minister present, a neighbor offered words of comfort at the graveside. Then the survivors, dressed in their everyday clothing, returned home. Everett Dick commented on the psychological implications of such a frontier death: "Bereavement is hard to bear in a home of comfort and ease where friends and kinfolk surround the mourners. It must have been far harder for the bereaved ones to return to a bare shack to face the hardships of frontier life without the helpmate, the parent, or the little child the light of the home" (Dick, 253–54).

Many popular ballads bemoaned the early death of young women. In the "safe" territories of Dakota, Nebraska, Utah, and Washington, women's death rates in 1859–60 were 22 percent higher than those of men, even after taking into account violent deaths, whereas in the eastern states the death rate was about the same for both sexes (Luchetti and Olwell, 27). Puerperal fever frequently resulted from unsanitary conditions during childbirth, and even when there were no fatal complications, if the child presented in breech position there was little anyone could do. Sometimes, to speed up a slow delivery, attendants held a quill of snuff to the mother's nose, the "paroxysms of sneezing bringing forth the child" (Bartlett, 266).

Sexual Practices on the Frontier

In part because they provided extra hands on the farm, children were welcome and families were often large. "Our poor man counts each one of his half dozen or half score a blessing ... stout hands and active heads are the very thing we need," editorialized one newspaper (Bartlett, 361). With infant mortality rates of as high as 25–30 percent and epidemics of measles, scarlet fever, or influenza wiping out whole families, a woman had to have been pregnant more than a half-dozen times to produce these large families. Some men, like Old Jules in Mari Sandoz's account of her family, believed that "women got to have children to keep healthy" (110). Some women thus practiced rudimentary birth control—hoping the rhythm method would work, utilizing pessaries for contraception, and nursing their babies as long as possible in the belief they could not then conceive. By word of mouth women passed on contraceptive techniques: the use of Vaseline—"a greased egg wouldn't hatch"; rock salt—though most avoided this because "it affected the mind"; and a concoction of cocoa butter and boric acid (Jameson, 152). Grace Fairchild reflected on her own fecundity: "To have six children in less than eight years is something of a record. You would have thought I was in a race to see how fast we could get that new country settled. I decided to call a halt," and for four years she didn't have a child. Once, though, she thought she was pregnant, "took a heaping tablespoon full of quinine" to induce an abortion, and went to bed. So sick she thought she would die, she decided "I'd better stop bucking nature so I could be around to look after the family we already had" (Wyman, *Frontier Woman* 29).

Though the homesteaders' frontier had far more Euro-American women than any other, men still outnumbered women. In 1870, when the sex ratio was about even throughout the country, there were 247 men for every 100 women in the West; as the area became more settled, the ratio decreased, but by the turn of the century it was still 128:100 (Underwood, 20). In 1880 Colorado had 129,131 men to 65,196 women; Montana Territory, 28,177 to 10,792; and Wyoming Territory, 14,152 to 6,637 (Bartlett, 243). This resulted, it may be hypothesized, in two almost antithetical responses to women: respect and domination.

The first was respect, codified if need be. Women—whether they were wives, schoolteachers, immigrant girls fresh off the boat, or prostitutes—were valued. When the bylaws of Yellowstone City, Montana, were written during the winter of 1884–85, there were only fifteen women and three hundred men in the camp. Hanging was established as the penalty for "murder, thieving or insulting a woman" (Bartlett, 249). Mollie Dorsey received so many proposals that she sighed, "We do not see a woman at all. All men, single or bachelors, and one gets tired of them" (Sanford, 39).

There was also a surprising sexual frankness. In April 1881 Charles Brown, trying to assure his wife, Maggie, back home in Virginia that he was not visiting Colorado prostitutes, wrote:

My virtue is all right and I think that it will remain so for I do not care to meddle with any of the women that I see here, but I look forward to something more soon [when she arrives]. I know that it will be the best in the world, so I am satisfied to think of how nice it will be and go and jack off. Now, don't blame me, for I do get awful hard up at times. (Schlissel, Gibbons, and Hampsten, 128)

Though there was occasional premarital sex between couples (Stewart, *Letters* 82–84), it was not really condoned. Marriages were opportunities for great celebration. Usually a jolly, rambunctious chivaree or party was held after the wedding:

The newly married couple occupied a wagon for sleeping apartments. The first notice they had of any disturbance was when ... most of the men and women ... took hold of the wagon, the men at the tongue pulling, the women at the back pushing, and ran the wagon a half mile out on the prairie. Then the fun began. Such a banging of cans, shooting of guns and every noise conceivable. . . .

The disturbance was kept up until midnight, when the crowd dispersed, leaving the happy couple on the prairie to rest undisturbed till morning, when they came [out] amid cheers and congratulation. (Luchetti and Olwell, 30)

Although much research suggests that one effect of the predominantly male society was respect for and joyful pursuit of women, an opposite, darker phenomenon also existed. Some men, like Mari Sandoz's character in *Old Jules*, believed that men had the right to "dominate women and coerce compliance with their wishes" (Graulich, 113). He thought nothing of blacking his wife's eyes, splitting her lip, or "clos[ing] her mouth with the flat of his long muscular hand." After pleading with Jules to castrate two calves before they were too big for her to hold, his wife could not "keep the larger one from kicking." Outraged, Jules dropped the castration knife into manure, stormed into the barn, and fashioned a whip from lengths of baling wire. Shrieking "I learn the goddamn balky woman to obey me when I say 'hold him,' " he slashed her repeatedly. With blood dripping from her face and arm, the abused woman staggered into the house, unstoppered "the red bottle with the [skull and] crossbones" with her teeth, and attempted suicide (Sandoz, 230–31). Though such spousal abuse did occur on the frontier, some women stood up to their men. After receiving a beating from her husband, one woman threw him out of the house and thenceforth supported herself by doing laundry and running a boarding house (Jameson, 154).

Entertainment for the Homesteaders   Although much of life on the homesteaders' frontier seems bleak, exhausting, and lonesome, people also enjoyed themselves. Work, coupled with a desire to see neighbors, resulted in "quilting bees, barn raisings, even communal butcherings" (Luchetti and Olwell, 29). People thought nothing of driving miles in a farm wagon, bringing some food with them, and spending all day and perhaps the night at a neighbor's house. Families played cribbage and cards, including Authors, at the kitchen table; when things grew more settled some families gathered around a melodeon and sang while another family member played the fiddle. Reading was popular and was sometimes the basis for other entertainment. Elinore Stewart remembers a "Leatherstocking Dinner" at which the host served "as many [foods] mentioned in the Tales as possible" (Stewart, *Letters* 154). Hamlin Garland remembers reading Cooper and Scott and Dickens but also Beadle's Dime Novels, farmers' newspapers, *Godey's Ladies' Book*, and the *New York Tribune*. As schools and churches appeared on the frontier, they provided social as well as educational or religious opportunities. Many people went to religious camp meetings as much for socialization as for salvation. The Grange offered "oyster suppers with debates, songs and essays"; the annual Grange picnic was "almost as well attended as the circus" (Garland, 165). And as farming diversified, the county fair became an event to anticipate.

Dances were a favorite pastime of nearly everyone:

> At the first hint of revelry, out came the hot pokers and rags for hair curling. Mail-order patent shoes appeared as if by magic, and chapped, wind-burned skin was softened with buttermilk and cornstarch. A thrifty woman usually had a long-hidden bit of ribbon to wrap around her waist, and might bundle up a few roses in a sachet the night before, to scent her clothing. Wrinkle-smoothers and hair tonics were applied liberally. . . . In Nebraska, dances broke forth in the soddies and machine sheds, with dozens of kerosene lanterns casting light into the dark shadows and throwing crazy dancing patterns across the dirt floor. The caller would shout out for a quadrille, and sets of four couples would swing and bend to the fiddler's lively "Old Zip Coon" and "Leather Breeches." Or they would eagerly wait for the fiddle to "pop" on "Pop Goes the Weasel," as the women arched hands and the men ducked under. (Luchetti and Olwell, 30)

LIFE IN THE TOWNS

And then they went to town. Literally. To those dwarfed by the immensity of the Plains, a trip to town—even if it was ostensibly to buy a sack of sugar and a pair of new boots, or to arrange for milling grain or to meet a relative arriving by train to take up a homestead—was an opportunity for socialization. The general store, the barber shop, Main Street itself provided opportunities to exchange information on crops, catch up on news and gossip, quaff a beer, or attend a political rally. Just as in California those who had provided goods and services to the miners prospered more than the miners, so, too, to Plains towns gravitated the "butcher, baker, bootmaker, banker, merchant, saloonkeeper, doctor [and] barber. Inevitably their ranks also included desperadoes, shysters, prostitutes and scalawags, but mostly they were serious men and women bound upon the honest mission of building a new society in the wilderness" (Wheeler, 19–20). Though the Civil War slowed the town-building process, the Homestead Act spurred it, until by 1890 there were villages of "at least some pretension every ten miles or so across the central grasslands" (Wheeler, 20).

The railroads were instrumental in establishing many towns. They had been granted up to twenty square miles of public land per mile of track as a subsidy to encourage construction. This land they could sell as they chose to finance laying the rails. Surveyors moved ahead of the tracks, selecting town sites every six to ten miles. The "team haul" principle was consciously applied; town sites were placed at the distance farmers could travel to town by horse and wagon and return in the same day (Nelson, 85; 192, n.5). Every seventy miles or so, transcontinental railroads established a main depot, or division point, where repair shops for rolling stock could be built.

Others also sought to establish towns. Through the Townsite Act of 1844, settlers and/or speculators could stake out 320 acres and take possession for $1.25 an acre. Usually such sites were divided into town lots of 125' by 25', with the profits from sales ranging from $50 to $1,000 per lot. At one point, what with surveyors working for the railroads and for others platting towns, a Missouri River steamboat captain observed he could make more money by "carrying survey stakes than by transporting passengers" (Wheeler, 64).

Many towns were established by special interest groups. For example, Neosha, Kansas, was founded by a group of vegetarians; Amana, Iowa, by Mennonites; Cheever, Kansas, by prohibitionists; and many Kansas towns by the New England Emigrant Aid Society, whose members were ardent abolitionists. Nicodemas, Kansas, was founded by "the colored people of Lexington, Kentucky," and Runnymede, Kansas, was established as a haven for dissipated young English aristocrats who spent their time playing tennis and riding to the hounds—after coyotes, not foxes (Wheeler, 66).

Most town plats were reasonably regular grids, drawn as "T towns" in which the railroad and Main Street formed a T. The railroad depot was usually at one end of Main Street; at the other end was a public building, such as a courthouse, with businesses lining the streets and banks being situated on prime corner locations (Nelson, 85). Probably two of the most unusual town plats were the Octagon Plan of Neosha, Kansas, and one designed by Frederick Law Olmsted in which there were no straight lines and the blocks were shaped like melons, pears, and sweet potatoes.

Once the town was platted, boosters aggressively encouraged settlers. Newspapers, sometimes called "mother's milk to an infant town," were at the outset vehicles for public relations and development rather than for newsgathering. The town promoters shipped such advertising pamphlets and propagandizing papers east to attract new settlers. It was observed that if a town had several papers, it must be desperately in need of promotion. An English visitor who asked how a young town could afford four newspapers was told that "it took four newspapers to keep up such a city" (Wheeler, 65). Other methods were also tried to promote new towns. Some railroads ran free excursion trains from the East, putting up potential settlers in the local hotels, sometimes established just for this purpose. Other towns auctioned off prime lots or, as a gimmick, offered free lots to desirable professionals, to the first couple married in the town, or to the first baby born there. Clearly such towns intended to project an air of permanence.

However, some promotional brochures projected an image vastly different from reality. An 1858 brochure for Sumner, Kansas, showed steamboat docks, a waterfront business district, a mill, a machine shop, a factory, four churches, fine residences on tree-lined streets, and even a domed college. In reality, the town then consisted of a couple of general stores dotted along one graded street, and about two hundred houses, most of them shabbily constructed of wagon boxes and sod slabs and roofed in canvas or straw. Beautifully produced, the brochure was later condemned as a "chromatic triumph of lithographic mendacity" (Wheeler; 54).

No matter how they were established, most towns that survived in their competition for railroad spurs, the right to be county seat, and settlers had certain common denominators: a blacksmith shop, a livery stable, a general store, one or more saloons, and a hotel. Conditions were often somewhat primitive. At one hotel a guest complained about the grimy condition of the roller towel; he was told that there'd been "26 men that went before you and you're the first one that complained" (Wheeler, 27). Grace Fairchild tells of a Fort Pierre, South Dakota, hotel infested with lice (Wyman, *Frontier Woman* 39–40). Main Street was unpaved—usually dusty but a wallow of mud after rain.

Initially town businesses were constructed of any materials that were at hand and presented a hodgepodge of styles. However, when lumber became available an almost universal style appeared. The false-front building with its phony windows and massive cornice may have been "unabashed braggadocio," an attempt to be imposing in an architectural manifestation of the town's boosterism. Some townsmen took advantage of prefabricated buildings brought from midwestern lumberyards by freight wagons or boxcars.

The general store was stocked with staples—whiskey and Bibles and everything in between. One proprietor proudly announced that he carried "anything you might call for, from a $500 diamond ring to a pint of salt" (Wheeler, 88). As a town became more established, other stores catered to more specialized needs: the meat market, combined drugstore and doctor's office, drygoods and clothing stores, and an emporium for boots and shoes. There were, in addition, offices for real estate/insurance/loan agents, dressmakers' shops, restaurants as well as saloons, and small establishments selling fruits and cold drinks. Aaron Montgomery Ward, a drygoods salesman who had traveled throughout the West and heard customers' complaints about prices, printed his first catalogue of only 167 items in 1882. His goal: to sell directly to the consumers and thereby save them the middleman's markup. Naturally storekeepers objected, referring to the mail-order house derisively as "Monkey Ward,"

"A Boom Lithograph of Sumner, Kansas." Reproduced courtesy of the Kansas State Historical Society, Topeka, Kansas. Town and railroad boosters often lured settlers to the West with "engraved romances" such as this lithograph of Sumner, Kansas. Frequently such advertising portrayed proposed rather than actual town improvements.

especially as the catalogue swelled to 2,000 items by 1875 and to 75,000 before the end of the century (Wheeler, 118).

For the farmer, the town provided an incredible gamut of entertainment ranging from brutal animal fights and boxing matches to lyceum lectures and Gilbert and Sullivan operettas. The offerings were kaleidoscopic: minstrel shows, brass bands, itinerant jugglers and magicians; prostitutes and taxi dancers—girls who were employed by saloonkeepers to dance with patrons for a fee of 25 cents a dance; freak shows and traveling zoos and stereoscope exhibits, which one proprietor called "choice works of art" but which the county judge deemed to be "obscene and lascivious pictures." Major actors played the West; Hamlin Garland remembers seeing Edwin Booth in *Hamlet*. The audiences, however, were not always sophisticated. During one performance of *Uncle Tom's Cabin*, just as the bloodhounds had almost caught up with the escaping Eliza, a drunken cowboy "came to her rescue" and shot the trained animals dead (Wheeler, 178). During election years political rallies, speeches, and debates offered both entertainment and intellectual stimulation. Baseball was popular; in one nearly endless game the Blue Belts of Milford, Nebraska, beat the Seward team by a score of 97 to 25! But the favorite, for most people, was the circus.

In contrast to the democracy of the Plains where no one was looked down on for poverty or unfashionable clothes, some townsmen considered themselves to be superior to the "hayseeds" and "clodhoppers" who reveled in such entertainment. These townsmen inaugurated a new trend in the West—joining organizations, many of which had women's auxiliaries, for philanthropic or recreational purposes. At first many of these, such as the local militias or fire companies, had primarily civic functions to help build the community and maintain public order. But when one examines a list of organizations established in Colorado towns between 1882 and the turn of the century, one sees that the frontier, that "border between civilization and savagery," was indeed gone.

A whole range of specific denominations—Baptist, Methodist, Episcopal, Catholic, Congregational, African Methodist Episcopal, and Christian Science—established churches, a far cry from the comparative ecumenicism of earlier days. Some provided outlets for Civil War veterans of both sides: the Grand Army of the Republic, and the Sons of Civil War Veterans. Fraternal organizations proliferated—Masons, International Order of Odd Fellows (IOOF), Knights of Pythias, the Independent Order of Good Templars—as did professional and trade organizations—the Western Colorado Stock Growers' Association, the Typographical Union, the International Brotherhood of Locomotive Engineers, the Real Estate Exchange, and the Mesa County Teachers Association. There were cultural organizations such as the Chautauqua Literary and Scientific Circle, the Shakespeare Club, or the Young Men's

Cultural Club; and others celebrated hobbies and recreation—the Jockey Club, the Rifle Club, the Amateur Dramatic Club, and the Grand Junction Wheel [bicycling] Club (Underwood, 129–31).

In short, in contrast to the unending labor of early days on the homesteads, people in towns scattered liberally across the Plains now had leisure to spend on recreational activities. This, as much as the Bureau of the Census announcement in 1890 that there was no more free land, marked the end of the frontier. Only the paroxysms of the Indian wars needed to be experienced before the process of transforming the Great Plains was complete.

6

The Indian Frontier and the Frontier Regulars: The Army and the Indians on the Great Plains

Although pop culture, especially the Western film, has dramatized big battles between the cavalry and the Indians (usually Apaches) and has created the cliché of the cavalry coming to the rescue with bugles blaring and guidons streaming, the average soldier on the Plains rarely saw combat and the average Indian participated only in small raids as forces other than the military brought the demise of traditional Indian culture. In the last third of the nineteenth century, the army and the Indians, though cast as adversaries, were in reality joint protagonists in a conflict more properly described as an inexorable movement west of eastern material and technological culture bent on taming and exploiting the last free land. The Indian lost everything, but it was not the army that gained. The process was especially ironic when one considers the actors' immediate pasts: most troops had endured the blood, brutality, and carnage of the Civil War, which was fought (at least in part) for freedom; most Indians were denied their freedom and autonomy in the process of unwilling or grudging acculturation to an alien culture.

This last third of the nineteenth century was a period in which the federal government vacillated; unable to establish a viable policy reconciling mutually exclusive goals, it often contradicted itself while responding reactively to external demands rather than proactively from carefully thought-out policy. It was a period of quick, sharp violence, when even those who were committed to doing good caused terrible suffering, a period in which progress, so fervently extolled in Whitman's

George Armstrong Custer (1836–76), U.S. Army officer and author. From George Armstrong Custer, *My Life on the Plains: or, Personal Experiences with Indians* (Norman: University of Oklahoma Press, 1962). New edition © 1962 by the University of Oklahoma Press, Norman, Publishing Division of the University. Fifth printing, 1986. Reproduced courtesy of the University of Oklahoma Press.

"Passage to India," brought agriculture and commerce westward and, in the bringing, irrevocably destroyed a way of life. It was a period in which a nation faced a dilemma of conscience in which well-meaning people—red and white—struggled to advance incompatible goals and, in the process, ranged in their behavior and thought between idealism and pragmatism.

It was a period perhaps best symbolized by a Zuni kachina—a "tan-

Sitting Bull (1803?–90), Hunkpapa military, religious, and political leader. Reproduced from the collections of the National Archives.

gible representation of a spiritual being or 'god' that objectifies particular truths or dynamics of life." This kachina, in the creation myth, came out of the underworld fastened back-to-back to a "person from an alien world. The deformity condemned the two to an eternity of physical union in which neither could see nor understand the other" (Utley, *Indian Frontier* xix). It was a period of tortured debates between the peace chiefs and hot-blooded young men, between Christian reformers and army strategists. It was a period bounded roughly by the Sand Creek Massacre (1864) and the Battle of Wounded Knee (1890). It was a period, ultimately, when the frontier ended as one group gained clear dominance over the other.

THE FRONTIER ARMY

The U.S. Army after the Civil War was the subject of usual peacetime debates over its size—and therefore appropriations, its role, and its means of attaining and maintaining professionalism. Being the enforcer, not the creator, of national policy, the army faced two major assignments—policing the South during Reconstruction, and maintaining order on the frontier. Both inevitably brought severe criticism from those opposed to the policies and from those whose lives were most directly affected.

Moreover, those in the frontier army were distant—physically, ideologically, and socially—not only from the centers of power but from the support of civilian families and friends. In 1866 one newspaper editor opined that a "respectable American citizen" would no more think of joining the Regular Army "than he would volunteer for the penitentiary." In 1878 the *New York Sun* referred to the rank and file as "bummers, loafers and foreign paupers" (Foner, 74). Albert Barnitz, writing from Fort Wallace, Kansas, to his wife, Jennie, observed that "it must be very amusing to people in Ohio to be told that certain of their acquaintances are really engaged in war, in these, to them, peaceful times! . . . and yet it is not a very laughable matter . . . to see a poor fellow . . . with his scalp gone, and his body full of bullet holes, and revenge arrows, and his clothes taken off and limbs gashed in every conceivable manner" (Utley, *Life* 80). Though Frances Roe, an officer's wife, enjoyed a visit back east, she discovered that "citizens and army people have . . . little in common" (Roe, 333).

The scorn heaped on enlisted men was extraordinary. One wrote, "Let a regular soldier go into any of the cities of the states and you will see all the citizens stick up their noses" (Foner, 74). (It is significant that both observers separate the army from the "citizens.") Even on the frontier, no one—except perhaps the Indian—was thought so poorly of as a soldier. Private David Barrow wrote in 1878 that "there are only two creatures who look upon a soldier here without scorn and contempt, and they are little children and dogs" (Foner, 95).

The role of the frontier army was varied—to build and garrison forts; to drive white buffalo hunters and squatters from Indian reservations; to provide escorts for army paymasters and the U.S. mails; to maintain civil order (e.g., when towns competing for the right to be the county seat resorted to gunfire); to supervise the distribution of rations to reservation Indians and to prevent theft by corrupt agents; to prevent smuggling of contraband liquor onto reservations in sacks of oats and corn for cavalry horses; to protect miners and railroad construction crews; to prevent attacks on stage lines, railroads, or telegraph agencies; to protect visiting dignitaries, politicians, and peace commissioners; to bring Indians into reservations, and to engage in combat those who refused.

General George Crook's changing assignments reveal changing relationships between the U.S. government and Indians of the Plains. After gold was discovered in the Black Hills on the Sioux reservation, he was ordered to "arrest any . . . persons attempting to go into the Black Hills and to destroy all their transportation, guns and property." Nonetheless, many "sifted in." In dealing with such miners and prospectors, who believed that as citizens of "these here United States" they could go where they pleased and do as they pleased, Crook was protecting Indian rights (Crook, 188–89). By 1876 his assignment was to "compel the Sioux and Cheyenne Indians, who were off their reservation, to go on it. They were . . . notified that they must either go on the reservation . . . or else the troops might attack them wherever found" (Crook, 189). This shift in policy may have been an acknowledgment of a reality as old as Americans' disdain for the Proclamation of 1763—we *will* cross freely into new territory—but that made the job of the army in the West no easier.

The army was spread too thin to accomplish all that was expected of it. From a peak of 56,815 in September 1867, the army's strength was reduced in 1874 by a series of congressional appropriations acts to a total of 25,000 enlisted men—with officers to a force of just over 27,000. Actual strength was usually 10 percent under the number authorized (Utley, *Frontier Regulars* 12–15). Two of the three military divisions—the Missouri and the Pacific—were in the West, separated by the Continental Divide.

The force reduction affected the number of men, not the number of posts that had to be manned. With 430 companies to man some 200 posts, it was the company or troop, rather than the regiment, that became the tactical unit. A company could range from 50 to 100 men, with the number being determined by the president (Rickey, 48–49). Robert M. Utley observes that

> [in the] typical year of 1881, actual enlisted strength of the 120 cav-
> alry troops averaged 56 (46 privates); of the 60 artillery companies
> and batteries, 40 (28 privates); and of the 250 infantry companies,
> 41 (29 privates). But the sick, imprisoned, detached and detailed to
> daily and extra duties made further inroads. Fortunate was the
> company commander who could actually muster three-fourths of
> the men carried on his rolls. (*Frontier Regulars* 16)

Utely notes that at the Battle of Big Hole in 1877, Colonel John Gibbon commanded six companies of the Seventh Infantry "numbering 15 offi-cers and 146 enlisted men, or about 24 men per company *and sustained a costly reverse*" [italics added] (16).

Who were these men—officers, non-coms, and enlisted men of the frontier regulars? In the postwar army one could gain a commission in four ways: through graduation from West Point, through direct appoint-ment from civilian life, through conversion of Civil War volunteer status, and, for some enlisted men, through passing stringent tests. The West Pointer was not always respected, perhaps in part because the Academy had been labeled during the Civil War as a seedbed for secession since so many of its graduates wore gray in command positions. Some felt the West Pointers rested on their laurels or were snobbish. "He presumes a good deal on his West Point education and I cannot see where it has benefited him," wrote Captain Albert Barnitz of one young lieutenant whom he described as "slovenly . . . lazy, and unmilitary. . . . I would not give one good non-commissioned officer for half a dozen lieutenants like him" (Utley, *Life* 172). Captain Charles King noted that in the Fifth Cav-alry there was a vast difference between classroom theory and field prac-tice: "it is my opinion that, while the best riders in the cavalry service are from West Point, the best horsemen are from the ranks" (King, 157). And the enlisted man H. H. McConnell wrote of the West Point officers he had served under, "I never saw one that could drill a squad, ride a horse, know how to wear a sabre without getting it tangled up with his legs, mount a guard, make out a ration return, or inspect a carbine. . . . [N]ot one in ten . . . could compute the ration allowances for one hun-dred men for ten days. I have heard that they were generally familiar with the science of mixed drinks and were 'up' in the mysteries of 'open-ing a jackpot' "—though with the caste system, he never witnessed these latter skills firsthand (McConnell, 219–20).

Among the excellent officers who owed their regular commission to Civil War service was General Nelson A. Miles. These men had seen combat, many in command positions, and though they had to adopt new tactics on the Plains, they provided an experienced officer cadre. The appointees direct from civilian life claimed at least two years of wartime experience; for this and for the taint of apparent political influence, they were often regarded with both jealousy and suspicion, though on the whole they performed as well as West Pointers. Officers commissioned from the ranks made up 13 percent of line leadership in 1874. Many had won their commissions during the Civil War; many others had served in foreign armies—87 of the 193 officers risen from the ranks were foreign-born, but few of them rose above the rank of captain (Rickey, 71–72; Utley, *Frontier Regulars* 18).

In the shrunken peacetime army few received promotions, which were usually based on seniority. An 1877 analysis of the promotion system showed that a new second lieutenant might reach the rank of major in 24–26 years and colonel in 33–37 years (Utley, *Frontier Regulars* 19). This stagnation in rank affected morale; not the least reason was that postwar pay scales fixed in 1870 ranged from an annual $3,500 for a colonel to $1,400 for an infantry second lieutenant. This sum, apparently exorbitant in comparison to enlisted men's pay of $13 a month, was considerably less than that for men in comparable positions in civilian life. Moreover, unlike enlisted men who were provided the basics of food and clothing, officers were responsible—at least while in garrison—for their own food, and in frequent changes of post they incurred still more expenses. Worse yet, each year awaiting the passage of the appropriations bill, they had to wonder whether their pay might indeed be cut.

A final factor causing confusion and conflict was the matter of brevet rank. At the close of the Civil War many officers, including staff officers, received honorary ranks—or brevets—higher than their actual rank. For line officers these were usually the reward for meritorious service in battle. Many regimental commanders could thus be addressed as "general" though their actual rank was colonel; company commanders, actual captains, might be brevet colonels or even major generals. Brevet Major General George Armstrong Custer, for example, was a lieutenant colonel of the Seventh Cavalry. But socially and often officially he was addressed by his brevet rank.

Captain Arthur T. Lee, a soldier-poet, summed up the essence of the brevets:

What Is a Brevet?

As Captain Forbes walked off parade,
Sam Green inquiringly said:
"Pray tell me, Cap.,—and tell me true,

Why all those officers in blue
Walk up and touch their caps to you:
They've leaves and eagles, them 'ere chaps,
Whilst you've but bars upon your straps.

"Why, Sam," says Forbes, "you *must* be green;
The reason's plainly to be seen:—
My straps, so humble in their place,
Are worth the symbol on their face.
Whilst leaves and eagles pay no debts:—
Those officers are all brevets."
    Says Green, "that puzzles me,—you bet;—
Cap, tell me,—what is a brevet?"
    "Well, Sam,—to put it through your pate,
You listen, whilst I illustrate,
You see yon turkey on the fence:—
That's turkey, Sam, in every sense;
Yon turkey-buzzard on the tree:—
He's *brevet* turkey:—do you see?"

        Moral
A Turkey has some value, Sam,
A Buzzard isn't worth a damn!   (Utley, *Life* xiii–xiv)

To fill the enlisted men's ranks, the postwar army could no longer depend on "legions of fresh young men fired by a sense of mission to save the Union." The pay was poor—ranging from $13 a month for privates to $22 a month for line sergeants. Though regulations required the paymaster to come every two months, the time between visits often stretched to six. In addition, the soldier was paid in greenbacks, which many shops and saloons would not accept; the soldier, exchanging his paper money for specie, lost money—15 percent, 20 percent, even 40 percent—in the exchange (Foner, 17). Thus, except when the civilian economy was in trouble, it was hard to attract enough enlistees who were better than mediocre.

Recruiting officers scoured the cities; consequently the urban poor and unskilled workers predominated. "Of 7734 enlistees in 1882, . . . 2373 identified themselves as laborers, 838 as soldiers, and 668 as farmers. There were also substantial numbers of teamsters, clerks, bakers, and blacksmiths," but few architects, teachers, or musicians. From 1865 to 1874 more than half of all recruits had been born in a foreign country, the majority in Ireland and Germany (Utley, *Frontier Regulars* 22–23). Most had little education; many were illiterate. H. H. McConnell, recalling his first night as a recruit in the Carlisle cavalry barracks, observed that although there were "a few young men who would have done credit to any walk of life," the vast majority were 'bounty jumpers,' blackguards and criminals of various degrees, or, at any rate, men who had sought the army as an asylum from the punishments that the law would have justly meted out to them had they remained in civil life" (Mc-Connell, 13). Charles King remembers that many of the recruits under his command had enlisted under false names, among them "Jackson Bewregard" and Jules Verne! He reflected, "If the police forces of our large Eastern cities were at a loss to account for the disappearance of . . . their 'regular boarders,' a flying trip to the Black Hills" would have found them. He suggests that many men enlisted as a way of getting free transportation to within easy striking distance of the gold mines (King, 163). But General George Forsythe counted among the men serving under him on a wagon escort in 1865 a wider, more positive cross-section: "a bookkeeper, a farm boy, a dentist, and a blacksmith, a young man of position trying to gain a commission and a salesman ruined by drink, an ivory carver and a Bowery tough" (Rickey, 18).

Few recruits had as their motive identification with the military lifestyle. Many were young men who saw the military as an economic opportunity despite the low army pay. William Hustede of the First Cavalry put it simply: "[I] was working in a grocery store for $2.00 per week—the army paid $13 per month" (Rickey, 19). Aside from the steady pay, some enlisted because of the lure of the West, some for adventure—many of these had been too young to participate in the Civil War. Still others, after 1876, were "Custer avengers" who enlisted when Congress raised the size of cavalry regiments to 100 men each after the debacle at Little Big Horn (Rickey, 21–22).

For most recruits the depots at Jefferson Barracks, Missouri; David's Island, New York; Columbus Barracks, Ohio; and Newport Barracks, Kentucky, were primarily induction centers. Basic training was minimal to nonexistent; until 1890 most military training was done in an operational unit. Few recruits had prior military training, so much of the instruction was designed to teach them "subordination, obedience, and their place in the army . . . the respect and obedience due at all times to commissioned and noncommissioned officers" (Rickey, 42). Recruits were hardened up by daily calisthenics. At the recruit depots many men "learned the virtues of a weekly bath under the supervision of a noncom every Saturday!" (Rickey, 43). At Newport Barracks, where malaria was feared, at least one daily routine was popular: each morning the recruits were issued three grains of quinine in an ounce of whiskey (Rickey, 42).

After such rudimentary training, the recruits were shipped west via land-grant railroads that were required to provide transportation, though not necessarily comfort, to the army. However, few frontier forts were located on railroad lines, so the recruits transferred to wagons, steamboats, or stagecoaches for the rest of the trip. Sometimes they marched hundreds of miles to their destination, fifteen miles a day being average. On such treks they quickly learned water discipline.

Desertion was one of the major problems for the postwar army; the proportions of the problem, however, are astounding. In 1866, from an army whose enlisted strength was 54,138, fully 14,068 deserted (Foner, 6). Though this may be explained in part by Civil War soldiers wanting an early return to civilian life, from 1867 to 1891 a full third of the men recruited eventually deserted (Rickey, 143). Captain Albert Barnitz of the Seventh Cavalry describes as many as ten non-coms and enlisted men leaving in one night (Utley, *Life* 44); on another occasion four deserters, when fired upon by guards, returned fire "quite briskly" (53); and from July 6 to 8, 1867, thirty-four men deserted and a plot was uncovered that would have taken a third of the command (86). In November 1867 Barnitz fully expects desertions immediately following payday; the men had not been paid for six months and were "sorely distressed for the want of little necessaries, even needles and thread, postage stamps and stationary" (128).

Among other causes suggested by officers analyzing the desertion problem was the generally poor quality of recruits, young men enlisting simply to get a free ride to the West, grievances about living conditions and about being forced to do nonmilitary manual labor, fear of Indians, drunkenness, and tyrannical superior officers. Barnitz obliquely blames Custer for the loss of 1,200 men by desertion from the Seventh Cavalry (Utley, *Life* 161), and Brigadier General Frederick W. Benteen (never one of Custer's admirers) blames his harshness for these mass desertions. During the summer of 1869, General Custer "had in use a hole dug in the ground about 30 × 30 feet, by about 15 feet deep, entrance by ladder, hole boarded over: *this was the guard house*, and a man even absent from a [roll] call was let down [into it. There were so many men there] I don't know how the prisoners laid down" (qtd. in Rickey, 146).

Nearly always, a hierarchical caste system was at work in the army. Rank literally had its privileges—in housing, food, justice, and severity of punishment. A private of the Thirteenth Infantry wrote, "In our regiment an enlisted man was a *thing* [italics added] apart, and he was given to understand **The Caste System of the Army** that there was a vast gulf between him and his officers" (Rickey, 69). At Fort Laramie in the 1880s officers' children were educated separately from enlisted men's (Rickey, 63). Officers' wives had civilian servants to help cook and clean and care for children; Frances Roe had, sequentially, several Chinese men, a Polish woman, and a Negro woman as cooks. In addition, officers had an enlisted man as servant, or "striker." These soldiers "perform service part military and part menial . . . fall heir to [the officer's] cast-off clothing, drink his whiskey, run errands for his wife, build chicken-coops, draw rations, attend his horses, and, in short, gobble up all the 'crumbs' of whatever kind that 'fall from his table,' hence the very expressive term *dog-robber*. . . . [Such men] have no pride about them, and still less self-respect" (McConnell, 107).

For some officers' wives, such as Frances Roe, the striker was valued less than a dog. She writes:

Findlay [our soldier cook] is so stupid he cannot appreciate the cunning things the little dog does. [Once the puppy snatched a sizzling steak meant for dinner but, despite burning his mouth, would not drop it.] Findlay ran after the little hound, yelling and swearing, and I ran after Findlay to keep him from beating my dog. Of course we did not have beefsteaks that day, but as I told [my husband], it was entirely Findlay's fault. He should have kept watch of things, and not made it possible for [the dog] to kill himself by eating a whole big steak!" (Roe 62–63)

On yet another instance her attitude toward enlisted men indicated the "vast gulf." After describing the rich social life among the officers and their wives—luncheons, card parties, and cotillions—she observes, quite seriously, "With all this pleasure, the soldiers are not being neglected. Every morning there are drills and . . . target practice . . . and of course there are inspections and other things" (Roe, 222).

Not all wives were as self-centered as Mrs. Roe. Jennie Barnitz, for example, notes that her husband's orderly had been standing by their front door in a cold, hard wind and prevailed upon her husband "to let him come in and [get] warm as there is no one here this evening." Though it's doubtful she would have invited him in if the house had been full of guests—such things just weren't done—she sees and treats him as a human: "I do pity the enlisted man" (qtd. in Utley, *Life* 130).

Among the men, despite distinctions between ranks made necessary by command structure, both officers and men often played on the same baseball team; and in the field, class distinctions were less obvious than on post (Rickey, 65, 66).

Although the caste system based on rank was sometimes insensitive and unpleasant, the prejudice experienced by **Blacks in** black soldiers was even more insidious. In 1866 Congress pro- **the Army** vided for four Negro regular army regiments, the Ninth and Tenth Cavalry and the Twenty-Fourth and Twenty-Fifth Infantry. When Indians, fascinated by their hair, called the Tenth Cavalry "Buffalo Soldiers," they proudly adopted the name and made the buffalo the central figure of the regimental crest. Before long, the term applied to all black soldiers.

To them, the army was a career superior to any they could find in civilian life. Though most were illiterate, requiring their white officers to perform paperwork usually handled by non-coms, "the blacks excelled in discipline, morale, patience and good humor in adversity, physical endurance, and sobriety" (Utley, *Frontier Regulars* 26). Complaints about drunkenness were rare, and their desertion rate was far lower than that of white troops. Most important, they performed so well on campaign and in combat that General Sherman, who admittedly preferred white troops, declared of them in 1874: "They are good troops, they make first-rate sentinels, are faithful to their trust, and are as brave as the occasion calls for" (Utley, *Frontier Regulars* 26).

Esprit de corps was high in the black regiments in part because of their excellent performance and in part because of solidarity from shared experiences with prejudice. Colonel Benjamin Grierson, like many white officers commanding black troops, was often the object of social and professional ostracism. In one instance at Fort Leavenworth the post commander, Colonel William Hoffman, ordered the "nigger troops" of the Tenth Cavalry not to form on parade so close to his Third Infantry. To the astonishment of their men, the two colonels verbally accosted one another when Grierson went to the defense of his troops (Utley, *Frontier Regulars* 27). As long as the Tenth was stationed at Leavenworth, Hoffman remained "contemptuous of Negro troops and apparently of officers who served with them" and quartered them on low ground that soon became a swamp, causing many men to be sent to the hospital with pneumonia; he refused to allow the black troops to march in review; and he harassed Grierson with complaints about the Tenth's "untidy quarters, alleged tardiness to meals [and] training methods" (Leckie, 13–14).

Such discrimination was not the product of a single bigoted officer. Custer refused to serve with Negro troops, turning down a colonelcy with the Ninth Cavalry, which, ironically, later rescued part of the Seventh at Wounded Knee (Leckie, 8, 255–58). Elizabeth Custer refers to the surgeon's servant as a "darky" (186). When one remembers that Custer did, after all, fight for the Union, this suggests the nearly universal prejudice (or condescension) toward blacks at the time and hints at what the Negro regiments must have faced.

Blacks were excluded from some branches of the army—artillery, ordnance, engineers, and signal corps—as being "outside their competence" (Foner, 135). Nor were black soldiers promoted from the ranks. One wrote bitterly to the New York *Freeman*, a Negro paper:

> Since the organization of the four colored regiments . . . not a single colored soldier has been promoted from the ranks. . . . It is not that they do not possess the necessary qualifications . . . but that the sentiment of the white men of the army is decidedly against it, and

any ambitious aspirant for shoulder-straps [officer's epaulets] . . . is promptly and effectually given to understand that "spades are not trumps" here. (Foner, 137–38)

Charles King unconsciously reflects the broader social climate when he comments on his friend, Captain Nick Nolan of the Tenth Cavalry, who "has an Ethiopian lieutenant (a West Pointer) and sixty of the very best darkies that ever stole chickens" (King, 8). The insensitive Frances Roe adds her insight: "There is one advantage in being with colored troops—one can always have good servants" (Roe, 55).

Despite widespread prejudice against them in both military and civilian communities, Negro troops generally performed well—perhaps because, as the Tenth Cavalry chaplain observed, they believed that the "colored people of the whole country are more or less affected by their conduct in the Army" (Utley, *Frontier Regulars* 27).

For all soldiers, life in the frontier army was difficult. When the *Army and Navy Journal* asked its readers to contrast mid-winter service in Montana, Dakota, and Idaho or mid-summer campaigning in Texas, New Mexico, and Arizona with anything known during the Civil War, respondents forcefully replied that the "latter was a mere picnic of pleasure compared to the former" (Foner, 14). The truth of this seemingly improbable assertion can be seen by examining the material surroundings of the frontier regular—his weapons, food, clothing, housing, and medical care; his duties both in garrison and in the field; and the discipline to which he was subjected.

Hardship for the Soldiers

Clothing. The soldier of the Indian wars might at first look like the little brother of the Civil War soldier wearing hand-me-downs, for from 1865 to about 1872, uniforms were Civil War surplus. Consequently the frontier regular suffered, as had his predecessor, from shoddy materials and poor workmanship that unscrupulous, profiteering suppliers had foisted on the War Department. The standard clothing issue provided at the recruit depot was a "navy-blue wool sack coat, two pairs of light-blue kersey trousers, two gray or dark blue flannel shirts, a couple of suits of wrist and ankle-length two-piece underwear, a caped overcoat of light-blue wool, a pair of rough boots or ankle-high brogans, a forage cap (or kepi), and a leather waist belt" (Rickey, 35).

Rarely did the uniforms fit, so the soldiers had them altered by the company tailor—at the soldier's expense, with the cost deducted from his pay. In 1872 the army introduced a new uniform with revised sizes and patterns, presumably more compatible with the human body. H. H. McConnell was none too sure: "None of the clothing issued was fit to wear until it had been altered from top to bottom. The clothing furnished was of four sizes—from number one to number four—and the [limited]

... stock on hand often necessitated the issuing of a number four garment to a number one man" (McConnell, 230). The tailor could usually alter these into "respectably fitting uniforms"; however, McConnell found little else good to say about the tailor, "a non-combatant, usually of the same kind as the dog-robber or the company clerk" (McConnell, 230). (Some of the combat soldier's resentment of the non-combatant is evident here. Later McConnell observed that most "real" soldiers regard band-members, clerks, tailors, and "extra-duty men of all kinds as ... shirking or getting out of legitimate duties" [266].)

The uniform, even altered by the tailor, had many shortcomings. The material tended to wear out quickly in the field or in garrison fatigue duty. It was far too hot for summer or for southern posts, and not nearly warm enough for winter on the northern plains. The long underwear and woolen socks itched, despite orders to change socks frequently and underwear once a week. The shoes were especially uncomfortable, made of stiff leather with the soles fastened by brass screws that conducted heat and cold and, worse, raised blisters and gouged holes in the wearer's feet. Shoes and boots, manufactured at the military prison at Fort Leavenworth, were so inexpertly crafted that rights and lefts were almost indistinguishable. One soldier solved the matter of fit by walking through a creek until the uppers were thoroughly soaked and then wearing the wet shoes for the entire day, thereby getting a "foot form and comfort." Soldiers usually rubbed soap on their feet and socks to avoid blisters from new shoes (Rickey, 124). There were no overshoes or rubbers; to protect their feet from the northern Wyoming winter, soldiers of the Eighteenth Infantry competed for burlap sacks with which they wrapped their feet to keep from freezing (Rickey, 123). Colonel Richard I. Dodge of the Eleventh Infantry wrote in 1887, "The shoe furnished the enlisted soldier is a disgrace to the civilization of the age.... Many a man is discharged from the service a cripple for life, from having been forced to wear the things called shoes now furnished by the Government" (Foner, 20).

Eventually changes—some official, some not—were achieved to make the uniform more serviceable. In the Southwest, clothing of lighter materials and colors was issued—white shirts and white canvas trousers, even the white cork helmets used by British troops in India. In the North, the Clothing Bureau experimented with all manner of furs and even canvas lined with sheepskin or blanket materials. One officer's wife described her husband: "[C]lad in buffalo skins, trousers and overcoat with the fur inside, mufflers over his ears, his hands encased in fur mittens, his face in a mask, leaving space sufficient only to see his way, he presents an appearance rivaling his Eskimo brother" (Utley, *Frontier Regulars* 76).

From individualism or necessity, frontier soldiers often created variant uniforms never thought of by Uncle Sam. Some cavalrymen adopted the more comfortable Indian moccasins, lined their pants with canvas, and wore shirts of many unregulation colors, including checks, often made by their wives; some were even seen in fringed buckskin. Charles King, campaigning with Crook, talks about troops making "rude leggins, moccasins, etc." from the skins captured from the Indians on the previous day when they defeated American Horse's band at Slim Buttes (King, 135). To the outside observer, frontier soldiers might look more like *banditti* than military men. A *New York Times* reporter described the arrival of the Fifth Cavalry at Fort Fetterman in July 1876:

> To a fastidious eye . . . there was something shocking in the disregard of regulation uniform, and the mud-bespattered appearance of the men; but it was a pleasure to see how full of vim, of spirit, and emphatically of fight, the fellows looked. . . . About the only things in their dress which marked them as soldiers were their striped pants and knee boots, both well bespattered with mud. Their blue Navy shirts, broad brimmed hats, belts stuffed with cartridges, and loose handkerchiefs knotted about the neck, gave them a wild, bushwhacker appearance. (qtd. in Utley, *Frontier Regulars* 77)

Food. One cannot discuss the frontier soldiers' food without considering whether it was eaten in garrison or in the field, and if in garrison, whether we're speaking of officers or enlisted men. Paragraph 1367 of Army Regulations in effect during 1868 clearly establishes "the ration," or the "established daily allowance of food for one person":

> twelve ounces or pork or bacon or canned beef (fresh or corned), or one pound and four ounces of fresh beef, or twenty-two ounces of salt beef; eighteen ounces of soft bread or flour, or sixteen ounces of hard bread, or one pound and four ounces of cornmeal; and to have, every one hundred rations, fifteen pounds of pease or beans, or ten pounds of rice or hominy; ten pounds of green coffee, or eight of roasted (or roasted and ground) coffee, or two pounds of tea; fifteen pounds of sugar; four quarts of vinegar; four pounds of soap; four pounds of salt; four ounces of pepper; one pound and eight ounces of adamantine or star candles; and to troops in the field when necessary, four pounds of yeast powder to one hundred rations of flour" (Custer, *Following* 205n.)

Because of their transient status, troops at the induction depots received the worst food in the army. The soldiers' health often took second priority to the cook's convenience. Second Cavalryman James B. Wilkinson reported that "at Jefferson Barracks [1882] pork meat was put around at tables the night before the following morning's breakfast. The meat would be spoiled, turned green, by morning. Some ate it—others did not." Any complaints made to officers resulted in only temporary improvement (Rickey, 39).

Breakfast at recruit depots was usually saltpork, fried mush, or "stew that had been cooked all night." Dinner was slumgullion stew with dried bread, and supper was "dry bread and coffee, with an occasional treat of three prunes" (Rickey, 39). One soldier hypothesized years later that the awful food may have been "necessary preparation for what was in the offing—field service against the anti-social redskins" (Rickey, 40). Not only was the recruit depot food unpalatable, but it was usually insufficient in quantity. Occasionally newspaper exposés resulted in noncoms being convicted of mismanagement of ration funds.

Even a cursory glance at the Army Regulations reveals a complete absence of fresh fruits and vegetables from the daily ration; the vinegar (four quarts per hundred rations) was the only attempt to combat scurvy. In part this was due to the difficulty and expense of transport to the western forts—though that was no excuse at recruit depots. For a while the army experimented with a variety of vegetables, "compressed into a large cake, thoroughly dried, requiring but a small quantity for a meal" (Rickey, 117). These, however, weren't popular.

Many officers recognized the need for fresh vegetables. Colonel Robert E. Johnson testified in 1876 that "the addition of one pound of potatoes or other vegetables to the daily ration would materially reduce the sick list" (Rickey, 117–18). At many posts, company gardens were planted. In 1869 at Fort Rice, Dakota, for example, troopers raised lettuce, radishes, spinach, squash, cucumbers, and new potatoes (Rickey, 119). Other soldiers bought canned fruit and tomatoes at the post commissary with their own funds, traded army-issue sowbelly with nearby Indians for fresh meat or vegetables, or purchased treats such as pickles, turkeys, onions, apples, raisins, butter, and spices from the company funds, which were established from the sale of issue rations. (Often surplus flour was sold; the regulations called for eighteen ounces of soft bread *or flour* per day; a pound of flour resulted in more than a pound of bread, and the surplus could thus be sold.)

Because the army wanted its soldiers to be prepared to fend for themselves in the field, food was usually prepared by the men themselves rather than by a cook. Men were detailed to ten-day tours as cooks and bakers. Not only was the food "miserably cooked," but "the man is in the kitchen [just] long enough to ruin his clothing without extra pay to replace it" (Utley, *Frontier Regulars* 85). Soldiers groused that cooks destroyed more men than Indians did (Foner, 21).

One officer observed, "nearly as much food is wasted as is used in the

Army from ignorance and inexperience of company cooks" (Rickey, 121). Much food was spoiled due to improper handling and storage and poor preservation techniques. Often ancient rations were full of worms and weevils. The bacon loaded at Fort Reno for the 1866 expedition into the Big Horn country was "so old and rotted that the . . . fat had commenced to sluff off from the lean, and it was . . . also full of mice, as was the flour" (Rickey, 122).

Bad as the food was in garrison, it could be worse in the field. In addition, the need to be a lean, mean combat force meant that men took only the essentials. General Crook noted that "in the field one eats only to live" and on the Yellowstone expedition of 1876 abandoned his wagon train with supplies and prohibited both officers and men from carrying more baggage than could be carried on the saddle: one blanket, one rubber blanket, coffee, sugar, bacon, and hardtack (Crook, 203). This expedition knew real hunger, existing for some days on half rations and then, finally, "for breakfast—water and tightened belts." When they captured American Horse's camp, "there had fallen into our hands 5000 pounds of dried meats and fruits. . . . This was a godsend, as we had already had to eat some of our horses. . . . To us who have to depend on them so much it seems like murder to kill horses." Nonetheless, to starving troopers, "fat colts are ever so much better than . . . beef" (Crook, 206). The infantry made a standing joke that "if we only marched far enough, they would eat all of the cavalry horses" (Crook, 209).

The hardships of this expedition tried the men in every way, not just by starvation. A young officer wrote of the suffering, particularly to the infantry:

> I have seen men become so exhausted that they were actually insane, but there was no way of carrying them except for some mounted officer or man to give them his own horse, which was done constantly. I saw men who were very plucky sit down and cry like children because they could not hold out. When there came a chance to fight, however, everyone was mad enough to fight well. (Crook, 206)

This passage also indicates that much time in the field was spent reconnoitering rather than fighting. Such privations captured the essence of many operations of the Indian wars; combat was an almost invigorating interlude in unending boredom and misery.

In extraordinary contrast was Eveline Alexander's recollection of the Fourth of July, 1866, as she accompanied her husband to his new posting. Camped near Fort Cobb in Indian Territory, "we passed a comfortable Fourth and drank to its many returns in a large tin cup of lemonade. We dined about seven: had tomato soup, wild turkey, beefsteak, green peas, and canned peaches for desert [*sic*]" (54). In October of that year the Alexanders entertained General Sherman at Fort Stevens, Colorado. Though their quarters was a tent, and though the day before the wind blew so hard that it broke some of her plates, overturned the soup, and blew dust into the blancmange she was preparing, the dinner was a success. In her rather self-mocking style Eveline writes: "It is the fashion after entertaining great men to publish the bill of fare, so I will note mine here. First course, beef vegetable soup; second, saddle of mutton with jelly, green peas, kirshaw squash, cabbage, and beets; third, soft custard blanc mange with cream and sugar, and coffee" (Alexander, 88–89). One must remember that her husband was a very junior officer entertaining the commander of the Division of the Missouri and that such a meal was far from typical.

Living Conditions. The fact that General Sherman was entertained in a tent suggests that many frontier regulars lived under canvas both in the field and on new posts. Rarely was the frontier fort surrounded by a stockade (Forts Phil Kearney and C. F. Smith on the Bozeman Trail were exceptions). Instead the buildings, constructed of whatever material was at hand—adobe, logs placed upright, even sod—simply sat on the plain like a collection of tiny houses exposed to the elements and looking more like a village than a military installation.

Many forts were temporary, being built and abandoned as military needs changed. In 1868 a permanent building required the permission of the secretary of war, and the 1872 appropriations act included a clause stipulating that construction of a new post costing more than $20,000 required congressional approval (Utley, *Frontier Regulars* 90 n.4). As long as many forts were in operation, "temporary" buildings, however squalid, continued to be used.

Sometimes the fort seemed a blemish on its surroundings. A young lieutenant wrote of Fort Bayard, New Mexico, in 1871:

The locality was all that could be desired, the Post everything undesirable. Huts of logs and round stones, with flat dirt roofs that in summer leaked and brought down rivulets of liquid mud; in winter the hiding place of the tarantula and the centipedes, with ceilings of "condemned" canvas; windows of four and six panes, swinging doorlike on hinges (the walls were not high enough to allow them to slide upward); low, dark, and uncomfortable. Six hundred miles from the railroad. (Utley, *Frontier Regulars* 81)

A similar isolation and squalor shocked a young bride arriving at Fort Harker, Kansas, in 1867 with her officer husband. Exhausted by the trip from Detroit by railroad, an ox-drawn freighter's wagon, and finally an army ambulance (a stagecoach-like vehicle), she brightened when her

"Fort Larned, 1867." Reproduced courtesy of the Kansas State Historical Society, Topeka, Kansas. This picture, first published in *Harper's Weekly* on June 8, 1867, was accompanied by the caption, "The western army could represent nothing more than a thin blue line on a vast tract of land."

husband announced they'd soon be home. But following his pointing finger, all she could see was "the stub of a stovepipe" protruding from the ground. Though "Old Glory" floated overhead, little else was as she expected. Indeed, her new home was a dugout. She remembered later:

> I gazed with disgusted disappointment around the bare, squalid room. Its conveniences were limited to one camp chair, two empty candle boxes and a huge box stove, red with rust and grime, its hearth gone and the space filled with a tobacco-stained hill of ashes, the peak of which was surrounded by "chewed quids" of unknown vintage.... The walls of the kitchen were ... supported by logs, while the ceiling was of the same material and covered with dirt. ... Canvas covered the ceiling and dirt sides [of the living room]. It sagged slightly in the center and trembled under the scampering feet of pack-rats and prairie mice. (Bartlett, 352–53).

At Fort Smith, Arkansas, in 1866, Eveline Alexander seems happy in a tent "lined with blue army blankets" that protect it from dampness and make it cooler on hot days. For a carpet she has a buffalo skin; on her bed, a red blanket. On raw evenings the tent is made cozy by "a camp kettle full of coals brought up from the company kitchen" (Alexander, 34–35).

At camp on Big Creek, Kansas, the Custers enjoyed the privileges of rank, having "as many rooms as some houses have" by finagling a collection of tents, each one being a "room"—a hospital tent about 14' by 16' for a sitting room, a 10' by 12' wall tent for a bedroom, a Sibley tent (modeled on a teepee, an example of reverse acculturation on the Plains) for the cook tent, and a real teepee of buffalo hides with "rude drawings representing the history of the original owner, his prowess at killing Indians at war with his tribe, the taking of the white man's scalp, or the stealing of ponies" (Custer, *Following* 71–75).

Of whatever construction, whether permanent or temporary, tents or brick buildings, a frontier post followed a distinctive layout. Officers' quarters faced enlisted men's barracks across a parade ground, in the center of which was the post flagpole. At either end of the rectangle and scattered nearby were "administrative offices, warehouses, workshops, corrals, and the post trader's store, and 'suds row,' homes of NCO's married to laundresses" (Utley, *Frontier Regulars* 82).

Officers' quarters were selected by rank, and in their journals some army wives express bitterness at being ranked out of quarters after they'd fixed them up to their personal preferences. If a man was killed in action, his widow's sorrow was made worse by having to move out as quickly as possible.

Although some officers' wives complained about having to share a double-family house—and thus hear what went on next door—enlisted men had no privacy. Privates and corporals bunked in one large room, whereas sergeants usually had small adjoining cubicles. Until the 1870s soldiers slept in pairs on bed sacks stuffed with straw or hay. One's "bunky" might become his closest confidant, but it could be aggravating never to be alone, even in bed. One enlisted man pleaded that "provision be made for the men to sleep singly and alone and not keep up the present barbarous and unhealthy system of having men sleep in couples summer and winter" (Foner, 18). In 1875 the change was put into effect, but conditions were still crowded. Cots were arranged along the wall about three or four feet apart. In lieu of a closet, a soldier placed all his possessions in a footlocker. The center aisle, thus, might be no wider than eight to ten feet between rows of cots. Often, especially in summer, barracks were so infested with roaches and bedbugs that soldiers longed to sleep outside. But men generally had to have permission from an officer to leave barracks after taps. Corporals and older soldiers usually had the best locations for cots—near the stove in winter and the windows in summer. Married enlisted men and their families often lived in "a collection of overcrowded sheds and shanties" whose location was unsanitary, thereby breeding disease (Foner, 17–19; Rickey, 81–82).

For many years—into the mid-1880s—there was no indoor plumbing in the barracks. Water was stored in barrels at the rear of the building. Kitchen slops were dumped in crude sewers near the barracks, and that collection of garbage and grease attracted swarms of flies during warm weather. Privies were erected over holes dug in the yards, were used until they filled, and then were moved, so that "backyards became literally honey-combed with deposits of filth" (Foner, 19). This was all the more dangerous at posts where water was pumped from wells rather than hauled from rivers. Despite army regulations that men must bathe once a week, at most posts there were no bathhouses for enlisted men.

Health and Disease. Under such conditions it is no surprise that as late as 1894 men quipped that if they wanted to be well taken care of "they [must] become inmates of either the military prison or a national cemetery" (Utley, *Frontier Regulars* 82). It may be surprising that soldiers' health was as good as it was, though one young private wryly observed, "Our health was excellent, it had to be, because medical attention was conspicuous by its absence." Nonetheless, every post or fixed detachment rated a surgeon or assistant surgeon, and the army acts of 1866 and 1868 provided for 222 medical officers (Utley, *Frontier Regulars* 8). However, getting them was often difficult; the low army pay and uncomfortable living conditions discouraged many doctors from seeking a military career. Consequently at many posts civilian contract doctors were hired. Routine care at the post hospital was provided by enlisted men detailed to this extra duty.

Disease caused more casualties than Indian arrows and bullets. Utley reports that each year, for every 1,000 men, army surgeons treated 1,800 cases; of these, about 1,550 were for disease and the rest were for accidents, wounds, and injuries. Of the thirteen deaths per 1,000, eight were from disease and five from wounds or accidents (*Frontier Regulars* 86). Army posts suffered from the same outbreaks of disease that affected other frontier settlements—diphtheria, typhoid, smallpox, influenza, and cholera. Though inoculation for smallpox had been practiced for years in the regular army, supplies of vaccine were sometimes inadequate. When Asiatic cholera swept the West in 1867, it caused more soldier deaths than did combat. The Seventh Cavalry, for instance, between 1866 and 1868 lost 36 men killed by Indians, 6 drowned, and 2 missing in action; in the same period 51 died of cholera (Rickey, 132). Scurvy was a constant problem in garrisons without gardens; at Fort Phil Kearney in the early spring of 1867 the post surgeon ordered the "scurvy gang" out to eat wild onions (Rickey, 132).

Venereal diseases, however, were the most common medical problem at western posts. Some soldiers arrived with the disease from recruit depots and eastern cities, but many contracted it from Indian women and frontier prostitutes. Colonel N.A.M. Dudley observed that two-thirds of the men in the post hospital at Fort Custer, Montana Territory, in 1886 suffered from venereal disease; he therefore argued for the creation of a large military reservation segregating his men from "the class of Indians that settle around a post [and who] have a large number of worthless, lewd women along, who are more or less diseased" (Rickey, 131).

There were no medics in the field in the Indian wars, and soldiers knew little about first aid. *The Soldiers Handbook* issued to all recruits provided a cursory discussion: cuts healed more quickly than bullet wounds; a wounded man should be placed on his back and given a drink of water; and there were two types of bleeding, venous and arterial, the latter requiring a tourniquet (Herschler, 52, 54).

At Fort Laramie, carbolic acid was in use as an antiseptic as early as 1870; there, too, anesthesia—either chloroform or ether—was used for surgery. But in contrast to official advice, soldier lore affirmed that to prevent infection one should spit tobacco juice into the wound. For most soldiers who were seriously wounded in combat, comrades applied bandages to staunch the bleeding, stabilized them as well as possible (often with a swallow of whiskey), and evacuated them. The vehicle of transport was often the Indian travois, which could go where a wheeled wagon could not. The jolting of almost any form of transportation, however, was excruciating; wounded soldiers "might as well be stretched on the rack as in an army wagon" (Rickey, 327).

Sickness was not only physical. Sometimes the mind could stand no more on this military frontier. Charles King writes of one survivor of the

Little Bighorn who could take it no more: "The Custer massacre had preyed upon his mind as to temporarily destroy his intellect, or make it too keen for the wits of the Medical Department." Whether he was insane or not was uncertain, for one of the detachment taking him east reported "he was the sensiblest man you ever saw by the time we got past Bismarck" (King, 95). Another soldier seemed genuinely psychotic. Taken to the post hospital at Fort Abraham Lincoln, he "almost constantly talked about Indians, and after he had tried to insert the tines of a fork in an ear to dig Indians out, he was placed in a straight jacket" (Rickey, 329).

Duties and Discipline. Many soldiers had little sympathy for such disorders, considering them to be merely cases of malingering. This was not surprising, for in garrison they were kept busy and in the field they faced real privations, even when they were not in combat. The daily routine was explicitly detailed in the post's general orders and accounted for virtually every minute of the soldiers' waking life. Elizabeth Custer observed that bugle calls regulated the day—"we needed timepieces only when absent from garrison or camp"—and claimed that even the cavalry horses knew and responded to bugle calls (Custer, *Following* v).

There was, of course, guard duty—two hours on, two off, for twenty-four hours. Whenever possible, officers tried to remedy the lack of training at recruit depots. Target practice, however, was often limited because with the new breech-loading weapons, the expensive ammunition was often in short supply. An officer in charge of the Gatling guns that accompanied the peace commissioners to Medicine Creek Lodge, Kansas, felt his men should be familiarized with the guns but was told he would have to pay for the ammunition for target practice himself; thus, the guns were not fired (Rickey, 99–100). The surgeon who accompanied Colonel Gibbon's column during the 1876 campaign against the Sioux felt the lack of training showed: "Cavalrymen . . . as a general thing are about as well fitted to travel through a hostile country as puling infants, and go mooning around at the mercy of any Indian who happens to catch sight and takes the trouble to lay for them behind the first convenient ridge" (Rickey, 101). He knew of what he spoke, for he participated in the relief of the Seventh Cavalry survivors of the Little Big Horn. In contrast to such inadequate training, General Nelson A. Miles was adamant that his Fifth Infantry participate in skirmishes in all sorts of weather; many historians believe that such careful preparation simulating combat field conditions allowed his men to prevail against Crazy Horse on the Tongue River in January 1877, despite being outnumbered two to one (Rickey, 103).

Nonetheless, one soldier wrote to his fiancée that most "soldiers in the Department of the Platte know better how to handle a pick & shovel than they do a gun" (Rickey, 93). Indeed, fatigue duty was so common a feature at most frontier forts that a group of disillusioned soldiers sent a petition to Congress in 1878 complaining of how they were used:

> We first enlisted with the usual idea of the life of a soldier; . . . but we find in service that we are obliged to perform all kinds of labor, such as all the operations of building quarters, stables, storehouses, bridges, roads, and telegraph lines; involving logging, lumbering, quarrying, adobe and brick making, lime-burning, mason-work, plastering, carpentering, painting, &. etc. We are also put to team-ing, repairing wagons, harness &. blacksmithing, and sometimes wood-chopping and hay-making. This in addition to guard duty, care of horses, arms, and equipments, cooking, baking, police of quarters and stables, moving stores & etc., as well as drilling, and frequently to the exclusion of the latter. (U.S. Senate, 487–88)

The arduousness of life in the field has already been suggested in the discussion of Crook's forces on the verge of starvation, snatching sleep in the rain, marching, exhausted, leading their emaciated horses through mud "so thick and sticky that whenever one raised a foot he brought up with it about ten pounds of clay" (Crook, 209).

THE INDIAN WARS

Charles King's account of a reconnaissance patrol on July 3, 1876, cap-tures the emotions and frustrations of the Fifth Cavalry. As the sun rises the men are grooming their horses, "the tap of the curry comb and the impatient pawing of hooves . . . music in the clear, crisp bracing air." As the men are inhaling morning coffee, word comes that Indians have been seen in the valley. The men "jump into boots and spurs . . . rattle the bits between the teeth of our excited horses," and move out at a "spanking gait" behind the scout, Buffalo Bill. Though this is the first chase of the campaign, "there is hardly a trace of nervousness" even among the new-est troops. As they deploy, left hands firmly grasping the "already foam-ing reins," right hands on their carbines, "excitement is subdued but intense." For most of the day the scouts see Indian sign, but the troop sees no Indians. Although once or twice the scouts get close enough to exchange shots, the day is one of frustration. After hours in the saddle the men catch sight of their foe, "miles ahead, and streaking . . . for the Powder River country as fast as their ponies can carry them." Though the company commander will not abuse his horses in a wild goose chase, "we have galloped thirty miles in a big circle before catching sight of our chase, and our horses are panting and wearied. . . . We head for home, reach camp, disgusted and empty-handed, about four P.M. Two 'heavy weights' . . . horses drop dead under them, and the first pursuit of the Fifth is over" (King, 21–22).

The rising and falling action of the day becomes a metaphor for much of the Indian wars and of the national debates on how to end them. Yet the outcome was inevitable. King concludes his narrative of campaigning with Crook with the observation that though "our engagements were indecisive at the time (and Indian fights that fall short of annihilation on either side generally are)," the campaign was ultimately successful: Sitting Bull driven to refuge "across the line" in Canada, his subordinates "broken up into dejected bands that, one after another, were beaten or starved into submission," and, the following year, "the grand ranges of the Black Hills and Big Horn, the boundless prairies of Nebraska and Wyoming were as clear of hostile warriors as, two years before, they were of settlers" (King, 170).

Robert M. Utley argues that until the middle of the nineteenth century the changes of Indian culture had been "evolutionary and mostly within the bounds of traditional culture. Henceforth they would be revolutionary and finally destructive of traditional culture" (*Indian Frontier* 30). Step by step, eastern woodlands Indians had been pushed onto the prairies and plains, adapting to their new environments as did the whites who pushed them. Cattlemen ranged up from the South; homesteaders, from the East; and miners, from the West, bringing with them new technologies. Some of these, like the breech-loading rifle, the Indians quickly adopted; but others, like the telephone, or "whispering spirit," left them awe-struck, literally shaken from hearing a comrade's voice from a house an eighth of a mile away and convinced that an army that had such inexplicable objects surely had powerful medicine (Miles, 317).

The four great transcontinental railroads and all their branch lines wrought even greater change—so great that General William Tecumseh Sherman observed in his final report as general of the army that although the actions of the army and the influx of settlers had been powerful forces for change, "the *railroad* which used to follow in the rear now goes forward with the picket line in the great battle for civilization with barbarism, and has become the *greater* cause" (qtd. in Prucha, 179). Jacob Cox, secretary of the interior, concurred:

> Instead of a slowly advancing tide of migration, making gradual inroads upon the circumference of the great interior wilderness, the very center of the desert has been pierced. Every station upon the railway has become a nucleus for a civilized settlement, and a base from which lines of exploration for both mineral and agricultural wealth are pushed in every direction. (qtd. in Prucha, 193–94)

The significance of the white flood was not lost on the Apache leader Cochise, who reflected, "Nobody wants peace more than I do. I have killed ten white men for every Indian I have lost, but still the white men are no fewer; and my tribe is growing smaller and smaller. It will dis-

Currier & Ives, *Across the Continent: "Westward the Course of Empire Takes Its Way,"* 1868. Reproduced courtesy of the Joslyn Art Museum, Omaha, Nebraska; Gift of Eugene Kingman. This lithograph, drawn by F. F. Palmer, shows how the "civilization" of the West grew up around the railroad.

appear from the face of the earth if we do not have a good peace soon" (Gard, 19). The reservation system sought to "remove Indians from the path of on-rushing whites" and thus save them from destruction (Prucha, 194). To this end, a whole new set of treaties was signed during the last third of the nineteenth century.

The legal basis for such treaties was Chief Justice John Marshall's decision in *Cherokee Nation v. Georgia*, 1831, which concluded that even though the Cherokees were a "distinct political society" capable of self-government, they were not truly a foreign nation; rather, the Indians were "domestic dependent nations" who "occupied territory to which the United States asserted a title independent of the Indians' will, which would take effect when the Indians give up possession" (Prucha, 76). Many of the treaties subsequently signed had included "in perpetuity" clauses guaranteeing protection and possession of new lands west of the edge of settlement, in the words of an old trade treaty, "for as long as the grass shall grow and the rivers run" (Nabokov, 152). Yet the Five Civilized Tribes who had been sent to Indian Territory witnessed the Oklahoma land rush; the Santee Sioux, after the 1862 Minnesota uprising, lost their reservation—as did the Winnebagos, who, ironically, had remained peacefully uninvolved; and after the discovery of gold in the Black Hills, the Great Sioux Reservation underwent drastic shrinkage.

At least one recent scholar has suggested that the purpose of treaty-making was to "benefit the national interest without staining the nation's honor" (Prucha, 36). A Georgia governor explained it less euphemistically: "Treaties were expedients by which ignorant, intractable and savage people were induced without bloodshed to yield up what civilized people had the right to possess by virtue of that command of the Creator ... —be fruitful, multiply, and replenish the earth, and subdue it" (Prucha, 36). If the earth was to be subdued, so too must be the Indians, who logically and instinctively recognized this fact. Thus, despite their recognition of the inevitable, there were many impediments to treaties involving land cession west of the Mississippi.

In some instances a treaty was not signed, or even approved of, by the whole tribe. From Jefferson's time onward, government officials had erred in selecting the leader with whom to deal; their external and arbitrary elevation of an individual to prominence—if not to power—caused schisms in tribal unity. And true tribal leaders, such as Red Cloud of the Oglala Sioux, constantly walked a tightrope between their white overseers and their own people. In many instances a rift developed between peace chiefs who were somewhat more pragmatic, willing to compromise in the face of the inevitable, and young warriors who were more idealistic and wanted freedom, not accommodation. Among the Kiowas during 1867, the peace chief Kicking Bird gained supporters while Satanta remained adamantly insolent to whites. And at the Medicine Lodge

Creek treaty council, Black Kettle and about 50 lodges came in early, while the remaining 200 lodges camped thirty miles away before eventually joining the talks (Utley, *Indian Frontier* 114).

Frequently the Indians didn't fully understand the implications of a treaty. Albert Barnitz observed that only with great difficulty were the Cheyennes persuaded to "touch the pen," or sign the Medicine Lodge treaty. In his journal entry of October 28, 1867, he tends to empathize with them: "*[T]hey have no idea that* they are giving up or that they have ever given up the country which they claim as their own, the country north of the Arkansas." Barnitz is well aware of the likely results of the white duplicity: "The treaty all amounts to nothing, and we will certainly have another war sooner or later . . . in consequence of misunderstanding of the terms of present and previous treaties" (Utley, *Life* 115). He does, however, record lighter moments of mutual experimental acculturation: Ten Bears practicing on an army bugle, and Senator Henderson trying on buffalo robes (112, 114).

The implications of lack of understanding were often quite serious. In Washington for a meeting with President Grant, Red Cloud was angry when he recalled that "in 1868 men came out and brought papers. We could not read them and they did not tell us truly what was in them. . . . When I reached Washington the Great Father explained to me what the treaty was, and showed me that the interpreters had deceived me" (Nabokov, 147). Newspapers reported the meeting. The *New York Times* editorialized: "The attempt to cajole and bamboozle [the Indians] as if they were deficient in intelligence, ought to be abandoned, no less than the policy of hunting them down like wild beasts." The *New York Herald* concurred: "Palaver has very little effect on the Indian character. . . . [F]aithlessness on our part in the matter of treaties, and gross swindling of the Indians . . . are at the bottom of all this Indian trouble" (Josephy, 394.)

Sometimes whites bargained in bad faith, speaking with "forked tongues." While peace commissioners negotiating for permission to open the Bozeman Trail promised that travelers would be confined to the roadway and would not be allowed "to molest or disturb the game in the country through which they passed," Colonel Carrington revealed that his orders were to build a chain of forts to protect the trail. The Indians were furious. Red Cloud did not mince words: "Great Father sends us presents and wants new road. But white chief goes with soldiers to steal road before Indian says yes or no!" (Josephy, 388–89). Some historians feel this led directly to the Fetterman massacre and thus to General Sherman's vow of "vindictive earnestness against the Sioux, even to their extermination, men, women and children" (Josephy, 391).

Sometimes the problem was one of translation. General Nelson A. Miles recalls one instance in which a translator ad-libbed a promo for a local trader, telling the Arapahos that the "Great Father hoped they would gather large quantities of buffalo robes and furs . . . , bring them all to Bent's fort, and sell them cheap." Miles wonders what the Indians thought of this "absurd message" (Miles, 336–37). Another instance was more tragic. When the army was trying to convince Crazy Horse to lead Oglala scouts against the Nez Percé, he finally agreed, saying "he would fight until not a Nez Percé was left." The bungling translator said he would fight "until not a white man was left." Crazy Horse was, naturally, arrested; he was killed in an escape attempt (Josephy, 407).

Some Indians simply did not want to be corralled. Sitting Bull told General Miles that "God Almighty made him an Indian, and did not make him an agency Indian either, and he did not intend to be one" (Miles, 226). Daklugie, telling of the choice he and other Apaches must make between a degraded life on the San Carlos reservation and life off the reservation hunted by troops of the United States and Mexico, remembered, "All of us knew that we were doomed, but some preferred death to slavery and imprisonment" (Josephy, 428). Others, like Chief Joseph of the Nez Percé, didn't want to abandon sacred land or land where their ancestors were buried.

Finally, many, being aware of past broken promises, simply did not feel they could trust the treaty negotiators. For example, in 1865 the Poncas, a small peaceful tribe, had been guaranteed a 96,000-acre reservation along the Missouri River north of the Niobrara. Only three years later, through the Fort Laramie treaty, the "United States—without consulting the Poncas—ceded the entire Ponca reservation to the Sioux, the Poncas' traditional enemies" (Prucha, 183).

Even an army general was not immune. Little Chief of the Northern Cheyennes surrendered to General Miles because he trusted him. "You have not lied yet, and I am going to surrender to you"; he believed Miles's promises that they could stay on the Yellowstone. Similarly, when Chief Joseph surrendered to Miles in northern Montana in October 1877, Miles promised they could return to Idaho in the spring. He was overruled by General Sherman, who declared the Nez Percé prisoners of war and ordered them to Fort Leavenworth, where many died (Prucha, 186–87). One wonders what these Indians thought of Miles. One wonders what Miles thought as his efforts of humanely bringing in Indians were undermined.

It seems certain that Indians would conclude that they could not trust the promises of the government or its agents. Perhaps of equal significance, such a fiasco reveals the deep divisions among those making Indian policy—a division between the hardliners and those who believed it was possible to "subdue by kindness." It is important to note that this dichotomy was not synonymous with the division between the military and civilians, for there were hardline civilians and humane officers.

General George Armstrong Custer was among the hardliners, though he didn't usually go so far as to demonize the Indian. He even once said that if he were an Indian, he would want to be free and not live on reservations. However, he rejected the noble savage "as described in Cooper's interesting novels" as untrue. Speaking from firsthand experience of war with the Plains Indian, he describes him as a "savage in every sense of the word; not worse, perhaps, than his white brother would be similarly born and bred, but one whose ferocious nature far exceeds that of any wild beast." He argued that the delegation Indians who visited Washington and the Indians whom peace commissioners met in council were one persona, "perhaps his most serviceable," but not a complete picture (Custer, *My Life* 13–14). Custer believed that many Indian agents either couldn't or wouldn't enforce the peace (28), and he verges on the bitterly sarcastic when he notes that Indians are receiving from traders the very same new weapons the army has only recently received (33). Ultimately, he argues, "no teaching, argument, reasoning or coaxing" will induce the Indian to change his mode of life unless it is "preceded and followed closely by a superior physical force. In other words, the Indian is capable of recognizing no controlling influence—[not eastern philanthropists, not Christian missionaries, not well-meaning teachers]—but that of stern arbitrary power" (Custer, *My Life* 148).

Colonel Richard I. Dodge believed Indians didn't "fight fair"—referring to their surprise attacks on wagon trains and their refusal to stand and fight; and he once wrote that the "noblest of virtues to the Indian are comprehended in the English words—theft, pillage, rapine and murder" (Dodge, 262). However, he blamed government policy for keeping "alive a warlike spirit by encouraging acts of aggression," specifically by having allowed hide hunters to deplete the buffalo herds, thereby leaving the Indians starving on reservations. Moreover, he condemned the ready access to alcohol as a catalyst to violence (350–58). He could not condone the Indians' violence, but he could understand its causes.

General William Tecumseh Sherman felt punishment under the law was the best deterrent to hostilities and depredations. "We can never stop the wild Indians from murdering and stealing until we punish them." Taking a shot at Indian agents, he observed that if a white man committed such acts he would go to prison, whereas "if an Indian commits these crimes, we give him better fare and more blankets. . . . Under this policy, the civilization of the wild red man will progress slowly" (qtd. in Custer, *My Life* 168–69).

Albert Barnitz believed peace councils to be shams. The "presents will be distributed, and the new guns . . . and in the Spring we will repeat the pleasant little farce of a Big Indian War, and a hand-full of men to carry it on. . . . The Indians," he wrote to his wife, Jennie, in August 1867, "must be thoroughly whipped before they will respect us, or keep any peace, and they haven't been whipped yet very much to speak of" (Utley, *Life* 95).

Many army officers respected their enemies and understood their motivations, even as they argued for tough policies. Some civilians were far less sympathetic. When Senator Doolittle spoke in Denver in 1865 on Indian policy, he asked what he thought was a rhetorical question—Should the Indians be placed on reservations and taught to support themselves, or should they be exterminated? "There suddenly arose such a shout," he recalled, "as is never heard unless upon some battlefield—a shout loud enough to raise the roof of the Opera House—'Exterminate them! Exterminate them!'" (Utley, *Indian Frontier* 102). And Frances Roe, reflecting in 1888 on the end of an era, remarked, "We have seen the passing of the buffalo and other game, and the Indian seems to be passing also. But I confess that I have no regret for the Indians—there are still too many of them!" (Roe, 359).

Most army officers did not develop such an "ideology of hostility" toward the Indians; rather, aware of the "fraud, corruption and injustice" they had suffered, officers were, as a class, ambivalent toward their foes. On the one hand, they felt "fear, distrust, loathing, contempt, and condescension"; on the other, "curiosity, admiration, sympathy, and even friendship" (Utley, qtd. in Prucha, 174). The eastern humanitarians, for the most part, were less ambivalent, many pointing to the Sand Creek Massacre (which was not the work of the regular army) as a chief illustration of why the military could not be trusted to civilize the Indians. Most of them were equally certain about what they wanted the Indian to become: a peaceful, Christian farmer, demonstrating the Puritan work ethic, living within the law on his own plot of land, and aspiring to U.S. citizenship. This goal, they believed, could best be accomplished by civilians—missionaries, teachers, and government officials of good moral character.

Such reformers who hoped to subdue the Indian by kindness initially found encouragement during the Grant administration. In 1873 the secretary of the interior set forth a comprehensive peace policy in which government and churches would cooperate to bring the benefits of civilization to Indians on reservations. By the end of the 1870s a set of priorities had emerged, supported by secretaries of the interior, commissioners of Indian affairs, and Christian reformers. These included:

1. to put Indians to work as farmers or herders, thereby weaning them from their "savage life" and making them self-supporting;

2. to educate young people of both sexes in order to "introduce to the growing generation civilized ideas, wants and aspirations";

3. to allot parcels of land to individual Indians, not to the tribe, in order to foster individual pride of ownership rather than tribal loyalty;

4. to dispose of surplus reservation lands remaining after individual titles had been obtained, with the money from sales to be used to provide for Indians' expenses; and

5. to treat Indians like all other inhabitants of the United States under the laws of the land. (Prucha, 194–95)

The Christian reformers were firmly convinced that Indians were capable of civilization and that it was the injustice or inefficiency of government that had impeded the process. However, they lacked any appreciation of Indian culture and approached their mission with "an ethnocentrism of frightening intensity" (Prucha, 199).

Ironically, many army officers—Miles, Crook, even Custer—had a better understanding of Indian culture than did these reformers. General Miles, for one, counseled patience: "Accustomed as they were from childhood to wild excitement of the chase, or of conflict . . . taught that to kill was noble and labor degrading, these Indians could not suddenly change their natures and become peaceful agriculturists" (Miles, 156). Preferring to avoid war and to bring hostiles into reservations without another campaign (Crook, 215), Crook went so far as to argue for decent treatment of those he'd known as adversaries. Addressing the West Point graduates of 1884, he concluded:

With all his faults, and he has many, the American Indian is not so black as he has been painted. He is cruel in war, treacherous at times, and not over cleanly. But so were our forefathers. His nature, however, is responsive to treatment . . . based on justice, truth, honesty and common sense. It is not impossible that the American Indian would make a better citizen than many who neglect the duties and abuse the privileges of that proud title. (qtd. in Gard, 20–21)

This debate between hardliners and peace advocates culminated in a debate as to whether the Department of the Interior or the War Department should be in charge of the Indians' acculturation. Most thinking people felt that it mattered less which manifested control than that the vacillations and contradictions in policy cease. The editor of the *Army and Navy Journal*, having analyzed the effects of ambivalence, concluded, "We go to [the Indians] Janus-faced. One of our hands holds the rifle and the other the peace-pipe, and we blaze away with both instruments at the same time. The chief consequence is a great *smoke*—and there it ends" (Josephy, 387).

INDIAN RESERVATIONS

To achieve peace in the West and to optimize the possibility of successful acculturation of the Indians, General Miles advocated "placing the Indians under some government strong enough to control them and just enough to command their respect" (Miles, 346). The realities of reservation life, however, impeded or compromised the process.

The first problem was the choice of site. Because settlers claimed the best land, many reservations were established in bleak, barren, unproductive, even unhealthy places. In 1863 General James H. Carleton ordered Kit Carson to move the Navajos to the Bosque Redondo, a reservation in sun-baked eastern New Mexico. Those who survived the Long Walk joined their traditional enemies, the Mescalero Apaches, in this sandy, barren land. They dug holes and trenches for shelter and slaughtered cows for hides to use as windbreaks and for shade. (There were no trees, as those that had grown in the immediate area had all been cut to build Fort Sumner.) Of Fort Sumner and the Bosque Redondo, Eveline Alexander, a cavalry officer's wife, wrote: "I never saw such an undesirable location for a post, and especially for a large Indian reservation" (116). Shocked by the conditions, and aware that "the Navajos in their native country beyond the Rio Grande were a wealthy tribe" (119), she concerned herself more than most army wives with the plight of the Indians (20). She wrote of the 8,000 Navajos living like prisoners of war. Rations were distributed every other day. "The daily ration . . . is three-fourths of a pound of flour and meat and a handful of salt to each Indian, little or big. Not much to support life on, one would think" (117). According to another contemporary account, "the brackish water they drank brought dysentery . . . [and] the reservation, situated on the edge of a treeless expanse of prairie, quickly depleted fuel close at hand. Resources of cedar and mesquite retreated farther and farther . . . until Navajos were traveling twelve to twenty miles for mesquite root, which they carried 'upon their galled and lacerated backs' " (Alexander, 160 n. 24). Although Eveline Alexander observed some Navajos hoeing corn (117), conditions were so bad that "Navajos had to be forced to work at bayonet point" (160).

In a report to Washington, General Carleton called all this

> a grand experiment to make civilized human beings out of savages . . . they . . . discard . . . their ways and learn how to be like white men. . . . To gather them together little by little into a reservation away from the haunts and hills and hiding places of their country and there . . . teach the children how to read and write; teach them the art of peace; teach them the truths of Christianity. Soon they

will acquire new habits, new ideas, new modes of life. (Josephy, 355)

The Indians perceived this process quite differently. Frederick Peso, whose people, the Mescalero Apaches, shared the Bosque Redondo, has declared, "The surest way to kill a race is to kill its religious ideals. Can anybody doubt that the white man attempted to do that? And when the Spirit is killed, what remains?" (Josephy, 355).

The physical impact of the reservation was not unique to the Navajos, of course. With a historian's objectivity, Robert M. Utley described the San Carlos reservation as "a terrible place to live" (*Indian Frontier* 196). Daklugie, Geronimo's nephew, also attempted a description: "The Creator did not make San Carlos. It is older than he. . . . He just left it as a sample of the way they did things before He came along. . . . Take stones and ashes and thorns, and, with some scorpions and rattlesnakes thrown in, dump the outfit on stones, heat the stones red-hot, set the United States Army after the Apaches, and you have San Carlos" (Josephy, 428).

General Miles was aware of the effect of climate as he argued for Indians to be returned to their native lands. "The climate and country of Montana and the Dakotas produced as fine physical specimens of the human race as have ever been found on this continent," he wrote of the Sioux (Miles, 254). "The forcing of strong, hardy mountain Indians from the extreme north to the warmer malarial districts of the South was cruel, and the experiment should never be repeated" (Miles, 347).

Helen Hunt Jackson took up the cause of the Native American in her exposé, *A Century of Dishonor*, a documented attack on the federal government's Indian policy. Describing the plight of the Northern Cheyenne during 1877 and 1878, she recounts how their hunts had been unsuccessful because game was gone, how their pony herd had been decimated, how rations had been reduced, and how malaria raged through the reservation, where the medical supplies were inadequate. She concludes that such a life on the reservation is hardly likely to appeal to the Indians' better nature and lead them to civilization:

> If it is to "appeal to men's better natures" to remove them by force from a healthful Northern climate, which they love and thrive in, to a malarial Southern one, where they are struck down by chills and fever—refuse them medicine . . . and finally starve them—then, indeed [this] might be said to have been most forcible appeals to the "better natures" of those Northern Cheyennes. What might have been predicted followed. (Jackson, qtd. in Jones, *American Frontier* 69–70)

Indians were literally dying to go home. Outbreaks were inevitable, and though not all were violent, some were, intensifying a cycle of frustration and retribution. Any Indian off the reservations was considered hostile. When a band of the Northern Cheyenne under Dull Knife decided to return north from Indian Territory, they automatically fell into this category. Additionally, by occasionally killing cattle along the way for food, they incensed settlers. Captured again, held at Fort Robinson, Nebraska, and told they would be returned south, they were adamant. "That is not a beautiful country. If we go there, we would all die. . . . We will not go." Said Dull Knife, "You may kill me here; but you cannot make me go back." While General Crook argued strongly with the Indian Bureau about a better location for them, the commander at Fort Robinson tried to starve them into submission, cutting off their rations and withholding water. The result was an outbreak, though escape was hopeless, with casualties among both soldiers and Indians before the seventy-eight surviving Cheyenne gave up. Ironically, wrote Crook, "Among the Cheyenne Indians were some of the bravest and most efficient of the auxiliaries who had [served with me] in the campaign against the hostile Sioux in 1876 and 1877. . . . I still preserve a grateful remembrance of their distinguished service, which the government seems to have forgotten" (Crook, 223–26).

Government Indian policy was not flexible enough to make exceptions, in effect illustrating the belief that "once you've seen one Indian, you've seen them all." A corollary to this inability to see Indians as individuals was the pattern, throughout the period of the Plains Indian wars, of indiscriminately punishing one group of Indians for the depredations of another.

Aside from totally inhospitable sites chosen for reservations, another major factor making reservations unworkable and intolerable was the role of the government agents. The chief duties of the agents were summarized in the *Instructions to Indian Agents* of 1880: to "induce the Indians to labor in civilized pursuits" (chiefly farming), to enforce the prohibition of alcohol, to provide and supervise education and industrial training (Prucha, 243–44), to ensure that licensed traders acted honestly and that agency physicians not only cared for the sick but countered the work of the medicine men (Prucha, 118). If the agent was a strong, ethical person, the reservation system might work, but General Crook believed that "ninety-nine hundredths" of Indian troubles were caused by agents (Crook, 229).

For one thing, before civil service reform the reservation personnel were appointed under a political patronage system in return for party loyalty. Not only did many such appointees have no humanitarian concerns, but when good agents were appointed, their tenure ended with a new party in the White House. Thus, programs had little to no continuity. Some agents engaged in fraud. On at least one occasion, instead of distributing annuity goods to Indians, an agent bartered them for furs and then sold the furs, pocketing the money (Miles, 337). By practicing such fraud some agents were able to save $40,000 in four years on an annual salary of $1,500 (Gard, 18). Some agents, apparently in cahoots with contractors and freighters interested in supplying the Indian Service, ignored commonsense ways to save government money. Elaine Goodale Eastman notes how the agents refused to buy surplus grain or beef from the Indians, preferring to import it. Moreover, until a new agent, Valentine McGillicuddy, insisted that Indians be hired to freight in the goods, contracts went to white freighters. Once reform was instituted in 1878, the Oglalas earned $45,000 in one year (Eastman, 81–82), indicating the magnitude of former corruption.

Minnesota during the 1850s was a "classic example of the corruption of the federal Indian system" (Utley, *Indian Frontier* 78). Long before the 1862 outbreak, Santee Sioux there had been nursing grievances against the whites: agents had been withholding food, traders selling "rancid bacon and wormy flour at exorbitant rates," and nearby "degenerate whites" seducing Indian women. When three hundred Indians died from eating spoiled food issued by a licensed trader at Sandy Lake, survivors asked for untainted food or money to buy some. The agent told them that the annual appropriation had been used up to pay the trader's claims for goods already purchased. When he was appealed to for relief, the trader, Andrew Myrick, only taunted the starving supplicants: "If they are hungry, let them eat grass" (Gard, 7). Urging reform, Minnesota's Episcopal bishop, Henry B. Whipple, in 1860 wrote to President James Buchanan that "a nation which sowed robbery would reap a harvest of blood" (Utley, *Indian Frontier* 78). The 1862 uprising proved him right.

Perhaps the most tragic illustration of the need for reform in the selection of Indian agents occurred on the Sioux reservations in 1890. After the competent and powerful agent, Valentine McGillicuddy, had fallen victim to the patronage system, the inexperienced and ineffectual Daniel F. Royer was appointed to the Pine Ridge Agency. Almost immediately the Sioux dubbed him "Young-Man-Afraid-of-Indians." When Ghost Dancers defied his orders to stop dancing, he panicked and telegraphed to the commissioner of Indian affairs, "Indians are dancing in the snow and are wild and crazy. . . . We *need protection and we need it now.*" Only five days later, on December 20, 1890, infantry and cavalry, complete with Hotchkiss rapid-fire cannons and Gatling guns, arrived at the Pine Ridge and Rosebud reservations (Viola, *After Columbus* 193; Prucha, 247). Instead of simply allowing the dance frenzy to subside, as someone who understood Indian culture might have done, Royer precipitated the sequence of events that led to the carnage at Wounded Knee.

There is no question that the central purpose of the reservation system was to change Indians' cultures, to "Americanize" them. As tribal identity began to change, "whole clusters of customs, activities, attitudes,

values, and institutions lost reliance and meaning and ... began to van-
ish" (Utley, *Indian Frontier* 236). Whereas warfare had once defined a
man's honor, provided a congerie of important rituals, and touched on
aspects of celebration and mourning, social structure, and individual
maturation, it was now proscribed. Whereas the hunt once not only provided most of a tribe's needs but also gave a sense of the rhythm of the
year, a calendar organically linked to nature, it was no longer possible.
Religion too had once linked man to nature in a profound sense of the
Creator's beneficence; these religions were now called "pagan" and some
of them forbidden. As even Custer was aware, this reordering of life was
cataclysmic. "The Indian has to sacrifice all that is dear to his heart"
(Custer, *My Life* 21).

One of the first priorities on the reservations was to make the Indian
a self-sufficient farmer, to teach him to plow and to plant and to harvest.
Seemingly innocuous, this process struck at some fundamental Native
American beliefs. Smohalla, a Wanapam dreamer-prophet, commented,
"You ask me to plow the ground! Shall I take a knife and tear my
mother's bosom? Then when I die she will not take me to her bosom to
rest. ... You ask me to make hay and sell it and be rich like white men!
But dare I cut off my mother's hair?" (Viola, *After Columbus* 188).

General Miles reported on one Indian who acquiesced to the idea of
planting a garden. He wanted to produce for himself "the best food the
white man had" and so wanted to plant a garden of raisins (Miles, 247).
Sometimes the "assistant farmers," frequently political appointees, knew
little more than their Indian pupils about farming. One, apparently as-
suming all root vegetables were alike, "directed his neophytes to cut
turnips in pieces and plant them in hills!" (Eastman, 79).

Education was, according to Francis Paul Prucha, "the ultimate reform." Whether the Indian was granted land in severalty (i.e., land
owned by individuals rather than tribes) and whether he received equal
treatment under the law were moot issues if he was not educated. At
the 1884 Lake Mohonk Conference, reformers summarized the goals of
Indian education:

> The Indian must have a knowledge of the English language that he
> may associate with his white neighbors and transact business as
> they do. He must have practical industrial training to fit him to
> compete with others in the struggle for life. He must have a Chris-
> tian education to enable him to perform the duties of the family,
> the State and the Church. (Prucha, 232)

To achieve these goals, schools—both day schools and boarding
schools—were established on the reservations. Elaine Goodale Eastman
taught in day schools on the Great Sioux Reservation. At her first school

she had about fifty students ranging in age from 6 to 16, none of whom knew any English. Fortunately she, unlike many educators, learned the Dakota language. Although it was official policy that only English could be used in the classrooms (a policy with which she took no public issue), she was able to communicate with her students' parents and thus help to avoid a potentially serious rift between generations and ways of life. Nonetheless, assimilation into the larger American society was a top priority, and so, with the help of philanthropist friends from the East who donated clothing and material, one of her first projects was to teach the older girls how to sew and to convince the boys to have their long hair cut.

Because manual training schools required greater expenditures to equip them with stock, farming implements, tools, and wagons, they had to be boarding schools. Many felt these were preferable to day schools in any case, for, as Indian Commissioner Ezra Hayt observed, "the demoralization and degradation of an Indian home neutralized the efforts of the schoolteacher" (Prucha, 233).

In 1878 there were 137 Indian schools of all kinds provided by the government, with about 3,500 students; by 1887 the numbers had grown to 231 schools and 10,000 students (Prucha, 234). The need, however, was still greater and was filled in part by "contract schools" provided by various religious denominations.

To many, the flagship of the Indian educational system was the Carlisle Indian School in Carlisle, Pennsylvania, established in 1879 by Captain Richard Henry Pratt. (Ironically, it was housed at first in the same barracks where cavalry recruits destined for the Indian wars had received their basic training.) Pratt's educational philosophy was simple: his students were to be prepared for complete integration into white society.

The first days at Carlisle were a tremendous shock for students. Luther Standing Bear described some of his experiences as he battled a sense of isolation and homesickness to learn the white men's ways. A member of the first class, he arrived to sleep the first night on the floor in a room with no furniture other than a stove. Worse, breakfast the next morning was only bread and water, and dinner was some meat, bread, and coffee. "How lonesome [we] were for [our] faraway Dakota homes where there was plenty to eat!" (Luther Standing Bear qtd. in Jones, *Christopher Columbus* 250).

If the students were to be Americans, they were to have American names; so, one day they arrived in the schoolroom to find the blackboard covered with columns of white marks. One by one the boys were called to the blackboard and told by the interpreter to point at one "word." As they did so, the teacher pinned a piece of cloth with a corresponding set of marks to the boy's shirt. Thus, one boy became "Luther." If one's personal identity is bound up with his name, each child was thus symbolically stripped of who he was.

Possibly the most traumatic event of the early weeks—because the boys were acutely conscious of how it redefined them—was their first haircut. Standing Bear writes:

> We all looked so funny with short hair. It had been cut with a machine and cropped very close. We still had our Indian clothes [for a few more days] but we were all bald-headed. None of us slept very well that night. . . . After having my hair cut, a new thought came into my head. I felt I was no more Indian, but would be an imitation white man. And we are still imitations of white men. (qtd. in Jones, *Christopher Columbus* 253)

Forbidden to speak their own languages, stripped of native dress, required to model themselves on white society, many Indian children were confused, lonely, and alienated, caught between two worlds. One young Chippewa woman could scarcely remember what had been. "Gone were the vivid pictures of my parents, sisters and brothers. Only a blurred picture of what use[d] to be. Desperately I tried to cling to the faded past which was slowly being erased from my mind" (qtd. in Josephy, 434).

Despite Pratt's intentions of full integration of his students into American society, the reality was that this was impossible. Many young people thus experienced a second culture shock when they returned to the reservation. Possibly the most extreme example of this was a young Sioux who returned to the Pine Ridge reservation shortly after the battle at Wounded Knee. Plenty Horses killed a cavalryman to prove that his education at Carlisle had not made him a white man (Viola, *After Columbus* 220).

The tragedy of the Indian wars and of the reservation life that followed was not in the number of deaths, which was relatively small, but rather in the destruction of a way of life. Francis Paul Prucha, a Catholic priest as well as a scholar on relations between the U.S. government and the Indians, preaches a eulogy for that way of life:

> The change was to be made from the nomadic life of a buffalo hunter to the sedentary life of a small farmer, from communal patterns to fiercely individualistic ones, from native religious ceremonials to Christian practices, from Indian languages and oral traditions to spoken and written English. For most of the reservation Indians the changes were a shattering experience, demoralizing rather than uplifting. (Prucha, 222)

New students at the Carlisle Indian School were allowed to keep their traditional dress only long enough for a "before" picture to be taken. The same three Sioux boys are shown three years later in their school uniform.

From across the cultural divide the Oglala holy man Black Elk wrote, remembering Wounded Knee:

I did not know then how much had ended. When I look back now from this high hill of my old age, I can still see the butchered women and children lying heaped and scattered all along the crooked gulch as plain as when I saw them with eyes still young. And I can see that something else died there in the bloody mud, and was buried in the blizzard. A people's dream died there. It was a beautiful dream. . . . The nation's hoop is broken and scattered. There is no center any longer, and the sacred tree is dead. (qtd. in Neihardt, 276)

Bibliography

Abbott, E. C. ("Teddy Blue"), and Helena Huntington Smith. *We Pointed Them North: Recollections of a Cowpuncher.* New York: Farrar & Rinehart, 1939.

Alexander, Eveline M. *Cavalry Wife: The Diary of Eveline M. Alexander, 1866–1867.* Ed. Sandra L. Myres. College Station: Texas A&M University Press, 1977.

Ambrose, Stephen E. *Undaunted Courage: Meriwether Lewis, Thomas Jefferson, and the Opening of the American West.* New York: Simon & Schuster, 1996.

Armitage, Susan, and Elizabeth Jameson, eds. *The Women's West.* Norman: University of Oklahoma Press, 1987.

Athearn, Robert G. *William Tecumseh Sherman & the Settlement of the West.* Norman: University of Oklahoma Press, 1956.

Bartlett, Richard A. *The New Country: A Social History of the American Frontier, 1776–1890.* New York: Oxford University Press, 1974.

Beard, Charles A., and Mary Beard. *The Rise of American Civilization.* Vol. 4, *The American Spirit: A Study of the Idea of Civilization in the United States.* New York: Macmillan, 1930.

Berthrong, Donald J. *The Southern Cheyennes.* Norman: University of Oklahoma Press, 1963.

Boorstin, Daniel. *The Americans: The National Experience.* New York: Random House, 1965.

Brown, Dee. *Bury My Heart at Wounded Knee: An Indian History of the American West.* New York: Henry Holt and Co., 1970.

———. *The Gentle Tamers: Women of the Old Wild West.* New York: Bantam, 1958.

Brown, Mark H., and W. R. Felton. *Before Barbed Wire: L. A. Huffman, Photographer on Horseback.* New York: Henry Holt and Co., 1956.

Bruff, J. Goldsborough. *Gold Rush: The Journals, Drawings, and Other Papers of*

J. Goldsborough Bruff: April 2, 1849–July 20, 1851. Eds. Georgia Willis Read and Ruth Gaines. New York: Columbia University Press, 1949.

Buck, Franklin A. *A Yankee Trader in the Gold Rush.* Boston: Houghton Mifflin, 1939.

Buffum, Edward Gould. *Six Months in the Gold Mines.* [1850]. Ann Arbor: University Microfilms, 1966.

Butler, Anne M. *Daughters of Joy, Sisters of Misery: Prostitutes in the American West 1865–90.* Urbana: University of Illinois Press, 1985.

Carnes, Mark C., and John A. Garraty, with Patrick Williams. *Mapping America's Past: A Historical Atlas.* New York: Henry Holt and Co., 1996.

Carriker, Robert C. "The American Indian from the Civil War to the Present." In Michael P. Malone, ed., *Historians and the American West.* Lincoln: University of Nebraska Press, 1983, 177–208.

Catlin, George. *Letters and Notes on the Manners, Customs and Conditions of the North American Indians . . .* New York: Dover Publications, 1973.

Chardon, Francis A. *Journal at Fort Clark, 1834–1839.* Ed. Annie Heloise Abel. Freeport, NY: Books for Libraries Press, 1932.

Chisholm, James. *South Pass, 1868: James Chisholm's Journal of the Wyoming Gold Rush.* Ed. Lola M. Homsher. Lincoln: University of Nebraska Press, 1960.

Chittenden, Hiram Martin. *The American Fur Trade of the Far West.* 2 vols. Stanford: Academic Reprints, 1954.

Chuinard, Eldon G. *Only One Man Died: The Medical Aspects of the Lewis and Clark Expedition.* Glendale, CA: Arthur Clark Co. 1980.

Clappe, Louise A.K.S. [Dame Shirley]. *The Shirley Letters: Being Letters Written in 1851–1852 from the California Mines.* Intro. Richard Oglesby. Salt Lake City, UT: Peregrine Smith Books, n.d.

Clark, C. M., M.D. *A Trip to Pike's Peak & Notes by the Way, etc.* San Jose, CA: Talisman Press, 1958.

Collinson, Frank. *Life in the Saddle.* Ed. Mary Whatley Clarke. Norman: University of Oklahoma Press, 1963.

Colt, Mrs. Miriam (Davis). *Went to Kansas.* [1862]. Ann Arbor: University Microfilms, 1966.

Crook, George. *General George Crook: His Autobiography.* Ed. Martin F. Schmitt. Norman: University of Oklahoma Press, 1960.

Crosby, Alfred W., Jr. *The Columbian Exchange: Biological and Cultural Consequences of 1492.* Westport, CT: Greenwood Press, 1969.

———. *Ecological Imperialism: The Biological Expansion of Europe, 900–1900.* New York: Cambridge University Press, 1986.

Custer, Elizabeth B. *Boots and Saddles.* New York: Harper, 1885.

———. *Following the Guidon.* New York: Harper and Brothers, 1890.

———. *Tenting on the Plains.* New York: Charles L. Webster & Co., 1887.

Custer, Gen. George Armstrong. *My Life on the Plains: or, Personal Experiences with Indians.* Norman: University of Oklahoma Press, 1962.

Demos, John. *Past, Present and Personal: The Family and the Life Course in American History.* New York: Oxford University Press, 1986.

DeVoto, Bernard. *Across the Wide Missouri.* Boston: Houghton Mifflin, 1947.

———. *The Course of Empire.* Boston: Houghton Mifflin, 1952.

———, ed. *The Journals of Lewis and Clark.* Boston: Houghton Mifflin, 1965.

————. *The Year of Decision: 1846.* Boston: Houghton Mifflin, 1942.

Dick, Everett. *The Sod-House Frontier, 1854–1890: A Social History of the Northern Plains from the Creation of Kansas & Nebraska to the Admission of the Dakotas.* New York: D. Appleton-Century Co., 1937.

Dodge, Richard Irving. *The Plains of the Great West and Their Inhabitants.* [1876]. New York: Archer House, 1959.

Durham, Philip, and Everett L. Jones. *The Negro Cowboys.* New York: Dodd, Mead & Co., 1965.

Dykstra, Robert R. *The Cattle Towns.* New York: Knopf, 1968.

Eastman, Elaine Goodale. *Sister to the Sioux: The Memoirs of Elaine Goodale Eastman, 1885–91.* Lincoln: University of Nebraska Press, 1978.

Embry, Jessie L., and Howard A. Christy, eds. *Community Development in the American West:* Provo, UT: Charles Redd Center for Western Studies, 1985.

Erdoes, Richard, and Alfonso Ortiz. *American Indian Myths and Legends.* New York: Pantheon Books, 1984.

Farragher, John Mack. *Women and Men on the Overland Trail.* New Haven: Yale University Press, 1979.

Ferris, Robert G. *The American West: An Appraisal.* Papers from the Denver Conference on the History of Western America. Santa Fe: Museum of New Mexico Press, 1963.

Field, Matthew C. *Prairie and Mountain Sketches.* Eds. Kate L. Gregg and John Francis McDermott. Norman: University of Oklahoma Press, 1957.

Fite, Gilbert C. *The Farmers' Frontier: 1865–1900.* New York: Holt, Rinehart and Winston, 1966.

Fletcher, Baylis John. *Up the Trail in '79.* Ed. Wayne Gard. Norman: University of Oklahoma Press, 1968.

Foner, Eric, and John A. Garraty, eds. *The Reader's Companion to American History.* Boston: Houghton Mifflin, 1991.

Foner, Jack D. *The United States Soldier between Two Wars: Army Life and Reforms, 1865–1889.* New York: Humanities Press, 1970.

Forbis, William H. *The Old West: The Cowboys.* New York: Time-Life Books, 1973.

Frantz, Joe B., and Julian Ernest Choate Jr. *The American Cowboy: The Myth & the Reality.* Norman: University of Oklahoma Press, 1955.

Frémont, John Charles. *The Exploring Expedition to the Rocky Mountains.* Intro. Herman J. Viola and Ralph E. Ehrenberg. Washington, DC: Smithsonian Institution Press, 1988.

————. *Narratives of Exploration and Adventure.* Ed. Allan Nevins. New York: Longmans, Green & Co., 1956.

Furnas, J. C. *The Americans: A Social History of the United States.* New York: G. P. Putnam's Sons, 1969.

Fuson, Robert H., trans. *The Log of Christopher Columbus.* Camden, ME: International Marine Publishing, 1987.

Gard, Wayne. *Frontier Justice.* Norman: University of Oklahoma Press, 1949.

Garland, Hamlin. *Main-Travelled Roads.* New York: Harper and Brothers, 1899 [1891].

————. *Son of the Middle Border.* New York: Macmillan Co., 1925.

Goetzmann, William H. "The Mountain Man as Jacksonian Man." *American Quarterly* 15 (1963): 402–15.

Goldman, Marion S. *Gold Diggers & Silver Miners: Prostitution and Social Life on the Comstock Lode*. Ann Arbor: University of Michigan Press, 1981.

Graulich, Melody. "Violence against Women: Power Dynamics in Literature of the Western Family." In Susan Armitage and Elizabeth Jameson, eds., *The Women's West*. Norman: University of Oklahoma Press, 1987, 111–26.

Hafen, LeRoy R. *The Mountain Men and the Fur Trade of the Far West*. Vols. 2, 5, 6, 8, 9. Glendale, CA: Arthur H. Clark Co., 1972.

Harger, Charles Moreau. "Cattle-Trails of the Prairies." *Scribner's Magazine* (June 1892): 732–42.

Hart, James D. *A Companion to California*. New York: Oxford University Press, 1978.

Herschler, N. *The Soldiers Handbook*. Washington, DC: U.S. Government Printing Office, 1884.

Hine, Robert V. *Community on the American Frontier: Separate But Not Alone*. Norman: University of Oklahoma Press, 1980.

Hoig, Stan. *The Sand Creek Massacre*. Norman: University of Oklahoma Press, 1961.

Holliday, J. S. *The World Rushed In: The California Gold Rush Experience*. New York: Simon and Schuster, 1981.

Irving, Washington. *Astoria, or Anecdotes of an Enterprize beyond the Rocky Mountains*. Ed. Richard Dilworth Rust. Boston: Twayne Publishers, 1976.

Isern, Thomas D. *Bull Threshers and Bindlestiffs: Harvesting and Threshing on the North American Plains*. Lawrence: University Press of Kansas, 1990.

Jackson, Donald Dale. *Gold Dust*. New York: Alfred A. Knopf, 1980.

James, Will S. *27 Years a Mavrick, or Life on a Texas Range*. [1893] facsimile. Austin, TX: Steck-Vaughan Co., 1968.

Jameson, Elizabeth. "Women as Workers, Women as Civilizers: True Womanhood in the American West." In Susan Armitage and Elizabeth Jameson, eds. *The Women's West*. Norman: University of Oklahoma Press, 1987, 145–64.

Jones, Mary Ellen, ed. *The American Frontier: Opposing Viewpoints*. San Diego: Greenhaven Press, 1994.

———, ed. *Christopher Columbus and His Legacy*. San Diego: Greenhaven Press, 1992.

Josephy, Alvin M., Jr. *500 Nations: An Illustrated History of North American Indians*. New York: Alfred A. Knopf, 1994.

King, Charles. *Campaigning with Crook and Stories of Army Life*. Ann Arbor: University Microfilms, 1966.

Larpenteur, Charles. *Forty Years a Fur Trader on the Upper Missouri*. Ed. Elliott Coues. New York: Francis P. Harper, 1898.

Lavender, David. *Bent's Fort*. Gloucester, MA: Peter Smith, 1968.

———. *The Fist in the Wilderness*. Garden City, NY: Doubleday & Co., 1964.

Leckie, William H. *The Buffalo Soldiers: A Narrative of the Negro Cavalry in the West*. Norman: University of Oklahoma Press, 1967.

Levinson, Robert E. *The Jews in the California Gold Rush*. New York: Ktav Publishing House, 1978.

Lewis, Alfred Henry. *Wolfville Nights*. New York: Frederick A. Stokes Co., 1902.

Limerick, Patricia Nelson. *The Legacy of Conquest: The Unbroken Past of the American West*. New York: W. W. Norton & Co., 1987.

Lowe, Percival G. *Five Years a Dragoon ('49 to '54) and Other Adventures on the Great Plains*. Norman: University of Oklahoma Press, 1965.

Luchetti, Cathy. *Home on the Range: A Culinary History of the American West*. New York: Villard Books, 1993.

Luchetti, Cathy, in collaboration with Carol Olwell. *Women of the West*. St. George, UT: Antelope Valley Press, 1982.

McConnell, H. H. *Five Years a Cavalryman: Or Sketches of Regular Army Life on the Texas Frontier*. [1888]. Freeport, NY: Books for Libraries Press, 1970.

McLear, Patrick E. "The St. Louis Cholera Epidemic of 1849." *Missouri Historical Review* 63 (1969): 171–81.

Malone, Michael P., ed. *Historians and the American West*. Lincoln: University of Nebraska Press, 1983.

Marryat, Frank. *Mountains and Molehills or Recollections of a Burnt Journal*. [1855]. Philadelphia: J. B. Lippincott Co., 1962.

Maximilian, Prince of Wied. *Travels in the Interior of North America, 1832–34*. Vols. 22, 23, 24 of *Early Western Travels 1748–1846*. Ed. Reuben Gold Thwaites. Glendale, CA: Arthur H. Clark Co., 1966.

Megquier, Mary Jane. *Apron Full of Gold: The Letters of Mary Jane Megquier from San Francisco, 1849–1856*. Ed. Robert Glass Cleland. San Marino, CA: Huntington Library, 1949.

Miles, Gen. Nelson A. *Personal Recollections and Observations of General Nelson A. Miles*. New York: Da Capo Press, 1969.

Milner, Clyde A. *A New Significance: Re-Envisioning the History of the American West*. New York: Oxford University Press, 1996.

Milner, Clyde A., Carol A. O'Connor, and Martha A. Sandweiss. *The Oxford History of the American West*. New York: Oxford University Press, 1994.

Minnesota Historical Society. *Aspects of the Fur Trade: Selected Papers of the 1965 North American Fur Trade Conference*. St. Paul: Minnesota Historical Society, 1967.

Morgan, Dale L., ed. *The West of William H. Ashley, 1822–1838*. Denver: Old West Publishing, 1964.

Morgan, Dale L., and Eleanor Towles Harris, eds. *The Rocky Mountain Journals of William Marshall Anderson: The West in 1834*. San Marino, CA: Huntington Library, 1967.

Mulford, Prentice. *Prentice Mulford's California Sketches*. Ed. Franklin Walker. San Francisco: Book Club of California, 1935.

———. *Prentice Mulford's Story: Life by Land and Sea*. New York: F. J. Needham, 1889.

Myres, Sandra L. *Westering Women and the Frontier Experience, 1800–1915*. Albuquerque: University of New Mexico Press, 1982.

Nabokov, Peter, ed. *Native American Testimony: An Anthology of Indian and White Relations: First Encounter to Dispossession*. New York: Harper and Row, 1979.

National Livestock Association. *Prose and Poetry of the Live Stock Industry of the United States*. [1904]. New York: Antiquarian Press, 1959.

Neihardt, John. *Black Elk Speaks*. Lincoln: University of Nebraska Press, 1932.

Nelson, Paula M. *After the West Was Won: Homesteaders and Town-Builders in West-ern South Dakota, 1900–1917.* Iowa City: University of Iowa Press, 1986.

Nevin, David. *The Old West: The Soldiers.* New York: Time-Life Books, 1973.

Nevins, Allan, ed. *Narratives of Exploration and Adventure by John Charles Frémont.* New York: Longmans, Green & Co., 1956.

Ogden, Peter Skene. *Snake Country Journals, 1827–28 and 1828–29.* Ed. Glyndwer Williams. London: Hudson's Bay Record Society, 1971.

Paul, Rodman W. *The Far West and the Great Plains in Transition: 1859–1900.* New York: Harper and Row, 1988.

Perez-Venero, Alejandro. "The 'Forty-Niners' through Panama." *Journal of the West* 11 (June 1972): 460–69.

Perkins, William. *Three Years in California: William Perkins' Journal of Life at Sonora, 1849–1852.* Berkeley: University of California Press, 1964.

Phillips, Catherine Coffin. *Portsmouth Square: The Cradle of San Francisco.* San Francisco: John Henry Nash, 1932.

Pomfret, John E., ed. *California Gold Rush Voyages, 1848–1849: Three Original Narratives.* San Marino, CA: Huntington Library, 1954.

Preuss, Charles. *Exploring with Frémont: The Private Diaries of Charles Preuss, Cartographer for John C. Frémont on His First, Second, and Fourth Expeditions to the Far West.* Trans. and eds. Erwin G. Gudde and Elisabeth K. Gudde. Norman: University of Oklahoma Press, 1958.

Prucha, Francis Paul. *The Great Father: The United States Government and the American Indians.* Abridged ed. Lincoln: University of Nebraska Press, 1986.

Purvis, Thomas L. *Revolutionary America: 1763 to 1800.* Almanacs of American Life. New York: Facts on File, 1995.

Read, Georgia Willis. "Women and Children on the Oregon-California Trail in the Gold-Rush Years." *Missouri Historical Review* 39 (October 1944): 1–23.

Rehwinkel, Alfred M. *Dr. Bessie.* St. Louis: Concordia Publishing House, 1963.

Reynolds, David S. *Walt Whitman's America: A Cultural Biography.* New York: Alfred A. Knopf, 1995.

Rhodes, Richard. *The Ungodly: A Novel of the Donner Party.* New York: Charterhouse, 1973.

Rice, Richard B., William A. Bullough, and Richard J. Orsi. *The Elusive Eden: A New History of California.* New York: Alfred A. Knopf, 1988.

Rickey, Don, Jr. *Forty Miles a Day on Beans and Hay.* Norman: University of Oklahoma Press, 1963.

Riley, Glenda. *Frontierswomen: The Iowa Experience.* Ames: Iowa State University Press, 1981.

Rischin, Moses, and John Livingston, eds. *Jews of the American West.* Detroit: Wayne State University Press, 1991.

Roe, Frances M. A. [In text the name is spelled Rae.] *Army Letters from an Officer's Wife, 1871–1888.* New York: D. Appleton and Co., 1909.

Ronda, James P. *Lewis and Clark among the Indians.* Lincoln: University of Nebraska Press, 1984.

Roosevelt, Theodore. *Memories of the American Frontier.* N.p.: Westvaco, 1977.

Royce, Sarah. *A Frontier Lady: Recollections of the Gold Rush and Early California.* Ed. Ralph Henry Gabriel. Lincoln: University of Nebraska Press, 1932.

Ruede, Howard. *Sod-House Days: Letters from a Kansas Homesteader, 1877–78*. Ed. John Ise. New York: Cooper Square Publishers, 1966.

Russell, Charles M. *Good Medicine: Memories of the Real West*. Garden City, NY: Garden City Publishing Co., 1930.

Russell, Osborne. *Journal of a Trapper*. Ed. Aubrey L. Haines. Lincoln: University of Nebraska Press, 1955.

Sandoz, Mari. *Old Jules*. Lincoln: University of Nebraska Press, 1962.

Sanford, Mollie Dorsey. *Mollie: The Journal of Mollie Dorsey Sanford in Nebraska and Colorado Territories, 1857–1866*. Lincoln: University of Nebraska Press, 1959.

Savage, William A., Jr. *The Cowboy Hero: His Image in American History and Culture*. Norman: University of Oklahoma Press, 1979.

———. *Cowboy Life: Reconstructing an American Myth*. Norman: University of Oklahoma Press, 1975.

Sawey, Orlan. *Charles A. Siringo*. Boston: Twayne Publishers, 1981.

Scamehorn, Howard L., ed. *The Buckeye Rovers in the Gold Rush*. Athens: Ohio University Press, 1965.

Schlissel, Lillian. *Women's Diaries of the Westward Journey*. New York: Schocken Books, 1982.

Schlissel, Lillian, Byrd Gibbons, and Elizabeth Hampsten. *Far from Home: Families of the Westward Journey*. New York: Schocken Books, 1989.

Schob, David E. *Hired Hands and Plowboys: Farm Labor in the Midwest, 1815–1860*. Urbana: University of Illinois Press, 1975.

Shinn, Charles Howard. *Mining Camps: A Study in American Frontier Government*. New York: Harper and Row, 1965.

Siringo, Charles A. *A Lone Star Cowboy*. Santa Fe, NM: N.p., 1919.

———. *A Texas Cow Boy, or Fifteen Years on the Hurricane Deck of a Spanish Pony*. Chicago: Siringo and Dobson, 1886.

Smith, Duane A. *Rocky Mountain Mining Camps: The Urban Frontier*. Bloomington: Indiana University Press, 1967.

Smith, Henry Nash. *Virgin Land: The American West as Symbol and Myth*. Cambridge, MA: Harvard University Press, 1950.

Soule, Frank, John H. Gihon, and James Nisbet. *The Annals of San Francisco*. New York: D. Appleton & Co., 1854.

Stewart, Elinore Pruitt. *Letters of a Woman Homesteader*. Boston: Houghton Mifflin, 1914.

Stewart, George R. *The California Trail: An Epic with Many Heroes*. New York: McGraw-Hill, 1962.

Sunder, John E. *Bill Sublette, Mountain Man*. Norman: University of Oklahoma Press, 1959.

Taylor, Bayard. *El Dorado, or Adventures in the Path of Empire*. 2 vols. New York: George P. Putnam, 1850.

Taylor, George Rogers, ed. *The Turner Thesis: Concerning the Role of the Frontier in American History*. 3rd ed. Lexington, MA: D. C. Heath and Co., 1972.

Turner, Frederick Jackson. "The Significance of the Frontier in American History." In George Rogers Taylor, ed., *The Turner Thesis*. 3rd ed. Lexington, MA: D. C. Health and Co., 1972, 3–28.

Tyson, James L., M.D. *Diary of a Physician in California: Being the Results of Actual*

Experience Including Notes of the Journey by Land and Water. Oakland, CA: Biobooks, 1955.

Underwood, Kathleen. *Town Building on the Colorado Frontier.* Albuquerque: University of New Mexico Press, 1987.

Unruh, John D., Jr. *The Plains Across: The Overland Emigrants and the Trans-Mississippi West, 1840–1860.* Urbana: University of Illinois Press, 1979.

U.S. Senate. "Sand Creek Massacre." *Report of the Secretary of War, Sen. Exec. Doc. 26.* 39 Cong. 2 sessions. Washington, DC: Government Printing Office, 1867.

———. "The Chivington Massacre." *Reports of the Committees.* 39 Cong. 2 sessions. Washington, DC: Government Printing Office, 1867.

Utley, Robert M. *Frontier Regulars: The United States Army and the Indian: 1866–1891.* Bloomington: Indiana University Press, 1973.

———. *The Indian Frontier of the American West, 1846–1890.* Albuquerque: University of New Mexico Press, 1964.

———, ed. *Life in Custer's Cavalry: Diaries and Letters of Albert and Jennie Barnitz, 1867–1868.* New Haven: Yale University Press, 1977.

Viola, Herman J. *After Columbus: The Smithsonian Chronicle of the North American Indians.* Washington, DC: Smithsonian Books, 1990.

———. *Diplomats in Buckskins: A History of Indian Delegations in Washington City.* Washington, DC: Smithsonian Institution Press, 1981.

———. *Exploring the West.* Washington, DC: Smithsonian Books, 1987.

Ward, Geoffrey C. *The West: An Illustrated History.* New York: Little, Brown, 1996.

Washburn, Wilcomb, ed. *The Indian and the White Man.* Garden City, NY: Doubleday & Co., 1964.

———. "Symbol, Utility and Aesthetics in the Indian Fur Trade." In Minnesota Historical Society, *Aspects of the Fur Trade: Selected Papers of the 1965 North American Fur Trade Conference.* St. Paul: Minnesota Historical Society, 1967, 50–54.

West, Elliott. *The Saloon on the Rocky Mountain Mining Frontier.* Lincoln: University of Nebraska Press, 1979.

Wheeler, Keith. *The Townsmen.* New York: Time-Life Books, 1975.

White, Lonnie J. *Hostiles and Horse Soldiers: Indian Battles and Campaigns in the West.* Boulder, CO: Pruett Publishing, 1972.

White, Richard. *"It's Your Misfortune and None of My Own": A New History of the American West.* Norman: University of Oklahoma Press, 1991.

Whitman, Walt. *The Portable Walt Whitman.* Ed. Mark Van Doren. New York: Penguin Books, 1974.

The Wild West. New York: Time-Life Books, 1993.

Wishart, David J. *The Fur Trade of the American West, 1807–1840.* Lincoln: University of Nebraska Press, 1979.

Woods, Daniel B. *Sixteen Months at the Gold Diggings.* [1851]. New York: Arno Press, 1973.

The World of the American Indian. Washington, DC: National Geographic Society, 1993.

Wyman, Walker D., ed. *California Emigrant Letters.* New York: Bookman Associates, 1952.

———. *Frontier Woman: The Life of a Woman Homesteader on the Dakota Frontier.* River Falls: University of Wisconsin–River Falls Press, 1972.

Index

Abilene, Kansas, 166, 171, 178–79, 181
Absaroka, 32
Accidents, 70–71
Acculturation, and adaptation, 7, 14, 79, 81–82, 114–15, 130–31, 211, 230, 242, 246–47
Agents. *See* Indian agents
Agriculture, and Indians, 247
Alcohol: in Army, 60, 65–66; among cowboys, 176–81; in fur trade, 12, 14, 30, 51; impact on Indians, 88
Alexander, Evelyn, 227–28, 230, 243
Alligators, 99
American character, 7–8
American Fur Company, 38, 88
American Horse, 225, 227
American Philosophical Society, 56
American River, 95, 136
Army and Navy Journal, 223, 242
Army Regulations, 225, 226
Ashley, William, 22–24, 30, 33, 34, 41–43
Assimilation, 57–58, 248–49
Assiniboine, 46
Astor, John Jacob, 16, 45

Astoria, 16
Atkinson, Gen. Henry, 35

Barnitz, Albert, 214, 216, 220, 238, 240–41
Barnitz, Jennie, 221
Bars, 113. *See also* Saloons and taverns
Beadle's Dime Novels, 2, 204
Beale, Lt. Edward F., 97
Bear Flag Republic, 95
Beaver, 12, 31–32, 57; trapping of, 32–33
Bennett, James Gordon, 167
Benteen, Brig. Gen. Frederick W., 220
Benton, Thomas Hart, 4
Biddle, Maj. Thomas, 51
Bison robes, 47; hunting, 47–48; processing, 48
Bitterroot Mountains, 62, 64
Black Elk (Oglala Sioux), 251
Black Hills, 121
Black Kettle (Cheyenne), 238
Bloomers, 114–15
Blue, Teddy, 160, 167
Boarding schools, on reservations, 248
Bodmer, Karl, 47, 78, 91

Boils, 69
Books, 127, 147–48
Boone, Daniel, 55
Boosterism, 166–67, 206–7
Boudin (poudinge) blanc, 64
Bozeman Trail, 238
Branding, 126, 168, 169–70
Brannan, Sam, 95, 96
Brevet rank. *See* U.S. Army
Bridger, Jim, 27, 30
British milk, 12
Brothels. *See* Prostitutes
Bruff, J. Goldsborough, 122, 125
Buck, Franklin A., 152–53
Buckeye Rovers, 117, 118, 122, 123, 125, 130
Buffalo, 33, 65, 158–62, 164; and government policy, 160, 162
Buffalo chips, 127
Buffalo dance (Mandan), 66, 68
Buffalo hunters, 160
Buffalo Soldiers, 221
Bullboats, 4, 45–46
Burke, Edmund, 9
Burial practices, 201–2
Busch, August, 167

Calafia, 93
California, 93–95, 98; population increase, 99
California banknotes, 94
"California frenzy," 97–98
California Star, 95
Campbell, Robert, 24, 30
Cannibalism, 118
Canot du maître, 19–20; *canot du nord*, 19–20
Card games. *See* Gambling
Carleton, Gen. James H., 243
Carlisle Indian School, 248–49
Carson, Kit, 27, 75, 243
Castoreum, 57
Cather, Willa, 190
Catlin, George, 82–91, 186; goals of, 83; significance of, 91
Cattle, 162. *See also* Longhorn
Cattle business, 166–67, 168, 171

Cattle drives, 171–75
Cattle ranching, 94
Cattle towns. *See* Cowtowns
Celebrations. *See* Christmas celebrations; Entertainment; Fourth of July
Census, Bureau of the, 5
Chagres, Panama, 110, 112–13
Chardon, Francis, 37, 47
Chatillon, Henry, 29
Cherokee Nation v. Georgia, 237
Chief Joseph (Nez Percé), 239
Children's labor, 194–95
Chimney Rock, 129
Chisholm Trail, 166
Cholera, 99, 102, 109, 120–21, 143, 232
Choteau, Auguste, 26, 62, 73
Christmas celebrations, 36, 50, 66, 178
Chuckwagons, 168–69, 175–76
Civil War, 180, 211, 216, 223
Civilization, concepts of, 6, 8, 82–83, 85–87, 181, 240–41
Clark, Gen. George Rogers, 56
Clark, William, 4, 22, 56–74 passim, 83
Clyman, James, 29, 38–39
Cochise (Apache), 235, 237
Cody, William H. "Buffalo Bill," 2, 91, 234
Coffee, 176
Colter, John, 38, 59, 75
Columbia River, 62
Columbus, Christopher, 4, 11, 12–13, 162
Conservation vs. exploitation. *See* Natural resources
Cooper, James Fenimore, 4, 29, 204
Cordelling (keelboats), 45
Corps of Discovery: assessment of, 71–74; discipline among, 59–60; hardships and hazards, 60; and Indians, 57, 58, 72–74; Jefferson's instructions to, 56–58; journals of, 57; leaders' skills, 56, 60–61; as military expedition, 59–60; pivotal moments of, 71; travel of, 61–62
Corps of Topographical Engineers, 4, 75

Cowboys, 164–82; duties of, 168–71; entertainment of, 177–81; food, 169, 175–46; hazards and hardships of, 171–72, 173; as heroes, 164–65; shelter of, 176–77; wages and expenses, 167–68
Cowboy songs, 174
Cowtowns 154, 166, 171, 178–82
Crazy Horse (Oglala Sioux), 233, 239
Creation legends, 182
Crime and punishment: in cowtowns, 181; in goldfields, 145–47
Crook, Gen. George, 215, 225, 227, 242, 245
Crosby, Alfred W., 162–63
Cross-cultural experiences, 60, 73
Cruzatte, Pvt. Peter 70. *See also* Corps of Discovery, hardships and hazards of
Cultural change, 58, 82–83, 85, 97. *See also* Indian education
Custer, Elizabeth, 222, 233
Custer, Gen. George Armstrong, 217, 219, 220, 222, 230, 240

Daguerrotype, 76
Daklugie (Apache), 239, 244
Dame Shirley (Louise Amelia Knapp Smith Clapp), 131, 132, 138, 140
Dana, Richard Henry, 94
Dances, 50, 149–50, 178
Day schools, on reservations, 247–48
Deerskins, 12
Delegation Indians. *See* Indian delegations
Democracy, 145
Denig, Edwin, 29
DeVoto, Bernard, 16–17, 21–22
Diaries, 100; of Charles Preuss, 78–82
Diarrhea, 50–51, 143, 195
Dime novels. *See* Beadle's Dime Novels
Discipline, military, 59–60
Disease. *See* Cholera; diarrhea; Dysentery; Injury and illness; Land-sea routes to California, disease and medical care; *Le mal de vache*; Malaria; Measles; Mental illness; Mercury poisoning; Poison oak; Rheumatism; Seasickness; Smallpox; Tick fever; Toothache; Typhoid; Venereal disease
Doctors, 144–45, 200, 231
Dogsled, 19
Dodge, Col. Richard I., 224, 240
Dodge City, Kansas, 166, 178, 180
Donner Party, 118
Drinking, 148
Dugout canoes, 46, 62
Dugouts, 62, 177, 195–97, 230
Dull Knife (Northern Cheyenne), 245
Dust Bowl, 75, 163
Dwight, Rev. Timothy, 8
Dysentery, 38, 69, 102, 143

Eastman, Elaine Goodale, 246, 247–48
Ecology, 116–17, 137, 162–64
Ellsworth, Kansas, 166
El Paso, Texas, 178
Emigrant route, 75
Emigrants, 75, 157
Emigrants' Guide to California, The, 77, 117
Entertainment: of Corps of Discovery, 65–68; at fur forts, 50; on oceangoing ships to California, 106–7; on overland routes to California, 128–30
Equipment, of mountain men, 25
Erosion, 163
Ethnocentrism, 6, 242
Ethnology, 57, 73, 91
Extermination, 241

Field, Joseph, 65
Field, Marshall, 167
Fitzpatrick, Thomas, 27, 75
Five Civilized Tribes, 237
Fleas, 69, 110, 114
Flint, Timothy, 9
Floyd, Sgt. Charles, 69
Food, 79–80; of Army, 225–28; of Corps of Discovery, 62–66; at fur forts, 17, 49–50; of mountain men, 25, 26, 35–38; on routes to Califor-

nia, 110, 113, 114, 115–16, 102–4, 127–28; of settlers, 199–200; of voyageurs, 21
Forbes, Capt. Cleveland, 102, 107–8
Foreign Miners' Tax, 154
Forsyth, George, 219
Forsyth, Nebraska, 154
Fort Griffin, Texas, 179–80
Forts: Abraham Lincoln, 233; Atkinson, 24, 43; Clark, 43, 45, 47, 52; Clatsop, 62, 64, 66, 68; Cobb, 227; Custer, 232; Detroit, 11; Fetterman, 225; Hall, 116. 117; Harker, 228, 230; Kearney, 117, 122, 129, 228; Laramie, 43, 116, 117, 129, 232; Larned, 229; Leavenworth, 43, 222, 224, 239; MacKenzie, 43; Mandan, 66; Michilimackinac, 11, 43; Osage, 43; Piegan, 43; Pierre, 43, 45; Reno, 227; Robinson, 245; Smith, 230; Stevens, 228; Sumner, 243; Tecumseh, 43; Union, 43, 45; William, 43
Forts, army construction of, 228–31
Forts, layout of in Army, 230
Four Bears (Mah-to-toh-pa) (Mandan), 52–53, 88–91
Fourth of July, celebrations, 40, 65, 107, 130, 178, 180, 227–28
France, 15
Fraud, 183, 184
Frémont, Jesse, 77–78
Frémont, Col. John Charles, 75–78, 95; application of science to exploration, 76–77; improvisation of, 76; as writer, 77–78
French and Indian War, 11, 15
Frontier thesis, 5–8, 81–82
Frostbite, 38
Funerals, 122
Fur fair at Montreal, 16–17
Fur forts, life in, 17–18, 47–51
Fur trade, 129; assessment of effects, 53; competition in, 24; crosscultural impact of, 12–14; economic impact of, 12; impact on Indian society and culture, 48, 51–53; linguistic influences of, 12; Montreal-Michilimackinac System, 16–22; Rocky

Mountain System, 22–43; Upper Missouri System, 43–53

Gambling, 113, 148–49, 180
Garland, Hamlin, 184, 189–90, 194–95, 199
Gender roles, 193–94. *See also* Women
General store, 207–8
Ghost Dance, 85, 164, 246
Gibbon, Col. John, 216, 233
Gift giving, in Native American culture, 13, 50
Gold, discovery of: in Black Hills, 215, 237; in California, 95–96
Gold fever, 96–99
Gold miners: clothing of, 141; demographics, 132–33; earnings, 137–39; entertainment, 147–50; food and drink, 141–42; hardships of, 139–41; health and disease, 143–45; homesickness, 150–42
Gold mining techniques: cradle, 134–35; dams, 136; flumes, 135; hydraulic mining, 136–37; inventions, 98, 99, 106–7; panning, 133–34; quartz mining, 137; sluices, 136
Gold rush, assessment of, 110, 128, 149, 154–55
Goldseekers, illusions of, 99–100, 129
Goldseekers, routes of. *See* Land-sea routes to California; Overland routes to California; Sea routes to California
Grant, Ulysses S., 162, 238
Grass, 118–19, 158, 163
Grasshoppers, 188
Great American Desert, 75, 77, 157
Great Falls of the Missouri, 61
Great Father, 65, 72, 74, 88
Great Plains, 74, 158, 186
Greenhorns, 78–82, 124, 126, 167
Grierson, Col. Benjamin, 222
Grizzly bears, 38–39, 63, 73, 144
Guidebooks, 117

Hangtown, California, 147
Hayt, Ezra, 248
Henry, Andrew, 22

Hide trade, 94
Hivernants, 15, 18
Holidays, celebration of, 50. *See also* Christmas celebrations; Fourth of July
Homesickness, 78, 81, 122–23, 150–52
Homestead Act, 8, 183–84, 205
Homesteaders, 163, 173; and homesteading, 157
Homesteads, 195–98
Horse races, 68, 83–84
Horse thieves, 34–35
Horses, 34–35, 62, 64, 114–15, 174–75, 227
Hotels, 113, 115, 207
Hudson's Bay Company, 13, 22, 76
Humanitarians, 241

Independence Day. *See* Fourth of July
Independence Rock, 129
Indian agents, 57, 240, 245–46
Indian culture: cultural change, 246–47; forces for change in, 235–37. *See also* Indian education
Indian delegations, 73–74, 82, 86–88, 240
Indian education, 247–49
Indian law, 48, 173
Indian wars, 235
Indians, 75–76, 82; relationship to nature, 163–64
Indians, individual nations: Apache, 243; Arapaho, 239; Arawak, 12–13; Arikara, 22, 24, 48–49, 60, 68, 72, 73; Assiniboine, 86–88; Blackfeet, 22, 38, 51, 71, 72; Cheyenne, 239, 244–45; Chinook, 68, 72; Crow, 22, 49, 173; Flatheads, 72; Gros Ventre, 49, 73; Hidatsa, 72; Iroquois, 82; Kiowa, 164; Mandan, 22, 49, 52–53, 58, 66–68, 72, 73, 84–85, 88–91; Mojave, 77; Navajo, 243; Nez Percé, 35, 64–65, 68, 72, 73, 239; Okanogan, 163–64; Oto, 60, 72; Osage, 73, 74; Pawnee, 73; Ponca, 239; Potawatomi, 74; Shoshone, 72; Sioux, 68, 72, 246; Ute, 33; Walla Walla, 77; Yakima, 22

Industrial ranching, 163
Infant mortality, 202
Inflation, 153–54
Initiation ceremonies, 15
Injury and illness, 38–39. *See also specific diseases*; Medical problems and care; Medicine
Insects, 188
International boundary, 16
International trade, 11, 55
Investment, 154
Irving, Washington, 8, 26

Jackson, Helen Hunt, 244
Jefferson, Thomas, 4, 6, 55, 73–74
Johnson, Andrew, 183
Johnson, Sir William, 11
Joint stock companies, 123–25

Kachina, 212, 214
Kearney, Maj. Stephen Watts, 35
Keelboat, 4, 23, 43–45
Kemble, Edward, 96
Kenton, Simon, 8
Kicking Bird (Kiowa), 237
King, Capt. Charles, 216, 219, 223, 225, 234–35

Lacrosse, 16
Lake Mohonk Conference, 247
Land, concepts of ownership and use, 14–15, 163–64, 182–85
Land Ordinance of 1785, 183
Land speculation, 181
Land-sea routes to California, 108–16; company organization and discipline, 109; cross-cultural issues, 109, 110, 114, 115; disease and medical care, 110, 112, 113, 115–16; flora and fauna, 110–11 114; food, 110, 113, 114, 115–16; lodging, 110, 113, 115; modes of travel, 113–15; Mexico route, 108–10; Panama route, 110–16; profiles of travelers, 111–12; terrain, 109–10, 114–15
Language, 12, 33, 51–52, 83–84, 168, 247
Larkin, Thomas O., 96

Larpenteur, Charles, 24–26, 30, 38
Latham, Dr. Hiram, 166
Law, 5, 8–9, 39, 56, 145–47, 173, 181, 188, 203
Le mal de vache, 26
Ledyard, John, 56
Lewis, Meriwether, 4, 56–74 passim; shot by Cruzatte, 70–71. *See also* Corps of Discovery
Limerick, Patricia Nelson, 163
Literacy, 177
Little Bighorn, 233
Livingstone, Robert R., 55
Long, Stephen H., 75
Longhorn, 165–66
Louisiana, 55–66
Louisiana Purchase, 4. 16, 55–56
Louisville, Kentucky, 43, 46

Mackenzie, Charles, 13
Mackinaw boat, 45
Mail, 129, 150–51
Malaria, 38, 112
Manifest Destiny, 8, 85
Marryat, Frank, 112
Marshall, James, 95–96
Marshall, John, 237
Mason, Richard B., 97
Maximilian (Prince von Wied), 8, 47, 78
McCormick reaper, 192
McCoy, Joseph, 166, 171
McGillicuddy, Valentine, 246
Measles, 200
Medical problems and care, 38–39, 50–51, 65, 69–71, 73
Medicine, 84–85; medicine man, 84–85
Meek, Joe, 32, 34
Megquier, Mary Jane, 104, 112–15
Mental illness, 102, 201, 227, 232–33
Mercury poisoning, 143
Mexican rule of California, 94–95
Mexican War, 97
Mexico, 8, 93–94, 109–10
Michaux, André, 56
Micheaux, Oscar, 190
Michilimackinac. *See* Forts

Miles, Gen. Nelson A., 216, 233, 238–39, 242, 243, 244
Military discipline. *See* U.S. Army
Miller, Alfred Jacob, 40, 91
Missionaries, 8, 40, 57, 157
Missions, 93–94
Missouri River, 43, 56, 61; hazards of, 23
Monroe, James, 55
Monterey, California, 93, 95
Montgomery Ward catalogue, 207, 209
Mormons, 8, 95, 121–22, 127
Mosquitoes, 21, 69, 121
Mountain men, 75, 78, 117, 124; assessment of, 27–30; duties and discipline, 25; equipment of, 25, 34; food, 25, 26, 35–38; and Indians, 39–40; literacy of, 30; skills of, 33–35; wages, 39
Muir, John, 162
Mules, 24, 25, 34–35, 114, 125–26
Murietta, Joaquin, 147
Music, 148, 178
Mythic frontier vs. reality, 1–5

Napoleon I (Napoléon Bonaparte), 55
Native Americans, 6, 14–15, 19, 85, 182. *See also* Indians
Nature: adaptation to, 14; exploitation of, 75, 99, 157
Natural hazards, 62, 70, 186–87
Natural resources, conservation vs. exploitation, 15, 75, 99
New Orleans, Louisiana, 55–56
New Orleans *Daily Picayune*, 97
New York Herald, 98
New York Tribune, 97, 110
Newman, John, 60
Newspapers, 97–98, 110, 206, 226, 238
Night watches, 110, 174
Nueva Helvetia, 95

Oceangoing ships, 98
O'Fallon, Benjamin, 24
Ogden, Peter Skene, 29
Olmstead, Frederick Law, 206
Oregon, 157

Organizations, philanthropic and recreational, 209–10

Overland routes to California, 116–18; climate and terrain, 118–19; disease, accidents and death, 120–22; entertainment, 128–30; food and drink, 127–28; joint stock companies, 123–25; modes of transportation, 119–20; psychological stress, 122–23; typical day, 125–27

Painting: Native American, 84, 89; portrait, 84–85

Painters, 91

Panama City, Panama, 110–11, 115–16

Panama, Isthmus of, 108, 110–16

Parkman, Francis, 29

Peace medals, 73, 88

Penn, William, 182

Perkins, William, 108–10, 140, 143, 149, 152

Pike, Lt. Zebulon Montgomery, 74–75

Pike, the, 111–12

Pine Ridge Agency. *See* Reservations

Pirogue, 46

Pittsburgh, Pennsylvania, 43

Plowing, 163, 164

Poison oak, 143

Polk, James K., 97

Pontiac, 15–16

Portable soup, 63

Prairie, 78

Prairie fires, 118, 187–88

Pratt, Richard Henry, 248–49

Pre-Emption Act of 1841, 183

Preuss, Charles, 76, 78–82; views on Frémont, 80–81

Proclamation of 1763, 4, 85, 215

Prostitutes, 113, 152, 180

Provost, Etienne, 25

Psychological problems, 122–23, 201, 227

Racism/racial prejudice, 147, 221–23

Railroad car, refrigerated, 167

Railroads, 108, 159–60, 166–67, 184, 188, 205–6, 235

Ranchos, 94, 95

Rats, 49, 140, 143

Rattlesnakes, 65, 128, 144, 189

Red Cloud (Oglala Sioux), 237, 238

Red Jacket (Seneca), 82–83

Reformers, Indian policy, 241–42

Rendezvous, 22, 40–43

Reservations, 82–83, 237, 243–48; Bosque Redondo, 243–44; Great Sioux, 247; Pine Ridge, 240, 249; Rosebud, 246; San Carlos, 239, 244; Sandy Lake, 246

Rheumatism, 38, 69, 143

Rockefeller, William, 167

Rocky Mountain, 23–24

Rocky Mountain Company, 94

Rocky Mountain trading system. *See* Fur trade

Rocky Mountains, 4, 129

Roe, Francis, 220, 221, 223, 241

Rogers, Robert, 13, 17

Roosevelt, Theodore, 167, 181

Roundup, 168–70

Routes to California. *See* Land-sea routes to California; Overland routes to California; Sea routes to California

Royce, Sarah, 118–19, 123, 127, 131, 132, 151–52

Royer, Daniel F., 246

Russell, Charles, 173

Russell, Osborne, 30, 33

Sacajawea (Shoshone), 59, 62, 72–73

Sacramento Valley, 95, 131

Saloons and taverns, 148, 180

Salt Lake City, Utah, 116, 118–19, 129

San Diego, California, 93

San Joaquin Valley, 94

Sand Creek Massacre, 4–5, 241

Sanitation, 120

Satanta (Kiowa), 237

Scientific instruments and exploration, 76

Scotts Bluff, 129

Sea routes to California, 100; entertainment, 106–7; food and drink, 102–4; hardships and disease, 100–102; passengers' behavior, 107–8; passengers' profiles, 104–6; the ships, 100

Seaman, 59

Seasickness, 100–102

"Seeing the elephant," 129

Serra, Fr. Junipera, 94

Service industries, 153–54

Settlers: clothing, 198–99; entertainment, 204–5; food, 199–200; hardships, 186–89; health and disease, 200; housing, 195–98; sexual practices, 202–4; work, 189–95

Sex, 39–40, 69, 202–4

Sheep, 162

Sherman, Gen. William Tecumseh, 162, 222, 228, 235, 238, 239, 240

Shields, John, 59

Sierra Nevada, 94, 118

Sitting Bull (Hunkpapa), 235, 239

Sloat, Commodore John Drake, 95

Smallpox, 15, 51–53, 58, 89, 91, 121, 232

Smith, Gen. Percifor F., 116

Smith, Henry Nash, 3

Smith, Jedediah, 23, 34, 38, 94

Smohalla (Wanapam), 247

Snowblindness, 38

Sod houses, 197

Sodbreaking, 190

Soldiers Handbook, The, 232

Soldier's portion, 58

Sonoma, California, 95

Spain, 93

St. Louis, Missouri, 22, 26–27

Staking claims, 145–46

Stampede, 173–74

Standing Bear, Luther, 248–49

Stanley, John Mix, 91

Steamboats, 4, 45–47, 206

Steamships, 102, 108, 116

Sublette, William, 24, 30, 51

Suicide, 145

Sutter, John Augustus, 95–96

Sweat lodge, 200

Swift, Gustavus, 167

Taverns. *See* Saloons and taverns

Taylor, Bayard, 110, 114, 115, 116, 117, 118, 140, 151

Taylor, Zachary, 120

Technology, impact on Native American culture, 235

Terminus, 4

Terrestrial Paradise, 93

Tick fever, 121, 166, 173

Toothache, 69, 102, 200

Tourists, 112, 129

Towns, on the Plains, 205–10

Townsite Act of 1844, 206

Trade goods, 12–14, 17–18, 41–43

Transportation 4, 19–21, 80. *See also* Bullboats; *Canot du maître*; Dogsled; Horses; Mules; Oceangoing ships; Pirogue; Railroads; Steamships

Trapping. *See* Beaver

Treaties: Fort Laramie, 239; Guadalupe Hidalgo, 96, 109; Indian, 237–39; Medicine Lodge Creek, 237–38; Paris, 16

Tumbleweed, 163

Turner, Frederick Jackson, 5–8, 81, 85. *See also* Frontier thesis

Two Years before the Mast, 94

Typhoid, 143

Tyson, James L., 100–101, 114, 115, 141, 144–45

U.S. Army: attitudes toward, 214–15; basic training, 219–20; blacks in, 221–23; brevet rank, 217–18; commissions in, 216–17; daily ration and food, 225–28; demographics of, 215–17; desertion, 220; duties and discipline, 215, 233–34; force reduction, 215–16; living quarters, 228–31; medical care, 219, 231–33; pay in, 217, 218; promotions in, 217; recruitment for, 218–19; role on frontier, 214, 215; uniforms of, 223–25

U.S. Army, units of: Fifth Cavalry, 216, 225, 234–35; Seventh Cavalry, 217, 220, 232, 233; Ninth Cavalry, 221, 222; Tenth Cavalry, 221, 222, 223; Third Infantry, 222; Fifth Infantry, 233; Seventh Infantry, 216; Eleventh Infantry, 224; Thirteenth Infantry, 220; Eighteenth Infantry,

224; Twenty-fourth Infantry, 221;
Twenty-fifth Infantry, 221
U.S. government, Indian peace poli-
cies, 211, 215, 239–42, 245
Union Pacific Railroad, 166–67
United States, diversity of geography
and climate, 3
United States Mail Steam Line, 108,
111
Upper Missouri Trading system. *See*
Fur trade

Venereal disease, 18, 39–40, 51, 69,
232
Violence, 39
Voyageurs, 18–21, 25

Wages, in fur trade, 19
Wagons, 126–27
Walker, Joseph, 75
Ware, Joseph, 77, 117
Warfington, Cpl. Richard, 59
Wayne, John, 2
Westering: effects of, 211; motives for,
8–9
West Point, 216, 242

Whipple, Bishop Henry B., 246
Whitman, Dr. Marcus, 76
Whitman, Walt, 8, 211–12
Wichita, Kansas, 166
Wi-Jun-Jon (Pigeon's Egg Head or
The Light), 86–88
Wister, Owen, 165
Wolverine Rangers, 123, 124–25, 128
Wolves, 38
Women, 104, 113–14, 123, 128, 130,
142, 149, 202–4; on cattle frontier,
178; on mining frontier, 151–53
Women's roles, 193–94
Woods, Daniel, 110, 140
Worms, 195, 200
Wounded Knee, 246, 249

Xenophobia, 120

Yellowstone, 46, 83, 88
Yellowstone National Park, 38, 75, 91,
159
Yerba Buena (San Francisco), 95
York, 59, 66, 70

Zuni kachina, 212, 214

About the Author

MARY ELLEN JONES is Director of American Studies and Associate Professor of English at Wittenberg University in Springfield, Ohio. Among other works, she is author of *The American Frontier* (1994), *Christopher Columbus and His Legacy* (1992), and *John Jakes: A Critical Companion* (Greenwood, 1996).